Teaching Science in the 21ST CENTURY

Teaching Science in the 21st CENTURY

Jack Rhoton and Patricia Shane, Editors

Arlington, Virginia

Claire Reinburg, Director
Judy Cusick, Senior Editor
Andrew Cocke, Associate Editor
Betty Smith, Associate Editor
Robin Allan, Book Acquisitions Coordinator

Printing and Production, Catherine Lorrain-Hale, Director
Nguyet Tran, Assistant Production Manager
Jack Parker, Electronic Prepress Technician
Linda Olliver, Cover and Book Design

National Science Teachers Association
Gerald F. Wheeler, Executive Director
David Beacom, Publisher

09 08 07 06 4 3 2 1

Library of Congress Cataloging-in-Publication Data

Teaching science in the 21st century / Jack Rhoton and Patricia Shane, editors.
p. cm.
Includes bibliographical references.
ISBN-13: 978-0-87355-269-1
ISBN-10: 0-87355-269-5
1. Science—Study and teaching—United States. 2. Science teachers—In-service training—United States. I. Title: Teaching science in the twenty-first century. II. Rhoton, Jack. III. Shane, Patricia.
Q183.3.A1T425 2005
507'.1273—dc22

2005025878

CONTENTS

Part II Professional Development: Implications for Science Teaching and Learning

Part III Leadership in Science Teaching and Learning

Part IV Building Science Partnerships and Collaboration

Part V Science of Learning Science

Foreword

JoAnne Vasquez

Alice came to a fork in the road. "Which road do I take?" she asked.
"Where do you want to go?" responded the Cheshire cat.
"I don't know," Alice answered.
"Then," said the cat, "it doesn't matter."
-Lewis Carroll, Alice in Wonderland

Science leaders throughout the country are looking for direction and wanting to know which road to take. This book of compiled issues and trends in science teaching and learning is the insightful contributions of leading science educators from across the country. It will begin to provide the much needed direction and insight.

Not since the Soviet Union's launch of the Sputnik satellite—48 years ago—has the need to improve science education in America been as clear and as urgent as it is today. America's competitive edge in the global economy, its strength and versatility all depend on an education system capable of producing a steady supply of young people well prepared in science and mathematics.

In the face of many converging trends, efforts to reform and strengthen science education have been largely piecemeal and unfocused, yielding only modest gains. For the past few years, conversations about educational standards, classroom practice, measurable achievement, and teacher quality have linked the phrases *No Child Left Behind* and *scientific research.* What do these conversations mean, and how might they affect people directly involved in science education? This book will help shed light on some of these topics and provide a starting place for science educators and administrators to focus on the future of science in our nation's classrooms.

By 2007–2008 all schools will be testing science. Will science become another "data-driven" reform? Will we have teachers teaching a garbage-in-garbage-out approach just to make certain their students pass the test? Will good science teaching become only for the very elite students as our rural and urban communities struggle to hold onto qualified science teachers, who too often flee to the burbs for better working conditions and wages? The future is not ours to predict. We do know, however, that, unless there are drastic changes within the nation's science classrooms, we will be raising a generation of students who have had their curiosity defused. And they will not know how to think critically and will not become the scientifically literate citizens we need.

True, we face an uncertain future in science education, but we know that knowledge is power. This book will provide the resources to give us that knowledge. On behalf of the National Science Education Leadership Association (NSELA), I am very grateful for the insight, leadership, and editing by Jack Rhoton and Patricia Shane. These two dedicated science educators have once again shed light on the critical issues facing all science educators.

JoAnne Vasquez, PhD
NSELA President, 2005–2006

Preface

As we move deeper into the 21st century, local, state, and national reports continue to remind us that standards, assessment, and accountability are common public policy concerns. They are, in fact, driving much of our effort as we strive to improve science education at all levels. These concerns originate and are embedded in research—as well as in the politics and economics of education, which include unparalleled public spending for education and increasing concern for our knowledge economy and the rapidly evolving competitive world. Implicit in these concerns are a multitude of issues ranging from how students learn science to building science partnerships and collaboration to the ramifications of the federal No Child Left Behind legislation. Even though opinions vary on how to approach the challenges in education, the mandate for establishing an accounting system for the outcomes of schooling for all students has never been clearer.

With the challenges in mind, this book addresses issues and outlines the practical approaches needed to lay the foundation upon which science teachers and science educators—at all levels—can work together to build effective science programs. The book shares the research, ideas, insights, and experiences of individuals ranging from science supervisors to university personnel to those who work for agencies representing science education. The authors discuss how to contribute to the success of school science and how to develop a culture that allows and encourages science leaders to continually improve their science programs.

The 21 chapters in *Teaching Science in the 21st Century* are organized into five major sections. This organization places each chapter within a general theme. The intent is not to provide an exhaustive coverage of each section, but rather to present a stimulating collection of essays on relevant issues. Those major themes are

Within the Science Classroom: The science classroom is a dynamic environment in which students have the freedom to explore and to question. As students learn, they share what they have learned with one another, and they connect that new knowledge to their existing knowledge of the world. We introduce this theme in "The Impact of Technology on the 21st Century Classroom." Next we consider the importance of a standards-based curriculum, planning and assessing science instruction and student learning, planning science experiences for diverse student populations, and how to get classroom teachers engaged in research.

Professional Development: Implications for Science Teaching and Learning: Within the environment of increased teacher and student expectations, teacher professional development is cited frequently as a key strategy for improving student learning. This theme emerges in four chapters that examine the effectiveness of high-stakes accountability systems in bringing about improvements in professional development and student learning.

Leadership in Science Teaching and Learning: In today's complex educational system it almost goes without saying that, without effective leadership at all levels, substantive change to bring about improved science programs will not happen. Successful science programs involve many participants—among them teachers, administrators, and science supervisors—playing different roles. This premise is highlighted in four chapters. See in particular "Leadership in Science Education for the 21st Century."

Building Science Partnerships and Collaboration: A number of individuals and programs have demonstrated the potential for catalyzing widespread improvements in science education by building and nurturing appropriate partners. Their approaches can overcome formidable barriers. This theme emerges most fully in "The Importance of Partnerships in Science Education Reform." Other topics include the role of professional learning communities for strengthening the science program, the impact of the No Child Left Behind legislation on science education, and alternative certification.

Science of Learning Science: One of the aims of science education is to teach students about our accumulated knowledge of the natural world and to help them learn to use the methods, procedures, and reasoning processes that produced that knowledge. This approach is introduced in "The Psychology of Scientific Thinking: Implications for Science Teaching and Learning." This theme is discussed at length in three other chapters: "Brain Research: Implications for Teaching and Learning as the 21st[st] Century Begins," "How Do Students Learn Science," and "Research in Science Education."

In addition to the themes described above, the need to address local, state, and national standards is prominent throughout this publication.

Previous publications in this NSELA/NSTA series are *Issues in Science Education, Professional Development Planning and Design, Professional Development Leadership and the Diverse Learner,* and *Science Teacher Retention: Mentoring and Renewal.*

Teaching Science in the 21st Century captures the latest research, trends, and best practices in science education. Science teachers and science leaders can use it to vitalize their teaching and programs for improved student learning in science. This book, therefore, is directed at science teachers, science department chairs, principals, science supervisors, curriculum directors, superintendents, university personnel, policy makers, and any other individuals who have a stake in science education. The final determinant of success in our effort to improve science education will be measured by the quality of science programs delivered to our students and student outcomes.

Jack Rhoton
Patricia Shane

About the Editors

Jack Rhoton is an educator with more than 30 years of experience, covering every level of education from elementary through graduate school. He teaches science and science education courses to preservice and inservice science teachers at East Tennessee State University, where he is professor of science education. He is a researcher in K–12 science, especially in the area of professional development and its impact on science teaching and learning.

He has served as president of the National Science Education Leadership Association (NSELA), president of the Tennessee Academy of Science (TAS), and president of the Tennessee Science Teachers Association (TSTA). He is editor of the *Science Educator*, a publication of NSELA. He is also director of the Tennessee Junior Academy of Science (TJAS), and editor of the *TJAS Handbook and Proceedings*. He is widely published and has directed numerous science and technology grants.

He has received many honors, including the National Science Teachers Association (NSTA) Distinguished Service Award, the East Tennessee State University Distinguished Faculty Award, the TAS Outstanding Science Teacher Award, and the Tennessee Science Teachers Association Distinguished Educator of the Year Award.

Patricia Shane is the associate director of the Center for Mathematics and Science Education and is an associate professor of education at the University of North Carolina at Chapel Hill, where she teaches and provides professional development for mathematics and science teachers. She works closely with the UNC-Chapel Hill Pre-College Program, which recruits underrepresented groups into math and science fields.

She has been the project director for numerous grants, including more than 30 Eisenhower grants, and has received awards for service in science education, including the National Outstanding Science Supervisor Award from NSELA.

She was a science, mathematics, and reading /language arts coordinator at the system level and worked as a classroom teacher and guidance counselor at the school level.

She is serving as the immediate past-president of NSELA and is a past-president of the North Carolina Science Teachers Association and the North Carolina Science Leadership Association. She is a former district director for both NSELA and NSTA and is a current board member of NSELA.

Acknowledgments

Many people worked with us to make this book a reality, and we would like to acknowledge their contribution. We would like to begin by thanking the staff at NSTA Press. Two of these exemplary professionals are Claire Reinburg and Betty Smith. We would also like to thank the many reviewers whose comments and suggestions were crucial in improving our work: James McLean, University of Alabama; Gerry Madrazo, Hawaii Department of Education; LaMoine Motz, Oakland County Schools, Michigan; and Martha Rhoton, Kingsport, Tennessee. No volume is any better than the manuscripts that are contributed to it; we appreciate the time and efforts of those whose work lies within the cover of this book.

We also want to thank and acknowledge the support, help, and suggestions of the NSELA board of directors: Nicola Micozzi, past president, for his suggestions and guidance in the early stages of the project, and executive director Peggy Holliday in the later stages of the project.

Finally, we would like to thank graduate assistant Rick Christian, East Tennessee State University, for his excellent work. Rick was instrumental in managing and wordprocessing the drafts of each manuscript.

Part I Within the Science Classroom

CHAPTER 1

The Impact of Technology on the 21st Century Classroom

Karen E. Irving

Little doubt exists that advances in educational technology have already transformed the American classroom. Teachers in the 21st century enjoy access to information and resources that their predecessors could not imagine: state-of-the-art information available on the internet 24/7 on the most arcane subjects; still images and video of events from all over the world and even the universe, data sets on population growth, the environment, ocean currents, weather patterns, sporting events, and a myriad other topics that are available for student analysis and research in classroom lessons and projects; virtual field trips to remote locations such as Antarctica and geologic sites with active volcanoes or isolated island communities; sophisticated representations of atoms and molecules that can be enlarged, color coded, and presented in multiple model systems; animations of processes such as protein synthesis and salt dissolving in water; and virtual planetarium software packages that allow teachers to "turn off the Sun" during daylight hours to allow students to visualize the constellations that are present in the daytime sky.

This chapter explores how educational technology has changed and will continue to change the ways that teachers teach and students learn in classrooms of the 21st century.

The chapter begins with a description of how students can learn *from* computers with tutoring systems and drill and practice software. Next, it explores the use of primary sources available on the internet, data sets, CD-ROMS, video, and animations that offer examples of how students learn *with* (rather than from) technology. Probeware peripheral devices hooked to handheld calculators or computers, digital imaging systems such as cameras or microscopes, and multimedia presentation systems and software offer new ways to collect, analyze, and display data as well as to motivate students and engage their interest. Connected classrooms promise improved formative assessment as teachers monitor student learning more closely and tailor their lessons to individual students' needs. Communication applications such as e-mail, discussion boards, chat rooms, teleconferencing equipment, and course management systems all enhance the choices teachers have to strengthen writing and speaking skills with the opportunity to facilitate communication with members of the education community. Online learning communities connect learners and teachers in remote locations and extend the educational opportunities to a greater number of students. In this era of testing requirement mandated by the No Child Left Behind Act (NCLB) of 2001 (2002), states are motivated to find more efficient and effective ways to measure student achievement. Computer-based assessments present the advantage of immediate feedback allowing schools to analyze data, decide on policy, and implement new programs in a timely fashion. Lastly, this chapter explores how preservice and inservice teachers can best be prepared for the educational technology challenges of 21st century classrooms.

For years science teachers have been using technologies such as pH meters, balances, overhead projectors, and optical microscopes in the classroom. In this chapter, educational technology tools will be characterized as computer- and calculator-based electronic devices used to complete an educational task.

Learning *From* Technology

Information delivery is the paradigm that learning *from* technology supports. In this way of thinking about learning, the computer (or teacher) provides information to students, students read and understand the information, and achievement occurs when students provide an adequate response to questions regarding the content of this information. The student serves as a passive recipient of knowledge. The teacher/computer functions as an information delivery system (Reeves 1998).

The literature contains mixed messages regarding the effectiveness of computer-based instruction, computer-assisted instruction, intelligent learning systems, and other computer tutoring systems. In 1995, a study of

101 eighth-grade students in Turkey on the use of computer-aided instruction in chemistry classrooms followed a pre- and posttest control group design. The authors found that students using the computer-aided instructional program on the mole concept and chemical formulas showed significantly higher scores than the control group recitation sections (Yalçinalp et al. 1995). In another study, Chang analyzed 159 Earth science students' achievement in Taiwan in a pre- and posttest control group experiment and found significant difference between the groups (Chang 2001). Students in the problem-based computer-based instruction group scored generally higher on total items as well as on knowledge and comprehension-level items than did students in the control group.

On the other hand, Wenglinsky in his study on the relationship between educational technology and student achievement in mathematics attempted to identify whether computer use was making a difference in mathematics, which kind of computer use had what kind of effect, and how differences among students impacted achievement. After controlling for socioeconomic status, class size, and teacher characteristics, findings from this large quantitative study of 6,227 fourth-graders' and 7,146 eighth-graders' scores on the National Assessment of Educational Progress (NAEP) pointed to lower achievement in groups with higher levels of drill and practice exposure to computers and higher achievement with "higher order" applications of technology in the classroom. Wenglinsky concluded that how computers are used in the classroom represents an important factor in student achievement (Wenglinsky 1998).

Another large-scale longitudinal study with the West Virginia Basic Skills/Computer Education Program (BS/CE) focused on reading, language arts, and mathematics with a gradual phase-in of technology equipment and training from kindergarten through third grade. Using regression analysis, researchers concluded that the BS/CE program was responsible for a significant portion of the total variance in the measured student achievement (Mann 1999). Kulik analyzed more than 500 individual papers on the impact of computer-based instruction, computer-aided instruction, and other drill and practice software in a large meta-analytical study. The findings from this work showed 9 to 22 percentile gains for the computer-using groups over control groups (Kulik 1994). In addition to improvement in student achievement data, Kulik found that computer-based instruction decreased the amount of time needed for students to learn. Johnston, in another review of the research on the effectiveness of instructional technology, reported effect sizes for computer-based training ranging from 0.20 to 0.46 depending on the population and effect sizes for instructional technology in general ranging from 0.15 to 0.66 standard deviations. Of note is that all effect sizes reported favorable findings when compared to traditional teaching methods (Johnston 1995).

As these studies indicate, use of computers for drill and practice or as a student tutor has some support in the literature. In the data-driven current educational climate, school districts bent on increasing student achievement on standardized tests have taken note. These research reports, however, often add the caveat that, while large quantitative studies point to achievement gains, closer examination of the data shows that educational technology is less effective when learning objectives are unclear. Limiting educational technology integration to learning *from* technology overlooks many contributions that technology can make in 21st century classrooms.

Learning *With* Technology

Knowledge construction is the paradigm for learning *with* technology. Rather than using technology as a source of information to pour into a passive learner, teachers employ technology to engage students with real-world problem solving, conceptual development, and critical thinking (Ringstaff and Kelley 2002). Student involvement with technology includes data collection, organization, analysis, and communication of results.

Use of primary data sources and interactive websites or software provides teachers with opportunities to engage students in inquiry-based science lessons from preschool to college level. These inquiry-based lessons enlist students in hands-on, minds-on science and encourage creative thinking and problem solving. Moore and Huber identified two types of internet sites as appropriate for inquiry-based lessons: 1) sites with data sets and interactive data visualization tools such as graphing programs, and 2) interactive sites that allow students to control virtual equipment and simulated resources (2001).

Data sets play a central role in the El Niño lesson in which students use monthly climate data (temperature and precipitation) from online databases to determine if the weather in their community varies from the norm during El Niño years. Students are introduced to spreadsheets, descriptive statistics (averages and standard deviations), and using graphing techniques to analyze the data (Bell et al. 2001). Other types of data sets that support inquiry lessons include athletic records, chemical element and periodic table data, and tidal information. The Center for Technology and Teacher Education at the University of Virginia offers a wealth of sample lessons for science and mathematics teachers that demonstrate how data sets can be integrated into lessons. These lessons can be accessed at *www.teacherlink.org*.

Interactive websites offer tools that students can use to learn about abstract science concepts. For example, students can change frequencies or wavelength and view the impact on wave formation and sounds at *www.mta.ca/faculty/science/physics/siren/Applets.html*; students can place seismometers and triangulate to locate the epicenter for an earthquake at *http://www.sciencecourseware.com/eec/Earthquake;* or students can view animations of water molecule visualizations to help them understand acids and bases at *www.johnkyrk.com/H2O.html*.

Software programs allow students to explore aspects of nature during the school day that would ordinarily be impossible. As part of an inquiry unit on Earth-Sun-Moon relationships, an Earth science teacher introduces her students to a virtual planetarium program.

Ida asks students to check their moon journals to recall where the Moon was located two days ago, where it was located yesterday, and where they expect to find the Moon today. Students share not only locations for Moon sightings from their journals, but also offer details about the shape and size of the Moon. Ida opens a virtual planetarium and shows images of the Moon's position and shape for the preceding few days to confirm students' observations. She asks, "If the Moon rises around 3:30 PM today, what time would it rise on Sunday? Will it rise earlier or later? What phase will the Moon have on Sunday?"

Ida continues the lesson: "Where do the stars go during the daylight hours?" Students consider possible answers, and agree that the stars must still be in the sky but that the power of the Sun's light makes it impossible to see them. Ida uses her virtual planetarium program to "turn off the Sun" and reveals the stars that students would see at Rural High School that day (Irving 2003).

In this lesson, Ida engages her students using both real data in their moon journals as well as virtual data from the planetarium software. Ida takes advantage of the unique features of this educational technology tool to allow her students to view the night sky during the daytime and to observe the apparent movement of heavenly bodies. She structures her lessons to engage students in learning by helping them formulate questions, collect evidence, make predictions, and apply the knowledge of the motion of the Moon to the motion of the stars.

Electronic data collection devices help teachers move the classroom to the field where students enjoy opportunities to use inquiry to develop questions based on their observations. Tools such as electronic probeware to collect pH, temperature, or oxygen levels link directly to handheld calculators or laptop computers and allow students to collect, record, and analyze data (Heflich et al. 2001). Middle and high school teachers in North Carolina engaged in a three-year technology-integrated project, Students as Scientists, developed by the University of North Carolina, Wilmington. The project included collecting and analyzing water samples from different sources in the Wilmington area and comparing their results to existing water-quality data available on the web (Comeaux and Huber 2001). Another example includes the use of motion detectors to help students understand kinematics graphing (Flores 2001; Friedler and McFarlane 1997).

Imaging devices such as digital cameras and digital microscopes offer additional opportunities for visualization in the science classroom. Students can observe the imbibation and germination of seeds using time lapse photography and digital microscopes. The transformation of a caterpillar into a chrysalis and the emergence of the butterfly captured in time lapse images as described below offer students windows into the subtle changes of nature that once could be learned about only in books (Bell and Bell 2002).

Ninth-grade biology students work in small groups at their low hexagonal laboratory stations finishing up an acid-base pH laboratory activity. Amy demonstrates the digital camera that students will use to record images during their inquiry projects. Students suggest recording close-up images of the plants at different stages of growth, images of the plants being treated with acid rain, images showing how the watering system functions to provide the plants with moisture, and images of the lighting system.

Amy next introduces the butterfly metamorphosis inquiry project. She asks her class to compare the experimental design of the acid rain project with this new observational project. In addition to the acid rain journal, students will record data daily in a butterfly journal. They will take pictures using a digital camera, record behavior using a digital microscope with both snapshot and video capture capability, make sketches by hand and record data describing the behavior of their caterpillars. Amy reviews the difference between observations and inferences with her students before she distributes the pillboxes with the caterpillars to her students (Irving 2003).

A different kind of educational technology use occurs in the connected classroom. Connected classroom technology refers to a networked system of personal computers or handheld devices specifically designed to be used in a classroom for interactive teaching and learning. These networked technologies include response systems, classroom communication systems, and newer systems included under the CATAALYST (classroom aggregation technology for activating and assessing learning and your students' thinking) name (Roschelle et al. 2004). Connected classroom systems offer opportunities for improved formative assessment through questioning and immediate feedback and allow teachers to tailor instruction to meet student needs (Black and Wiliam 1998; Fuchs and Fuchs 1986). Students beam answers anonymously to a receiving station and histograms of student answer choices are displayed. Data logs are archived for later analysis. Discourse that occurs in a safe environment through the public examination of problem solving and alternative conceptions helps students understand their role as critical listeners and thinkers in the classroom (Artzt and Yaloz-Femia 1999). In the connected classroom, teacher adaptive expertise allows formative assessment that can monitor students' incremental progress and keep them oriented on the path to deep conceptual understanding.

Improving Communication *With* Technology

The classroom, especially at the secondary level, has been described as a culture of isolation (Schlagal et al. 1996). Electronic communities for students and teachers offer a wealth of opportunities to break down barriers between people and provide settings for idea sharing and peer support (Bull et al. 1989; Casey 1994; Bodzin and Park 2002). Teachers use online communities, electronic bulletin boards, lesson plan banks, and listservs to stay connected to the larger educational community outside their classroom. Web-based forums promote reflective thinking for preservice science teachers in remote student teaching placements (Bodzin and Park 2002,

2000). In addition to supporting reflective practice, the public nature of the discourse encourages participants to respond thoughtfully (Yore 2001). Pairing inservice teachers and preservice students provides opportunities for improved teacher-student teacher communication, and also focuses on technology transfer from the university teacher education classrooms to inservice teachers (VanMetre 2000). The Teacher Institute for Curriculum Knowledge about the Integration of Technology (TICKIT) at Indiana University used asynchronous web-based conferencing for K–12 teachers from rural Indiana schools. Online debates focused participants around a particular content and resulted in greater content-based discussion than face-to-face forums (Bonk et al. 2002).

Teleconferencing technologies offer the opportunity for teachers and students in remote locations to have two-way audio and video communications. Cybermentoring with elementary and secondary schools has been explored in Washington State with telephones, e-mail, web design, and both low- and high-end videoconferencing systems. Recent projects pairing university faculty and students with K–12 students and teachers included fourth-grade science mentoring and ninth-grade Earth science curriculum planning projects (Maring et al. 2003). Online courses with high-end video conferencing are already in use for courses offered to Japanese students. Professors at Stanford, the University of California, Davis, and California State University, Hayward, offer pre-MBA courses to students in Tokyo's Hosei University. With complete multimedia capabilities, the videoconferencing system allows Japanese students to see live presentations of classes offered in California. Professors and students have access to a full palate of writing utensils to annotate and save slides from class lectures and discussions (Shinkai 2004).

The Rural Technology Initiative (RTI) sponsored by McREL (Mid-Continent Research for Education and Learning) provides quality training in technology integration for mathematics and science teachers and administrators in remote rural locations in Colorado, Kansas, Missouri, Nebraska, North Dakota, South Dakota, and Wyoming. This project provides training targeted at increasing student achievement through the use of technology and effective teaching strategies. Online courses save schools the travel, substitute, and hotel expenses usually associated with traditional professional development opportunities. Videoconferencing, an internet portal, and teleconferencing are part of the online delivery system for this professional development. Science teachers receive college credit in science technology integration to help teachers meet the NCLB highly qualified teacher requirements (REL Network 2004).

Course management systems have become more popular on college and university campuses as well as for schools in the K–12 sector. Although initially courseware companies suggested that these tools would help reach 'distant' students, the audience for courseware tools is mostly local students in traditional educational programs. Convenience for large numbers of resident students as well as off-campus adult students plays an important role in the use of course management systems. These applications allow professors to build course content, offer chat rooms for guided discourse, link to electronic resources on other websites, and manage course grades. Course management tasks such as planning, organizing, structuring, tracking, reporting, communication arrangements, and expectations were tracked by Nijhius and Collis in their study of 51 instructors' use of web-based course management systems at the University of Twente, Netherlands, during one academic year (2003).

Assessment and Educational Technology

In this era of NCLB testing requirements, states are searching for more efficient and effective ways to determine student achievement. Computer-based assessments offer the advantage of immediate feedback, allowing schools to analyze data, decide on policy, and implement new programs in a timely fashion. Traditional testing formats often take weeks or months to score and return to schools. According to *Education Week's* Technology Counts report in May 2003, 12 states and the District of Columbia are already using or piloting computerized exams. All except one of these programs are internet-based (Edwards 2003).

The demands of NCLB can be seen as either support for or hindrance to computerized testing. Although technology offers the potential for streamlined assessment and accountability options, schools need computers for students to take tests online. With budgets limiting school options, it seems unlikely that many school systems will be able to take advantage of this opportunity without an infusion of capital. The secure conditions required to limit opportunities for cheating on high-stakes tests represent another problem. Students across a state must take the test in a limited time and under the same conditions as all other students. The questions become: How many computers are needed, and can the connections needed to internet websites be guaranteed across the state at the same time? Equipment often varies from school to school, complicating the issue of fairness. If some students in a state take paper-and-pencil tests and others take computerized versions, is one group or the other advantaged? Do students with outdated computers suffer compared to their peers with more modern technology resources (Olson 2003)?

Although high-stakes testing raises many issues for educators, low-stakes diagnostic computerized testing offers many possibilities for improving student performance. The logic is that success on low-stakes tests will lead to improved performance on their high-stakes cousins. In addition to low-stakes individual classroom use of computer-based testing, many experts predict that most states and districts will use online test preparation programs to help raise student scores on high-stakes assessments. Twelve states already have computer-based practice exams available to help students prepare for state-mandated tests (Borja 2003).

Opportunities for special education students to fully participate in the classroom through the use of assistive technologies are the focus of research efforts in both the special education and educational technology communities (Rose 2001; Hitchcock et al. 2002). Inexpensive, efficient test delivery and rapid scoring as well as an opportunity to make state tests more accessible to special populations of students argue in favor of computerized testing programs. Special education students may serve as test populations as educators experiment with new technology-based assessment systems. In Indiana, electronic portfolios are used to measure the progress of students with disabilities. A videotape of oral reading ability collected annually provides a unique and highly individual view of a student's progress over a multiyear period (Goldstein 2003).

Other innovative programs in computerized assessment include Indiana's plan to create a deep online test item bank with each item linked to appropriate state standards and Oregon's efforts to produce an online writing assessment. Adaptive testing, where students are pitched questions from the computer test bank that are chosen based on performance on earlier items, provides useful diagnostic information for educators, but does not meet the demands of NCLB to assess each student against the grade-level standards set by the state. South Dakota developed an adaptive online testing program, but has made it voluntary for schools and has added a paper-and-pencil test to meet the requirements of the NCLB legislation (Olson 2003; Trotter 2003).

Preparing Teachers for the 21st Century Classroom

Professional science and education organizations have stated positions regarding the preparation of science teachers (AAAS 2002, 1998; ISTE 2002; NCATE 1997; NRC 2000; Willis and Mehlinger 1996). Common aspects of the recommendations offered for teacher preparation include a) providing skills training for educational technology in the context of science teaching; b) modeling appropriate uses of educational technology to teach science in preservice methods classes; c) providing opportunities for preservice teachers to practice using educational technology in science teaching; d) providing opportunities for preservice teachers to observe inservice teachers model educational technology use for science teaching; and e) providing opportunities for preservice science teachers to use educational technology during their student teaching experience.

The early literature regarding student teacher use of technology in secondary science teaching revealed that despite attempts to provide technology training for preservice science teachers, little transfer of this knowledge to their secondary classrooms occurred during their teaching (Barton 1993; McFarlane 1994; Kennedy 1996; Parkinson 1998; Byrum and Cashman 1993). Simply teaching novice teachers how to use technology proved insufficient preparation for them to integrate the same skills into their classroom teaching. Findings from recent research projects indicate that participants who complete a sustained technology-enriched preparation program report feeling adequately prepared to teach science using technology both during student teaching and during their first year in the classroom (McNall 2003; Irving 2003).

ePCK, electronic pedagogical content knowledge, includes the knowledge classroom teachers need in addition to the knowledge of their content domain, pedagogy, and curriculum in order to integrate educational technology successfully into their teaching. Shulman (1986) first described pedagogical content knowledge (PCK) as the teacher's knowledge of the best ways to teach particular concepts, which concepts are apt to cause confusion for students, common misconceptions for students in a particular domain, a wide variety of teaching strategies from which to select the best approach for a particular student group, and the most appropriate demonstrations, laboratory exercises, analogies, images, diagrams, problems, and explanations to make a subject transparent for students. Expert teachers not only have a deep conceptual understanding of the topics they teach, but they also understand why students are challenged when learning some topics and not others.

Two important aspects of ePCK for integrating technology into science teaching include being able to recognize the connection between the technology, the science content, and the pedagogy for a lesson, and being able to recognize how the technology can help students dispel or avoid misconceptions in a particular domain. As with science content, it is not enough to have a deep understanding of educational technology to be able to teach effectively using its tools. Teaching involves identifying the match between the learner's prior knowledge, how the new content fits with the already known, and the strategy the teacher chooses to present new topics. Teacher knowledge of educational technologies that offer compelling animations, interactive simulations, images, data sets, data collection and analysis tools, and communication tools that fit the curriculum topics for their science discipline is an important element of ePCK.

Not every domain in a science class will fit the use of educational technology equally well. Hands-on activities where students manipulate objects and create artifacts in the classroom offer compelling strategies for many science concepts. However, many concepts in science are abstract, complex, and invisible without the aid of special technologies, or too subtle for ordinary viewing in the classroom. Electronic technologies offer science teachers a host of powerful tools to help students visualize these concepts. ePCK knowledge involves the developing process of recognizing the parts of a science curriculum that would benefit from the use of educational technology tools to illuminate abstract or complex topics. Knowing about the technology, knowing how to use the technology, knowing how the technology fits the curriculum, knowing how the use of the technology contributes uniquely to the lesson and helps students avoid or dispel misconceptions regarding the content in a particular domain constitute important aspects of ePCK.

Teacher education programs face the dual burdens of constantly changing educational technology as well as a climate of rising expectations for technology use in teaching and learning. Despite these challenges, an excellent example of an integrated technology enrichment program is provided for student teachers at the University of Virginia (Bell and Hofer 2003; Cooper and Bull 1997).

In this program, students learn not only learn how to use educational technologies but also are encouraged and required to envision, plan, and implement lessons using technology with objectives clearly tied to the national and state standards. The sequential mode of instruction—from the introductory course focusing on word processing, e-mail, and networking—through an educational technology course with a science- and mathematics-specific syllabus followed by a year-long science methods class where educational technology is routinely modeled in appropriate and effective ways provides a sustained approach to technology integration. Students spend time identifying resources, learning how to use them, thinking about how they fit the curriculum objectives of their specific disciplines, designing lessons to include these technologies with a guiding framework provided by the Flick and Bell standards for effective and appropriate integration in science classrooms (Flick and Bell 2000), and finally reflecting on the successes and failures of their implementation efforts.

Conclusion

What are the messages to educators about the impact of educational technology in 21st century classrooms? Sweeping changes have occurred in the workplace where faxes, computer networks, e-mail, and teleconferencing alter the daily routines of modern people. Policy makers, business leaders, and parents urge educators to prepare students for the high-tech world of the contemporary community. School boards and superintendents have amassed impressive resources to wire and equip the school houses of America to allow students and teachers access to the powerful interactive technologies of the future. Not only will students in the 21st century learn *with* technology, but colleges of education have an obligation to help their preservice teachers learn about and implement educational technology in their teaching and learning.

An important message that can be gleaned from the research on educational technology in classrooms of the 21st century is that technology represents a means, not an end. Educators and policy makers recognize that in addition to infrastructure, maintenance, and reliability, an essential condition for success is that teachers must have *ePCK, electronic pedagogical content knowledge*. Teachers must know not only how to use the technology but also how to teach with technology in appropriate and effective ways. Technology alone does not improve instruction or student achievement; rather, technology works when it serves clear educational goals and is implemented in pedagogically sound ways.

Karen E. Irving

is an assistant professor of Mathematics, Science, and Technology in the School of Teaching and Learning at The Ohio State University and co-director of the West-Central Excel Center for Excellence in Science and Mathematics. She received the 2004 National Technology Leadership Initiative Science Fellowship Award for her work in educational technology in science teaching and learning.

References

American Association for the Advancement of Science (AAAS). 2002. *Project 2061: Blueprints online* 1997 [cited July 23 2002]. Available at *www.project2061.org/tools/bluepol/blpframe.htm.*

American Association for the Advancement of Science (AAAS). 1998. *Blueprints for reform.* New York: Oxford University Press.

Artzt, A., and S. Yaloz-Femia. 1999. Mathematical reasoning during small–group problem solving. In *Developing mathematical reasoning in grades K–12: 1999 yearbook*, eds. L. Stiff and F. Curio. Reston, VA: National Council of Teachers of Mathematics.

Barton, R. 1993. Computers and practical science: Why isn't everyone doing it? *School Science Review* 75 (271):75–80.

Bell, R., and L. Bell. 2002. *Invigorating science teaching with a high-tech, low-cost tool* [website]. The George Lucas Educational Foundation 2002 [cited 02/06/11 2002]. Available from *http://glef.org/techtoolarticle.html.*

Bell, R., and M. Hofer. 2003. The Curry School of Education and long-term commitment to technology integration. *Contemporary Issues in Technology and Teacher Education.*

Bell, R., M. Niess, and L. Bell. 2001. El Niño did it: Using technology to assess and predict climate trends. *Learning and Leading with Technology* 29 (4):18–26.

Black, P., and D. Wiliam. 1998. *Inside the black box: Raising standards through classroom assessment.* London: King's College London.

Bodzin, A. M., and J. C. Park. 2000. Factors that influence asynchronous discourse with preservice teachers on a public, web-based forum. *Journal of Computing in Teacher Education* 16 (4): 22–30.

Bodzin, A. M., and J. C. Park. 2002. Using a nonrestrictive web-based forum to promote reflective discourse with preservice teachers. *Contemporary Issues in Technology and Teacher Education* 2 (3).

Bonk, C., L. Ehman, E. Hixon, and L. Yamagata-Lynch. 2002. The pedagogical TICKIT: Web conferencing to promote communication and support during teacher professional development. *Journal of Technology & Teacher Education* 10 (2): 205–33.

Borja, R. 2003. Preparing for the big test. *Education Week's Technology Counts 2003*, May 8, 23–26.

Bull, G., J. Harris, J. Lloyd, and J. Short. 1989. The electronic academic village. *Journal of Teacher Education* 40 (4): 27–31.

Byrum, D., and C. Cashman. 1993. Preservice teacher training in educational computing: Problems, perceptions and preparations. *Journal of Technology and Teacher Education* 9 (1): 20–24.

Casey, J. 1994. TeacherNet: Student teachers travel the information highway. *Journal of Computing in Teacher Education* 11 (1): 8–11.

Chang, C. 2001. Comparing the impacts of a problem-based computer-assisted instruction and the direct–interactive teaching method on student science achievement. *Journal of Science Education & Technology* 10 (2):147–53.

Comeaux, P., and R. Huber. 2001. Students as scientists: Using interactive technologies and collaborative inquiry in an environmental science project for teachers and their students. *Journal of Science Teacher Education* 12 (4): 235–252.

Cooper, J., and G. Bull. 1997. Technology and teacher education: past practice and recommended direction. *Action in Teacher Education* 19 (2): 97–106.

Edwards, V. B. 2003. Tech's answer to testing. *Education Week*, May 8, 8–10.

Flick, L., and R. Bell. 2000. Preparing tomorrow's science teachers to use technology: Guidelines for science educators. *Contemporary Issues in Technology and Teacher Education [Online serial]* 1 (1): 39–60.

Flores, A. 2001. SSMILes#51: Inclined planes and motion detectors: A study of acceleration. *School Science & Mathematics* 101 (3):154–161.

Friedler, Y., and A. E. McFarlane. 1997. Data logging with portable computers: A study of the impact on graphing skills in secondary pupils. *Journal of Computers in Mathematics & Science Teaching* 16 (4): 527–550.

Fuchs, L. S., and D. Fuchs. 1986. Effects of systematic formative evaluation: A meta–analysis. *Exceptional Children* 53 (3):199–208.

Goldstein, L. 2003. Spec. ed. tech sparks ideas: Testing tools for children with disabilities attracts mainstream attention. *Education Week Technology Counts 2003*, May 8, 27–30.

Heflich, D. A., J. K. Dixon, and K. S. Davis. 2001. Taking it to the field: The authentic integration of mathematics and technology in inquiry-based instruction. *Journal of Computers in Mathematics and Science Teaching* 20 (1): 99–112.

Hitchcock, C., A. Meyer, D. Rose, and R. Jackson. 2002. Providing new access to the general curriculum: Universal design for learning. *TEACHING Exceptional Children* 35 (2): 8–17.

Irving, K. E. 2003. Preservice science teachers' use of educational technology during student teaching. PhD diss., Curry School of Education, University of Virginia, Charlottesville, VA.

ISTE. 2002. *National standards for technology in teacher preparation.* International Society for Technology in Education [cited Dec 20, 2004. Available from *http://cnets.iste.org/teachers/*].

Johnston, R. 1995. The Effectiveness of Instructional Technology: A Review of the Research. Paper read at Proceedings of the Virtual Reality in Medicine and Developers' Exposition, June 1995, at Cambridge, MA.

Kennedy, J. 1996. Essential elements of initial teacher training courses for science teachers: A survey of tutors in the UK. *Research in Science and Technology Education* 14: 21–32.

Kulik, J. A. 1994. Meta–analytic studies of findings on computerized instruction. In *Technology assessment in education and training*, eds. E. Baker and H. O'Neil. Hillsdale, N.J.: Lawrence Erlbaum.

Mann, D. 1999. Documenting the effects of instructional technology: A flyover of policy questions. In *Secretary's Conference on Educational Technology*. Washington, DC: US Department of Education.

Maring, G. H., J. A. Schmid, and J. Roark. 2003. An educator's guide to high-end videoconferencing.

McFarlane, A. 1994. IT widens scope for acquiring key skill. *Times education supplement*: xi.

McNall, R. 2003. Beginning secondary science teachers' instructional use of educational technology during the induction year. PhD diss., Curry School of Education, University of Virginia, Charlottesville, VA.

McREL Launches Rural Technology Institute. 2004. Mid Continent Research for Educational Learning 2004. Retrieved December 18, 2004, from *www.relnetwork.org/news/2004–08/10–McREL.html.*

Moore, C. J., and R. Huber. 2001. Internet tools for facilitating inquiry. *Contemporary Issues in Technology and Teacher Education* 1 (4): 451–464.

National Research Council (NRC). 2000. *Inquiry and the National Science Education Standards.* Washington, DC: National Academy Press.

NCATE. 1997. *Technology and the new professional teacher: Preparing for the 21st century classroom.* Washington, DC: National Council for Accreditation of Teacher Education.

Nijhuis, G., and B. Collis. 2003. Using a web-based course-management system: An evaluation of management tasks and time implications for the instructor. *Evaluation and Program Planning* 26 (2):193–201.

Olson, L. 2003. Legal twists, digital turns. *Education Week's Technology Counts 2003*, May 8, 11–16.

Parkinson, J. 1998. The difficulties in developing information technology competencies with student science teachers. *Research in Science & Technological Education* 16 (1): 67–78.

Reeves, T. C. 1998. The impact of media and technology in schools: A research report prepared for the Bertelsmann Foundation. Retrieved December 18, 2004, from *www.athensacademy.org/instruct/media_tech/reeves0.html.*

Ringstaff, C., and L. Kelley. 2002. *The learning return on our educational technology investment: A review of findings from research.* San Francisco: West Ed RTEC.

Roschelle, J., W. R. Penuel, and L. Abrahamson. 2004. The networked classroom. *Educational Leadership* 61 (5): 50–54.

Rose, D. 2001. Universal design for learning. *Journal of Special Education Technology* 16 (4): 64–67.

Schlagal, B., W. Trathen, and W. Blanton. 1996. Structuring telecommunications to create instructional conversations about student teaching. *Journal of Teacher Education* 47 (3):175–183.

Shinkai, Y. 2004. Videoconferencing system brings Japanese students face-to-face with U.S. professors. In *T H E Journal*: T.H.E. Journal.

Shulman, L. S. 1986. Those who understand: Knowledge growth in teaching. *Educational Researcher* 15: 4–14.

Trotter, A. 2003. A question of direction: Adaptive testing puts federal officials and experts at odds. *Education Week's Technology Counts 2003*, May 8, 17–21.

United States Department of Education Office of Elementary and Secondary Education. 2002. *No Child Left Behind: Closing the Gap in Educational Achievement.* Washington, DC: USDOE.

VanMetre, S. 2000. Productive partnerships. *The Delta Kappa Gamma Bulletin* 67 (1): 38–40.

Wenglinsky, H. 1998. *Does it compute? The relationship between educational technology and student achievement in mathematics.* Princeton, NJ: Educational Testing Service.

Willis, J. W., and H. D. Mehlinger. 1996. Information technology and teacher education. In *Handbook of Research on Teacher Education*, eds. J. Sikula, T. J. Buttery and E. Guyton. New York: Prentice Hall International.

Yalçinalp, S., O. Geban, and I. Özkan. 1995. Effectiveness of using computer-assisted supplementary instruction for teaching the mole concept. *Journal of Research in Science Teaching* 32 (10):1083–1095.

Yore, L. D. 2001. Heightening reflection through dialogue: A case for electronic journaling and electronic concept mapping in science classes: A commentary on Germann, Young-soo, & Patton. *Contemporary Issues in Technology and Teacher Education [Online serial]* 1 (3).

CHAPTER

2

The Science Curriculum: Trends and Issues

Rodger W. Bybee

Among the 21st century issues and trends in science education, one must acknowledge the fundamental importance of the science curriculum. It is the one component that brings together social aspirations, content standards, research on learning, appropriate assessments, and meaningful professional development. Changing a district's or a school's science program often begins with the need for or timing of a textbook adoption. I would note that the fundamental importance of the curriculum is longstanding (Kliebard 1992), and that there are contemporary trends that relate directly to the curriculum (Ravitch 1995) and the theme of national standards in general (Cobb 1994) and science in particular (NRC 2002). Because contemporary policies often have not acknowledged the fundamental form and function of curricula, I will address several themes central to school science curricula.

In recent times one can cite the Sputnik era in which we reformed the curriculum programs based on the Soviet Union's perceived lead in the race to space; the national-risk era in which we reformed policies based on pending economic doom; the standards era in which we reformed policies, programs, and practices based on the low levels of achievement of U.S. students compared to their peers in other countries and our goal of being first in the world. As we begin the 21st century, we have the era of the No Child Left Behind (NCLB) Act of 2001 (2002) in which assessments—international, national, state, and local—represent the dominant forces for educational reform. We have perspectives from reforms past and present, but one lesson stands out—the reforms that had the most impact affected three areas: they changed the curriculum, they improved teaching, and they provided professional development for teachers.

In this chapter I begin with a discussion of standards and then develop the connections between standards and the science curriculum. The third section addresses the design and development of science curricula, and I use our work at BSCS as the basis for this discussion.

Standards

- *The power of standards lies in their capacity to change the fundamental components of the educational system.*

The standards, as a set of national or state policies, provide a comprehensive approach to changing science education policies, programs, and practices. By their design, standards direct attention to these domains and inform decisions about various components of the educational system. To the degree various agencies, organizations, institutions, and districts embrace the standards, they have the potential to bring greater coherence and unity to diverse components such as state frameworks and assessments, teacher education, continuing professional development of science teachers, textbook adoptions and implementations, and resources and support for science education K–12.

Contrast the potential influence of standards on the instructional core and student achievement with the possibility of improving student achievement through educational ideas such as vouchers, charter schools, site-based management, wiring schools for the web, and purchasing computers. To be clear, I am not opposed to such ideas. They embrace important goals, but they are distant from those factors that have the highest probability of enhancing student learning.

- *A standards-based approach to educational improvement emphasizes what all students should know and be able to do.*

Using standards shifts our perspective on improving education from inputs, that is, changes that we assume will enhance achievement such as time in school, homework, and use of instructional technologies to outputs such as defining the goals for 13 years of school science education. The intention is to define clearly the goals of education and then change the various means of achieving those ends. Of course, educational change never works out as planned, but this is a new perspective, a different way of thinking about reform and achieving higher levels of student achievement.

Taking a school district as an example, the district uses standards as the basis for identifying goals for the science education program—what all students should know and be able to do. The district could then either select or design assessments aligned with those outcomes and do the same for curriculum materials and instructional strategies. Such an approach, I propose, would result in greater coherence for the school science program. In marked contrast, many districts pay little attention to standards, go directly to selection of textbooks, and independently implement a commercially available textbook. School personnel then complain that the text does not align with the valued outcomes, administrators apply pressure for higher test scores, and local media decry the appalling results, regardless of what they are.

Curriculum

- *The content of national and many state standards emphasizes fundamental concepts of life, Earth, and physical science and expands the traditional domains to include the contexts of inquiry, technology, personal and social perspectives, and the history and nature of science.*

Although it may seem that this discussion places standards at the center of science education, it is the science curriculum and teaching that matter most. In the end, students learn the content they are taught. And this directs attention to the content of the curriculum. Indeed, the standards help define that content. This said, school districts make decisions about the textbooks and materials used in the science program, and teachers decide the particular emphasis and activities that students will experience. It is worth noting that the national standards recommend the development of fundamental scientific concepts and intellectual abilities as opposed to the current emphasis on facts, information, and topics.

One insight from TIMSS (1996, 1997, 1998) and comparisons of U.S. curricula with high-achieving countries shows the need to reduce the number of science topics students encounter in a school year and to focus efforts on fundamental concepts and abilities (Schmidt et al. 1996, 1997). The national standards do this. However, those standards assume that those with responsibility for curricular reform would reduce topics and reform programs so the topics in school programs present opportunities to learn fundamental science concepts. Instead, schools have viewed standards as topics that must be added to current programs. Such was not the intention of the standards-based reform of the science curriculum.

The national standards present a new view of inquiry. Based on the historical importance of scientific inquiry, or the processes of science, the standards extend current views from process skills such as observing, inferring, hypothesizing, and the like, to a development of cognitive abilities such as reasoning, critical thinking, and using evidence and logic to form explanations. In addition, the standards recommend that students develop some understanding of scientific inquiry. Science as inquiry thus becomes a part of content for the science curriculum and not just teaching strategies.

Finally, the standards provide a context within which such fundamental concepts can be presented. Technology, personal and social perspectives, and history and nature of science all provide appropriate contexts for use in curriculum reform.

- *The standards provide the basis for a science curriculum that is educationally coherent, developmentally appropriate, and scientifically honorable.*

If a school district uses standards as the basis for deciding the content of a school program, then it is important to make further decisions about how the content should be organized. Most school science programs lack coherence. That is, topics do not represent an organized and coordinated K–12 structure for content. The parts should make a whole. Rather, most programs present a grade-level, course orientation, especially at the secondary level. Curricular coherence requires a strong vertical perspective that is then complemented by the traditional course or horizontal view.

By developmentally appropriate, I am referring to a curricular perspective that includes the number, duration, repetition, sequencing, specificity, and difficulty of science concepts in the curriculum. Decisions relative to these issues should be based on students' developmental and learning capacities (NRC 1999) and the fundamental concepts and intellectual abilities as presented in the standards.

I use the term *scientifically honorable* to express the idea that science concepts must be accurate, given the age and developmental level of students. In general, the national standards have recognized this criterion in the K–4, 5–8, and 9–12 grade-level orientations for content. Another essential feature of scientifically honorable is expressed by the requirement of fundamental topics at the heart of the sciences that cause some groups concern. I cite biological evolution as an example of this point. Omitting fundamental concepts, as opposed to topics, that are central to science disciplines for a curriculum is *not* scientifically honorable. Holding the line on socially controversial concepts is a part of our educational responsibility to science. In a very real sense, representatives of states, school districts, and professional science teachers are the first line of defense in battles over the integrity of science.

The Science Curriculum and Teaching

- *Science teaching should consist of coordinated and systematic strategies that provide opportunities to learn for a diversity of students.*

In the section on curriculum I stated that "In the end, students learn the content they are taught." Here I propose that how much students learn is directly influenced by how they are taught. To be more specific, I will give an example of coordinated and systemic strategies for teaching. My example is the 5E model used in contemporary BSCS materials and enjoying some popularity in state frameworks and many local programs. The 5Es consist of Engage, Explore, Explain, Elaborate, and Evaluate (see Table 1).

Table 1: BSCS 5E Instructional Model

BSCS 5e Instructional Model	
Engage	The instructor accesses the learners' prior knowledge and helps them become engaged in a new concept by reading a vignette, posing questions, presenting a discrepant event, showing a video clip, or conducting some other short activity that promotes curiosity and elicits prior knowledge.
Explore	Learners work in collaborative teams to complete lab activities that help them use prior knowledge to generate ideas, explore questions and possibilities, and design and conduct a preliminary inquiry.
Explain	To explain their understanding of the concept, learners may make presentations, share ideas with one another, review current scientific explanations and compare these to their own understanding, and/or listen to an explanation from the teacher that guides the learners toward a more in-depth understanding.
Elaborate	Learners elaborate their understanding of the concept by conducting additional lab activities. They may revisit an earlier lab and build on it or conduct an activity that requires an application of the concept.
Evaluate	The evaluation phase helps both learners and instructors assess how well the learners understand the concept and whether or not they have met the learning outcomes.
From: *Profiles in Science: A Guide to NSF-Funded High School Instructional Materials* (2001). The SCI Center, BSCS, page 45.	

Although simple, the 5E model provides a coordinated and systematic approach to teaching that provides students opportunities and time to learn.

Designing Standards-Based Science Curricula

Design refers to a process of identifying a goal and selecting the means to achieve that goal. My use of the term *design* is intentionally associated with engineering and technology and applied to the science curriculum. For many, the dominant model of curriculum includes thinking of a topic, clarifying science content, developing one or several activities associated with the topic, and finally figuring out some form of assessment. Fundamentally, this approach centers on activities and gives reduced emphasis to considerations of student learning as an important constraint in curriculum development. Viewing curriculum as a design problem holds promise of improving the quality of instructional materials and subsequently student achievement.

Recently, several books have used the term *design* in reference to curriculum in general and science curriculum in particular. There is a very helpful book by Grant Wiggins and Jay McTighe, *Understanding by Design* (1998), the National Research Council publication *Designing Mathematics or Science Curriculum Programs* (NRC 1999), and *Designs for Science Literacy* (AAAS 2001) developed by the AAAS Project 2061. I have found *Designs for Science Literacy* quite informative as it addresses the attributes of design (e.g., designs are purposeful, deliberate, require compromise, can fail, and have stages), essential elements of design (e.g., designs have goals, such as achieving scientific understanding, and constraints, such as developmental abilities of students), and that designs require decisions (e.g., benefits and costs, risks, and trade-offs). Some fundamental issues of curricular design include curriculum specifications, student learning, and national standards.

Design Specifications: Student Learning

As I mentioned, design is a deliberate effort to attain a specific goal. Achieving scientific literacy states a purpose for science education. In *Achieving Scientific Literacy* (Bybee 1997), I discussed definitional aspects of the term *scientific literacy.* Here, the specifications for student learning should focus on science concepts and understanding as well as the abilities and processes of scientific inquiry. The national standards define, at a fairly specific level, what students should know and be able to do. These standards are the learning outcomes for the science curriculum.

While identifying and clarifying goals, one has to consider the limits of what can be done. In curriculum development, time and budget are clear examples. Other examples include discipline and grade level. In this discussion, I wish to emphasize one particular class of constraints; namely, what we know about how students learn. By analogy, if you are building a bridge, the laws of nature impose constraints on the design. If you are developing a curriculum, what we know about student learning imposes constraints on the design. Enhancing student achievement will rely on implementing research that has advanced our understanding of how students learn science. The National Research Council reports *How People Learn: Brain, Mind, Experience, and School* (Bransford et al. 2000), *How People Learn: Bridging Research and Practice* (Bransford et al. 1999), and the more recent *How Students Learn: Science in the Classroom* (NRC 2005) present a major synthesis of research on human learning. The findings from these NRC reports have both a solid research base and clear implications for curricular design. The following three findings are from *How People Learn: Bridging Research and Practice.*

> Students come to the classroom with preconceptions about how the world works. If their initial understanding is not engaged, they may fail to grasp the new concepts and information that are taught, or they may learn them for purposes of a test but revert to their preconceptions outside the classroom (p. 10).

The first finding relates to science teaching; specifically, how we structure experiences to draw out students' current understandings, bring about some sense of the inadequacy of the ideas, and provide opportunities and time to reconstruct ideas so they are consistent with basic scientific concepts.

A second finding refers to the conceptual foundation of a curriculum.

> To develop competence in an area of inquiry, students must: (a) have a deep foundation of factual knowledge, (b) understand facts and ideas in the context of a conceptual framework, and (c) organize knowledge in ways that facilitate retrieval and application (p. 12).

The science curriculum should incorporate fundamental knowledge and be based on, and contribute to, the students' development of a strong conceptual framework. Research comparing performance of novices and experts, as well as research on learning and transfer, shows that experts draw upon a richly structured information base. Although factual information is necessary, it is not sufficient. Essential to expertise is the mastery of concepts that allow for deep understanding. Finally, there is a finding related to students' ability to think about their thinking.

> Students can be taught strategies that help them monitor their progress in problem solving (p. 13).

Research on the performance of experts suggests that they monitor their understanding of a scientific investigation. They note the requirement of additional information, the alignment of new information with what is known, and they use analogies that may provide insights and advance their understanding. For experts, there are often internal conversations grounded in the processes of scientific inquiry. The latter can be learned if taught in the context of science subject matter and investigations. This finding has clear implications for the theme of teaching science as inquiry.

Design Specifications: Rigor, Focus, and Coherence

Criticisms about the lack of rigor in the U.S. curriculum center on its content, particularly the conceptual orientation of programs. For example, one can ask whether a curriculum is oriented toward scientific concepts fundamental to a discipline, or timely topics that may be interesting but do not emphasize scientifically fundamental concepts or processes. Lack of focus refers to the depth of treatment of content. For example, content may only receive brief and superficial time in the curriculum. Finally, concerns about coherence refer to the connections among science concepts and inquiry abilities in both horizontal and vertical dimensions of the curriculum. The cumulative effect of the lack of these qualities is a lack of student achievement. Because qualities of rigor, focus, and coherence can be addressed as issues of curricular design, I believe it important to introduce them, along with understanding of student learning, as issues in curricular design.

To the questions of *rigor,* school science programs should be based on fundamental or essential scientific concepts and inquiry abilities. Documents such as the *National Science Education Standards* (NRC 1996), *Benchmarks for Science Literacy* (AAAS 1993), and *TIMSS Assessment Frameworks and Specifications* (IAEA 2001) have answered questions about what students should know and be able to do. (See Table 2 for an example from the national standards.)

Table 2: Example from the National Science Education Standards

Design Specification: Rigor
Rigor centers on the content of the curriculum, particularly the conceptual orientation of science disciplines.
Example from the *National Science Education Standards:*
Life Cycles of Organisms (Grades K–4)

However, identifying the content for school science is not enough. One must attend to other curricular and instructional issues.

Design of programs must address the focus and coherence for the organization of content. *Focus* is the depth of treatment for fundamental concepts and procedures. It is a measure of the time and opportunities given within classes, courses, and across the extended curriculum; for example, units, courses of study, and the K–12 science programs. Table 3 presents an example of depth from the national standards.

Table 3: Example from the National Science Education Standards

Design Specification: Focus
Focus refers to the depth of treatment of content. Example from the *National Science Education Standards:* Life Cycles of Organisms (Grades K–4)
• Plants and animals have life cycles that include being born, developing into adults, reproducing, and eventually dying. The details of this life cycle are different for different organisms. • Plants and animals closely resemble their parents. • Many characteristics of an organism are inherited from the parents of the organism, but other characteristics result from an individual's interactions with the environment. Inherited characteristics include the color of flowers and the number of limbs of an animal. Other features, such as the ability to ride a bicycle, are learned through interactions with the environment and cannot be passed on to the next generation.
From: National Research Council. (1996). *National Science Education Standards,* page 129. Washington, DC: National Academy Press.

Coherence is the number of concepts and procedures developed in a period of study (e.g., lesson, unit, course) and within a school program (e.g., elementary, middle, high school, college). It is a measure of the connectedness among science concepts and procedures that students experience during their study of science. Note these are both horizontal (that is, courses) and vertical (that is, school science programs) dimensions to curricula coherence. F. James Rutherford (2000) has written about coherence in high school programs. The following is from his essay.

> If coherence in high school science courses is a desirable property, then one can reasonably argue that it should be present at every level of content organization: lessons, units, courses, sequences of courses, and entire curricula. Thus, the topics and activities making up a science lesson or chapter ought to connect with one another to tell a (very limited) story, with, as it were, a discernable beginning, middle, and end. Similarly, the lessons or chapters making up a science unit should connect one another in interesting ways to tell a complete (but still limited) story, and units should connect with one another in interesting ways to tell a more comprehensive story. Notice that two conditions must prevail at each level of organization: All of the parts forming a unit or course must be coherent, and all of those parts must join together to form a conceptual whole (p. 22, 23).

For school science programs, this is a place where less is more. That is, fewer concepts studied in greater depth will result in more learning.

Curriculum Design and Development at BSCS

I begin this discussion with an example. *BSCS Science: An Inquiry Approach* is currently under development (funded by the National Science Foundation in 2000) and is conceptualized as a standards-based science program for grades 9 through 11. We explicitly used the National Science Education Standards as the conceptual basis for designing and developing this program (see Table 4). Each year of the program begins with a two-week "Science As Inquiry" unit and is followed by three core units (eight weeks each): Life Science, Earth-Space Science, and Physical Science. In each of these core units, the first several chapters are devoted to helping students build conceptual understanding of the core concepts. The latter chapters help the students understand how these core concepts play a part in problems and events in the integrated setting of the natural world. The final unit uses problems and projects that are relevant to the lives of high school students to develop an integration of ideas across the sciences.

Table 4: *BSCS Science: An inquiry approach framework for grades 9–11*

Units	*Major Concepts Addressed at Each Grade Level*		
	Grade 9	Grade 10	Grade 11
	Abilities necessary to do and understandings about scientific inquiry with a focus on:		
Science as Inquiry	• Questions and concepts that guide scientific investigations	• Design of scientific investigations • Communicating scientific results	• Evidence as the basis for explanations and models • Alternative explanations and models
Physical Science	Structure and properties of matter Structure of atoms Integrating chapter	• Motions and forces • Chemical reactions • Integrating chapter	• Interactions of energy and matter • Conservation of energy and increase in disorder • Integrating chapter
Life Science	• Cell structure and function • Behavior of organisms • Integrating chapter	• Biological evolution • Molecular basis of heredity • Integrating chapter	• Matter, energy, and organization in living systems • Interdependence of organisms • Integrating chapter
Earth-Space Science	• Origin and evolution of the universe • Origin and evolution of the Earth system • Integrating chapter	• Geochemical cycles • Integrating chapter	• Energy in the Earth system • Integrating chapter
Science in a Personal and Social Perspective; Science & Technology	• Personal and community health • Natural and human-induced hazards • Abilities of technological design	• Population growth • Natural resources • Environmental quality	• Science and technology in local, national, and global challenges • Understandings about science and technology
History and Nature of Science addressed throughout grade levels and units • Science as a human endeavor • Nature of science • History of science			

Design Studies. Since the mid-1980s, curriculum development at BSCS has been initiated with a design study. These studies involve a current review of science education at the level or levels under study, national and state priorities, careful consideration of curricular elements such as content, instructional strategies, use of laboratory investigations, tests and assessment exercises, and issues of implementation and professional development. One of the BSCS design studies results in a detailed curriculum framework and specifications for a new program (see Table 5).

These design studies have helped identify what to include in the program; for example, student materials, teacher editions, and implementation guides. Further, the design studies have clarified the goals and constraints as best we could before initial development. One of the important and enduring outcomes of this work has been the BSCS 5E model. Since the mid-1990s, BSCS has used the National Science Education Standards as the basis for several aspects of curricular design; e.g., content and professional development.

Table 5: BSCS design studies and core programs

New Designs for Elementary School Science and Health (BSCS and IBM 1989)
♦ *Science for Life and Living: Integrating Science, Technology, and Health* (1992)
♦ *BSCS Science T.R.A.C.S. (1999)*
New Designs for Middle School Science (BSCS and IBM 1990)
♦ *Middle School Science & Technology* (1999)
Developing Biological Literacy (1993)
♦ *BSCS Biology: A Human Approach* (1997)
♦ *Biological Perspectives* (1999)
Making Sense of Integrated Science: A Guide for High Schools (2000)
♦ *BSCS Science: An Inquiry Approach (9–11)* (available)
♦ *BSCS Science: An Inquiry Approach (6–8)* (proposed)

Backward Design. Beginning in the late 1990s, we have incorporated the backward design process described by Grant Wiggins and Jay McTighe in *Understanding By Design* (1998). In this process, we begin with a content standard and determine acceptable evidence of student attainment for that content. Then, we decide what learning experience would develop students' knowledge and understanding of the content.

The BSCS 5E model for instruction provides a concrete example of this process. After identifying the standard and stating the content outcomes, we go to the evaluate activity and design an activity that would assess students' knowledge and understanding of the content.

Forward Development. After clarifying the desired outcomes and means to assess for those outcomes, we design and develop the experience that will provide students with the opportunities to learn the content.

Again, using the BSCS 5E model, we develop the engage, explore, explain, and elaborate activities. This process may result in further clarification and modifications of the evaluate activities (see Table 6).

Table 6: The backward design process and the BSCS 5E model

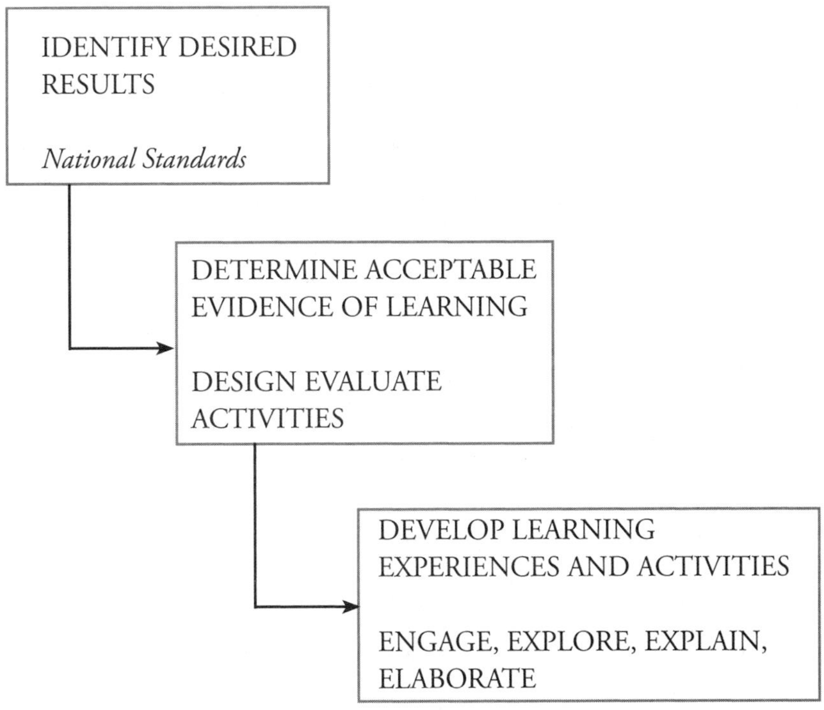

Conclusion

In this chapter, I reviewed some of the intended and actual effects that national standards have on the science curriculum. The review draws upon a major policy report, *Investigating the Influence of Standards* (NRC 2002), research from the Third International Mathematics and Science Study (TIMSS) as reported in *Why Schools Matter: A Cross-National Comparison of Curriculum and Learning* (Schmidt et al. 2001), and my work on *National Science Education Standards* for the United States and the development of curricular materials at BSCS.

This discussion leads to several conclusions about national standards and curricular reform. Each of the following conclusions also suggests a component of evaluation:

First, gaining widespread acceptance and agreement on what science teachers should teach and what students should learn is required. Indeed, this is a major function of standards.

Second, there is a need for greater consistency and coherence within the educational systems: purposes, policies, programs, and practices.

Third, much greater emphasis should be placed on the work of those who translate policies to programs and implement programs and practices.

Fourth, the greater the freedom of professionals to design their own programs and practices, the higher is the need for professionals who understand multiple facets of standards, curriculum design, development, and implementation.

Fifth, one must consider economical, political, and pedagogical factors influencing the selection and implementation of standards-based programs.

Finally, for the evaluation of student learning, one should consider the full and stable implementation of materials and the degree to which the innovative features of the curriculum are being practiced the way developers intended.

The whole issue of national standards and curricular reform presents the problems of changing a complex system. It may be among the most difficult stakes science educators encounter. But to the degree we are successful, it provides teachers and students opportunities for achieving higher levels of scientific literacy.

Achieving scientific literacy will require a curriculum that is rigorous, focused, and coherent. Briefly, rigor was discussed as content that is conceptually fundamental; focus is a measure of attention given scientific concepts and procedures; and coherence is a measure of connectedness among the concepts and procedures students experience during their study of science. Based on design principles of rigor, coherence, and focus, this discussion addressed student learning and curricular design including the scope of content and instructional sequences that will enhance student learning. The discussion included examples of curricular materials from BSCS programs and the process of designing and developing contemporary instructional materials.

Rodger W. Bybee

is the executive director of the Biological Sciences Curriculum Study (BSCS). Before this he was executive director of the Center for Science, Mathematics and Engineering Education at the National Research Council. Author of numerous journal articles, chapters, books, science curricular, and textbooks, he also directed the writing of the content standards for the National Science Education Standards. Honors included the National Science Teachers Association Distinguished Service Award.

References

American Association for the Advancement of Science (AAAS). 1993. *Benchmarks for science literacy.* New York: Oxford University Press.

American Association for the Advancement of Science, Project 2061. 2001. *Designs for science literacy.* New York: Oxford University Press.

Bransford, J., M. Pellegrino, and W. Donovan, eds. 1999. *How people learn: Bridging research and practice.* Washington, DC: National Academy Press.

Bransford, J., A. Brown, and R. Cocking, eds. 2000. *How people learn: Brain, mind, experience, and school.* Washington, DC: National Academy Press.

BSCS and IBM. 1989. *New designs for elementary school science and health.* Colorado Springs, CO: BSCS.

BSCS and IBM. 1990. *New designs for middle school science.* Colorado Springs, CO: BSCS.

BSCS and IBM. 1992. *Science for life and living: Integrating science, technology, and health.* Dubuque, IA: Kendall/Hunt Publishing.

BSCS and IBM. 1993. *Developing biological literacy.* Colorado Springs, CO: BSCS.

BSCS and IBM. 1997. *BSCS biology: A human approach.* Dubuque, IA: Kendall/Hunt Publishing.

BSCS and IBM. 1999. *Biological perspectives.* Dubuque, IA: Kendall/Hunt Publishing.

BSCS and IBM. 1999. *Middle school science & technology.* 2nd ed. Dubuque, IA: Kendall/Hunt Publishing.

BSCS and IBM. 1999. *BSCS science T.R.A.C.S.* Dubuque, IA: Kendall/Hunt Publishing.

BSCS and IBM. 2000. *Making sense of integrated science: A guide for high schools.* Colorado Springs, CO: BSCS.

BSCS and IBM. The SCI Center. 2001. *Profiles in science: A guide to NSF-funded high school instructional materials.* Colorado Springs, CO: BSCS.

Bybee, R. W. 1997. *Achieving scientific literacy: From purposes to practices.* Portsmouth, NH: Heinemann.

Cobb, N., ed. 1994. *The future of education: Perspectives on national standards in America.* New York: College Entrance Examination Board.

International Association for the Evaluation of Educational Achievement (IAEA). 2001. *TIMSS assessment frameworks and specifications 2003.* Boston, MA: Lynch School of Education, Boston College.

Kliebard, H. 1992. *Forging the American curriculum: Essays in curriculum history and theory.* New York: Routledge.

National Research Council (NRC). 1996. *National Science Education Standards.* Washington, DC: National Academy Press.

National Research Council (NRC). 1999. *Designing mathematics or science curriculum programs: A guide for using mathematics and science education standards.* Washington, DC: National Academy Press.

National Research Council (NRC). 1999. *Global perspectives for local action: Using TIMSS to improve U.S. mathematics and science education.* Washington, DC: National Academy Press.

National Research Council (NRC). 2002. *Investigating the influence of standards: A framework for research in mathematics, science, and technology education.* Washington, DC: National Academy Press.

National Research Council (NRC). 2005. *How students learn: Science in the classroom.* Washington, DC: National Academy Press.

No Child Left Behind Act (NCLB) of 2001. 2002. Public Law 107–110–January 8, 2002. 107th Congress. Washington, DC.

Ravitch, D. 1995. *National standards in American education: A citizen's guide.* Washington, DC: The Brookings Institution.

Rutherford, F. J. 2000. Coherence in high school science. In *Making sense of integrated science: A guide for high schools*, 21-29. Colorado Springs, CO: BSCS.

Schmidt, W. H., D. Jorde, L. S. Cogan, E. Barrier, I. Gonzalo, U. Moser, K. Shimizu, T. Sawada, G. A. Valverde, C. McKnight, R. S. Prawat, D. E. Wiley, S. A. Raizen, E. D. Britton, and R. G. Wolfe. 1996. *Characterizing pedagogical flow: An investigation of mathematics and science teaching in six countries.* Boston, MA: Kluwer Academic Publishers.

Schmidt, W. J., D. E. Wiley, C. C. McKnight, G. A. Valverde, and R. T. Houang. 1997. *Many visions, many aims,* vol 2. Boston, MA: Kluwer Academic Publishers.

Schmidt, W. H., C. C. McKnight, R. T. Houang, H. Wang, D. E. Wiley, L. S. Cogan, and R. G. Wolfe. 2001. *Why schools matter: A cross-national comparison of curriculum and learning.* San Francisco: Jossey-Bass.

Third International Mathematics and Science Study (TIMSS). 1996. *Pursuing excellence: A study of U.S. eighth-grade mathematics and science teaching, learning, curriculum, and achievement in international context.* Washington, DC: National Center for Education Statistics.

Third International Mathematics and Science Study (TIMSS). 1997. *Pursing excellence: A study of U.S. fourth-grade mathematics and science achievement in international context.* Washington, DC: National Center for Education Statistics.

Third International Mathematics and Science Study (TIMSS). 1998. *Pursuing excellence: A study of U.S. twelfth-grade mathematics and science achievement in international context.* Washington, DC: National Center for Education Statistics.

Wiggins, G., and J. McTighe. 1998. *Understanding by design.* Alexandria, VA: Association for Supervision and Curriculum Development.

CHAPTER

3

Classroom Assessment in the Service of Student Learning

Janet E. Coffey

Talk about testing dominates talk about assessment. The focus of conversations about the two often turns to outcomes—to what has been learned. As any teacher knows, however, testing is not the whole of assessment activity. Within any classroom, assessment encompasses a wide range of activities and serves multiple purposes: it is the means by which we gauge what has been learned and the means by which learning goals can be achieved. In short, classroom assessment must facilitate learning as well as measure it.

Science education reform literature acknowledges this close relationship between assessment and learning. The *National Science Education Standards*, for example, presents the view that assessment and learning are two sides of the same coin (NRC 1996). In a document that accompanies Project 2061's Science Benchmarks, AAAS (1998) states: "Classroom assessment remains the most important direct influence on students' day to day learning" (p. 162).

This chapter takes a closer look at the tight link between assessment and learning, specifically at how classroom assessment can be organized to better support and facilitate student learning. After reviewing the literature, the discussion turns to features of assessment activity in classrooms where assessment works in the service of student learning. An example illustrates the ways in which assessment can catalyze improved learning.

Background

A growing body of research literature underscores the importance of attending to classroom assessment in efforts to improve student learning. In numerous research studies, student learning gains appear substantial in classrooms in which teachers attend regularly to formative assessment, or to activities undertaken that provide information that can feed back to modify teaching and learning activities (Black and Wiliam 1998a; NRC 2001). This use of assessment data—to inform teaching and learning—stands in contrast to summative assessment, which provides useful outcomes data but does little to shape practice.

The literature offers the metaphor of a gap to help in understanding the role assessment can play in supporting learning (Sadler 1989; Black and Wiliam 1998b). If one side of the gap represents the place where students sit with respect to learning goals (point A) and the other represents those learning goals (point B), assessment becomes a critical mechanism for ensuring that the gap is bridged. Yet, in many conversations about assessment, the focus stops with an inference concerning student understanding (point A), and at times includes how much it falls short of point B or the goals. Assessment that facilitates learning not only helps the teacher know where the student is starting from (point A) but also highlights for the student where he or she is headed (point B) and reveals productive actions to help the student reach this point.

Although the gap metaphor lacks the complexity inherent in any classroom activity, it does capture the possibility that assessment can provide teachers and students with information that can inform actions that bridge the gap. The research literature also identifies critical assessment practices that can contribute to the bridging of the gap, moving students from where they are to learning goals. Improving questioning practices (Minstrell and van Zee 2003), articulating explicit assessment criteria (Fairbrother et al. 1995; Stiggins 2001), providing quality feedback (Kluger and DeNisi 1996; Bangert-Drowns et al. 1991; Dweck 1986; Butler 1987), and engaging students in their own assessment (White and Frederiksen 1998; Wolf et al. 1991; Coffey 2002) have been shown to enhance the learning that goes on in the classroom.

On one level, most teachers recognize the practices as existing within their teaching repertoire. All teachers ask questions. All teachers give feedback. All teachers use some criteria for their grading. In all classrooms, students are involved in assessment, even if only as passive recipients. Despite the prevalence of these teaching practices, however, the classroom assessment research literature also signals the paucity of practice: Classroom assessment is rarely used in such a way that it supports student learning (Black and Wiliam 1998a).

The degree to which assessment supports student learning is contingent not on the existence but on the *quality* of these activities—the quality of the information collected and the ways in which that information is used. In classrooms, questions are ubiquitous, but do they elicit students' understandings and underlying rationales, and even promote connections not yet made? All teachers pay attention to something as they observe students at work in their classrooms. Is it the substance and reasoning of student thinking they are attending to? From their position in the classroom, teachers learn a lot about a student's understanding, but does that information inform teaching, or does it remain in a grade book or in the teacher's head? Teachers make judgments about student understanding, but are those determinations based on criteria important to the subject area? Are students just recipients of assessment, or are they involved in assessment in meaningful ways? These questions can guide reflection on and modification of classroom assessment as one moves from assessment *of* learning to assessment *for* learning. In many ways, when assessment supports learning, it is difficult to tease apart from teaching, learning, and curriculum. Using assessment in the service of student learning is less about incorporating drastically new teaching practices than it is about better leveraging and improving existing everyday practices.

To consider this everyday assessment in action, we will turn to an example from middle school classrooms characterized by active assessment.

Learning From Connections: Five Features That Support Learning

"What did I get?" "What is my grade?" are questions teachers hear regularly from students. These questions and their variations indicate the prominence of grades in classroom assessment conversations. In and of itself, the questions are not problematic; yet, many teachers can attest, the focus on grades often comes at the expense of attention to and interest in learning.

Connections was a middle-school choice program in a large public middle school in the San Francisco Bay Area (Coffey 2002). The teaching staff explicitly sought to address the issues raised by focusing on grades. From the start of the school year, teachers were committed to organizing assessment in such a way as to shift the students' focus from grades and test scores to their own learning. According to the founding teacher:

"... if you ask people about how they did in school, they'll say their grades, with no sense of what they learned .... That is not what we should remember about school. It just isn't what we should remember about learning, and you aren't going to create lifelong learners if you do that ..." (Coffey 2002).

To address this concern, the teachers made assessment an explicit part of their teaching and curriculum and an active part of their students' learning experiences.

The forms that assessment activities took in Connections were many and varied. Teachers engaged students in conversations about student work, and they provided regular feedback on class work, homework, lab activities, and student projects. Students set learning goals and reflected on them, talked with peers about improving work, and generated evaluation criteria. Students took tests and quizzes and reviewed their teachers' corrections. Teachers provided time for revision, sent home regular reports on progress on key district indicators, and, with students, established next steps.

In the fall, assessment looked as it did in many classrooms: students asked for their grades and resisted efforts to be actively involved in assessment activities. "Isn't that your job?" they would ask teachers when asked to reflect on and evaluate their work. Teachers persisted in their efforts to shift the focus of assessment to learning. By midyear, an assessment culture began to emerge in which students participated in and with assessment, and the focus was on the quality of work they were producing and on what they were learning (Coffey 2002). The following five features marked the supportive assessment ethos:

- Student involvement
- Organized around meaningful criteria
- Embedded in everyday activity
- Provided immediate and relevant feedback to students (and teachers)
- Focused on progress and improvement

In Connections, the features gave rise to assessment activity that was inextricably linked to the teaching and learning to which it was so integrally a part.

Student Involvement

The gap metaphor provides imagery for how the involvement of students is so essential: Teachers cannot learn for their students. Although teachers play many roles—they assist and support, and organize and create learning experiences—students ultimately are responsible for their own learning.

Too often, students are the recipients of assessment—assessment is done to them rather than with them. In Connections, teachers involved students as critical partners in the assessment process. Assessment was something students *did,* alongside their teachers and peers. Teachers engaged students in reflection and conversations about what made something good and what could be improved. Teachers inserted their sense of quality into the class discussion and pointed out aspects of work that may have been overlooked.

A scenario from a sixth-grade science classroom may prove illuminating. Maria and Jamie had designed an investigation to explore erosion rates with a range of soil coverage and to consider possible consequences for the local watershed. For their investigation, the girls had removed 12-inch-square swatches of four different types of grasses along with several inches of the topsoil in which it was planted, placed the samples in a large aluminum pan, and propped the pans up on the same angle of slope. Twice daily they poured the same amount of water on the soil and measured the amount of runoff, recorded the clarity of runoff, and measured the thickness of the remaining topsoil.

As part of their project, they determined how they wanted to be evaluated. From previous scientific investigations and associated assessment-related conversations, they were beginning to develop criteria about what feedback would prove useful before they completed the final version to turn in to the teacher. The two girls included topics such as explanation of the problem, project design, data collection, and explanation of implications among the areas they sought feedback on from teachers and peers after their presentation. Other categories for which they wanted comment were presentation and delivery of information and, last, two open questions: "What did you learn?" and "What questions do you still have?"

Since September, students had reflected on their own work and that of their peers at all stages. For Maria and Jamie, the preparation for their presentation was no exception. At various times during the course of the project, the teacher had facilitated a conversation about the types of issues and questions students should pay attention to as they did work. These reinforced the class's emerging shared criteria and added new issues to help extend and deepen their ideas of what constituted quality. As Maria and Jamie discussed ways to organize a presentation on what they had learned, the two girls referred to the drafts of background research, pages of data, and charts they had constructed for data collection and analysis.

We will continue with this example, but it provides a sense of how students can engage in assessment activity and alludes to the ways in which this involvement can become consequential. In the case of Connections, as students engaged meaningfully with assessment activity—including participating in assessment conversations about what makes good work, reflecting on their work in light of meaningful criteria, and reviewing the work of their peers—they began to develop a deeper understanding of what constituted quality work in a particular realm, in this case, what it meant to engage in a scientific investigation. They began to use these new understandings to inform their own work and to ask their peers critical questions (Coffey 2002).

Organized Around Meaningful Criteria

Assessment goes far in highlighting what is important and worthwhile (Lampert 2001). When assessment is organized around meaningful criteria, it helps students develop an awareness of practice and plays a role in conveying important principles and boundaries that undergird subject matter disciplines (Cole et al. 1999; White and Frederikson 1998; Coffey 2003).

Let us return to the example of Maria and Jamie. During their class presentation, Jamie and Maria reported on the results of their erosion investigation. Based on their results, Maria said they believed the city should seed the creek bed with a serpentine grass and periodically care for it so that it did not get too overgrown. They presented data to help make this case. The serpentine sample that was not cut had the greatest overall clarity of runoff in their trials, but it also had a high rate and amount of runoff, which they reasoned might not be good for other reasons. The more manicured sample of serpentine had less runoff. During the ensuing discussion of their work, after no one else remarked on their use of data, the teacher commented that she thought they did a good job using data to support their recommendation and added that using data was an important thing that scientists did in their jobs.

Evaluative words help label practice, be it a more traditional concept or a feature of scientific practice that teachers would like to see students develop. When the teacher remarked to the class that Maria and Jamie's use of data to support their particular recommendation was good, she was supporting a key tenet of science: the use of data as evidence or argumentation. In Connections, the teacher wanted students to support justification with data and would take opportunities to highlight this key idea and others she wanted her students to cultivate. In addition to helping inform her students' understandings of what was a good response in science, these instances provided examples of how and what they did in the classroom connected to what occurs in the broader scientific community.

Meaningful assessment criteria serve another important role. Well-articulated criteria can help guide teachers to pay attention to what matters most. Questions such as, What am I assessing? Is it worthwhile? and What does it convey to my student about science as a discipline? can inform a teacher's framework for actual assignment design, what she pays attention to when looking at work, how she listens, what she looks for as evidence of understanding, and how she responds to her students.

In short, assessment focuses on what counts. It conveys messages about practice and about the relationship among concepts and facts. A corollary exists with external testing. Teachers are aware of the powerful force external tests play in shaping the curriculum—for better or for worse. Similarly, meaningful criteria works inside the classroom to shape what is emphasized and what students learn.

Embedded in Everyday Activity

With their participation in daily classroom activities, teachers are in a unique position to gain insight into their students' understandings, actions, behaviors, interests, and motivations (Hammer 1997; Moss 1994). They do not need to rely solely on traditional tests to measure understanding and abilities. They are privy to an array of activities and conversations that can provide useful information from which they can draw inferences about what a student understands and what supports he or she may need to move forward (Hein and Price 1994). Teachers need to create and seek out opportunities to observe and listen to their students; they need to consider the design of assignments to elicit useful information; and, importantly, they need to use that information thoughtfully to shape subsequent instruction.

All pieces of student work, even contributions during class discussions, become possible occasions for assessing understandings, scientific thinking, and abilities. As Maria and Jamie worked on their investigation during class time, the teacher could circulate and listen to their conversations, identifying the sense they were making of their data as well as areas that she may be able to provide support. As the class discussed Maria's and Jamie's presentation, the teacher could listen closely to the comments and explanations, asking follow-up and clarification questions if necessary. And students could begin to engage in similar reflection as they learned to observe and listen to their peers.

Certainly, observations and careful consideration of students at work and of the products of their work will not completely replace tests and quizzes as mechanisms to gauge understanding. Used effectively, however, access to the rich information available as students work and engage in discussion can enable the teacher and the students to achieve more depth and complete understandings.

Embedding assessment in everyday activity may be particularly important in terms of supporting developing skills and understandings of scientific inquiry. Many of the skills at the heart of inquiry are difficult to capture on a paper-and-pencil or time-constrained test. Some practices are best assessed over time as students engage in inquiry or an inquiry-oriented activity.

Provided Quality Feedback

Teachers must not only interpret and make meaning of the information they gather through assessment activities; they must also *use* the information to adapt their teaching to meet the needs of their students. As stated above, students should be involved in the process too. In some important sense, feedback is at the heart of an assessment system supportive of learning (Black and Wiliam 1998b).

Here too, teachers need to attend to the quality of information provided as feedback. In terms of feedback to Maria and Jamie, the teacher in the example above could have stopped at "good work" or even a letter grade. The nature of those responses does little to help the girls know what to do to improve their work. Saying why something was good—in the example of Maria and Jamie, their use of data from their investigation to support their recommendation— helps them know to do the same thing next time. Because the teacher provided the feedback orally, other students benefited as well.

Any distinction between formative and summative assessment comes down to issues of how the information is used. Educational researchers have the luxury of making distinctions between the two, teasing them apart. Teachers, facing multiple demands and sometimes-competing priorities, do not always share that luxury. They need to make the most of all assessment activity and use it to feed into teaching decisions as often and as efficiently as possible. If teachers listen to student explanations, and do so in realms of importance, and pay careful attention to student work, they can provide individualized feedback and also note trends that can be addressed to the class as a whole. A teacher cannot possibly provide detailed feedback on every piece of work a student completes, which further speaks to the importance of focusing what is most important to assess and building in student involvement. As students get better at assessment, they can share responsibility with their teachers.

Focus on Progress and Improvement

Providing opportunities for students to make use of assessment information accompanies regular and substantive feedback. If a primary goal of schooling is to promote student learning, classrooms should be organized and aligned to achieve this. One such vehicle is to value progress and improvement and allow room for revision.

Maria and Jamie received other comments on their work when they presented it to their classmates: some peers weren't clear what exactly they were investigating, others offered ideas for the presentation or data, and others raised concerns about whether they had done enough data collection and analysis to make a recommendation. Their teacher asked them to comment on the limitations of their study, particularly their design. Maria and Jamie could address these questions and issues and incorporate responses in their next iteration before they submitted the final copy to the teacher, so the teacher was evaluating their strongest piece of work at the time. Had they not been able to make use of the feedback, it might have had less impact.

Maria, Jamie, and their classmates had numerous other opportunities across the course of the year to collect and analyze data. The district indicators helped the teacher and students identify key skills and concepts that spiraled across multiple units. As part of the BEAR assessment system, Mark Wilson and colleagues at University of California at Berkeley have developed a blueprint that articulates key skills and benchmarks of progress that can inform assessment design and be tracked across a single year or even multiple years (Wilson and Scalise 2003; Wilson and Draney 1997). The rubriclike scale along key dimensions of what it means to do science provides a mechanism to challenge all students to improve their work. For one, it provides criteria for more sophisticated responses. Second, it helps connect what could otherwise seem disparate units. On a five-point scale, for example, a "3" is a meaningful step on the way to a "5." Accompanied by the scaling criteria and sense of the progress continuum, feedback from one assignment can feed forward to the next.

In Connections, teachers built in opportunities for revision and held students accountable for making them. In the same way as other teachers, they made attempts to revisit skills or ideas from one unit to the next. Progress reports, geared in part to district guidelines, provided teachers and students a chance to consider evidence of progress along numerous dimensions and communicated this progress to parents. Students also set academic goals and reflected on the progress towards those goals.

Taking Stock From Connections

Perhaps more meaningful than the collection of features was the synergy that can arise from the interplay among the features in an assessment system. In Connections, the arrangement of these features and the resultant participation required of students became significant in many ways (Coffey 2002). Data and analysis suggests that, in general, the ways in which the assessment activity worked was consequential in the following ways: the focus for the students became the work, not the grade; students developed more clear notions about what constituted quality; the quality of student work improved across the school year; and the ways in which students approached their work changed. The notion that a clearer idea of criteria for quality work coupled with an ability to engage in ongoing reflection on one's work in light of that criteria would contribute to improved participation in science class—and subsequently enhance science learning—is consistent with current learning theory (Bransford et al. 1999).

A Connections student described assessment as "how we help ourselves help each other." The supportive mechanism implied in the student's description is a far cry from other common descriptors, including "how a teacher knows what I know and don't."

Creating a classroom culture in which assessment supports learning requires an ongoing commitment. Teachers need to identify what is important to assess, what counts as evidence of understanding, and then use this to guide their assessment activity. Classroom norms and expectations of how assessment works need to be altered. In many classrooms, assessment remains in the hands of the teacher. Shifting to more distributed responsibilities takes time and intention. Students need to learn how to reflect and how to comment on work constructively and meaningfully. Teachers need to scaffold the necessary skills to help their students engage meaningfully in everyday assessment activities. Assessment in these moments becomes an integral part of the curricula.

Changing assessment practice will not happen overnight. No one formula exists that will ensure that assessment serves learning. Rather, teachers need time to carefully consider their existing assessment practices and employ modifications that make sense within the frame of their own strengths, styles, and priorities.

As we read in the literature, and we see in the case above, it is this everyday assessment—the collection of dynamic assessment-related activities that occurs regularly among teachers and students, formally and informally—that may prove to be most powerful in terms of supporting student learning. And, as we see from classrooms where assessment works powerfully, the specific components are not nearly as important as the underlying features from which they stem and to which they contribute.

Janet E. Coffey

is an assistant professor in the Department of Curriculum and Instruction at the University of Maryland, College Park. She received her PhD in science education from Stanford University. She has participated on numerous research efforts to better understand the intersections of assessment and learning, and has worked with teachers in assessment-centered professional development. She has taught middle school science.

References

American Association for the Advancement of Science (AAAS). 1998. *Blueprints for reform.* Washington: DC: AAAS.

Bangert-Drowns, R. L., C-L. C. Kulik, J. A. Kulik, and M. T. Morgan. 1991. The instructional effect of feedback in test-like events. *Review of Educational Research* 61 (2): 213 –238.

Black, P., and D. Wiliam. 1998a. Assessment and classroom learning. *Assessment in Education* 5 (1): 7–74.

Black, P., and D. Wiliam. 1998b. Inside the black box: Raising standards through classroom assessment. *Phi Delta Kappan* 80 (2): 139–148.

Bransford, J. R., A. L. Brown, and R. R. Cocking, eds. 1999. *How people learn: Brain, experience, and school.* Washington, DC. National Academy Press.

Butler, R. 1987. Task-involving and ego-involving properties of evaluation: Effects of different feedback conditions on motivational perceptions, interest and performance. *Journal of Educational Psychology* 79 (4): 474–482.

Coffey, J. E. 2002. *Making connections: Engaging students in assessment.* Doctoral dissertation. Stanford University.

Coffey, J. E. 2003. Involving students in assessment. In eds. J. M. Atkin and J. E. Coffey, *Everyday assessment in the science classroom.* Arlington, VA: National Science Teachers Association Press.

Cole, K., J. E. Coffey, and S. V. Goldman. 1999. Using assessments to improve equity in mathematics. *Educational Leadership* 56 (6): 56–58.

Dweck C. S. 1986. Motivational processes affecting learning. *American Psychologist.* Special issue. *Psychological science and education* 41 (10): 1040–1048.

Fairbrother, R., P. Black, and P. Gill, eds. 1995. *Teachers assessing pupils: Lessons from science classrooms.* Hatfield, UK: Association for Science Education.

Hammer, D. 1997. Discovery teaching, discovery learning. *Cognition and Instruction* 15 (4): 485–529.

Hein, G., and S. Price. 1994. *Active assessment for active science.* Portsmouth, NH: Heinemann.

Kluger, A. N., and A. DeNisi. 1996. The effects of feedback interventions on performance: A historical review, a meta-analysis, and a preliminary feedback intervention theory. *Psychological Bulletin* 119 (2): 254–284.

Lampert, M. 2001. *Teaching problems and the problems of teaching.* New Haven: Yale University Press.

Minstrell, J., and E. van Zee. 2003. Using questioning to assess and foster student thinking. In eds. J. M. Atkin, and J. E. Coffey, *Everyday assessment in the science classroom.* Arlington, VA: National Science Teachers Association Press.

Moss, P. A. 1994. Can there be validity without reliability? *Educational Researcher* 23 (2): 5–12.

National Research Council (NRC). 1996. *National Science Education Standards.* Washington, DC: National Academy Press.

National Research Council (NRC). 2001. *Classroom assessment and the National Science Education Standards.* Washington, DC: National Academy Press.

Sadler, R. 1989. Formative assessment and the design of instructional systems. *Instructional Science* 18: 119–144.

Stiggins, R. J. 2001. *Student-centered classroom assessment.* Columbus, OH: Merrill Prentice Hall.

White, B. Y., and J. R. Frederiksen. 1998. Inquiry, modeling and meta-cognition: Making science accessible to all students. *Cognition and Instruction* 16 (1): 3–118.

Wilson, M., and K. Draney. July, 1997. Developing maps for student progress in the SEPUP Assessment System. University of California, Berkeley: BEAR Report Series, SA–97–2.

Wilson, M., and K. Scalise. 2003. Reporting progress to parents and others: Beyond grades. In eds. Atkin, J. M., and J. E. Coffey, *Everyday assessment in the science classroom.* Arlington, VA: National Science Teachers Association Press.

Wolf, D., J. Bixby, J. Glen III, and H. Gardner. 1991. To use their minds well: Investigating new forms of student assessment (31–74). In ed. G. Grant, *Review of research in education.* Washington, DC: American Educational Research Association.

CHAPTER

4

Engaging Teachers in Research on Science Learning and Teaching

Emily H. van Zee and Deborah Roberts

Professional Development Standard C of the National Science Education Standards recommends that professional development activities for teachers "provide opportunities to learn and use the skills of research to generate new knowledge about science and the teaching and learning of science " (NRC 1996, 68). This chapter considers four issues underlying this standard:

What does it mean for a teacher to be a researcher?

How do teachers inquire into science learning and teaching?

Why would they undertake such inquiries?

In what ways do they use and communicate their findings?

What Does It Mean for a Teacher to Be A Researcher?

In her essay "Teaching as Research," Eleanor Duckworth (1987) articulated the following vision:

> I am not proposing that school teachers single-handedly become published researchers in the development of human learning. Rather I am proposing that teaching, understood as engaging learners in phenomena and working to understand the sense they are making, might be the sine qua non of such research.

This kind of researcher would be a teacher in the sense of caring about some part of the world and how it works enough to want to make it accessible to others. He or she would be fascinated by the questions of how to engage people in it and how people make sense of it and would have time and resources to pursue these questions to the depth of his or her interest, to write what he or she learned, and to contribute to the theoretical and pedagogical discussions on the nature and development of human learning (1987, p. 168).

This word *research* recognizes teachers as legitimate participants in efforts to improve instruction through explorations of questions about student learning. Such usage is controversial, however, as some prefer to reserve the word *research* for more formal investigations (Hammer and Schifter 2001; Richardson 1994).

In this chapter *research* refers to a continuum of acts associated with generating knowledge. At one end of the continuum, acts of research include a fleeting question about student thinking that emerges in the midst of a discussion: the teacher is identifying an issue that could be explored. Most teacher research involves articulating questions of interest, developing interpretations of data collected while teaching, modifying instruction in light of these interpretations, and perhaps sharing findings with colleagues. The more intentional and systematic the process, the more others perceive these efforts to be research. Acts of research at the opposite end of the continuum include reporting results at professional meetings and in refereed publications, particularly results from teachers who undertake extensive studies.

The findings of teacher research apply only to the context within which the study was conducted but may be more valid for that context than findings from studies conducted in many locations with randomized designs. Teacher research techniques can be used to examine whether findings from a formal study with generalizable results apply to a teacher's own students. Judgments of the quality of teacher research typically include trustworthiness and transferability (Lincoln and Guba 1985) rather than reliability and generalizability because the latter are rarely feasible in studies teachers conduct in their classrooms. Roth (forthcoming) proposes "evidence-based reasoning" and "worthwhile questions" as appropriate aspects to be considered. Although findings from one study in one classroom would not be generalizable, findings from a variety of settings in which teacher-researchers have focused on an issue can be discussed in terms of their broader implications. Assertions about questioning practices, for example, have been made on the basis of a series of individual case studies (van Zee et al. 2001).

Inquiring into one's own teaching practices and students' learning also is known as the "scholarship of teaching and learning" (Hutchings 2000), "self-study" (Dinkelman 2003), "critical reflection" (Nichols et al. 1997), "classroom inquiry" (Hubbard and Power 1993, 1999), "teacher inquiry" (Hammer and Schifter 2001), "action research" (Feldman 1996), "research on practice" (Richardson 1994), and "practitioner research" (Zeichner and Noffke 2001). Such research captures the "wisdom of practice" (Shulman 2004) and contributes knowledge generated from the unique perspective of the instructor.

How Do Teachers Inquire Into Science Learning and Teaching?

Conducting research in the midst of teaching is challenging. A good way to start is to listen closely to what students are saying (Paley 1986). Most teacher-researchers undertake qualitative studies in which they collect and interpret data such as videotapes of instruction, copies of student writings and drawings, e-mail messages, anecdotal records, reflective journals, interviews, and surveys (Cochran-Smith and Lytle 1993; Hubbard and Power 1993, 1999; Mills 2003; White and Gunstone 1992). Descriptive statistics and other quantitative methods also can be used effectively (McLean 1995).

An Example

An article published in a journal for teachers, *Science and Children,* provides an example of teacher research. In "Kids Questioning Kids: Experts Sharing," Marletta Iwasyk wrote about ways in which her first-grade students asked questions of one another during conversations about light and shadows (1997). She stated the issue she was exploring, described how she conducted the research, included information about the curricular context, provided a transcript as example data, and shared her interpretations as follows:

> I believe that children are capable of being teachers and while engaged in the teaching process, they reinforce and solidify their own learning.... To examine how this happens in my classroom, I conducted a case study....

> The case study involved analysis of transcripts of students discussing the subject of shadows in which two students became the "teachers" or "leaders" and the rest asked questions for clarification or gave input of their own.
>
> To document the discussions, I used a tape recorder with a microphone placed on a desk near the seated children. I also placed a video camera high in an unobtrusive corner. The camera was trained on the seats in the middle of the circle where I placed the "leaders" of the discussion. If other students had something to contribute, I asked them to step to the middle of the circle where I knew they would be visible to the camera…
>
> On the very first sunny day of school in the fall, we begin our study of shadows.… The sidebar lists some suggestions for various shadow activities.… Many questions arise.… In the beginning I do not answer any of the questions; instead, I ask the children to think about the questions and discover how they can find the answers for themselves. If they make early conclusions about what they observe, I do not acknowledge any answer as right or wrong.…
>
> See *Student Conversations* [in a box on a page] for an example of dialog that took place during a discussion of shadows … One of the questions asked and discussed was "Why doesn't it [the shadow] have the color you have on?" This student wondered why the shadow wasn't the same color as skin.… Just as questions can help children clarify their own thinking, the teacher can learn much about the students by listening to their discussions. It was very enlightening for me to observe thinking processes as the children gave explanations … (1997, pp. 42–46).

Iwasyk's case study adds to the literature an example of inquiry learning and teaching within a specific context. The children's questions illustrate unexpected ideas that teachers are likely to hear if they encourage students to talk about what they think. Iwasyk developed this case study while participating in a teacher-researcher group exploring student and teacher questioning during conversations about science (van Zee et al. 2001).

Experiences in a Teacher-Researcher Group

Participants in teacher-researcher groups support one another as they explore their own questions about learning and teaching. In her book *Talking*

Their Way Into Science: Hearing Children's Questions and Theories, Responding With Curricula, Karen Gallas, a first- and second-grade teacher, described the process as follows:

> My research on Science Talks began in 1989 when I first joined the Brookline Teacher Research Seminar. At that time I started to tape and transcribe Science Talks, and with the help of seminar members began to try and make sense of them. In the early stages of this work, Sarah Michaels [faculty member at Clark University] was extremely helpful to me, both because she encouraged me to pursue my interest and because she showed me how to look at complex data in a thoughtful and open way. Since then, the members of the seminar have continued to be interested and creative in their responses to the many transcripts I have shared. Their dedication to understanding children's intentions and meanings is always a source of support and inspiration (1995, p. vii).

Role of University Researchers

The role of university researchers in facilitating teacher-researcher groups differs substantially from the role of university researchers in initiating research projects in schools. In the latter projects, university researchers typically generate the questions explored, design the strategies or curricula that participating teachers try to implement, interpret data collected in the teachers' classrooms without involving the teachers in these analyses, and refer to participating teachers with pseudonyms, if at all, in publishing findings. In contrast, the role of university researchers in facilitating teacher-researcher groups is to foster the *teachers'* inquiries through organizing meetings, gathering resources, and supporting the teachers as the teachers generate issues, design ways to explore those issues, collect data, develop interpretations of their data, and present findings. Although the focus of the group may reflect the university researcher's interests (e.g., Michaels and Sohmer [forthcoming]), the teachers undertake their own studies and author or co-author reports of their findings.

Support From School Administrators

The importance of school administrators in fostering teacher research was acknowledged by the teachers (Patty Jacobs and Caryn McCrohon) and university researchers (Maureen Reddy and Leslie Herrenkohl) who were co-authors of the book *Creating Scientific Communities in the Elementary Classroom*:

> We have also been helped by a number of other people whom we would like to thank. Five years ago, Joan Merrill, with characteristic foresight, recognized the potential of our collaboration. As principal of the Goddard School of Science and Technology, she often speaks about "inviting children into learning." Her belief that a school can be a community of inquiry, for adults and children alike, has also invited us into learning (Reddy et al. 1998, p. ix).

Such administrative support may include arranging schedules so teacher-researchers can meet regularly, providing a place to meet and resources, promoting an environment where teachers are motivated to undertake in-depth looks at their students' learning, using the findings to guide school decision making and long-range planning, and encouraging dissemination of results.

Districtwide Initiatives

Some school districts have started teacher-research groups facilitated by school district personnel. The Fairfax County, Virginia, public schools, for example, undertook a concerted effort to improve instruction through teacher research (Mohr et al. 2003). Not only did the district sustain a network of teacher-researchers over many years, but it also sponsored a regional teacher-researcher conference each spring at which participating teachers presented their studies. In the book *Teacher Research for Better Schools*, the authors offer recommendations for teacher colleagues, school-level administrators, central office administrators, teacher educators, professional developers, parents, and school communities.

Teacher Research in Preparation and Professional Development

Pekarek, Krockover, and Shephardson recommended that "the notion of teachers as researchers ought to be incorporated in science teacher preparation and professional development programs" (1996, p. 112). One approach is to reconceptualize science teaching methods courses with a reflection orientation (Abell and Bryan 1997). Another is to engage prospective teachers in inquiries into science learning and teaching, particularly if these can be in collaboration with practicing teacher-researchers (van Zee 1998; van Zee et al. 2003).

High-quality professional development programs engage teachers in long-term learning about science and about learning and teaching (Stiles and Mundry 2002). An example is described by Wendy Saul, who collaborated with teachers on a project to integrate science and literacy. Some of the participating teachers became authors of chapters in several books. In *Science Workshop: Reading, Writing, and Thinking Like a Scientist*, Saul reflected upon the teachers' learning experiences as follows:

> [The co-authors] are teachers whose classrooms have changed not as a result of a new curriculum package but because of intense professional discussions and extensive reading. They have learned from and with colleagues whose insights and questions made the strange familiar and the familiar strange. They have explored, investigated, and analyzed scientific phenomena themselves so that they could understand what children engaged in schoolwork need to think about and feel and understand. The public recital of their experiences represents a commitment not only to a workshop model, but to a profession that values intelligence, community, and caring (2002, pp. 15-16).

One of the participants, Charles Pearce (1999), wrote a book, *Nurturing Inquiry: Real Science for the Elementary Classroom.* It provides a detailed account of how he gets started and sustains inquiry throughout the year in his fifth-grade classroom.

Why Would Teachers Undertake Inquiries Into Science Learning and Teaching?

Primary motivations for undertaking teacher research include the learning that occurs as well as the satisfaction of sharing new understandings with others. A kindergarten teacher, Vivian Paley, reflected on the difference between participating in a researcher's study and undertaking her own studies as follows:

> Until I had my own questions to ask, my own set of events to watch, and my own ways of combining all of these with teaching, I did not learn very much at all ... I have studied the subject [of children's play] through teaching and writing, and I cannot do one without the other.

> For me, the tape recorder is a necessity. I transcribe each day's play and stories and conversations and then make up my own stories about what is happening ... [The children's] fantasies propelled me further into surprises and mysteries, and I hungered after better ways to report what I heard and saw, and to find out what it all had to do with teaching (Paley and Coles 1999, p. 16, 18, 20).

Another motivation is the desire to design effective instruction that addresses one's commitments. *In Connecting Girls to Science: Constructivism, Feminism, and Science Education Reform,* for example, Elaine Howes wrote about her high school biology study:

> Listening to students is pedagogically consistent with my feminist commitments and with my desire to create and study instruction that attends to "science for all." This study of contexts in which I tried—and succeeded to differing degrees—to really hear what these students were saying forms the core of this book. While I concentrate on students' ideas and beliefs, I also include my reflections on their ideas and how these might inform instructional and curricular choices. Thus this teacher-research project originated in my commitments, which led to the development of specific instructional contexts, which in turn allowed me to hear students' voices in ways that are typically absent in traditional instruction. (2002, p. 5).

Teachers who systematically analyze their students' learning and own teaching practices contribute to the knowledge base and help bring into view questions that need to be asked. Detailed accounts of what individual instructors consider inquiry learning and teaching to be, for example, can provide an empirical base upon which to build a deeper understanding of what "learning science through inquiry" means. The potential of engaging teachers in this way was recognized many decades ago by John Dewey, who wrote in *Progressive Education and the Science of Education:*

> The method of the teacher ... becomes a matter of finding the conditions which call out self-educative activity, or learning, and of cooperating with the activities of the pupils so that they have learning as their consequence.... A series of constantly multiplying careful reports on conditions which experience has shown in actual cases to be favorable or unfavorable to learning would revolutionize the whole subject of method (1928/1959, p. 125–126).

Generating knowledge through such case studies is a feasible way for teachers to contribute to the research enterprise. For example, Roberts (1999) reported on ways parents became involved when she asked her students to watch the Moon. Simpson (1997) reflected on ways she engaged students in collaborative dialogues. Phyllis Whitin, with assistance from David Whitin, recorded her students' year-long exploration of bird behaviors in *Inquiry at the Window: Pursuing the Wonders of Learners* (Whitin and Whitin 1997). Another teacher author, Ellen Doris (1991), included transcripts of dialogues, copies of students' writings and drawings, and photos in documenting her students' inquiries in *Doing What Scientists Do: Children Learn to Investigate Their World.* When serving as texts or supplements in courses for teachers, such journal articles and books ground discussions of inquiry learning and teaching in specific contexts.

In What Ways Do Teachers Use and Communicate Their Findings?

Teacher-researchers use their findings in ongoing efforts to improve instruction. For example, in "Conceptual Development Research in the Natural Setting of a Secondary School Science Classroom," Jim Minstrell, a high school physics teacher, described his use of data to inform his teaching practices:

> The initiative for my research in alternative conceptions grew out of the frustrations of my own teaching experiences, particularly the frustration that my very rational (to me) instructional activities were less effective than I desired .... Data for this study were gathered in the context of the activities in [two] physics classes. Typically, prior to studying a new unit, a pre-instruction quiz was administered to determine the extent to which students were using alternative conceptions. They were usually paper-and-pencil quizzes and included questions designed to be sensitive to alternative conceptual structures. Some questions were adapted from those used by other researchers ... other questions were developed based on difficulties identified in my classes in earlier years. Other data on alternative initial conceptions came from tape recordings of large- or small-group discussions within the classes. I monitored the tenacity of the alternative conceptions, as would any teacher, by paying careful attention to what they said in discussions, wrote in lab reports, and did on tests that I constructed (1982, p. 131).

Minstrell communicated his findings in presentations at professional meetings and in publications for teachers and researchers (Minstrell 2001; Minstrell and Kraus 2005). By applying for grants, he obtained funding for release time to conduct his research more systematically than would have been otherwise possible. The funding enabled him to create a community of teacher-researchers within his school as he coached two mathematics teachers to use his approach to teach several of his physics classes. He also invited university researchers to join him, his colleagues, and his students in investigating physics learning. This enabled him to draw on university resources to accomplish some of his research goals. Building on his ongoing studies, Minstrell constructed a system of "facets of knowledge" that guided his design of instruction and assessments in many physical science contexts (Minstrell 2001). These facets formed the bases for computer diagnostic programs that students could use to check their understandings, now available free as tools for assessment at *www.Diagnoser.com*.

Teacher-researchers communicate their findings in a variety of ways. These may include talking informally with their grade-level team members, leading discussions at school faculty meetings, and presenting district-wide workshops on the issues they are exploring. They also may present their findings at local conferences for teacher-researchers and at national meetings such as Teacher-Researcher Day at National Science Teacher Association (NSTA) conventions. They may publish their findings in school district or state organization newsletters, journals for teachers, discipline specific journals, research journals, and books.

Teacher-researchers also may contribute to the public conversation about learning and teaching by developing documentary websites that enable anyone with internet access to explore their experiences and perspectives on issues they have formulated and examined. The Carnegie Foundation for the Advancement of Teaching, for example, has mounted a "Gallery of Teaching and Learning" with "snapshots of practice" that K–12 and higher education Carnegie Scholars have developed. Emily Wolk's snapshot documents the participatory action research that she undertook with elementary students to examine and modify a dangerous intersection near her school (*http://gallery.carnegiefoundation.org/ewolk*). Denis Jacobs, a college chemistry professor, developed a snapshot that presented an alternative approach to general chemistry in which he addressed the needs of at-risk students with cooperative learning strategies (*http://gallery.carnegiefoundation.org/djacobs*). Deborah Smith, a science teacher educator, documented ways in which she engaged science-phobic preservice teachers in her course on methods of teaching science in elementary school (*http://gallery.carnegiefoundation.org/dsmith*). Teacher-researchers interested in developing their own web-based snapshots of practice can use the Foundation's freely available KEEP (Knowledge, Exchange, Exhibition, Presentation) Toolkit to communicate their studies to others (at *www.carnegiefoundation.org/KML/KEEP/index.htm*).

Reflection

Teachers act as researchers every day as they listen closely to their students, consider what to do next, how and why, and pause to wonder about some aspect of what is happening in their classrooms. Those who undertake systematic studies contribute to the research enterprise when they make their findings public through workshops, presentations, and publications. University researchers can foster teacher research by supporting teachers in their inquiries. School administrators can create environments in which teachers are motivated to take an in-depth look at teaching and learning in their classrooms. Thus teacher research has the potential to improve instruction directly by engaging teachers in seeking to understand deeply how their students learn. Teacher research also has the potential to influence science teaching practices through generation of findings that are credible to other teachers in the field.

Emily H. van Zee

is an associate professor of science education at the University of Maryland, College Park. She collaborates with teachers in development of case studies of science learning and teaching. She is a Carnegie Scholar in teacher education and participant in the Carnegie Academy for the Scholarship of Teaching and Learning.

Deborah Roberts

is the instructional specialist in elementary science for the Montgomery County Public Schools, Maryland. She engages teachers in research as part of the Howard Hughes Student Inquiry Project. She is a K–12 Carnegie Scholar and participant in the Carnegie Academy for the Scholarship of Teaching and Learning.

References

Abell, S. K., and L. A. Bryan. 1997. Reconceptualizing the elementary science methods course using a reflection orientation. *Journal of Science Teacher Education* 8: 153–166.

Cochran–Smith, M., and S. Lytle. 1993. *Inside/outside: Teacher research and knowledge.* New York: Teachers College Press.

Dewey, J. 1928/1959. Progressive education and the science of education. In *Dewey on education selections.* M. S. Dworkin, ed. 113–126. New York: Teachers College Press.

Dinkelman, T. 2003. Self-study in teacher education: A means and ends tool for promoting reflective teaching. *Journal of Teacher Education* 54 (1): 6–18.

Doris, E. 1991. *Doing what scientists do: Children learn to investigate their world.* Portsmouth, NH: Heinemann.

Duckworth, E. 1987. *The having of wonderful ideas and other essays on teaching and learning.* New York: Teachers College Press.

Feldman, A. 1996. Enhancing the practice of physics teachers: Mechanisms for the generation and sharing of knowledge and understanding in collaborative action research. *Journal of Research in Science Teaching* 33: 512–540.

Gallas, K. 1995. *Talking their way into science: Hearing children's questions and theories, responding with curricula.* New York: Teachers College Press.

Hammer, D., and D. Schifter. 2001. Practices of inquiry in teaching and research. *Cognition and Instruction* 19 (4): 441–78.

Howes, E. 2002. *Connecting girls and science: Constructivism, feminism, and science education reform.* New York: Teachers College Press.

Hubbard, R. S., and B. M. Power. 1993. *The art of classroom inquiry: A handbook for teacher research.* Portsmouth, NH: Heinemann.

Hubbard, R. S., and B. M. Power. 1999. *Living the questions: A guide for teacher-researchers.* York, ME: Stenhouse.

Hutchings, P. 2000. *Opening lines: Approaches to the scholarship of teaching and learning.* Palo Alto, CA: Carnegie Foundation for the Advancement of Teaching.

Iwasyk, M. 1997. Kids questioning kids: "Experts" sharing. *Science and Children* 35 (1): 42–46.

Lincoln, Y., and E. Guba. 1985. Emerging criteria for quality in qualitative and interpretive research. *Qualitative Inquiry* 1 (3): 275–289.

McLean, J. E. 1995. *Improving education through action research: A guide for administrators and teachers.* Thousand Oaks, CA: Corwin Press.

Michaels, S., and R. Sohmer. (forthcoming). The "two puppies" story: The role of narrative in teaching and learning science. To appear in *Narrative interaction.* U. Quasthoff and T. Becker, eds. Amsterdam: Benjamins.

Mills, G. 2003. *Action research: A guide for the teacher-researcher.* 2nd ed. NJ: Merrill.

Minstrell, J. 1982. Conceptual development research in the natural setting of the classroom. In *Education for the 80's: Science*, ed. M. B. Rowe, 129–143. Washington, DC: National Education Association.

Minstrell, J. 2001. Facets of students' thinking: Designing to cross the gap from research to standards-based practice. In *Designing for science: Implications for everyday, classroom and professional settings.* eds. K. Crowley, C. D. Schunn, T. Okada, 415–444. Mahwah, NJ: Lawrence Erlbaum.

Minstrell, J., and P. Kraus. 2005. Guided inquiry in the science classroom. In *How students learn: History, mathematics, and science in the classroom*, eds. M.S. Donovan and J.D. Bransford, 475–524. Washington, DC: National Academy Press.

Mohr, M. M., C. Rogers, B. Sanford, M.A. Nocerino, M. MacLean, S. Clawson, and A. Lieberman. 2003. *Teacher research for better schools.* New York: Teachers College Press.

National Research Council (NRC). 1996. *National Science Education Standards.* Washington, DC: National Academy Press.

Nichols, S. E., D. Tippins, and K. Wieseman. 1997. A "toolkit" for developing critically reflective science teachers. *Research in Science Education* 27 (2): 175–94.

Paley, V. 1986. On listening to what the children say. *Harvard Educational Review* 56 (2): 122–131.

Paley, V., and R. Coles. 1999. *The boy who would be a helicopter.* Cambridge, MA: Harvard University Press.

Pearce, C. 1999. *Nurturing inquiry.* Portsmouth, NH: Heinemann.

Pekarek, R., G. H. Krockover and D. P. Shephardson. 1996. The research-practice gap in science education. *Journal of Research in Science Teaching* 33: 111–114.

Reddy, M., P. Jacobs, C. McCrohon, and L. R. Herrenkohl. 1998. *Creating scientific communities in the elementary classroom.* Portsmouth, NH: Heinemann.

Richardson, V. 1994. Conducting research on practice. *Educational Researcher* 23 (5): 5–10.

Roberts, D. 1999. The sky's the limit: Parents and first-grade students observe the sky. *Science and Children* 37: 33–37.

Roth, K. (forthcoming). Science teachers as researchers. In *Handbook of research on science education.* S. K. Abell and N. G. Lederman, eds. Mahwah, NJ: Erlbaum.

Saul, W., J. Reardon, C. Pearce, D. Dieckman, and D. Neutze. 2002. *Science workshop: Reading, writing, and thinking like a scientist.* 2nd ed. Portsmouth, NH: Heinemann.

Shulman, L. S. 2004. *The wisdom of practice: Essays on teaching, learning, and learning to teach.* San Francisco: Jossey–Bass.

Simpson, D. 1997. Collaborative conversations: Strategies for engaging students in productive dialogues. *The Science Teacher* 64 (88): 40–43.

Stiles, K. E., and S. Mundry. 2002. Professional development and how teachers learn: Developing expert science teachers. In *Learning science and the science of learning*, ed. R. W. Bybee, 137–151. Arlington, VA: NSTA Press.

van Zee, E. H. 1998. Fostering elementary teachers' research on their science teaching practices. *Journal of Teacher Education* 49: 245–254.

van Zee, E. H., M. Iwasyk, A. Kurose, D. Simpson, and J. Wild. 2001. Student and teacher questioning during conversations about science. *Journal of Research in Science Teaching* 38:159–190.

van Zee, E. H., D. Lay, and D. Roberts. 2003. Fostering collaborative inquiries by prospective and practicing elementary and middle school teachers. *Science Education* 87: 588–612.

White, R., and R. Gunstone. 1992. *Probing understanding*. London: Falmer Press.

Whitin, P., and D. J. Whitin. 1997. *Inquiry at the window: Pursuing the wonders of learners*. Portsmouth, NH: Heinemann.

Zeichner, K., and S. Noffke. 2001. Practitioner research. In *Handbook of research on teaching*, ed. V. Richardson. 4th ed., 298–330. Washington, DC: American Educational Research Association.

CHAPTER

5

Celebrating Diverse Minds: Using Different Pedagogical Approaches

Hubert M. Dyasi

Science and science education communities have embraced the notion of science for all American children as a democratic alternative to teaching science only to select groups of students. To facilitate its implementation without distorting the nature of science and of appropriate pedagogy and attendant assessments, the American Association for the Advancement of Science—the AAAS—(1989, 1993) and the National Research Council—the NRC—(1996) have produced comprehensive publications. The National Science Foundation, which has provided significant funding for science education, has long adopted a policy of funding quality science education development programs that pay particular attention to the education of children of traditionally underserved groups in science, such as minorities, girls, English language learners, and children with limited educational and physical abilities.

The idea of science for all has been echoed nationwide. In many colleges and universities admission requirements include passing grades in science. State departments of education, professional science and science teaching associations, nonprofit science education agencies, formal and informal science education institutions, and most school districts subscribe to the notion. The New York State Education Department, for example, requires fourth- and eighth-grade students to take statewide science tests, and high school students to successfully complete three science courses to earn a high school diploma. Other states have similar regulations.

Local school districts have followed suit. The Board of Education of the City of New York, for example, has published science performance standards in which it

> resolved to abolish the practice of expecting less from poor and minority children and children whose first language is not English. These performance standards are intended to help bring *all* students to high levels of performance (Board of Education of the City of New York 1999, p. 4, emphasis added).

For science for all children to be successfully implemented, however, inclusive quality pedagogical approaches are essential, approaches that are authentic not just to the nature and content of science but also to children's diverse cultural and personal strengths. At the same time, school systems will have to be aware of and avoid pitfalls that led to unequal access to science learning in the past. The question is: What do quality approaches look like? I attempt to answer this question.

Identifying Pitfalls

A large proportion of minority children speak and write English differently from the standard ways of the majority. This difference has been linked to their sometimes unimpressive performance in paper-and-pencil reading and writing tests and interpreted as lack of understanding, sometimes even as lack of capability to develop understanding. As a result, many minority children have been labeled as children with learning difficulties and have either not been taught science at all or have been expected only to read difficult science textbooks and to memorize scientific words and concepts that have neither meaning nor relevance to their interests or their lives (Weber and Dyasi 1985). There has also been a widespread, invalid presumption that only academically gifted students benefit from learning science, and, therefore, only gifted children should be taught science. Since academic giftedness has been associated with privilege, mostly children from privileged homes enrolled in science while children from low socioeconomic and minority communities were tracked out of science (Aldridge 1992). Thus, presumptions of incapacity have been imposed on academically challenged students and on students from low socioeconomic environments. All pedagogical approaches must not only dismiss these presumptions of incapacity to learn science, they must also de-mystify science.

Authentic Science and Requisite Pedagogical Practice

In the 1960s nationally funded secondary and elementary and middle school science education programs represented authentic science. Secondary programs produced physics, chemistry, and biology textbooks, support materials, and kits, while elementary and middle school programs emphasized student engagement in authentic scientific activities focusing on processes of science, science subject matter, and a combination of both. The latter programs developed modules on selected science areas, such as electricity, rather than textbooks. Kits accompanying the modules contained commonly available household materials, supplies, and tools or equipment, which made it easier for both students and teachers to relate to school science activities. Some programs added a story line to their modules to portray the incremental and dynamic nature of scientific knowledge.

All the programs' curriculum materials shared an investigative pedagogical approach marked by explorations, extended practical investigations, teacher as guide, use of familiar materials, and a focus on the practical and intellectual processes of doing science. One elementary science program in particular, The Elementary Science Study, developed at Education Development Center, directly discussed open inquiry as an essential component of its pedagogical approach:

> Rather than beginning with a discussion of basic concepts of science, ESS puts physical materials into children's hands from the start and helps each child investigate through these materials the nature of the world around him. Children acquire a great deal of information, not by rote but through their own active participation. We feel that this process brings home even to very young students the essence of science—open inquiry combined with experimentation (ESS 1970, p. 7).

Other programs, for example the Science Curriculum Improvement Study (SCIS) and the Biological Sciences Curriculum Study (BSCS), developed inquiry-oriented science learning cycles.

Meta-analyses of learning studies on these early elementary and middle school science programs showed they had a more positive impact on

students' growth in science learning than traditional programs in general achievement, analytic skills, process skills, related skills (reading, mathematics, social studies, and communication), and in attitude towards science (Bredderman 1983; Shymansky et al. 1983).

Newer science programs developed in the 1980s and 1990s—FOSS, Science and Technology for Children, Insights, Science Education for Public Understanding Program, Chemunity—built upon and extended the science pedagogical work of the earlier programs and also took into account contemporary understandings on cultural, gender, differential abilities, and assessment issues in the learning of science. The kind of science and science education embodied in these programs served as a point of departure for establishing consensus on authentic science for schools as well as on appropriate pedagogy and assessment. The NRC's National Science Education Standards (NSES), the AAAS's Benchmarks, and position statements of various science and science teaching associations are definitive representations of the consensus.

To illustrate: according to the NSES, school science content encompasses eight related strands: unifying concepts and processes—for instance, system, order, evidence, models, constancy, equilibrium, and form and function; science as inquiry; life science; physical science; Earth and space science; science and technology; science in personal and social perspectives; and history and nature of science. The Benchmarks portray a similar image, emphasizing common themes in science. Scientific inquiry is presented as a major epistemology in all science.

Science as Inquiry and the Learning of Science

Science as inquiry has long been recognized as a most important aspect of epistemology in science (see for example, Bruner 1961; Dewey 1910; Piaget 1975; Schwab 1962). It is the NSES, however, that have most recently highlighted it as "basic to science education and a controlling principle in the ultimate organization and selection of students' activities" (NRC 1996, 105). The NSES further claim that engaging students in science inquiry helps them to develop

- understanding of scientific concepts,
- an appreciation of how we know what we know in science,
- understanding the nature of science,

- skills necessary to become independent inquirers about the natural world, and
- the dispositions to use the skills, abilities, and attitudes associated with science.

Achievement of high attainment levels in these five areas is, therefore, a hallmark of quality science education. To enable students to reach those levels the NSES recommend, *among other things*, that

> Students at all grade levels and in every domain of science should have the opportunity to use scientific inquiry and develop the ability to think and act in ways associated with inquiry, including asking questions, planning and conducting investigations, using appropriate tools and techniques to gather data, thinking critically and logically about relationships between evidence and explanation, constructing and analyzing alternative explanations, and communicating scientific arguments (NRC 1996, p. 105).

Because children at all grades are at different academic and intellectual levels of maturity and represent diverse cultural and geographical groups, this recommendation implicitly calls for matching specific pedagogical strategies to a broad inquiry-based pedagogical approach. Hence the NRC produced *Inquiry and the National Science Education Standards*, a practical guide for teaching and learning science through inquiry (NRC 2000).

Humans as Learners

Many research studies of human learning have been carried out, as evidenced in the NRC's publication, *How People Learn: Brain, Mind, Experience, and School* (Bransford et al. 1999). Of all the findings in the research studies analyzed in the publication, Donovan et al. (1999) have highlighted three that have a solid research base and have particular relevance to education, namely,

1. Students come to the classroom with preconceptions about how the world works. If their initial understanding is not engaged, they may fail to grasp new concepts and information presented in the classroom, or they may learn them for purposes of a test but revert to their preconceptions outside the classroom (p.10).
2. To develop competence in an area of learning, students must: (a) have both a deep foundation of factual knowledge; (b) understand

facts and ideas in the context of a conceptual framework, and (c) organize knowledge in ways that facilitate retrieval and application (p. 12).

3. A "metacognitive" approach to instruction can help students learn to take control of their own learning by defining learning goals and monitoring their progress in achieving them (Donovan et al., 1999, p. 13).

The first finding confirms our practical knowledge that long before they enter school, children are curious and learn a great deal about phenomena in their world. They ask questions in order to understand a world in which they can orient themselves and function; this is true for all children whether or not they are gifted (Weber 1973; cf. Duckworth 1987; Isaacs 1930). Further,

> … a child's inquiry takes place in a world of people and things. In the process of his questioning he accumulates answers that are the "facts" of science. He focuses on this or other thing, and his focusing is concrete: He asks what the thing can do and what it means. Long before and even after he has acquired words, his asking can be observed in his actions, and his tentative solutions in his adaptations of his actions (Weber 1973, p. 4).

The learning is often spontaneous, joyful, and self-directed; it is also dynamic, non-linear, and long-term. We believe that this kind of learning can apply with necessary changes to older children in school.

We believe that inquiry can serve as an all-embracing culture of learning. Findings from research studies on learning such as those reported by Driver et al. (1985, 1994), Duschl and Gitomer (1991), Osborne and Freyberg (1985), Tobin (1991), and those highlighted by Donovan et al. (1999) can inform pedagogical strategies within the inclusive culture of inquiry-based teaching and learning.

Inclusive Science Pedagogy and the Culture of Science Inquiry

We identify learning science by inquiry as an overarching culture and approach to learning within which pedagogical strategies bearing an imprint of its essential characteristics can be mobilized to meet the science education needs of culturally and cognitively diverse students. It should be overarching because it is not just a pervasive human attribute, but also a central epistemological feature of the culture of science. Ipso facto, an inquiry-based pedagogy of science education is an inclusive science pedagogy. Inquiry is not a teaching strategy. Teaching strategies are specific mechanisms used at opportune times to meet specific, short-term goals: lecturing, reading, discussing, concept mapping, and questioning are examples of teaching strategies that may be useful at one time or another. They fit in the culture of inquiry insofar as they are used to support rather than to supplant learning by inquiry.

An inclusive science pedagogy is a deep professional commitment to successfully create congruence between children's attributes and science inquiry in classrooms. At that level, it is a community and culture that builds upon children's strengths and cultural and cognitive capital, utilizing artifacts from their immediate physical and cultural environments as initial resources in science learning. It then progressively and successfully links them with significant authentic science content and with artifacts and intellectual and physical tools associated with the scientific enterprise. In that culture, scientific thinking and reasoning are a constant in all science learning activities. The degree to which they are applied, of necessity, varies to match different children's motivational and intellectual attributes. A good match allows every member of a classroom community to experience success and to learn that his or her contributions are identified, recognized, and acknowledged. Variations can be found in examples of phenomena to be investigated, science tools and equipment, the degree of complexity and number of variables and relationships to be kept in mind, and the pace of activity. These variations are judiciously manipulated to bring about optimum learning levels among diverse students.

In such classroom communities, there are many examples of natural phenomena that students can investigate directly; and there are displays of students' scientific investigations at various levels of complexity and at various stages of progress towards completion. There are also sufficient quantities of and a wide range of scientific tools and equipment for carrying out and documenting students' inquiries—hand lenses, ordinary and analytic measuring devices, computers, and specialized equipment. Students' science notebooks showing evidence of deep, extended, and repeated inquiries as well as of shorter-term firsthand inquiries into phenomena of nature are major sources of reference during inquiries. They contain pictorial and symbolic representation of data and evidence and records of students' scientific reflective abstractions (or "science news" making) that go beyond phenomenological levels of knowledge. Further, the notebooks show evidence of "public" communications of students' science news and scientific justifications, based on accepted standards of scientific evidence and lines of scientific reasoning linking observations initially to conclusions and eventually to a big scientific idea (or childhood version of scientific research council conferences).

One would also see a classroom library of suitable science stories such as accounts of authentic science inquiries that led to discoveries, accounts of the development of selected scientific ideas, current science problems and efforts to solve them, examples of children's science inquiries written by children, easy-to-read biographies of female and male scientists from ethnic groups represented in the class, science inquiry-based software, and videos of representations of scientific understandings that are often inaccessible from direct concrete investigations—such as photosynthesis—that are otherwise inaccessible through direct inquiries. Most important, the learning environment would exude the feelings of psychological, intellectual, and physical safety we should see and feel in a learning environment. These kinds of classrooms exist many places across the country.

In its educational work with inner city schools in New York City, the Workshop Center at the City College (City University of New York) successfully developed and employed an inclusive pedagogy in a culture of inquiry. For example, students conducted initial inquiries into familiar fruits, red cabbage, and household chemicals such as vinegar, baking soda, and detergents, using a variety of ordinary tools such as spoons, plastic medicine cups, droppers, and stirrers until they understood the concept of indicator, acid and base reactions, and neutralization and the procedures involved to arrive at those understandings. Only then did they use less common materials and equipment such as pH paper and standard laboratory apparatus and chemical reagents to arrive at the same understandings. The positive impacts of these practices on teachers and students are discussed in Dyasi (1992) and Dyasi and Dyasi (2003). Similarly, results from an exploratory study of the effects of "an instructional congruence framework (i.e. instruction that creates congruence "between students' cultural expectations and classroom interactional norms [and] between academic disciplines and students' linguistic and cultural experience," Lee 2004, p. 67) on elementary school teachers of science and their students indicate that important educational benefits accrue in science teaching and learning for teachers and students alike (ibid.).

Although the school plays a vital role in the adoption and support of inclusive science pedagogy, the science teacher's pedagogical strategies are pivotal in its implementation. Pedagogical roles of the teacher discussed in the science teaching standards of the NSES are excellent examples of possibility for inclusive science pedagogy. The Standards recommend that during inquiry-based science lessons, teachers of science "focus and support students' inquiries," "orchestrate discourse among students about scientific ideas," "challenge students to accept and share responsibility for their learning," "*recognize and respond to student diversity and encourage all students to participate fully in science learning*," and "encourage and model the skills of scientific inquiry, as well as the curiosity, openness to new ideas and data, and skepticism that characterize science" (NRC 1996, p. 32, emphasis added). These roles are also highlighted in many inquiry-based science education materials produced in the last 20 years. The issue we are discussing here, however, goes beyond "recognize and respond to student diversity and encourage all students to participate fully in science learning," to knowing what to actually do to meet that pedagogical responsibility. For example, what should a teacher do as a positive and productive initiative to celebrate diverse minds in the classroom when using inquiry-promoting pedagogical approaches?

The National Research Council has answered this question (NRC 2000). It has highlighted essential features of science inquiry during science lessons. Learners "ask scientifically oriented questions," "give priority to evidence that permits development of explanations and their evaluation," "formulate explanations from the evidence," "evaluate their explanations while considering alternative explanations," and "communicate and justify their proposed explanations" (NRC 2000, p. 25). The NRC also provides a continuum of pedagogical strategies for addressing the needs of students at different stages of mastery of abilities and knowledge necessary to do science inquiry. If a teacher's objective, for example, is to engage learners in scientifically oriented questions, depending on the student's abilities, she or he can have students (a) pose their own questions to investigate, (b) select among questions to pose a new question, (c) sharpen or clarify a question provided by the teacher or other source, or (d) engage in questions provided by the teacher. If the objective is to enable students to communicate and justify explanations, the teacher may have able students form reasonable and logical arguments to communicate explanations, but it may be necessary to coach less able students before they can carry out the task. Other students may be able to accomplish the task only if they are provided with guidelines to help them sharpen communication, and still others need to be given steps and procedures for communication. Similar variations in strategy may be necessary with other essential features of science inquiry (NRC 2000, p. 29).

Some students cannot fruitfully proceed with science inquiries without consulting a book, other people, the internet, or a variety of other sources. They may need to know a fact, a mathematical value, a constant, a name of an organism, or a conventional way of organizing data, or it may be a case of finding out how others dealt with the question at hand and how they met attendant challenges. Perhaps a student is looking for ideas on how to comfortably enter and transform his or her "zone of proximal development" into knowledge (Vygotsky 1962)—or to push further and further out of his or her "proximal zone of ignorance" (St. John 1998). Students who recognize a need to consult a book for these purposes are becoming connoisseurs of their own knowledge and of where it is lacking in a given situation—a positive condition for learning. In this case, students are not hapless visitors to the resources but inquirers who search also for scientific evidence supporting the facts they find in the source. Their effort will promote continuing growth of their abilities to do science inquiry and can give them ownership of the means and products of their science inquiries (Alberty and Weber 1973; Harlen 2000).

Teachers further celebrate diverse minds in their classrooms by carefully framing their questions. Reasoning questions can be phrased to invite students to participate or *require their ideas rather than the "right answer;"* for example, "Why, do you think, the bulb failed to light?" instead of "Why did the bulb fail to light"? Insertion of the words, "do you think," dramatically focuses the question on reasoning (Harlen 2001). Harlen has identified different kinds of useful questions, such as attention-focusing questions ("do you notice…"?); measuring and counting questions ("how many?" "how long?" "how often?"); action questions ("what happens if you do this or that?"); and problem-posing questions ("can you find a way to increase the velocity of the cart?"). Teachers also make judicious choices about timing different kinds of questions and students they select to respond. For example, students need more time to think about and to frame their response to questions that ask for an extended response than to closed-ended questions that require only a "yes" or "no." In a class of students with vastly varying educational abilities, a teacher might select slower students to answer closed-ended questions and ask them more open-ended questions when they work in small inquiry groups. To accommodate students who lack verbal facility or have other educational shortcomings, teachers can encourage them to draw, act out, or demonstrate their responses or illustrate them through concept maps and cartoons.

Within inquiry-based pedagogical approaches teachers may model science inquiry in the classroom or laboratory to help students. Modeling can occur when a teacher joins a small group with questions, noticings, and wonderings about their inquiries or shares with them his or her genuine puzzles, or thinks aloud or otherwise support them in their inquiries. Playing back to students their own questions and their thinking about their inquiry activities and accepting their thinking as valid and important—because it is, to them—helps students develop an awareness of their thought processes and a sense of ownership of questions, inquiry activities, and findings. Student ownership of science inquiry activities is especially important for the shy and academically challenged and for students from cultures that expect children to do what they are told without question.

A teacher can further assist students in their inquiries by highlighting important scientific findings from their work and emphasizing how scientific findings can be anchors around which to build subsequent findings. The teacher can make a finding even more meaningful by singling it out and asking students where they think, in their experience, the finding holds true and why they think so—or students, in instances students have not experienced, ask them where the finding could be used to explain observed phenomena. In addition, the teacher might offer specific instances in which the finding applies and other instances that are superficially similar but to which the finding does not apply and ask students to deconstruct them to demonstrate how the finding is or is not applicable. An interesting example is whether Fourier analysis applies in our hearing of sounds and whether it also applies when a radio tunes to a specific frequency.

Many teachers use available human and physical resources from outside the classroom. Local scientists who are successful at working with young students, parents, technologists, crime detectives, journalists, and others should be regular features in a culture of science inquiry. So should field trips to local science-based establishments such as science museums, water purification plants, construction sites, rivers, and oceans. These trips, however, should always be carefully planned to give students questions that require them to provide good, reliable answers. In this way they serve as supports to learning science through inquiry.

A teacher cannot accurately make judgments of the level of students' science inquiry abilities without relying on good evidence-based formative assessment (see Black and Wiliam 1998; Atkin et al. 2001). Much of the evidence the teacher needs to make judgments is in the teacher's own inquiries into (a) students' actions, discussions, and primary records of their work; (b) his or her own teaching; and (c) the nature and characteristics of instructional materials used. The illustrations below regarding students' actions that follow are drawn directly from Harlen 2000, p. 28-30.

To judge science inquiry abilities a teacher may check against specific indicators. For example check (a) observation—whether students succeed in identifying obvious differences and similarities; can identify similarities between objects where differences are more obvious than similarities; distinguish from many observations those which are relevant to the problem at hand; (b) interpretation of evidence—whether students compare their findings with earlier predictions; notice associations between changes in one variable and another; recognize that any conclusions are tentative and may have to be changed in light of new evidence; (c) communicating and reflecting—whether students listen to others' ideas and look at their results; use tables, graphs, and charts when these are suggested to record and organize results; record and present results in forms commensurate with the type of information presented and the audience; and (d) respect for evidence—whether students realize when the evidence doesn't fit a conclusion based on expectations, even though they may challenge the evidence rather than the conclusion; check parts of the evidence that don't fit an overall pattern or conclusions; accept only interpretations or conclusions for which there is supporting evidence; recognize that no conclusion is immune to challenge by further evidence.

A teacher's answers to questions should help determine the selection of phenomena to use and directions and levels of subsequent students' inquiries. The teacher's responsive actions will hopefully be unfettered by scheduling, material resources, pressures of inordinately long science syllabi, and narrowly conceived accountability requirements.

All the pedagogical adjustments and variations suggested are compatible with an inclusive classroom culture of science inquiry; indeed, they are essential mechanisms for enabling students to progress in quality science learning. They are desirable professional strengths in science teachers—knowledge of science and sensitivity to students' cultural norms, abilities, and dispositions; valid professional judgments of realistic expectations from students' efforts; mastery of classroom organization in mixed-ability classes; and an informed commitment to cultivating a vibrant learning classroom community. They are not substitutes for students' direct experience of authentic science inquiry, and they are not end points in students' development. If they are so regarded, that would be contrary to how people learn and would engender feelings of inferiority and a sense of worthlessness in students of different academic abilities and socioeconomic levels, and in children of different cultures. They would be antithetical to authentic science for all children.

Hubert M. Dyasi

is professor of science education at the City University of New York, where he also directs science teacher development programs for schools. He is author of numerous journal articles, book chapters, and national science education reports of the National Research Council. He has been honored as Visiting Scholar at the University of Oxford (England) and at the California Institute of Technology, as a Fellow of the National Institute for Science Education, and as a recipient of the Exploratorium's 2005 Outstanding Educator Award.

Acknowledgments

I am grateful to Nancy Pelaez, University of California, Fullerton, and Richard Frazier, North Central Missouri University, for helping me in the clarification and enrichment of some of the ideas expressed in this chapter.

References

Alberty, B., and L. Weber. 1973. *Continuity and connection: Curriculum in five open classrooms.* New York: The City College Workshop Center.

Aldridge, B. G. 1992. Project on scope, sequence, and coordination: A new synthesis for improving science education. *Journal of Science Education and Technology* 1(1): 13–21.

American Association for the Advancement of Science (AAAS). 1989. *Science for all Americans.* New York: Oxford University Press.

American Association for the Advancement of Science (AAAS). 1993. *Benchmarks for science literacy.* New York: Oxford University Press.

Atkin, J.M., P. Black, and J. Coffey (eds.). 2001. *Classroom assessment and the National Science Education Standards.* Washington, DC: National Academy Press.

Black, P. J., and D. Wiliam. 1998. Assessment and classroom learning. *Assessment in Education* 5 (1): 7–74.

Board of Education of the City of New York. 1999. *Performance standards: Science.* New York: Board of Education of the City of New York.

Bransford, J. D., A. L. Brown, and R. Cocking (Eds.). 1999. *How people learn: Brain, mind, experience, and school.* Washington, DC: National Academy Press.

Bredderman, T. 1983. Effects of activity-based elementary science on student outcomes: A quantitative analysis. *Review of Educational Research* (4): 499–518.

Bruner, J. S. 1961. *The process of education.* Cambridge: Harvard University Press.

Dewey, J. 1910. *How we think.* Lexington, MA: D.C. Heath.

Donovan, M.S., J. D. Bransford, and J. W. Pellegrino, eds. 1999. *How people learn: Bridging research and practice.* Washington, DC: National Academy Press.

Driver, R., E. Guesne, and A. Tiberghiem. 1985. *Children's ideas in science.* Philadelphia: Open University Press.

Driver, R., A. Squires, P. Duck, and V. Wood–Robinson. 1994. *Making sense of secondary sciences: Research into children's ideas.* London: Routledge.

Duckworth, E. 1987. *The having of wonderful ideas and other essays on teaching and learning.* New York: Teachers College Press, Columbia University.

Duschl, R. A., and D. H. Gitomer. 1991. Epistemological perspectives on conceptual change: Implications for educational practice. *Journal of Research in Science Teaching* 28 (9): 839–858.

Dyasi, H. 1992. Developing confidence in primary school teachers to teach science—A practical approach. In *Innovations in the science and technology education Volume IV*, ed. D. Layton, 23–37. Paris: UNESCO.

Dyasi, H., and R. Dyasi. 2003. The Workshop Center at City College of New York. In *Designing professional development for teachers of science and mathematics*, eds. S. Loucks–Horsley, N. Love, K. Stiles, S. Mundry and P. W. Hewson, 283–293. Thousand Oaks, CA: Corwin Press.

Elementary Science Study. 1970. *ESS reader*. Newton, MA: Education Development Center.

Harlen, W. 2000. *Respecting children's own ideas*. New York: The City College Workshop Center.

Harlen, W. 2001. *Primary science: Taking the plunge*. Portsmouth, NH: Heinemann.

Isaacs, S. 1930. *Intellectual growth in young children*. London: Routledge and Kegan Paul.

Lee, O. 2004. Teacher change in beliefs and practices in science and literacy instruction with English language learners. *Journal of Research in Science Teaching* 41 (1): 65–93.

National Research Council (NRC). 1996. *National science education standards*. Washington, DC: National Academy Press.

National Research Council (NRC). 2000. *Inquiry and the national science education standards: A guide for teaching and learning*. Washington, DC: National Academy Press.

Osborne, R.J., and P. Freyberg. 1985. *Learning in science: The implications of children's science*. Auckland: Heinemann.

Piaget, J. 1975. *The development of thought*. New York: Viking Press.

Schwab, J.J. 1962. *The teaching of science as enquiry. The Inglis Lecture 1961*. Cambridge: Harvard University Press.

Shymansky, J., W. C. Kyle, and J. M. Alport. 1983. The effects of new science curricula on student performance. *Journal of Research in Science Teaching* 20 (5): 387–404.

St. John, M. 1998. *"Wait, wait! Don't tell me!" The anatomy and politics of inquiry*. New York: The City College Workshop Center.

Tobin, K.G. 1991. *Constructivist perspective on teacher learning*. Paper presented at the 11th Biennial Conference on Chemical Education, Atlanta, GA.

Vygotsky, L. S. 1962. *Thought and language*. Cambridge, MA: MIT Press

Weber, L. 1973. But is it science? In *Science in the open classroom*, ed. R. Dropkin, 3–15. New York: The Workshop Center for Open Education.

Weber, L., and H. Dyasi. 1985. Language development and observation of the local environment: First steps in providing primary-school science education for non-dominant groups. *Prospects* XV (4): 565–576.

Part II Professional Development: Implications for Science Teaching and Learning

CHAPTER

6

Leading Professional Development for Curriculum Reform

James B. Short

The purpose of curriculum reform in science education is to improve student learning.

The most effective strategy for improving student learning is to impact teaching practices.

Adopting high quality, inquiry-based instructional materials can support effective teaching and improve the science curriculum implemented in a district.

Understanding how to effectively implement high-quality, inquiry-based instructional materials is grounded in teachers' knowledge and beliefs about learning and teaching and the content of their discipline. The link between each of these levels of curriculum reform is effective professional development.

What are the components of effective professional development in science teaching and learning? What do professional development providers need to know and be able to do in order to design learning experiences that challenge teachers' beliefs and change their practice? And most important, how does one develop the leadership to sustain professional development for curriculum reform in science education? These are important questions to consider as reform efforts progress toward a future that includes higher standards for qualified teachers and greater accountability for student learning.

Over the past five years, with funding from the National Science Foundation, the Biological Sciences Curriculum Study (BSCS) developed a long-term professional development program to support standards-based curriculum reform at the secondary level. The National Academy for Curriculum Leadership (NACL) is a three-year program in which district-based leadership teams learn about tools and strategies for selecting and implementing inquiry-based, reform-oriented instructional materials. School districts from across the country have participated in the program, which is now being replicated as a regional program in Washington State. The ideas about curriculum leadership and professional development presented in this chapter are based on this work.

Curriculum Reform

Curriculum reform in science education is a systemic approach that involves both developing new instructional materials and learning new ways of using them (Anderson 1992). Putting curriculum reforms into practice is a difficult and demanding process that requires a vision of reform, flexibility and support for change, collaboration among teachers to learn, and leadership at different levels (Anderson 1995). One way to participate in curriculum reform is to select and use instructional materials based on the National Science Education Standards (referred to as the Standards) (NRC 1996) in their approach to content, assessment, teaching, and professional development. Instructional materials aligned with the Standards include inquiry as a part of the science content, incorporate instructional strategies and embedded formative assessments that promote a student-centered approach to learning, and require ongoing professional development for sustainable implementation.

Reform-oriented instructional materials incorporate contemporary research on learning (NRC 2000) that challenge teachers to think differently about learning and teaching science. Instead of a textbook that provides only what to teach, these instructional materials also provide support for how to teach. Because incorporating these supports into instructional materials makes them look different, most teachers need a rich form of ongoing professional development to help them learn how to use such materials effectively. Due to the substantial changes in practice that may be required to implement reform-oriented instructional materials, many teachers will require shifts in their knowledge and beliefs. To support curriculum reform that involves the selection and implementation of reform-oriented, standards-based instructional materials, effective professional development must challenge teachers' beliefs about and understandings of science content, best teaching practices, and contemporary views of learning. This chapter describes the need for effective professional development that transforms teachers' beliefs and practices. Curriculum leadership becomes what professional development leaders need to know and be able to do to support curriculum reform that is focused on reform-oriented, standards-based instructional materials.

The ultimate goal of curriculum reform is to improve student learning through better teaching practices. One way to improve these teaching practices is to develop stronger instructional systems and support systems. In particular, supporting teachers with a mix of reform-oriented, standards-based instructional materials and effective professional development focused on transforming their beliefs and practices adds up to a powerful combination for improving instruction. Districts can develop better support systems by building improvement infrastructures that include resources and people (such as professional development providers, coaches, and curriculum specialists) that are positioned and funded to improve the system and its instructional supports (St. John 2002). Curriculum leadership defines a key piece of the improvement infrastructure. This chapter describes the knowledge, capabilities, and ways of thinking and acting needed by leaders of professional development and curriculum reform.

Curriculum Leadership

Curriculum leadership typically has been defined as leading the development of new instructional materials that support a reform agenda (Gross 1998; Henderson and Hawthorne 2000). Instructional materials are defined as the collection of textbooks (containing units and lessons), teacher's guides, and ancillary materials and activities that are adopted for use in schools for teachers to use in teaching. Instructional materials are important aids to initiating and sustaining curriculum reform in science education because they are tangible vehicles for embodying the essential ideas of a reform (Powell and Anderson 2002). Standards-based instructional materials help teachers enact a reform agenda by offering concrete ways for them to become facilitators of learning, helping students construct understandings, organizing the science content around large conceptual themes, and addressing the nature of science overtly so that students participate in self-directed inquiries (NRC 2000).

Although varying definitions of leadership pervade the literature, many are often confused with definitions of a leader, and the terms are often used interchangeably, viewing leadership as the work of the leader (Lambert et al. 2002). For the purpose of this chapter, curriculum leadership is defined as being more about understanding adult learning and the process of change, building relationships, and facilitating professional development than as being a set of behaviors for leading in the traditional sense. Instead of leading the development of new instructional materials, curriculum leadership, in this sense, is about supporting a district's improvement infrastructure through selecting and implementating reform-oriented instructional materials that were developed to address the goals of the Standards.

Given that national and state standards provide a vision of improving the science literacy of all students, the focus of reform is to affect changes in teacher practice that result in improved student learning. Standards-based instructional materials can support changes in teacher practice and provide opportunities for student learning, but materials alone cannot sustain reform.

The changes in practice suggested by the Standards and incorporated into reform-oriented instructional materials are substantial. In their extensive review of research about learning to teach, Putnam and Borko (1997) begin by saying, "For teachers to move successfully toward these new visions of classrooms will require in many cases major changes in their knowledge, beliefs, and practice . . . . To make the changes being asked of them, teachers must reflect deeply and critically on their own teaching practice, on the content they teach, and on the experiences and backgrounds of the learners in their classrooms" (p. 1224). The implication for curriculum reform and professional development is that some teachers will require shifts in their knowledge and beliefs to effectively implement and sustain the recommended changes in practice.

The research on professional development is clear that "professional development [should] help teachers understand (a) subject matter, (b) learners and learning, and (c) teaching methods" (Loucks-Horsley and Matsumoto

1999, p. 262). Cohen and Ball (1999) reinforce this idea in their work in mathematics education, which describes a model focused on teaching and surrounded by models for professional development and leadership development (see Figure 1). This diagram (based on an adaptation by Seago and Mumme 2000) illustrates how student learning, adult learning, and learning to lead professional development are related to one another. This view of leadership development provides a conceptual framework for thinking about the role curriculum leadership plays in supporting professional development providers who create learning environments for teachers to engage in conversations about Standards-based instructional materials and the intersections between teaching, students, and science content.

Figure 1: Circles of learning and leading

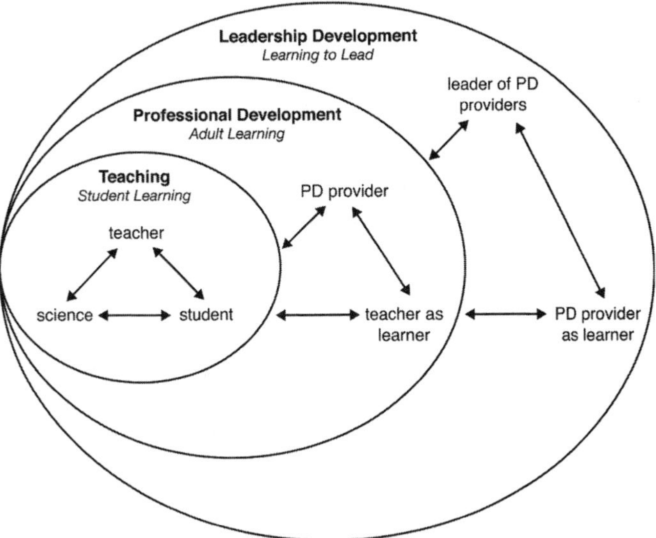

The diagram begins with a representation of the relationships involved in teaching students—the relationships between teacher and student, student and content, and teacher and content. As Carroll and Mumme (2001) explain,

> This dynamic relationship is one that includes the teacher knowing the content, not just the specific content of a lesson, but a deeper understanding of where that content resides in the curriculum, what is important for students to know, and how students come to learn it. The teacher also needs to know about her students in particular and student thinking and learning in general. She needs to know how students learn the content—how she brings the student and the content together to create a learning environment. Teaching occurs in a context, and teaching

involves understanding the complexities of how the context interacts with the goals for learning the content (p. 9).

In the middle level of the diagram, professional development, the content becomes the work of teaching, the learner is the teacher, and the instructor is the professional development provider. Carroll and Mumme (2001) explain,

> Here the [professional development provider] needs to know the content—the content being taught and the complex relationships that this entails. The [professional development provider] also needs to know about the learner—this time, teachers. They need to know how adults learn and what will help them learn the content (teaching). The [professional development provider] needs to understand her role in facilitating learning (teaching teachers) (p. 9).

In the outer level of the diagram, leadership development, the content is professional development and the learner is the professional development provider. Carroll and Mumme (2001) describe the knowledge required of the instructor at this level as even more complex, involving knowledge of the work of teaching, of professional development, and of supporting the work of professional development providers. This level provides additional insights into the concept of curriculum leadership and the task of supporting professional development providers who are, in turn, supporting teachers. The remainder of this chapter will further explore professional development and leadership development in order to develop a better understanding the role of curriculum leadership in standards-based science reform.

Professional Development

Research indicates there is a strong relationship between high-quality professional development and the kinds of teaching practices that are advocated by curriculum reform in science education (Supovitz and Turner 2000). Furthermore, there is a promising indication that large-scale, high-quality, inquiry-based professional development set within a context of standards-based systemic reform can be a powerful mechanism for sustained and positive impact on teachers' attitudes, preparation, and teaching practices (Supovitz et al. 2000).

For effective professional development to support adult learning, the knowledge base on learners and learning needs to be considered. Teachers and principals need to be engaged in learning experiences that confront traditional beliefs and participate in field experiences where they can experiment collaboratively. The conventional wisdom has been that changing teacher beliefs should be the primary work of professional development, for when one believes differently new behaviors will follow (Loucks-Horsley et al. 2003). Research on teacher change, however, indicates that changes in beliefs often come only after teachers use a new practice and see the benefits to their students (Ball and Cohen 1999). This means that effective professional development experiences must include opportunities for teachers to apply new practices in their classrooms and reflect on their experiences. Professional development providers must extend their work with teachers beyond workshops and institutes and include strategies such as coaching and mentoring, looking together at student work, and analyzing the results of commonly developed assessments.

From the hallmark study of mathematics reform in California (Cohen and Hill 1998), researchers learned that reform focused only on adding new instructional materials and changing some practices can result in a patchwork quilt of reform in which some reform practices—often the ones that fit with a teacher's prior ideas—are adopted and others ignored. What is needed is that teacher learning and professional development engage teachers in strategies that produce transformative learning, that is, "changes in deeply held beliefs, knowledge, and habits of practice" (Thompson and Zeuli 1999, p. 342).

To implement standards-based reform, professional development must challenge teachers' knowledge and beliefs about learners, the process and learning, and effective teaching. Professional development strategies intended to transform teachers' practices often result instead in teachers' assimilating new techniques and tools into established patterns of teaching, leaving basic modes of instruction undisturbed (Thompson and Zeuli 1999). Curriculum leadership involves helping professional development providers understand how to design and facilitate transformative learning for adults. Only when teachers' beliefs, perceptions, and experiences are challenged in an environment conducive to learning can the realities of standards-based reform be confronted in productive ways. The first step is viewing professional development as helping adults change their beliefs and construct new knowledge rather than as training teachers in new strategies.

Dimensions of Curriculum Leadership

Based on the dimensions of technological literacy (NAE 2002), curriculum leadership encompasses three interdependent dimensions: (1) knowledge; (2) capabilities; and (3) ways of thinking and acting. In practice, it is impossible to separate the dimensions from one another. A capable leader in professional development most likely also knows something about adult learning and effective professional development. So, although such a framework can be helpful in thinking and talking about curriculum leadership, it is important to remember the dimensions are arbitrary divisions. Curriculum leadership focused on supporting transformative professional development has a unique combination of knowledge, capabilities, and ways of thinking and acting.

Knowledge

Four aspects of knowledge involved in curriculum leadership include

- understanding the change process,
- using the research on how people learn to develop coherence in curriculum,
- applying science as inquiry and the nature of science to provide congruence within the science curriculum, and
- using a process of deliberate design in professional development that includes evaluation.

The Concerns-Based Adoption Model (CBAM) provides a framework for understanding the change process and its impact on individuals. Based on Frances Fuller's work on stages of teacher development (1969), the CBAM (Hall and Hord 2001) is an empirically based conceptual framework that outlines the developmental process individuals experience as they use an innovation (i.e., a curricular program or teaching process that is new to the individual) and participate in associated professional development. The concept of concerns was developed to describe individuals' perceptions, feelings, motivations, frustrations, and satisfactions as they progress through different stages in using the innovation (Hall and Loucks 1978). Curriculum leadership involves knowing how to collect information about the change process on an ongoing basis and use it to inform professional development and facilitate the management and implementation of the change process.

The knowledge aspects of *coherence and congruence* are based on Bybee's (2003) use of these ideas to frame the teaching of science. Curricular coherence is based on contemporary research on learning (NRC 2000). Coherence refers to the number of concepts developed in a uniform set of experiences (e.g., lessons and units) and within a school program (e.g., elementary and secondary science courses). Coherence is a measure of the connectedness among the science concepts that students experience. Instructional congruence focuses on how teaching science as inquiry brings together content and pedagogy in a way that broadens and deepens student learning, and ultimately students' understanding and appreciation of science. This means that scientific inquiry is a prominent theme for both teaching and content. Based on the Standards, all students should develop the abilities necessary to do scientific inquiry and the understandings about inquiry and the nature of science.

A final aspect of the knowledge dimension of curriculum leadership is the process of designing professional development. Effective professional development is the result of *deliberate designing*. Loucks-Horsley et al. (2003) have created a professional development design framework that includes several components to consider when designing learning experiences for teachers. These critical inputs into the design process include how knowledge and beliefs inform a commitment to standards and a vision for reform; how context factors determine what kinds of data you consider about student, teacher, and organizational learning needs; how critical issues like equity, scaling up, and building capacity inform goal setting and planning; how professional development strategies are chosen after goals are clearly established; and how evaluation plays a feedback role in the design process.

One of the critical issues facing professional development leaders is linking the results of effective professional development to improved student learning outcomes. Planning for what you want students to learn is different than planning for what teachers are going to do. Guskey (2003) states, "Planning backward compels staff development leaders to consider crucial evaluation questions up front, before any program or activity begins" (p. 29). A useful way to facilitate the planning-backward process is to begin with evaluating student learning, teacher practice, and organizational support to inform and design the outcomes for professional development (Guskey 1999).

Capabilities

Capabilities involved with the development of collaborative groups are described by Garmston and Wellman (1999) and can be applied to the concept of curriculum leadership. Based on these ideas, the five capabilities involved in curriculum leadership include

- efficacy,
- flexibility,
- craftsmanship,
- consciousness, and
- interdependence.

Efficacy refers to knowing that one has the capacity to lead professional development and reform initiatives that make a difference and be willing and able to do so (Garmston and Wellman 1999). According to the authors, confident leaders regard events as opportunities for learning, are motivated by and committed to achieving shared goals, learn from experiences, focus resources where they will make the greatest difference, know what they know and do not know, and develop strategies to learn what is needed. In leading professional development, this means knowing the punch lines, or what is important, in the piece you are teaching, understanding that dips will occur during learning, trusting the people and the process to get out of the dips, and predicting the outcomes to be better prepared to handle what surfaces during the learning process.

Flexibility refers to honoring and valuing diversity within and outside groups, attending to both rational and intuitive ways of thinking, having the ability to collectively shift perspectives, and using a wide array of thinking and process skills (Garmston and Wellman 1999). According to the authors, flexible leaders can navigate the internal tensions related to confusion and ambiguity and get unstuck by generating multiple actions for moving ahead. In leading professional development, this means being able to monitor and adjust your plans, knowing when to tell and when to let learners struggle on their own, and incorporating different learning styles into activities and tasks.

Craftsmanship refers to learning and deepening one's knowledge, skills, and effectiveness through elaboration, clarity, refinement, and precision (Garmston and Wellman 1999). According to the authors, leaders using this capability invest energy in honing and inventing better ways to do

their work, honor the journey from novice to expert, manage time effectively, and continually improve inter- and intragroup communications. In leading professional development, this means making the content of the professional development relevant and contextual for the learner, providing a conceptual framework so the learner can see the whole and the parts of what they are trying to learn, and using both inductive and deductive professional development strategies to support the learning of all adults.

Consciousness refers to being aware of one's thoughts, feelings, behaviors, intentions, and their effects (Garmston and Wellman 1999). According to the authors, leaders using this capability monitor group decisions, actions, and reflections based on values, norms, and common goals. In leading professional development, this means monitoring the needs of the group, using reflective strategies that involve journaling and small group conversations, and establishing and routinely revisiting norms or behaviors for working together, sharing ideas, and talking with each other.

Interdependence refers to valuing and trusting the process of dialogue, having awareness of multiple relationships and identities within groups, and regarding disagreements as sources of learning and transformation (Garmston and Wellman 1999). According to the authors, leaders using this capability regard knowledge as fluid, provisional, and subject to new interpretation with additional experience. In leading professional development, this means challenging the thinking of others, using evidence to develop shared understanding, and embracing resistance as learning opportunities. Working with a cofacilitator and depending on the structure of teams and the roles on a team are additional ways of using this capability in professional development.

Ways of Thinking and Acting

Three ways of thinking and acting involved in curriculum leadership include

- developing norms for working collaboratively,
- communicating a vision and a plan, and
- using transactional and transformational leadership to facilitate the change process and adult learning.

Collaborative cultures come into existence and thrive because of common values and ways of working together. Developing shared norms and values is central to building a community of learners in professional development. Garmston and Wellman (1999) describe seven *norms of collaboration* that, when consciously attended to over time, produce skilled communication and increased clarity and cohesion within working groups. They are pausing, paraphrasing, probing for specificity, putting ideas on the table, paying attention to self and others, presuming positive intentions, and pursuing a balance between advocacy and inquiry (Garmston and Wellman 1999). In professional development, establishing norms and revisiting them not only models good classroom practice with teaching students but also lays the foundation for developing highly effective teams and professional learning communities.

Effective leaders provide a *vision and plan*. According to Bybee (1993), providing leadership means continually reaffirming your vision while simultaneously adjusting your plan. He explains that some leaders have a plan, but no vision—they are managers. Other leaders may have a vision but no plan—they are utopian. Providing curriculum leadership requires both a plan of directed action and flexibility. Bybee states, "One must give a sense of direction *and* be responsive to those with whom one is working. Being too rigid and authoritarian is ineffective; being too flexible and laissez-faire is equally ineffective" (p. 151). In leading professional development, the Standards provide a vision for curriculum reform in science education. There are also standards to guide the design of professional development (NSDC 2001). The professional development design framework (Loucks-Horsley et al. 2003) provides a conceptual tool for planning effective learning experiences that includes feedback loops to monitor and adjust your designs.

Leading professional development also requires two different types of leadership, *transactional and transformational*. Based on the work of Burns (1978), Bybee (1993) provides descriptions of these two types of leadership. Transactional leadership means letting followers know what is expected and what they will receive for meeting those expectations. This type of leadership focuses on services and rewards. Transformational leadership identifies the motives and aspirations of followers and seeks to engage individuals on a personal level. This type of leadership focuses on the needs of others. Both types of leadership are needed in leading professional development. Examples of transactional leadership include establishing an agenda and time frames for sessions; honoring time commitments by beginning and ending sessions on time; and setting clear expectations for the work participants engage in during professional development experiences. Examples of transformational leadership include taking care of the personal needs of participants—the temperature of the room, comfortable chairs, good food, and occasional breaks—and finding out their motivations for change. Because transformative professional development and adult learning are about changing beliefs and practices, knowing what motivates adults to consider a change in their practice or alter their beliefs is crucial.

Implications for Reform

It is clear that more effective teaching practices supported by high quality, inquiry-based instructional materials have great potential to improve student learning. Effective professional development that challenges teachers' knowledge and beliefs about learning and the implications for teaching is also needed. This chapter has considered two additional issues to support curriculum reform: the need for transformative professional development and the need for curriculum leadership to support the improvement infrastructure that includes professional development providers in science education.

Three implications for curriculum reform in science education emerge from this chapter. First, effective professional development is about leading adult learning, which means providing experiences so that individuals can deal with the uncertainties of change and develop some common understandings about reform-oriented, standards-based instructional materials. Second, for professional development to support curriculum reform, it needs to transform the beliefs and practices of teachers. And finally, professional development leaders are needed to support the learning of professional development providers by exploring the dimensions of curriculum leadership and investing in the local improvement infrastructure.

James B. Short

is a science curriculum coordinator for Denver Public Schools and is primarily responsible for supporting the redesign of the K–12 science program. Previously he was director of the National Academy for Curriculum Leadership, a program developed with funding from the National Science Foundation at the BSCS Center for Professional Development. His work includes both classroom implementation and working with schools and larger systems on building the capacity for standards-based science reform involving K–12 instructional materials.

References

Anderson, R. D. 1992. Perspectives on complexity: An essay on curricular reform. *Journal of Research in Science Teaching 29*: 861–876.

Anderson, R. D. 1995. Curriculum reform: Dilemmas and promise. *Phi Delta Kappan 77* (1): 33–36.

Ball, D. L., and D. K. Cohen. 1999. Developing practice, developing practitioners: Toward a practice-based theory of professional education. In *Teaching as the learning profession: Handbook of policy and practice*, eds. L. Darling-Hammond and G. Sykes, 3–32. San Francisco: Jossey-Bass.

Burns, J. M. 1978. *Leadership.* New York: Harper and Row.

Bybee, R. W. 1993. *Reforming science education: Social perspectives and personal reflections.* New York: Teachers College Press.

Bybee, R. W. 2003. *The teaching of science: Content, coherence, and congruence.* Colorado Springs, CO: Biological Sciences Curriculum Study.

Carroll, C., and J. Mumme. 2001. *Leadership for change: Supporting and developing teacher leaders in mathematics renaissance K–12.* Retrieved April 9, 2001, from *http://temat.enc.org/carroll.shtml.*

Cohen, D. K., and D. Ball. 1999. *Instruction, capacity, and improvement.* (CPRE Research Report No. RR-043). Philadelphia: University of Pennsylvania Consortium for Policy Research in Education.

Cohen, D. K., and H. C. Hill. 1998. State policy and classroom performance: Mathematics reform in California. *CPRE Policy Briefs* (RB–23–January, 1–14). Philadelphia: University of Pennsylvania Consortium for Policy Research in Education.

Fuller, F. F. 1969. Concerns of teachers: A developmental conceptualization. *American Educational Research Journal* 6: 207–226.

Garmston, R. J., and B. M. Wellman. 1999. *The adaptive school: A sourcebook for developing collaborative groups.* Norwood, MA: Christopher-Gordon.

Gross, S. J. 1998. *Staying centered: Curriculum leadership in a turbulent era.* Alexandria, VA: Association for Supervision and Curriculum Development.

Guskey, T. R. 1999. *Evaluating professional development.* Thousand Oaks, CA: Corwin Press.

Guskey, T. R. 2003. Scooping up meaningful evidence. *Journal of Staff Development* 24 (4): 27–30.

Hall, G. E., and S. M. Hord. 2001. *Implementing change: Patterns, principles, and potholes.* Needham Heights, MA: Allyn and Bacon.

Hall, G. E., and S. F. Loucks. 1978. Teacher concerns as a basis for facilitating and personalizing staff development. *Teachers College Record* 80: 36–53.

Henderson, J. G., and R. D. Hawthorne. 2000. *Transformative curriculum leadership.* 2nd ed. Upper Saddle River, NJ: Prentice-Hall.

Lambert, L., D. Walker, D. P. Zimmerman, J. E. Cooper, M. D. Lambert, M. E. Gardner, and M. Szabo. 2002. *The constructivist leader.* 2nd ed. New York: Teachers College Press.

Loucks-Horsley, S., N. Love, K. E. Stiles, S. Mundry, and P. W. Hewson. 2003. *Designing professional development for teachers of science and mathematics.* 2nd ed. Thousand Oaks, CA: Corwin Press.

Loucks-Horsley, S., and C. Matsumoto. 1999. Research on professional development for teachers of mathematics and science: The state of the scene. *School Science and Mathematics* 99 (5): 258–268.

National Academy of Engineering (NAE). 2002. *Technically speaking: Why all Americans need to know more about technology.* Washington, DC: National Academy Press.

National Research Council (NRC). 1996. *National science education standards.* Washington, DC: National Academy Press.

National Research Council (NRC). 2000. *How people learn: Brain, mind, experience, and school (Expanded Edition).* Washington, DC: National Academy Press.

National Staff Development Council (NSDC). 2001. *Standards for staff development (rev).* Oxford, OH: NSDC.

Powell, J. C., and R. D. Anderson. 2002. Changing teachers' practice: Curriculum materials and science education reform in the USA. *Studies in Science Education* 37: 107–136.

Putnam, R. T., and H. Borko. 1997. Teacher learning: Implications of new views of cognition. In *The international handbook of teachers and teaching,* eds. B. J. Biddle, T. L. Good, and I. F. Goodson, vol. II, 1223–1296. Dordrecht, The Netherlands: Kluwer Academic Publishers.

Seago, N., and J. Mumme. 2000. *Video cases for mathematics teacher development: What we are learning.* San Francisco, CA: WestEd. Unpublished paper.

St. John, M. 2002. The improvement infrastructure: The missing link or why we are always worried about "sustainability." Retrieved May 13, 2004, from *http://sustainability2002.terc.edu/invoke.cfm/page/123/show/print.*

Supovitz, J. A., D. P. Mayer, and J. B. Kahle. 2000. Promoting inquiry-based instructional practices: The longitudinal impact of professional development in the context of systemic reform. *Educational Policy* 14 (3): 331–356.

Supovitz, J. A., and H. M. Turner. 2000. The effects of professional development on science teaching practices and classroom culture. *Journal of Research in Science Teaching* 37 (9): 963–980.

Thompson, C. L., and J. S. Zeuli. 1999. The frame and the tapestry. In *Teaching as the learning profession: Handbook of policy and practice,* eds. L. Darling-Hammond and G. Sykes, 341–375. San Francisco: Jossey-Bass.

CHAPTER 7

Advancing Student Achievement Through Professional Development

John H. Holloway

Kindergarten through twelfth grade teacher competence, in both subject matter and pedagogy, is critical for advancing student achievement in science. The National Science Foundation (NSF 1996), however, has found that only about two-thirds of first- through eighth-grade teachers completed at least one college course in science and fewer than 30 percent said they feel well qualified to teach science.

Additionally, Lowery (1998) points out that many educators see no need to change from a show-and-tell type of instruction to methods that help students understand science by constructing meaning for themselves through exploration and using prior knowledge. Levitt's (2002) research supports this by suggesting that many elementary teachers perceive their role in teaching science as primarily a dispenser of facts. Wenglinsky's research (2002) has shown that professional development has a strong influence on teachers' classroom practices and, as a result, becomes the key mechanism for helping students meet high standards. To help teachers raise student achievement levels, Schmoker (2002) proposes that schools design professional development that, by focusing on assessed standards and reviewing student achievement data, directly impacts student learning.

In spite of this growing awareness about the importance of linking professional development directly to student achievement, this type of training seldom occurs. Research done by Parsad et al. (2001) found that teachers were most likely to have taken part in professional development that focused on the integration of educational technology into the grade or subject taught. What kinds of professional development offerings, then, can schools provide that are designed to directly affect gains in student achievement? Can schools use student performance as part of the professional development process? How can schools be sure that the training provided did, in fact, produce any of the observed gains in student performance?

Connecting a Professional Development System to Student Achievement

Professional development typically is offered to teachers to serve a variety of purposes that includes providing training in new teaching techniques, helping teachers understand new mandates and regulations, giving teachers assistance in implementing new technology tools, and a myriad of other job-specific topics. In many districts this training is given at one session with little follow-up, feedback, or coaching. But to effect student achievement gains, educators must think differently about professional development. This new concept must view teacher training as a job-embedded system, specifically designed as an agent for promoting increased student learning rather than as occasional, isolated events. Sparks and Hirsh (1997) believe there must be some significant shifts in our thinking on professional development to have this training more clearly focused on student achievement. According to these professional development experts, this paradigm must include:

- a new focus on student needs and learning outcomes,
- a greater use of multiple forms of job-embedded learning,
- classroom-based investigations by teachers into the teaching and learning processes,
- continuous improvement in performance for everyone who affects student learning; and
- a belief that staff development is an indispensable process for advancing student growth.

A unified system of professional development must focus on the needs of the students rather than simply those of the teachers and school leaders. Training must be delivered in a variety of innovative ways to accommodate the limited time most teachers have and should become part of the ongoing classroom instructional process, rather than the "one-shot, sit and get" delivery mode. Most important, professional development must be part of the continual learning process for the entire school community, and that community must view the training system as a vital part of the entire reform process. We must begin to think about all these factors that contribute to effective professional development experiences rather than just the training event itself.

For schools to educate all students to higher levels, educators must think of professional development as a sequential process that begins by engaging educators in learning experiences and culminates with specific benefits to students. The learning process would continue as educators have a chance to analyze the direct effects staff development has on student learning. Both teachers and school leaders place greater value on professional development when they see it result in improved student learning (Mizel 2003). The National Staff Development Council (NSDC 2004) has created the *NSDC Standards for Professional Development* to help guide this more-focused view of professional development for higher student achievement. NSDC believes that to improve student learning, professional development must

- consider and apply knowledge about human learning and the change process in planning training for teachers and school leaders;
- use multiple sources of information to evaluate and guide improvement of professional development initiatives and demonstrate its impact; and
- use available data to inform training decisions.

Although these points are only a very brief summary of all the NSDC Standards, they form an initial platform upon which to begin building a professional development system.

Guskey (2003) analyzed several recently published lists of characteristics of effective professional development. These lists came from national professional associations and organizations as well the U.S. Department of Education. According to his analysis, several of these lists failed to include any of the NSDC Standards that are directly linked to improving student achievement. Instead, Guskey found the lists typically involved surveys of the opinions of researchers and educators. He did find, however, that typically a National Institute for Science Education (NISE) analysis and an Educational Testing Service (ETS) study showed a direct link between their identified characteristics and specific measures of student achievement. He found for that most of the lists mention sufficient time and other resources as essential to effective professional development. But most lists failed to mention that the time must be well organized, carefully structured, and purposefully directed. He found that fewer than half the lists mentioned the importance of using analyses of student learning data to guide professional development activities, and only four lists stressed that professional development should be based on the best available research evidence.

Criteria are beginning to emerge that link professional development to improved student learning and opportunities for educators to become better consumers of offerings. The list of characteristics for focusing professional development on increased student performance is growing. Some of the most critical criteria are:

- focusing on the needs of the students,
- providing delivery modes that accommodate the participants' time and schedule and that allow the training to become embedded in practice,
- bringing together teachers, school leaders, and other appropriate stakeholders responsible for student progress into the training process,
- using appropriate data to inform professional development planning decisions, and
- monitoring and assessing the impact of the training on student learning.

Although these few points can begin to help districts construct a professional development system, what can teachers and school leaders do to begin this process?

An Evidence-Centered Approach to Inform Professional Development

One way to get a jumpstart on helping teachers and school leaders become engaged in understanding how to advance student learning is to have them analyze student classroom data—the evidence of student learning. We want to use this evidence to begin to answer two questions: "What teacher behaviors or school conditions contributed to this evidence?" and "What can I learn from this evidence to better inform future instructional decisions?" This simple, initial activity in data analysis can be the beginning of a professional development system that directly links past teacher behaviors to evidence of learning. More important, it helps teachers reflect on their practices. By looking at student data in an organized and focused way, schools can begin to identify professional development needs and prioritize valuable, scarce resources more effectively. By gathering evidence of student learning, collected in both formative and summative assessments, we gain a powerful tool to guide professional development and teacher collaboration (Holloway 2003). The National Education Association agrees that student classroom data can become both the actual substance of professional development and the basis for making decisions about educators' on-the-job learning, including decisions pertaining to professional development resource allocation, content, and delivery (NEA 2003).

Jones and Courtney (2002) have been investigating how to help teachers look at evidence of student learning, make judgments about the evidence, and use the information to inform instructional decisions. They point out that simple classroom science activities in the early grades, such as planting seeds, are a natural part of early childhood instruction and provide settings in which teachers can observe how children are making sense of the world around them. Evidence of learning comes from notes of children's conversations and actions and other forms of classroom projects and constructions. This evidence forms the classroom-based data that helps teachers learn how children are thinking about science. The evidence gathering and documentation process starts to help teachers gain a deeper understanding of individual student growth and changes in the class as a whole and what teaching behaviors produced these changes. They have found that some specific principles are needed to guide teachers through the classroom-based documentation process, such as

- collecting a variety of forms of evidence over time,
- collecting evidence on groups of children as well as individuals,
- describing evidence of children's learning without judgment and discussing it with colleagues,
- interpreting evidence of individual and group understanding by connecting to learning goals and identifying patterns of learning, and
- applying this new information and understanding to improve instruction and curriculum and assessment.

Through ongoing professional development, teachers can master this evidence-centered, progress monitoring system. It will help them to continually and more accurately gauge the learning of the youngest children and adjust their teaching and planning to address the needs of each student. Once mastered, this progress-monitoring strategy becomes a sustained, self-directed professional development system embedded in the teaching process.

Stearns and Courtney (2000) found that as teachers begin to rely on evidence of student learning to make better instructional decisions, they realize a need for new kinds of classroom assessments. These investigators looked at elementary science units taught by the teachers who were trying to align the units with science standards. At first, teachers concentrated on subject-matter passages found in the textbooks, partly to reinforce their own understanding of the central science concepts. Then, after examining student work and reflecting on their own classroom experiences, the teachers revisited the standards with deeper questions, such as "What does this mean at the second-grade level as compared to the fourth?" (p. 52). Because the acquisition of science knowledge is cumulative, they found it best if students continually check their growing understanding of scientific principles based upon their prior learning. Stearns and Courtney found that, when teachers understand this concept of the accumulation of science learning, their sense of their role in influencing assessment design increases. Through training, teachers began to learn how to create better evidence-gathering devices (e.g., tasks or assessments) that provided opportunities for students at different places along the learning continuum to show their understanding. These teachers also learned how to recognize evidence of student learning in work samples rarely characterized by a unique correct answer. And they found that one of the most effective activities was to give teachers an opportunity to engage in reflective discussions at and across grade levels about the content standards and assessment. In their grade-level discussions, teachers analyzed students' responses to the tasks with three basic questions in mind:

- Did the task reveal whether students were achieving the learning goals?
- Did the task provide students with multiple ways of responding?
- Was the task accessible to all students?

Black and Wiliam (1998) believe that teachers need to know about their pupils' progress and difficulties with learning so they can adapt their own work to meet pupils' needs. They believe that schools can improve student achievement by training teachers in how to use formative assessment results to provide the necessary evidence to gear instruction to individual students' needs. Some evidence of student learning occurs during structured, teacher-led classroom discussions. Sometimes, however, teachers fail to take advantage of this data-gathering strategy, or they collect misinformation because, in some cases, they are looking for a particular response and lack the flexibility or the confidence to deal with the unexpected. In these cases, many teachers try to direct the pupil toward giving the expected answer. In compensating for their own lack of content knowledge, teachers redirect the discussions and fail to credit creative attempts by students to construct their own meaning. Done over time, this sends a message to the students that they are not required to think out their own answer but must simply come up with the preconceived correct answer. When using classroom dialogue to assess student understanding and to inform future instructional decisions, teachers should first ask themselves: "Do I really know enough about the understanding of my pupils to be able to help each of them?" (p. 144).

By using evidence of student performance as a professional development activity and to inform professional development decisions, we begin to realize a job-embedded system of training and more effective targeting of training resources. This can occur, however, only if teachers become more comfortable with teaching the content, staging effective classroom discussions, and understanding some basic principles of assessment. How do we know if this training is actually producing the observed gains in student achievement or if the progress is due to some other, unrelated variable?

Verifying the Link Between Professional Development and Student Achievement

Program evaluation of professional development initiatives helps decision-makers determine if

- the intervention accomplished its goals,
- the training should be continued, and
- the training should receive resources at the current levels.

In order to conduct a program evaluation several factors must be considered:

- What are the claims of the program?

- What evidence will we collect to monitor change?
- What types of instruments must we develop or use to gather the evidence of change?
- Can we devote enough time to measure change over months and years?
- Which type of evaluation design is best suited for our study and available resources?
- How do you know it was the professional development that caused the change?

The effects that professional development have on student learning frequently take several months or even years to emerge. Unfortunately, because of changes in leadership, shifts in resource allocation priorities, or changes in external mandates, many initiatives are not given the necessary time to show student growth. Educators must begin to appreciate this fact and be committed to a more formal look at the results of training programs.

What should districts look for in assessing the quality of their professional development initiatives to determine if they do, in fact, make any difference in improving student achievement? Guskey (2000) believes that one could imagine five levels of professional development evaluation. From lowest to highest, they are

- participant reaction
- participant learning
- district support for the training
- participant implementation of the training
- student learning resulting from the training

The lowest level, *participant reaction* to the training, usually provides the least valuable information about the effect the training has on student achievement, but this is what most school districts use to justify the training. Participants at this level are typically surveyed to find, for instance, if they enjoyed the training or for some other, similar subjective opinion. This information might help inform revisions for future training, but it provides little information about the impact the training will have on teaching and student learning. One way to partially improve the quality of the responses for this low-level training assessment is to use an instrument that requires participants to give short answers to simple phrases. For instance, a rating sheet could ask participants to complete sentences such as

- One thing new that I learned today was ….
- The most important thing I learned today that I will use tomorrow is ….
- I was most interested in ….
- To really implement what I learned today, I will need ….

These open-ended phrases tend to elicit more valid responses that can then be used to plan future training and as starting points to monitor training impact on teaching and learning.

The next level is *participants' learning*. What did the participants learn? How do we know? Although we still are not sure if the participants will translate this new knowledge into gains in student achievement, it might provide more information for improving the next training session.

The third level is *district support* for the training and for the change the training is intended to produce. The chances that the professional development will reach its intended goals are increased when teachers and school leaders see a strong district commitment to providing time and resources for training programs and then support ongoing efforts to sustain any change.

The next level of professional development is the *participants' use* of the newly acquired skills or knowledge. Did the participants apply the new learning to their practices, and what evidence can be found to support this conclusion?

The highest level of professional development evaluation is *student learning gains*. Did this training bring about the intended outcomes in learning or in other student attributes that affect learning, such as improved student attendance or behavior, or reduced dropout rates? At these higher levels of program evaluation, we begin to determine the effects of the essential purpose of the training.

How can schools tell if it is the professional development or some other reform initiative that caused an increase in student performance? A *process study* can describe the implementation of various professional development or other reform initiatives introduced into a school. This study can be conducted over one or more years, with a report each year. The specific goals of the evaluation will change each year to reflect the change process of educational reform. For example, in the first year of the study, a goal might be simply to look at the implementation of school leader training and its influence on school culture and the teaching and learning of science. Questions asked in this first year might be: How is the school leadership training integrated into the school's reform efforts? What leadership skills do principals learn from this training? What skills are integrated into practice? How is school culture affected by changes in leadership? Data sources might include:

- pre- and post-surveys of school culture,
- several principal surveys given during the year,
- observations of teachers and students in the school, and
- principal interviews.

Another study could be a *random assignment evaluation* of the training program. Examples of questions to be asked are:

- Does this training improve learning in specific content areas?
- What factors influence the impact of the training?

To answer these questions, students must be randomly assigned to two different groups of teachers: those who have undergone this training—the experimental group—and those who have not received this training—the control group. Data is then collected from both sets of classrooms from sources such as

- pre- and post-assessment,
- baseline test scores,
- background school records, and
- teacher surveys.

Another type of study is the *interrupted time series analysis.* In a district-wide school reform effort, random assignment usually is not feasible. In an interrupted time series, the time period before the intervention is used to project what would happen if, in fact, the school reform—or interruption—had not occurred. The impact of the reform is the difference between the projection and the actual level of achievement. For instance, to control for factors that may influence the change, a matched control group can be used to control for things like change in student demographics. A question guiding this type of study could be: Is the school's reform effort improving student achievement in the district? Data sources to answer this question could be:

- five years of retrospective standardized test scores in the district,
- annual test scores,
- five-year retrospective demographics, and
- current school records.

What Do I Do Tomorrow?

We know that most single, isolated training sessions fail to deliver the results in the classroom we are expecting. To provide educators with professional development offerings that affect student learning, districts must think about creating a system of training that is job-embedded and ongoing. Districts must begin to think of teachers and school leaders as classroom researchers who use their daily practice to learn about their students and to identify what works best for these students. To do this, these educators must be given guidance and support in understanding the basic concepts of evidence-centered instruction, including

- What do I want my students to know and be able to do when I finish this teaching episode or unit?
- What standards will I use to measure my students, and how closely have I aligned my instruction to these standards?
- What evidence will show me what my students have learned, both individually and as a group?
- How can I best capture and make judgments about that evidence?
- Now that I know this about my students, what do I do tomorrow?

By creating a system of ongoing teacher training based on a reflection of one's practice on classroom learning, coupled with a strategy for monitoring the effectiveness of the system, we begin to create teacher-researchers with the ability to look at the evidence of learning and to directly link that to teacher and student growth.

John H. Holloway

is a director at Educational Testing Service (ETS) in Princeton, New Jersey, in the Elementary and Secondary Education Division. He is the author of numerous journal articles, books, and book chapters. Before joining ETS, John served as a high school science teacher, assistant principal, and high school principal. While serving as principal, John was an adjunct college instructor at both the undergraduate and graduate levels. He received an ETS divisional leadership award in 2002.

References

Black, P., and D. Wiliam. 1998. Inside the black box: Raising standards through classroom assessment. *Phi Delta Kappan* 80 (2): 139–141.

Guskey, T. 2000. *Evaluating professional development.* Thousand Oaks, CA: Corwin Press.

Guskey, T. June 2003. What makes professional development effective? *Phi Delta Kappan* 84 (10): 248–251.

Holloway, J. 2003. Linking professional development to student learning. *Educational Leadership* 61 (3): 85–87.

Jones, J., and R. Courtney. 2002. Documenting early science learning. *Young Children* 57 (5): 34–41.

Levitt, K. 2002. An analysis of elementary teachers' beliefs regarding the teaching and learning of science. *Science Teacher Education* 86 (1): 1–24.

Lowery, L. 1998. How new science curriculums reflect brain research. *Educational Leadership* 56 (3): 26–31.

Mizel, H. 2003. Facilitator: 10; refreshments: 8; evaluation: 0. *Journal of the National Staff Development Council 24* (4): 10–13.

National Education Association (NEA) Foundation for the Improvement of Education. 2003. *Using data about classroom practice and student work to improve professional development for educators.* Washington, DC: Author. Retrieved August 27, 2004, from *www.nfie.org.*

National Science Foundation (NSF) Division of Research, Evaluation and Communication, Directorate for Education and Human Resources. 1996. *The learning curve: What we are discovering about U.S. science and mathematics education.* Suter, L. E., ed. Washington, DC: National Science Foundation.

National Staff Development Council. 2004. *NSDC standards for professional development.* Retrieved August 27, 2004, from *www.nsdc.org/standards.*

Parsad, B., L. Lewis, and E. Farris. 2001. *Teacher preparation and professional development: 2000.* Washington, DC: National Center for Educational Statistics, U.S. Department of Education.

Schmoker, M. 2002. Up and away. *Journal of the National Staff Development Council* 23 (4): 10–13.

Sparks, D., and S. Hirsh. 1997. *A new vision for staff development.* Alexandria, VA: ASCD.

Stearns, C., and R. Courtney. January 2000. Designing assessments with the standards. *Science and Children* 37 (4): 51–55, 65.

Wenglinsky, H. 2002. How school matters: The link between teacher classroom practices and student academic performance. *Education Policy Analysis Archives* 10 (12). Retrieved August 27, 2004, from *http://epaa.asu.edu/epaa/v10n12.*

CHAPTER

8

Building Ongoing and Sustained Professional Development

Jack Rhoton and Brenda Wojnowski

Perhaps at no other time in our educational history has the spotlight shone more brightly on the need for quality professional development. This new focus has been brought to center stage by more than two decades of educational reform efforts. Recognizing that science teachers and administrators represent the major link between the curriculum and student learning, expert practitioners, researchers, and policy makers emphasize professional development as an essential mechanism for deepening teachers' content knowledge and developing their teaching practices.

Since the release of the National Science Education Standards (NRC 1996), professional development aimed at retraining practicing teachers to meet the content and process standards has intensified. A recent stimulus to this concern can be traced directly to the enactment of the No Child Left Behind Act of 2001 (NCLB 2002), which emphasizes the importance of high-quality professional development to assure that all teachers are highly qualified and that all students reach high levels of achievement. Bringing this ambitious goal to fruition hinges in large part, however, on the quality of teachers. Student learning will be transformed only if high standards are reflected in teachers' classroom practices (Desimone et al. 2002; Loucks-Horsley et al. 1998; NSDC 2004; NCTAF 1996).

In recent years, a body of research has emerged on characteristics of effective professional development, teacher learning, and teacher change (Hargreaves and Fullan 1992; Hawley and Valli 1999; Leiberman 1996; U.S. Department of Education 1997; Loucks-Horsley et al. 1998; Sparks and Loucks-Horsley 1989; Stiles et al. 1996; Rhoton 2001). These characteristics or principles of professional development highlight

- improved teacher content and pedagogical knowledge as well as student learning,
- appropriate data to inform professional development planning decisions,
- active learning environments,
- links to high standards,
- teachers in leadership roles;
- school-based and job-embedded strategies,
- teachers and administrators working together,
- extended duration and long-term commitment, and
- continuous evaluation.

Even though these prominent characteristics and particular approaches of effective professional development, as well as others, are quite visible in the literature, very few systematic research studies have been conducted on the extent to which these characteristics contribute to better teaching and improved student learning (see, in particular, Guskey 2003). Some recent studies are beginning to show, however, along with the experiences and wisdom of expert practitioners, that professional development that incorporates all or most of these characteristics can have substantial, positive influence on teachers' practices and student achievement (Garet et al. 2001; Rhoton and Bowers 2001; Loucks-Horsley et al. 1998; U.S. Department of Education 1999).

Even though most reform initiatives have directed the largest resource investment to teachers' professional development, researchers and expert professional developers have seen much of this investment as supporting ineffective practices. Although educators may recognize the importance of new training models for improving science teaching practices, professional development strategies remain largely unchanged, detached from the realities of the classroom, and ineffective for promoting long-term change (Elmore et al. 1996; Stiles et al. 1996). Even as we go deeper into the 21st century, too much of what is promoted as professional development is dominated by stand-alone workshops and short after-school meetings.

Moreover, teachers have typically perceived their professional development programs as ineffective, poorly planned, and lacking in relevance to their instructional practices (Sparks and Loucks-Horsley 1990).

A Professional Development Model

What does an effective professional development program look like when it captures the elements of effective professional development and supports an ongoing, sustained approach for science teaching and learning? One thing we have learned is that short-term, one-shot workshops do not greatly enhance teachers' learning or the transfer of that learning into teachers' classrooms. The East Tennessee State University Science Partnership (ETSUSP) provides an example of one way in which an ongoing, sustained professional development support system can assist middle and high school science teachers in improving their knowledge of science content and pedagogy and engage students in meaningful science learning experiences.

Figure 1: ETSUSP professional development model

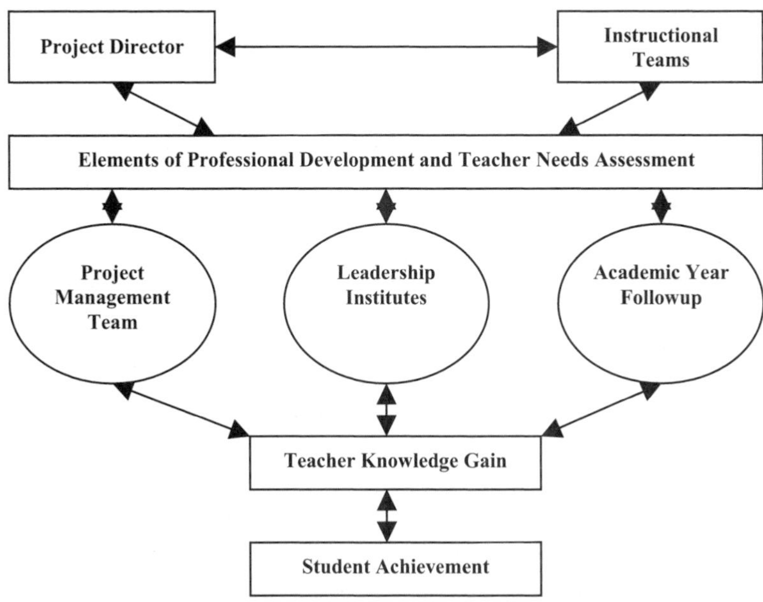

The ETSUP has established a collaborative relationship, extending over more than a decade, with various funding agencies and local school districts in the Upper East Tennessee Educational Cooperative (UETEC) to develop and implement a model of professional development for middle and high school science teachers.

The model (Figure 1) emerging from this 15-year partnership differs from traditional professional development paradigms. First, it offers sustained professional development support and teacher training throughout the academic year. Second, it requires the simultaneous development of instructional skills, administrative insights, and content expertise. Third, it is a grassroots effort involving teachers who implement and maintain the change.

The model accommodates three-member teams, composed of middle and high school science teachers, in the ETSU service area. Since the inception of the program, 375 teachers have been trained and more than 30 principals have been directly involved in the activities of the model. The ETSU model captures many of the principles of effective professional development as described in the professional development literature (see Table 1 for a comparison).

Table 1: Principles of effective professional development for science teachers

Cited by various sources	ETSU Framework and Model
Focus on content knowledge, pedagogy, and leadership	Science institutes for content, pedagogy and leadership
Focus on student learning	Analysis of teaching and learning
Collective participation	Teacher teams
Links to high standards	State and national standards
Opportunities for teachers to be engaged in leadership roles	Teachers as mentors
Bringing together various stakeholders	Project management team
School-based and job embedded	School-site professional development
Use of data to inform professional development decisions	Analysis of student classroom data
Monitoring and assessing	Assessment each year

The model allows teachers to have control over their own needs. The following sections describe each component of the model and provide insights into the ways in which the program is addressing professional development issues.

Focus on Content and Pedagogical Knowledge

Effective science teachers need a deep understanding of science content and pedagogy (Rhoton and Bowers 2001). Researchers and expert practitioners agree that content knowledge can have a positive influence on student achievement, especially in secondary science (Blair 2000; Whitehurst 2002; Wenglinsky 2000).

To build opportunities for participants to gain enhanced content and pedagogical knowledge, the ETSU model makes available summer science leadership institutes for middle and high school science teacher participants. The institutes run from two to six weeks each summer and are taught by ETSU science faculty and science educators. Institutes focus on both science content (inquiry in science) and inquiry in teaching and learning. Participants engage in a variety of science investigations in the areas of biology, chemistry, and physics, with topics for investigation driven by the participants, student data, and local and state science standards. Investigations and institute activities are presented in the context of how the teacher participants can implement them effectively in their own classrooms.

In addition to learning science content, participants explore questions and ideas about their students' learning, their teaching, and their curricular approaches. These conversations prepare the participants for examining meaningful ways to connect their students' understanding with accepted practices of teaching and learning, thereby providing for a seamless integration of content and scientific ideas with knowledge of student learning and pedagogical practices.

Each participant in the project receives the science supplies and equipment necessary for his or her science curriculum, graduate credit, and a stipend for participating in the project.

After participants return to their schools to implement the science program, university science faculty provide ongoing support for them by visiting them in their schools during the academic year. During these visits university faculty can gather information from teachers and principals as they implement the professional development model as well as support teachers in their classroom environment. Program participants work with their peers by leading monthly science inservice training sessions, observing peer teachers, teaching model science lessons, and assisting their peers in analyzing and selecting instructional materials for their classrooms.

The Principal's Role in Science Education

In our lengthy professional development work, we have learned that the school administrator plays an important role in maintaining an effective school science program. The instructional management role of the principal is complex, shaped and constrained by many issues. Current reform initiatives in science education, moreover, compel the secondary school principal to think of new ways to accomplish standards-based reform in his or her school. For example, there are matters of teacher time, structural arrangements, cultural norms, and teacher learning, all of which affect student learning, either directly or indirectly.

The detached manner in which professional development for science teachers is typically handled compounds the problem. Programs may be coordinated from the district office and conducted during after-school hours or during summer months, perhaps on a local college campus or other off-school location. In many cases, principals may not even be aware of the type of inservice training their teachers have received. Similarly, teachers are seldom aware of their principals' academic backgrounds or preparation in specific subject areas. Consequently, teachers and principals alike may despair of improving science instruction and never realize their mutual interest or the others' resourcefulness in developing constructive programs. Clearly, they need effective channels of communication to ensure the combination of administrative and instructional insights and cooperation needed for reform of science teaching.

The teaching and learning of science are generally perceived to take place in the context of an individual teacher working with a group of students in an individual classroom, but teaching is not a solitary activity. Many dynamics affect the teaching and learning of science in a school or even in a single classroom. Having a clear set of standards for classroom practice is an important part of the equation, but real, long-lasting change calls for a principal's playing an active role. The principal who recognizes the crucial importance of school- and district-based initiatives can use his or her influence, power, and authority to help shape critical approaches to science education reform efforts (see Figure 2). Changes in educational practices rarely happen quickly, and pervasive and permanent changes rarely come from without. Successful programs involve many participants—including teachers, science coordinators, and administrators—playing different roles (NRC 1996).

Figure 2: Approaches principals can take to support science education reform

Creating an instructional organization and climate that are conducive to school-based initiatives and innovations
Creating a clear vision of effective science teaching and learning, as well as goals that reflect content knowledge
Providing high-quality instructional materials that support a coherent presentation of important science concepts
Providing the necessary resources to make materials available to all students
Supporting alternative assessment methods that more accurately measure students' deep understanding, not just short-term recall, of science ideas
Supporting ongoing and long-term professional development of science teachers
Maintaining class size appropriate for the science discipline
Hiring new science teachers who are well grounded in science content, the processes of science, and learning theory
Supporting environments in which all students can learn science in some meaningful way
Communicating to teachers about research and innovative practices outside the school district
Allowing teachers to visit innovative science programs both within and outside the school district
Encouraging grant proposal writing to supplement school resources
Pairing induction teachers (new science teachers) with compatible mentor teachers in an effort to provide neophytes with role models at the beginning of their teaching careers

Project Management Team

The project director of the ETSU summer institutes works closely with each layer of the project and serves as a vital link among the ETSU science faculty, local education agencies (LEAs), and the Project Management Team (PMT). In addition to the project director, the PMT consists of central office curriculum directors with decision-making authority, middle and high school principals, university science professors, and middle and high school science teachers, all of whom represent participating school districts. For nine months before each of the summer leadership institutes, members of the PMT meet monthly to establish an agenda based on the needs assessment described below. The PMT designs the summer institutes and follow-up academic year professional development activities for the subsequent year. The PMT meets throughout the academic year to realize the project goals and build leadership capacity.

Using Data to Inform Professional Development Planning Decisions

To examine student learning more closely and to collect evidence to inform the professional development process, institute participants, working in conjunction with the PTM, examined videotapes of science lessons from their classrooms, explored questions and concerns about their students' learning and analyzed data from classroom assessment and end-of-course exams. This data analysis assisted the PMT and the teacher participants in identifying, prioritizing, planning, organizing, and making resource allocations for the professional development activities during the summer leadership institutes and the professional development activities during the academic year. As the ETSU professional model has matured, this data analysis has become increasingly important in informing both the professional development process and the teaching process.

Focus on Standards

According to the National Science Education Standards, "Learning science is something that students do, not something that is done to them. In learning science, students describe objects and events, ask questions, acquire knowledge, construct explanations of natural phenomena, test those explanations in many different ways, and communicate their ideas to others" (NRC 1996, 20). This approach is consistent with the East Tennessee State University Science Partnership Model, which considers students active constructors, rather than passive receivers, of knowledge. Accordingly, students who bring their own view of the world into the classroom are encouraged to be engaged in the learning process. An important role of the teacher in this process is to create learning environments that allow students to engage in problem solving and higher-order thinking so they can integrate information and build on their own understanding of a particular topic or idea (Anderson 1998).

School-Based and Job-Embedded

When university faculty make their monthly school site visits during the academic year, they can accomplish two other objectives. They can gather information from teachers and principals and provide support to participants as they implement the professional development model. During the visits, model lessons are presented. Visits, however, do not provide the continuous networking inherent in the professional development model. The project model gives participants an opportunity to develop a networking force for improving middle and high school science teaching and learning in the participants' schools.

The model allows for several kinds of communication and networking between and among teacher participants, both within the classroom and across the science program. Teacher participants play the role of sensitive facilitators to establish a climate in which team members build mutual trust and share what they have done in their classrooms. The professional development model allows for the teachers to network in the following ways:

- Members of the science department are granted a minimum of one-hour release time each week throughout the academic year to discuss and share information and classroom feedback. During this time science teachers may elect to discuss content and methodologies or reflect on classroom events of that week. These meetings are also used by participants to share information from the summer institute with their colleagues.
- Once a month, science teachers in targeted districts observe their colleagues teaching a science lesson using the methodologies and content gained during the summer institute. During their weekly meetings, teachers share feedback from the lessons and reflect on the appraisal of the lessons taught. These sessions provide insight, solutions to problems, and support and encouragement to one another. Teacher participants receive a great deal of input from one another and benefit from sharing of ideas from their own classroom experiences.
- Teacher participants lead professional development sessions for their colleagues four times during the school year (two days of in-service time already in place and two additional days of release time granted by the school district).
- Principals in participating schools meet with science faculty in their schools each month to provide information and resources concerning science teaching and learning and to reduce barriers that impede effective science teaching.

Major rewards of the program have been the personal renewal of middle and high school science teachers' expertise in science content and pedagogical skills, increased focus on active student participation and student learning, frequent teacher-teacher and teacher-student interaction, and implementation of lessons that provide an accurate portrayal of disciplinary knowledge, nature, and structure.

An important outcome of this model has been continuous and ongoing professional development opportunities for participating school districts. To track and document change systematically, each participant completes a log and turns it in to the project staff each month. These data revealed the following outcomes for participating schools:

- Planned and systemic scheduling of professional development in each participating school.
- Professional development that accommodates participants' needs and is embedded in practice.
- Networking of stakeholders (teachers, curriculum supervisors, principals, and university staff) who are responsible for student achievement in the training process.
- Sharing of support materials and resources in support of the science program.
- Using student data to inform professional development decisions.

Local school support for middle and high school science has increased throughout the duration of the project.

Participant and Student Evaluation

Various data collection instruments have been used to determine if participants and their students grew significantly in science content knowledge and attitudinal perceptions as a result of the institutes. One component of the evaluation model was designed to determine if participants grew significantly in academic science content knowledge as a result of the institutes. Data on performance in science were gathered through pre- and posttests for each institute. Although participant performance varied in the institutes conducted from 1992–2003, the project group as a whole showed significant overall gains ($p < .01$) of approximately 21% in content mastery. Greatest gains were observed in physical science (14.2%) and Earth science (12.4%). Gains of 11.6% and 9.2% were observed in life and environmental sciences respectively.

Student Learning

The ultimate criterion for the success of any educational program is student performance. To evaluate this dimension of institute effect, ETSU compared performance of pupils taught by teachers (institute) with students from the same grade and subject taught by other teachers in the same school (home) and with students in the same grade and subject but attending schools in a district not participating in the institutes (control). Comparisons extended over 11 years. Baseline data were gathered on student science mastery each fall during the project study period. Pretest data on the performance of institute, home, and control groups were analyzed across grade levels by using a series of t-tests to compare the mean content score of each group with each other group. Posttests were administered near the end of the school year, and the same comparisons were carried out on these data to assess student gains ($p < .01$ in most cases, and $p < .05$ in others). As a group, the institute students made larger gains than either the home or control groups. As a whole, they showed significant gains of approximately 10% in mastery.

Summary

The ETSU Science Partnership is bringing about a restructuring of the system as it pertains to building and maintaining ongoing and sustained professional development in science teaching and learning at the middle and high school levels in Northeast Tennessee. Clearly, the 10 participating school districts in the UETEC are benefiting from the effects of the ETSU Science Partnership. Participants learn during their preparation for leadership that those benefits should be shared with other teachers in the school and school districts. A major asset of the project's activities has been to establish collaborative relationships with educational institutions, agencies, and other groups interested in improving middle and high school science teaching and learning. Perhaps the greatest benefit is that the schools are discovering within their own ranks the leadership needed to find and follow a new impetus and direction for ongoing and sustained professional development to support science teaching and learning.

Jack Rhoton

is professor of science education at East Tennessee State University. During his career as middle and high school science teacher, district supervisor, administrator, professor, and officer of several state and national professional organizations, he has published widely, served as leading principal investigator on numerous grant projects, and made presentations throughout the United States and in Europe. He has received numerous awards for teaching and service, including the National Science Teachers Association Distinguished Service to Science Education Award.

Brenda Shumate Wojnowski
is the president of Inventive Education, a subsidiary of the National Inventors Hall of Fame. An award-winning former teacher, she has taught at the elementary, middle, and secondary levels and has served as a high school curriculum administrator. She has held various university positions overseeing professional development programs and curriculum development projects and was named to the Academy of Outstanding Faculty Involved in Extension at North Carolina State University. She has numerous grants, contracts, and publications to her credit.

References

Anderson, R. 1998. The research on teaching as inquiry. Paper prepared for the Center for Science, Mathematics, and Engineering Education, National Research Council, Washington, DC.

Blair, J. 2000. ETS study links effective teaching methods to test-score gains. *Education Week* 20 (8): 24–24. Retrieved from *www.edweek.org/ew/ewstory.cfm?slug=08ets.h20.*

Desimone L., A. Porter, M. Garet, K. Yoon, and B. Birman. 2002. Effects of professional development on teachers' instruction: Results from a three-year longitudinal study. *Educational Evaluation and Policy Analysis* 24 (2): 81–112.

Elmore, R.F., P. L. Peterson, and S. J. McCarthy. 1996. *Restructuring in the classroom: Teaching, learning, and school organization.* San Francisco: Jossey-Bass.

Garet, M., A. Porter, L. Desimone, B. Birman, and K. Yoon. 2001. What makes professional development effective? Analysis of a national sample of teachers. *American Education Research Journal* 38 (4): 915–945.

Guskey, T. 2003. What makes professional development effective? *Phi Delta Kappan* 84 (10): 248–251.

Hargreaves, A., and M. G. Fullan. 1992. *Understanding teacher development,* London: Cassell.

Hawley, W. D., and L. Valli. 1999. The essentials of effective professional development: a new consensus. In *Teaching as the learning profession: Handbook of policy and practice,* eds. Darling–Hammond, L., and G. Sykes, 127–150. San Francisco: Jossey-Bass.

Leiberman, A. (Ed.). 1996. Practices that support teacher development: Transforming conceptions of professional learning. In *Teacher learning: New policies, new practices,* eds.

M. W. McLaughlin, M. W., and I. Oberman, 185–201. New York: Teacher College Press.

Loucks-Horsley, S., P. W. Hewson, N. Love, and K. E. Stiles. 1998. *Designing professional development for teachers of science and mathematics*. Thousand Oaks, CA: Corwin.

National Commission on Teaching and America's Future (NCTAF). 1996. *What matters most: Teaching for America's future*. New York.

National Staff Development Council (NSDC). 2004. *NSDC Standards for Professional Development*. Retrieved September 24, 2004, from *www.nsdc.org/standards*.

National Research Council (NRC). 1996. *National science education standards*. Washington DC: National Academy Press.

No Child Left Behind Act (NCLB) of 2001. 2002. Public Law 107–110–January 8, 2002. 107th Congress. Washington, DC.

Rhoton, J. 2001. School science reform: An overview and implications for the secondary school principal. *National Association of Secondary School Principals Bulletin* 85 (No.623): 10–23.

Rhoton, J., and P. Bowers, eds. 2001. *Professional development planning and design*. Arlington, VA: NSTA Press.

Sparks, D., and S. Loucks-Horsley. 1989. Five models of staff development for teachers. *Journal of Staff Development* 10 (4): 40–57.

Sparks, D., and S. Loucks-Horsley. 1990. Models of staff development. In *Handbook of research on teacher education*. Houston, W.R, ed. New York: Macmillan.

Stiles, K., S. Loucks-Horsley, and P. W. Hewson. 1996. *Principles of effective professional development for mathematics and science education: A synthesis of standards* (NISE Brief, Vol. 1). Madison, WI: National Institute for Science Education.

U.S. Department of Education. 1997. *Achieving our goals: Goal 4. Teacher education and professional development*. Washington, DC.

U.S. Department of Education, National Center for Education Statistics. 1999. *Teacher quality: A report on the preparation and qualifications of public school teachers* (NSES 1999–080). Washington, DC.

Wenglinsky, H. 2000. *How teaching matters. Bringing the classroom back into discussions of teacher quality. A policy information center report.* Princeton, The Milken Family Foundation and Educational Testing Service.

Whitehurst, G. J. 2002. Scientifically based research on teacher quality: Research on teacher preparation and professional development. Presented to the White House Conference on Preparing Tomorrow's Teachers, March 5. Published as Appendix C of *Improving Teacher Quality State Grants. Title 11, Part A. Non–Regulator Draft Guidance.*

CHAPTER

9

Best Practices for Professional Development for the 21st Century

Karen J. Charles and Patricia M. Shane

"Strategic and intentional," a friend of mine said recently. "We want all of our professional development decisions to be strategic and intentional." As the team leader for Project Grad Atlanta, a whole-school reform model, she makes professional development decisions every day and is determined that those decisions pay dividends in the classroom. She participated in the highly regarded Technical Assistance Academy for Mathematics and Science Services sponsored by the Southeast Eisenhower Regional Consortium at SERVE and is a regular attendee at the annual conference of the National Staff Development Council (NSDC). While the academy offers math and science staff developers a five-year professional experience designed to improve their skills at implementing and sustaining reform initiatives (Charles 1999), NSDC provides a rich literature-and research-base on professional development as its own field of study. For the friend, both experiences—the content-rich academy and the process-rich NSDC conferences—have converged, making her well-grounded in professional development and well-prepared for the decisions she makes. Consider the following as examples of how NSDC supports professional developers.

Key Issues in Professional Development

In the last seven years, the themes of the *Journal for Staff Development,* published monthly by the national Staff Development Council, have included: Powerful Designs, Ideas That Work, How Educators Learn, Data-Driven Staff Development, Evaluation, Teacher Quality, Content Specific Staff Development, and Mathematics and Science. We read this to imply that to support *teacher quality* in *mathematics and science*, we should *design powerful, content-specific staff development* that is *data-driven* and *evaluated*, and is based on using *ideas that work* and knowing *how educators learn*. These themes provide the framework for this chapter and serve as a launch pad for a discussion of what is important in professional development today, what the key issues and trends are, and how we can continually improve the planning and implementing of effective professional learning experiences for educators that have positive results for student learning. Examples of the best ideas in the field of professional development today are drawn from a new book, *Powerful Designs for Professional Development* (Easton 2004).

Student Achievement Issues in Science

Although many states still do not test science with the same rigor with which they test reading and mathematics, several large-scale assessments give us a reliable indication of U.S. students' performance in science. Within the United States, the National Assessment of Educational Progress (NAEP) has reported student achievement in mathematics, science, reading, writing, U.S. history, civics, geography, and the arts since 1969 (NCES 2004). Although student scores are not disaggregated by race and gender, NAEP scores are often presented by comparing regions of the country and exposing regional achievement gaps. Useful tools on the National Center for Education Statistics (NCES) website offer the chance to compare state, regional, and national averages and to explore trends and related data. For example, NAEP 2000 science results showed that scores for high school seniors declined since 1996, that teachers' majors are related to student success in science in the eighth grade, and that students scored higher when learning in an activity-based environment (NCES).

The point that we live in a global society—thanks to exponential advancements in communication, technology, and transportation—was harshly driven home in 1995 when results from the Third International

Mathematics and Science Study (TIMSS) revealed that U.S. students, when compared on mathematics and science tests to their international counterparts in more than 40 countries, scored well in elementary school, below average in middle school, and near or at the bottom in high school (U.S. Education Department of Education 1995). TIMSS showed that our students were not the best in the world, as indicated by the Goals 2000 report (U.S. Department of Education 1994), and Americans were shocked.

The United States participated in a repeat of TIMSS (called TIMSS-R) in 1999, hoping that the 1995 fourth-grade cohort would carry their good showing with them as they advanced to eighth grade. Sadly, their scores dropped and mirrored those of the 1995 eighth-grade cohort. Whatever was happening, analysts were left to conclude that long-term exposure to the U.S. school system was debilitating—the longer the exposure, the weaker the student! While TIMSS was adorning the mathematics and science landscape with catch phrases like *mile-wide and an inch deep, less is more,* and *splintered vision,* insightful U.S. educators kept asking—"What can we learn from TIMSS? What are the implications for us?" One clear and consistent finding across all of the highest-performing countries was the focus on professional development. In many countries, professional development is collaborative, job-embedded, and focused on student needs. It takes place during the workday and involves a high level of teacher participation and interaction (Lewis and Tsuchida 1997).

This should not come as a surprise. For years, leading professional developers in the United States have been advocating for long-term professional development based on teacher and student needs and designed to improve student achievement, yet we had to look at other countries to see these ideas in action. Although there have been changes in professional development emphasis, design, and delivery in this country, they have been more evolutionary than revolutionary. By contrast, professional practices in other countries look radically different from common practices and expectations in the United States. So, although the news media concentrated on TIMSS scores, serious educators began investigating and analyzing the connection between high student achievement and well-prepared teachers. One compelling professional model, Japanese Lesson Study, is discussed in a later section.

Although TIMSS introduced America to the harsh lights of the international stage and the global economy, the current federal legislation, the No

Child Left Behind (NCLB) Act of 2001 (2002) is mandating an agenda of accountability rich in testing and reporting protocols. As with TIMSS, immediate and repetitive media attention has focused on scores and student achievement. In fact, student achievement is *the* measurement of success under NCLB, and, because the data is disaggregated by student subpopulations (race and gender, for instance), the success rates of various groups of students can be determined. Schools must attain *adequate yearly progress* (AYP), a metric determined largely by student scores in mathematics and reading (and soon to be included, science) or be sanctioned by penalties described in the NCLB legislation. All students' scores, disaggregated by subgroup, are used to determine AYP, so schools can no longer depend on one average score (high performance pulling up low performance) to determine success. Although teaching skills must improve to reach the growing diversity represented in our national student population, NCLB requires that the professional development designed to address teaching quality include only research-based practices and strategies. Now we are back to NSDC's "strategic and intentional" as well as *data-driven ideas that work.*

Although NAEP tells a story of slow but steady improvement, it also points out achievement gaps between and across various regions of the country. TIMSS exposes gaps between the United States and our economic partners and competitors, and NCLB (with assistance now from NAEP) illuminates the most compelling gaps—those within the United States between and among subgroups of students, between rural and urban schools, between the privileged and the poor. As educators, we have a moral responsibility to acknowledge, address, and erase these gaps. Professional development that targets improved teaching quality offers some answers.

Teacher Quality Issues in Science

Loucks-Horsley (Sparks 1997) identified several major teacher quality issues that professional development for science teachers can address. The issues she lists express concerns about teachers' content knowledge and pedagogical skills: lack of adequate preparation, including the absence of a science requirement in some elementary certification programs; lack of inquiry-based instructional strategies; the need to stay current within the discipline; and lack of awareness about the science standards.

Several studies from the past 10 years support Loucks-Horsley's concerns about content knowledge. In 1994, a Cornell University study found that student achievement in science and mathematics was greatly influenced by teachers' knowledge of both subject matter and teaching theory (George Lucas Educational Foundation 2001). Other studies (Education Trust 1998; Marzano 2003) reveal that students with underprepared teachers can often experience academic losses from which there is little hope of recovery. In other words, there is no room for a "well, they'll get it next year" attitude. Learning opportunities missed are learning opportunities lost, and teaching quality is at the heart of the matter.

As with *A Nation at Risk* (NCEE 1983) in the eighties, *What Matters Most: Teaching for America's Future* (NCTAF 1996) pulled no punches in the nineties. With an emphasis on the critical importance of teachers and teacher competency, the report states,

> On the whole, the school reform movement has ignored the obvious: what teachers know and can do makes the crucial difference in what children learn. And the way school systems organize their work makes a big difference in what teachers can accomplish. New courses, tests, and curriculum reforms can be important starting points, but they are meaningless if teachers cannot use them well. Policies can only improve schools if the people in them are armed with the knowledge, skills, and supports they need. Student learning in this country will improve only when we focus our efforts on improving teaching (National Commission on Teaching and America's Future 1996, p. 5).

The Role of Standards in Professional Development

Several things occurred in the nineties that have had rippling effects on professional development in general and science-specific professional development in particular. In general, the NSDC published its *Standards of Staff Development* (NSDC 1995, 2001), and evaluation experts such as Tom Guskey (1998, 2000, 2001) began promoting the need for evaluating staff development along a continuum of defined and targeted outcomes. Specifically, the *National Science Education Standards* (NRC 1996) and *Benchmarks for Science Literacy* (AAAS 1993) began to crystallize the scope and sequence of science content and process skills and provide recommendations and resources for the professional development of science teachers.

The NSDC standards are the product of research conducted by NSDC with educators and districts searching for ways to make professional development more effective. Hayes Mizell points out that educators in decision-making roles about local professional development needs have been responsive to the guidance offered by the standards. He says that:

> Each day, central office administrators make quiet but fateful decisions, perhaps unconsciously, that affect the context, process, and content of staff development. If you are in this position, knowledge of the staff development standards and their application to science educators is imperative (Mizell 2001, p. 20).

The NSDC standards center on three major themes: context, process, and content. Within each theme are guidelines considered by NSDC to be essential in providing the level of professional development that will increase student learning (NSDC 2001). First, through the context standard, NSDC emphasizes the need for educators to work collaboratively in learning communities and for leaders to guide and support teachers' plans for continuous instructional improvement and to provide the resources necessary to accomplish these plans. These structures are necessary parts of the setting and culture in which the new practices will take place. Second, the process standards defines the "how" strategies that need to be embedded in professional development plans. These include using disaggregated student data and research-based practices, evaluating the process throughout its duration, and planning with attention to adult and student learning principles and needs. Finally, the content standard stresses equity, teacher quality, and family involvement. It reminds planners of the importance of understanding the needs of all students and their families and of improving quality teaching by improving teachers' content knowledge and instructional and assessment practices. *Tools for Growing the NSDC Standards* (NSDC 2001) is a useful tool for gauging a district's professional development readiness.

NSDC has also been a place where serious professional developers could go to study the principles of adult learning and change theory. Novice staff developers often do not understand that adult learners have unique needs. Adults must see an immediate application for what they are experiencing and it must be relevant in their world (Knowles 1973; Mundry 2003). In other words, an immediate application for one person is not necessarily an immediate application for another person. A passionate staff developer who does not connect his or her presentation to the needs of the participants is in peril, but that alone is not enough. Veteran professional developers also understand change—that it is a process, not an event, and that it is experienced by different people at different rates (Hall and Hord 1987). They cannot be impatient or set unrealistic deadlines for new practices to begin demonstrating success. They can, however, design their program with a clear commitment to the expected outcomes and plan for those outcomes from the start.

The Role of Evaluation in PD Design

Since the mideighties, Thomas Guskey has been offering insights and guidance about the relationship between professional development and its evaluation. In a variety of publications (Guskey 1998, 2000, 2001) he clarifies the use of his five-step model in planning as well as in evaluating staff development initiatives. Thus, it is our premise that evaluation should have a major role in professional development planning. This role will only intensify as NCLB requires that states and districts use only research-based professional strategies when planning professional opportunities for educators. Guskey's five levels of evaluation are participants' reactions, participants' learning, organizational support/change, participants' use of new knowledge and skills, and student learning outcomes. To plan program evaluations that address all of these levels, Guskey recommends what he calls "backward planning" (Guskey 2001, 2003). By first agreeing on the desired student outcomes, one can determine teacher practices that will produce these outcomes, the organizational supports needed, the skills and knowledge that will promote these practices, and so on. Backward planning steers planners away from event-driven planning and puts the focus on establishing goals for learners and learning (Guskey 2003).

A wonderful example of how evaluation should influence and guide professional development is seen the in the work of Shinohara and Daehler with their work on the Science Cases for Teacher Learning Project. Writing with Joan Heller, they explain,

> The aim of the Science Cases for Teacher Learning Project is to develop teachers' pedagogical content knowledge (Shulman 1986)—their understanding of what makes learning a science topic easy or difficult, and knowing how to present and explain the material to make it easier for learners to understand (Heller et al 2003, p. 37).

To accomplish this goal, they describe how developing an evaluation framework allowed them to improve their professional development design continuously. Having a framework forced them to define their expected outcomes and design questions that could explicitly suggest modifications to their professional development design. If, for instance, the process and content of a specific session did not lead to the intended shifts in teachers' beliefs and practices, they knew they needed to revisit and revise the process and content of the session. The framework also required that they identify the key features of their professional development model. In this case, they planned for participants to experience the following: exploration of scientific meanings, focus on student thinking, critical analysis of practice, and the culture of a learning community. By putting evaluation outcomes up front, professional development designers are able to use evaluation data to refine their efforts and improve their resources. Heller, Daehler, and Shinohara (2003) state that:

> This framework is not intended to be prescriptive, linear, or hierarchical. It is a tool to help determine whether case discussions have an impact and, if so, what and where that impact may be. This evaluation framework evolved as the work proceeded. With each analysis, we gained a clearer understanding of both what might be important to look at and how to assess each aspect (p. 39).

Professional Development Specific to Science and Mathematics

By peeling away the layers of data associated with TIMSS, U.S. researchers are learning more about professional development and the strategies that support changes in science and mathematics teaching and learning. Prominent TIMSS researchers Heibert and Stigler (2004) point out that teaching is a cultural activity and that "changing teaching means changing the culture of teaching, not distributing more recommendations or holding more workshops" (p. 13). Their recommendations for changing the culture around professional development practices are drawn from comparisons of professional development in TIMSS countries and emphasize providing teachers "… vivid examples that illustrate alternative ways of teaching" (p. 14). These vivid examples should include "… studying the ways teachers present problems to students, asking students to develop problem-solving methods, comparing solution methods, looking for patterns, and comparing one problem to others ... [analyzing] student work and [making] inferences about students' thinking" (p. 14). TIMSS points us to lessons we already know: professional development should be "situated in teachers' practice, connected to the curriculum, focused on clear student learning goals and student thinking, and continuing over time" (p. 15).

One of the most prolific and recognized authors and champions for professional development for science and mathematics teachers was Susan Loucks-Horsley. Her contributions to the field have been a major influence in moving professional development from one-shot workshops in search of a purpose to long-term learning experiences with well-defined goals. She and her colleagues (Loucks-Horsley et al. 2003) moved beyond the notion of professional development models by describing 15 professional development strategies and suggesting that by designing an array of experiences tailored to the needs of the participants, professional developers could begin to create their own unique models (Loucks-Horsley et al.). Besides elaborating the strategies, however, the authors proposed purposes for each. Professional developers now knew which worked best if they were trying to (a) develop awareness, (b) build knowledge, (c) translate new knowledge into practice, (d) practice teaching, or (e) reflect deeply on teaching and learning. Alignment discussions began taking place. Since that time, practitioners have invested immeasurable amounts of time and effort expanding and refining these 15 strategies as well as developing and researching more. One result of this intense effort to enrich the field of professional development is *Powerful Designs for Professional Learning* (Easton 2004).

Powerful Designs

Powerful Designs represents a type of next generation of resources for professional developers. Easton invited more than 20 of the nation's best professional developers to contribute a chapter to the book; the result is a must read for any serious professional developer. As a sign of the times, a CD with handouts accompanies the book. On the following pages is an abbreviated form of the planning matrix that Easton provides for professional developers. It expands greatly on the five purposes mentioned above and includes advice on who should be involved and how the sessions should be structured. This chapter explores a few of the strategies most relevant to science educators (Japanese Lesson Study, Case Discussions, and Data Analysis) and introduces the planning matrix (Tables 1 and 2) created to make the best use of the strategies.

Table 1: Matrix of selected professional development designs and related questions

	Who to Involve				Individuals or Groups			How				
	Teachers	Administrators	IHE staff*	Community	Both	Pairs	Large groups	In school	Out of school	Low cost	Medium cost	High cost
Action Research	X	X	X		X			X			X	
Assessment	X	X					X	X	X			X
Case Discussions	X	X					X		X		X	
Critical Friends Groups	X	X	X				X	X			X	
Data Analysis	X	X	X	X			X		X			X
Immersion in Practice	X	X					X	X	X			X
Journaling	X	X			X			X		X		
Lesson Study	X	X					X	X	X		X	
Mentoring	X	X	X			X		X			X	
Peer Coaching	X	X	X			X		X			X	
Portfolios	X	X			X			X		X		
Shadowing Students	X	X		X	X			X			X	
Standards in Practice	X	X					X	X			X	
Study Groups	X	X	X	X			X	X			X	
Train the Trainer	X	X	X			X		X	X			X
Tuning Protocols	X	X	X				X	X			X	

Adapted from Easton 2004.

* institute of higher education staff

Table 2. Matrix of selected professional development designs and their purposes

	What and why											
	Gather school data	Create learning community	Look at curriculum assessment	Focus on pedagogy and instruction	Look at classroom	Look at whole school	Look at student work	Is reflective	Good for involving others	Good for problem solving	Yields concrete product	Is experiential
Action Research	X		X	X	X	X	X			X		
Assessment			X								X	
Case Discussions			X	X								
Critical Friends Groups		X		X			X			X		
Data Analysis	X									X		
Immersion in Practice			X	X		X						X
Journaling				X				X				X
Lesson Study			X	X	X	X				X	X	X
Mentoring		X		X	X		X	X	X	X		X
Peer Coaching		X		X	X		X	X		X		X
Portfolios	X			X	X		X	X		X	X	
Shadowing Students	X				X		X		X			X
Standards in Practice			X				X			X	X	X
Study Groups			X			X				X		
Train the Trainer						X	X	X	X		X	X
Tuning Protocols		X		X	X							

Adapted from Easton 2004.

Japanese Lesson Study

Twenty-three heart surgeons in Maine, New Hampshire, and Vermont agreed in 1993 to observe each other regularly in the operating room and share their know-how, insights, and approaches. In the two years after their nine-month-long project, the death rate among their patients fell by an astonishing 25 percent. Merely by emphasizing teamwork and communication instead of functioning like solitary craftsmen, the study showed, all the doctors brought about major changes in their individual and institutional practices. For teachers who, like heart surgeons, have traditionally worked as isolated professionals, the experiment holds a powerful lesson. If their goal is to lower the "death rate" of young minds and see them thrive, many educators now emphatically believe, they can do it better together than by working alone (Cushman 1996).

Imagine the collective power of teachers working together, exposing themselves and their work to the observations of their colleagues, and ultimately improving their practice like these New England doctors. This is the purpose of Japanese Lesson Study. Catherine Lewis encountered the power of lesson study firsthand when in Japan doing research for a different purpose. She noticed that while observing in classrooms and compiling her field notes, she was also learning from the science lessons she was experiencing. She became a student of lesson study and the research lessons it produces long before TIMSS introduced the concepts to U.S. educators. Lewis explains that lesson study is a teacher-led activity that requires collaboration and a deep commitment to improving instructional practice and student learning (Lewis 2004).

First, we must distinguish between lesson study (a collaborative *process*) and the study lesson (the collaboratively developed *product*). In lesson study, teachers are engaged in an ongoing process of planning, observing, and revising study lessons. This is a far different process than that of the lesson planning that we are familiar with in the United States. In lesson study, teachers agree on a topic, consider a unit plan and where the lesson fits in the unit, examine existing resources, share their own ideas and experiences, select or design a task, and—most importantly—discuss and anticipate student thinking. This rarely happens in one meeting. Once the lesson has been refined and an instructional guide has been written, one member of the team teaches the lesson and the rest observe. Often more observers are present than were on the development team. After the lesson, the observers convene with the teacher and the lesson is discussed. Observers ask questions and make suggestions. The teacher shares her or his insights from the teaching experience. In many instances, team members decide to refine the lesson for a second trial. Although the study lesson is clearly a visible and tangible product, it's the process that is the real professional development nugget. Over the course of a year, a lesson study team may produce only a few lessons, but the experience of the process—the collaboration and sharing, the insights about student thinking—is what teachers find invaluable. Lewis writes,

> Throughout the process of lesson study, teachers have opportunities to deepen their own content knowledge as they compare various curricula and standards, select and modify a lesson, try the problem themselves, anticipate student thinking, and analyze student responses to the lesson (Lewis 2004, p. 139).

Case Discussions

Researcher-practitioners at WestEd, one of the nation's federally funded regional educational laboratories, have produced resources that facilitate case discussions for science and mathematics educators. In *Powerful Designs* (Easton 2004), Barnett-Clarke and Ramirez explain the rationale behind case discussions and suggest them as a way to ease into lesson study. Like lesson study, case discussions also help teachers deepen their subject matter knowledge and pedagogical reasoning and improve their ability to analyze student thinking. Cases are examples of real classroom situations, real student answers, and real instructional actions that teachers explore in an attempt to challenge their own knowledge and skills about both content and pedagogy. For strong science examples of case discussions, we suggest the work of Shinohara and Daehler, colleagues of Barnett-Clarke and co-project directors of the Science Cases for Teacher Learning Project at WestEd (Heller et al. 2003). These developers have designed two sets of case discussions—one around magnetism and one around electricity. In these professional development sessions, teachers investigate a series of student tasks, examine student responses, interpret student thinking, and discuss their own misconceptions related to the tasks. Their work and the work of Barnett-Clarke and Ramirez demonstrates that

> Cases help teachers examine, articulate, reformulate, and realign their beliefs, values, and practice. Using cases that intentionally target issues with no clear-cut solutions allows teachers to weigh the positive and negative consequences of particular instructional decisions in a case, refine their thinking, and develop a clearer understanding of how their teaching decisions impact students (Barnett-Clarke and Ramirez 2004, p. 79).

Data Analysis

Although we might be familiar with data analysis for use in curriculum planning, its role in professional development is essential. Since NCLB will require science testing by 2007, science teachers and curriculum specialists need to be prepared for a barrage of new data concerning student achievement. Bernhardt (2004) suggests that beyond telling us what students know and can do, data are windows into whether processes, programs, and procedures are working or not. Data on student learning should point school leaders back to the classrooms in which learning occurs. Science scores will uncover students' strengths and needs, but what does that say about teachers' strengths and needs? Can our student data help pinpoint strategies and topics for professional development planning? When we uncover our students' weaknesses, we should realize that we may have uncovered the focus of the next professional development opportunities. If kids are struggling with chemistry, there's no need for the workshop on the planets. Data analysis is at the heart of school improvement.

Recommendations

Powerful Designs is PD 101 at its best; the reader gets a complete lesson on leading professional development strategies and the tools to recreate them. A few other tools to add to your professional developer's repertoire include *Evaluating Professional Development* (Guskey 2000), *Designing Professional Development for Teachers of Science and Mathematics* (Loucks-Horsley et al. 2003), *Change in Schools: Facilitating the Process* (Hall and Hord 1987). These works will ground you in the best of professional development practices and insights. None will give you answers; all will challenge your ability to read between the lines.

In Summary

Professional development planning is always the result of a need for change. It can be designed to improve existing practices or to establish new ones, but it involves change nonetheless. As Robin Fogarty (2001) writes, "…change begins with a personal journey of one," and in describing his "adopter" types, Rogers (1962) reminds us that change will be quick for some and painfully slow for others. Fogarty (2001) recounts the four primary influences along her journey of personal change as the influence of a reading (*Teacher*, by Sylvia Ashton-Warner), the influence of a school culture, the influence of a mentor, and the influence of a student. Although all of our personal professional journeys are unique, we can learn professional development lessons from Fogarty's reflections and can use these lessons to soften the resisters. First, the role of professional reading cannot be overemphasized, and professional developers should look for opportunities to include reading and the reflection it inspires into professional learning experiences. Second, consider the culture you are creating within your professional development community. Are there norms, is there respect, a joy of learning, a collaborative and risk-free environment, and a clear and attainable shared purpose?

Third, do you as a staff developer continue to pay attention to your own growth and learning; do you have a professional network or mentor with whom you challenge yourself? And, last, do you listen to your participants when they provide you signals and feedback that require modifications to your work or that challenge your beliefs? Resisters, in particular, will be watching for your ability and willingness to shift gears on the fly. Doing so may demonstrate your acceptance of change—the same behavior you are seeking from them. In sharing her influences, Fogarty has also provided a template against which to check some of our more subtle professional development decisions.

Through our many combined years of planning learning experiences for student and adult learners, we have come to propose that there are three gifts that teachers can give their students. We believe that it is our responsibility to help all learners—children and adults— (a) develop and deepen confidence in knowing how to learn so learners can recognize when and what to learn in new or unfamiliar circumstances and can plan for their own learning; (b) develop and nurture a sense of inquiry so that curiosity will lead to unanswered questions and experimentation will lead to possible answers; and (c) develop the ability to seek and recognize connections between and among facts and ideas, observations and inferences, and theories and phenomena. These same gifts and insights are what we believe should be the strategic and intentional goals of all professional development designs.

Karen J. Charles

is a research evaluation specialist at RTI, International, in Research Triangle Park, North Carolina. Prior to coming to RTI, she worked for 12 years across the southeast with the Eisenhower Consortium at SERVE as a science and mathematics professional developer. She is the 2005–2006 president of the North Carolina Science Leaders Association.

Patricia Shane
is the associate director of the Center for Mathematics and Science Education and is an associate professor of education at the University of North Carolina at Chapel Hill (UNC—Chapel Hill) where she teaches and provides professional development for mathematics and science teachers. Her honors include the National Outstanding Science Supervisor Award from NSELA.

References

American Association for the Advancement of Science (AAAS). 1993. *Benchmarks for science literacy*. New York: Oxford University Press.

Barnett-Clarke, C., and A. Ramirez. 2004. Case discussions. In *Powerful designs for professional development*, ed. L. B. Easton, 75–84. Oxford, OH: National Staff Development Council.

Bernhardt, V. 2004. Data analysis. In *Powerful designs for professional development*, ed. L. B. Easton, 111–118. Oxford, OH: National Staff Development Council.

Charles, K. 1999. Building capacity—Step by step and state by state. *The Common Denominator* 3 (1). Eisenhower Consortium at SERVE.

Cushman, K. 1996. Looking collaboratively at student work: An essential toolkit. *Horace* 13.

Easton, L. B. 2004. *Powerful designs for professional learning*. Oxford, OH: National Staff Development Council.

Education Trust. 1998. Good teaching matters. *Thinking K-16* 3 (2).

Fogarty, R. 2001. The roots of change. *Journal of Staff Development* 22 (3).

George Lucas Educational Foundation. 2001. *http://www.glef.org/php/article.php?id=Art_788*.

Guskey, T. 1998. The age of our accountability. *Journal of Staff Development* 19 (4).

Guskey, T. 2000. *Evaluating professional development*. Thousands Oaks, CA: Corwin Press.

Guskey, T. 2001. The backward approach. *Journal of Staff Development* 22 (3).

Guskey, T. 2003. Scooping up meaningful evidence. *Journal of Staff Development* 24 (4).

Hall, G., and S. Hord. 1987. *Change in schools: Facilitating the process*. Albany, NY: State University of New York Press.

Heller, J., K. Daehler, and M. Shinohara. 2003. Connecting all the pieces. *Journal of Staff Development* 24 (4).

Hiebert, J., and J. Stigler. 2004. A world of difference: Classrooms abroad provide lessons in teaching math and science. *Journal of Staff Development* 25 (4).

Knowles, M. 1973. *The adult learner: A neglected species*. Houston, TX: Gulf Publishing.

Lewis, C. 2004. Lesson study. In *Powerful designs for professional development*, ed. L. B. Easton, 135-148. Oxford, OH: National Staff Development Council.

Lewis, C., and I. Tsuchida. 1997. Planned educational change in Japan: The case of elementary science instruction. *Journal of Educational Policy* 12 (5).

Loucks-Horsley, S., N. Love, K. Stiles, S. Mundry, and P. Hewson. 2003. *Designing professional development for teachers of science and mathematics.* Thousand Oaks, CA: Corwin Press.

Marzano, R. 2003. *What works in schools: Translating research into practice.* Alexandria, VA: Association for Supervision and Curriculum Development.

Mizell, H. 2001. How to get there from here. *Journal of Staff Development* 22 (3).

Mundry, S. 2003. Honoring adult learners: Adult learning theories and implications for professional development. In *Science teacher retention: Mentoring and renewal,* eds. J. Rhoton and P. Bowers, 123–132. Arlington, VA: NSTA Press.

National Center for Education Statistics (NCES). 2004. *http://nces.ed.gov/nationsreportcard/about/.*

National Commission on Excellence in Education (NCEE). 1983. *A nation at risk.* Washington, DC: U.S. Government Printing Office.

National Commission on Teaching and America's Future (NCTAF). 1996. *What matters most: Teaching for America's future.* New York: NCTAF.

National Research Council (NRC). 1996. *National Science Education Standards.* Washington, DC: National Academy Press.

National Staff Development Council (NSDC). 1995. *Standards for staff developmen*t (revised 2001). Oxford, OH: National Staff Development Council.

National Staff Development Council (NSDC). 2001. *Tools for growing the NSDC standards.* Oxford, OH: National Staff Development Council. Available online at *www.nsdc.org/bookstore.htm.*

Rogers, E. 1962. *Diffusion of innovation.* New York: The Free Press.

Shulman, L.S. 1986. Those who understand: Knowledge growth in teaching. *Educational Researcher* 15 (2):4-14. Cited in Heller, Daehler, and Shinohara 2003.

Sparks, D. 1997. Reforming teaching and reforming staff development: An interview with Susan Loucks-Horsley. *Journal of Staff Development* 18 (4).

U.S. Department of Education. 1994. The National Education Goals. At *http://www.ed.gov/pubs/goals/summary/goals.html.*

U.S. Department of Education. 1995. *Attaining excellence: A TIMSS resource kit.* Pittsburgh, PA: Superintendent of Documents.

U.S. Department of Education. 2002. No Child Left Behind (NCLB). Available online at *www.ed.gov/nclb.*

Part III Leadership in Science Teaching and Learning

CHAPTER

10

Leadership in Science Education for the 21st Century

Rodger W. Bybee

In the early decades of the 21st century, science educators face some problems unique to our times and some common to all eras. A quick review of headlines from several weeks of *Education Week* produces a list of problems and issues requiring leadership.

- The Bigger Picture: U.S. Education in Global Context (February 9, 2005)
- Researchers Cite Uniform Standards in Singapore's Sciences (February 9, 2005)
- Charter Studies Offer Caution on Achievement (February 9, 2005)
- Philadelphia Officials Hire Firm to Craft High School Core Content (February 9, 2005)
- Researchers Connect Lower Achievement, High School Exit Tests (February 2, 2005)
- Teachers Torn Over Religion, Evolution (February 2, 2005)

These headlines offer some insights into the variety of issues requiring leadership at all levels of the science education community. A few other trends and issues belong on this list: international perspectives, core elements of science education, inquiry, integrity of science, and professional development of science teachers. Some of the issues will be with us for the relative brief time of political administrations, and some trends have a longer and deeper educational perspective. After a brief discussion of leadership, I will elaborate on these five trends important to contemporary science education.

Leadership in Science Education

One of the consistent requirements of leadership is that leaders have vision, which has various interpretations. Leaders may, for example, have a long-term perspective, see large systemic issues, present future scenarios, or discern fundamental problems and present possible solutions rather than spending time and energy setting blame for the problems. Depending on their situations, leaders have diverse ways of clarifying a vision. Some may do so in speeches, others in articles, and still others in policies. One leader's vision may unify a group, organization, or community while another's vision may set priorities or resolve conflicts among constituencies. A leader's vision likely will have many sources and result from extensive review and careful thought. This is especially true in today's complex educational system.

Leadership in science education extends from science teachers to the secretary of education and the president. It does not reside with a few people in key positions. Science education consists of numerous systems and subsystems, all with individuals who have power, constituents, and goals that contribute to a better science education for students. Not all in the science education community can or should be involved in constructing international assessments, developing curriculum materials, presenting the arguments for scientific inquiry, defending the integrity of science, or providing professional development. But all of us do have our roles and responsibilities that relate to these and many other leadership opportunities, and that is what will ultimately make a difference for students.

For me, the fundamental purpose of science education is achieving high levels of scientific literacy for all students. Such a broad and, I would argue, deep perspective touches critical components of the science education system, national, state, and local school science programs, and classroom practices of curriculum, instruction, and assessment. The fundamental purpose is comprehensive and inclusive. This is the vision required of science education leaders in the 21st century.

Although visions of "science for *all* students" or "*no* student left behind" have become part of every state's standards and school district's science framework, many leaders seem to have missed the fact that such statements explicitly highlight equity. By all students we mean *all students*. The goal should be clear and unambiguous, but achieving the goal presents a complex array of problems. Now is the time to restate and renew our efforts to make sure that all students have adequate and appropriate opportunities to learn science. I point to the issue of equity—and its frequently cited countervailing force, excellence—because they pervade all of education, not just science education. In later sections I discuss five trends that are unique to science education.

Contemporary justification for a vision of improved science education resides in themes such as education and the economy, basic skills for the workforce, and thinking for a living. Such themes differ from earlier justifications such as the space race and a nation at risk. In many respects the economic rationale has emerged from the realization that the U.S. economy is part of a global economy and that the educational levels of the our citizenship influence the rate and direction of our country's economic progress.

The complement to a vision of science for all students is having a plan to enact that vision within the leader's context. The vision centers on students' learning science, so how can we think about the contexts within which leaders should work and identify important initiatives?

To enhance all students' scientific literacy, we must focus on the interactions between teachers and students, especially those interactions that enhance learning. This, I believe, is a critically important educational perspective, one that contrasts with contemporary political points of view. Examples of enhancing learning include placing curriculum materials, instructional strategies, classroom assessments, and continuous professional development in the foreground of the leader's vision. Examples of contemporary political views include emphasizing school choice, charter schools, and vouchers as means to achieve higher levels of student literacy in science.

Leaders work in increasingly complex educational systems. The time has passed when, for example, a leader can facilitate the selection of curriculum materials and trust that all will be well with their use and, ultimately, student achievement. Now, the complex system of science education includes political, economic, and social factors, as well as educational issues. Effective leaders must recognize multiple factors, varied components, and different aspects of the system as they implement their plans.

As the leader moves from a vision and plan to initiatives and actions within the education system, paradoxes will appear. What do I mean by paradoxes? A paradox is a statement or situation that on the surface seems contradictory. Earlier I mentioned an often-heard paradox in education—equity for all students versus excellence for a few students. A paradox differs from a dilemma. A dilemma involves the selection of one alternative from two equally balanced alternatives. Dilemmas often defy satisfactory solutions; paradoxes may satisfactorily resolve themselves. For example, a leader must maintain continuity with past science programs and institute change with new curricula. Leaders often express paradoxes as tensions, contradictory directions, or conflicting issues. Leaders must be masters of the paradoxes they confront. Let me list a few of the paradoxes faced by leaders.

- Leading and managing
- Symbolism with substance
- Consistency with flexibility
- Making quick decisions while taking time for review and consideration
- Encouraging risk-taking while providing security
- Handling situations uniquely while planning for the whole

Along with the central importance of resolving the tensions of paradoxes, I would list the importance of a leader's ability to recognize and address the political realities of his or her work. My first insight here is that the leader has to recognize that initiating changes means addressing the politics. All issues are not solely educational. Indeed, it may be the case that all educational issues ultimately may be political. The paradox embedded here can be stated as achieving educational goals while addressing political realities. I have found that either-or thinking often expresses the paradox, while both-and thinking provides insights into the resolutions.

Experience teaches another lesson for those in leadership positions. If you are leading, you cannot avoid conflict and controversy. And the larger the system and greater the change, the more controversy you will experience. It can be thought of as "achieving your goals requires enduring criticism." And the criticism often is unfair, constant, and personal.

Leadership for the Next Decade

This section describes five areas that will be central to leadership in the coming decade. They are

- introducing international perspectives,
- centering on the educational core,
- maintaining an inquiry orientation,

- upholding the integrity of science, and
- integrating professional development into school science programs.

Careful review reveals continuity with the past and change and innovation for the future. Within each category I have tried to identify some issues the leader will face, although each leader has a unique environment he or she must navigate.

International Perspectives

Since the 1960s, the United States has been part of the tradition of international comparative studies of mathematics and science education. Recently, the results of two studies, PISA (Program for International Student Assessment) 2003 (Lemke et al. 2004) and TIMSS (Trends in International Mathematics and Science Study) 2003 (Gonzales et al. 2004), once again have engaged our interest. The primary domain for PISA 2006 will be science, which should affect the work of science education leaders. At some times and in some categories, the United States does better than other countries. But more often than not, we are about average. Occasionally, we are among the lowest-achieving of all countries in this assessment. This discussion is not about the results of the 2003 assessments. These can be reviewed in *Pursuing Excellence: Eighth-Grade Mathematics and Science Achievement in the United States and Other Countries From the Trends in International Mathematics and Science Study* (Gonzales et al.) and *International Outcomes in Learning Mathematics Literacy and Problem Solving: PISA 2003 Results From the American Perspective* (Lemke et al.).

Beginning in the 1990s, I became intrigued with a paradox that accompanies these international assessments. Inevitably, we compare our results—as one nation—to other countries. Yet, states and school districts decide what students should know and what curriculum to implement.

With the release of comparative results, the inevitable commentaries express varying degrees of concern about the results. If the United States does as well compared to other countries as we did at fourth-grade on the 1995 TIMSS, we hear comments that we really should have done better. After all, we should be first in the world. If we do poorly as our physics and advanced mathematics students did on the Third International Math and Science Study—no countries performed more poorly, that is, we are last in the world—then commentaries express deep concern, because these students represent our best and brightest.

Now, let us examine the paradox in detail. Recall that a paradox consists of seemingly contradictory views that nonetheless may be resolved. For example, we want our leaders to be bold and take new initiatives and at the same time to be accommodating and maintain past programs. With international assessments we compare the United States to other nations, and we do this assuming the U.S. results represent one nation. At the same time, we maintain an educational system that defends the right of 50 states and approximately 15,000 local districts to make decisions about what students should know and be able to do, how they should be taught, and what content and processes should be assessed. Here we see the two contradictory aspects of the paradox. We maintain a system with wide and significant variation, but value assessment results as though we were one unified system.

How might this paradox be resolved? The basic challenge centers on maintaining the rights of states and local jurisdictions to determine the curriculum, instruction, and assessments and, at the same time, attaining higher student achievement as a nation.

The No Child Left Behind Act of 2001 (NCLB) legislation must be considered because it is a dominating influence on science education, and it will continue with the introduction of assessment for science in the 2007–2008 school years. The NCLB uses assessment results as a punitive means to assure that schools make adequate yearly progress in student achievement. To meet this goal, the law requires states to set high standards, assure highly qualified teachers, and implement yearly assessments—all at the state level. But note that states are still setting the standards and implementing the assessments. Most financial support for changes designed to accommodate the NCLB mandates goes directly to the states. So, NCLB avoids establishing a national curriculum, and I predict it holds little promise to attain higher student achievement—as one nation. Because design of NCLB yields decisions about standards, curriculum, instruction, and assessment to the 50 states, it does not avoid the fundamental causes for incoherence at the core of the educational system.

I can propose a resolution to the paradox. The national standards and the forthcoming science framework for the 2009 National Assessment of Educational Progress (NAEP) hold promise of both maintaining the rights of states and the school districts to select instructional programs and achieve higher levels—as a nation.

First, it is important to understand that use of NAEP framework and standards such as the National Science Education Standards (NRC 1996) is voluntary.

Second, the framework standards define and describe what students should know and be able to do. The NAEP framework and national standards include the science understandings and abilities students should develop as a result of their K–12 education. They do *not* prescribe the structure, organization, balance, and presentation of content and processes in classrooms. To be clear, national standards and assessment frameworks are not lessons, classes, courses of study, or school science programs.

This said, they do have the capacity to influence core components of the educational system; namely, curriculum, instruction, classroom assessments and other complementary aspects of the system such as teacher education, initial certification, and continued professional development of teachers and administrators. National standards and the 2009 NAEP framework can serve as a weak force field that, over time, influence decisions about state standards, adoption requirements, textbooks, teacher education programs, and state and local assessments. Greater alignment among core components of the educational system will enhance student learning and result in higher levels of achievement as a nation. So the 2009 NAEP Framework and national standards may resolve the paradox by nature of their influence on state and local systems while they contribute to greater consistence and coherence within the educational system.

Educational Core

In the coming decade, and future decades for that matter, leaders will have to center on the core elements of science education. You may ask what I mean by the core elements of science education. As an initial definition, I suggest Richard Elmore's.

> By "the core of educational practice," I mean how teachers understand the nature of knowledge and their students' role in learning, and how these ideas about knowledge and learning are manifest in teaching and class work. The "core" also includes structural arrangements of schools, such as the physical layouts of classrooms, student grouping practices,

> teachers' responsibilities for groups of students, and relations among teachers in their work with students, as well as processes for assessing student learning and communicating it to students, teachers, parents, administrators, and other interested parties (Elmore 2004, p. 8).

Note several features of this quotation critical for science education. First Elmore cites the importance of leaders' understanding of the nature of scientific knowledge and their students' role in learning science. This feature centers on the science teacher and has direct implications for professional development. Second, he underscores how ideas about scientific knowledge and students' learning of science are realized in the classroom. I translate this to the traditional categories of curriculum and instruction. Third, he recognizes broader programmatic and systemic factors such as classroom student grouping, teachers' responsibilities and collegiality, and finally the processes of assessment of student learning. Certainly assessment will be on the leaders' agenda for the foreseeable future. The basic categories of the educational core can be identified in traditional terms of curriculum, instruction, and assessment with the underlying foundation of student learning and the continuous professional development of science teachers. I discuss professional development in the last section.

I have tried to express this issue of centering on the educational core without using contemporary jargon such as "constructivist" or "hands-on, minds-on instructional materials." Further, I would point out contemporary initiatives that may be included but in my view are largely political and distinctly different from what I am describing as the educational core. I refer to school choice, vouchers, charter schools, and home schooling. So what should the leader consider relative to curriculum, instruction, and assessment?

The foundation for science teaching has to be a rich understanding of learning. *How Students Learn: Science in the Classroom* (NRC 2005) provides three principles for leaders.

- *Engage prior understandings.* Learning results when new understandings are constructive on a foundation of extant understandings and experiences.
- *Understandings consist of factual knowledge and conceptual frameworks.* The concept of learning science with understanding has two elements: (1) factual knowledge that must be placed on a conceptual framework to be well understood; and (2) concepts given meaning by multiple

representations that are rich in factual detail. To be clear, learning with understanding has a complementarity of facts and big ideas. It is not either facts or concepts, and it is not one more than the other.

- *The importance of self-monitoring.* This principle is intended to help students guide their own learning by defining goals, clarifying strategies, and monitoring their progress in achieving them.

Although the three principles of how students learn science have a research base and have clear implications for practice, they are more general than required for classroom science teachers. It also should be clear that they apply directly to the educational core. The challenge for leaders is to identify instructional materials that include a framework of scientific concepts and complementary facts; an instructional sequence that engages prior understandings and provides opportunities for students to develop new understandings and meanings through multiple and varied experiences; and finally, assessments that provide feedback to the student and teacher about the degree to which learning has occurred.

Inquiry Orientation

Leaders in science education have the obligation to clarify a basic confusion that persists about scientific inquiry as it applies to education programs and to confront the controversial view that an inquiry orientation is just play and not intellectually rigorous. Critics reduce teaching science as inquiry to its simplest and most inappropriate form and summarily dismiss the content and process. Unfortunately, inquiry has become associated with an ambiguous instructional approach and not recognized as a viable and appropriate set of educational outcomes; namely, the cognitive abilities and conceptual and factual understandings aligned with this central feature of the scientific enterprise. One hears arguments that inquiry approaches (note that use of terms such as *approaches* and *strategies* assume that inquiry refers to teaching methods) are not effective for learning all science content, because the process takes too long. The term is misinterpreted, it is extended to its most unreasonable position, and it is dismissed as not viable. We need to mount efforts to clarify what the education community means by scientific inquiry—it is a content goal; i.e., students should understand scientific inquiry and develop cognitive abilities. Inquiry also can be instructional approaches to achieve these goals.

No doubt some confusion about teaching science as inquiry emerges from the fact that inquiry is both a set of instructional strategies (e.g., laboratory investigations and activities) and educational outcomes (e.g., knowledge such as "science advances through legitimate skepticism" and abilities such as "thinking critically and logically to make relationships between evidence and explanations").

Scientific inquiry has a long, rich, and appropriate place in school programs. Leaders can begin by applying a general understanding from the educational core, namely, how teachers understand the nature of scientific knowledge and enhance that understanding by applying the principles of learning discussed in the previous section, "Educational Core." The obvious extension is how to apply appropriately the ideas about scientific inquiry in teaching and class work. I have discussed various aspects of scientific inquiry in prior works (Bybee 1997, 2002, 2005).

A valuable resource for leaders is *Inquiry and the National Science Education Standards* (NRC 2000). This guide for teaching and learning contains discussions of inquiry as it is described in the standards and applied in classrooms. It includes clarifying examples of inquiry in science and assessments of inquiry in classrooms and makes the case for inquiry by making connections to our knowledge about how students learn.

Integrity of Science

My introduction made reference to a headline about teachers' being "torn" over religion and evolution. This headline reveals a continuing issue for leaders at all levels of the science education community. In the early years of the 21st century and for coming decades, the challenges will continue. Some fundamental groups continually attempt to infuse the school curriculum with religious doctrine, and they use the science curriculum in general and biological evolution in particular as the point of entry. Often the assault centers on state or local school boards and attempts to set policies that allow alternative "theories" about the origin and evolution of life.

The most recent form of these attempts to infuse the science curriculum with religious explanations is "intelligent design." Proponents of this view argue that organisms are just too intricate and complicated to have evolved, so they infer that the complexity of living systems shows there must have been deliberate design. The reasonable extension of this inference is that an intelligent designer must exist. Advocates of intelligent design do not explicitly state who or what the intelligent designer might be, but it does not take students long to answer the question: "Like, who is the designer? It must be God, right?" I find this view to be an insult to science education and an assault on the integrity of science. The view is by its own rationale grounded in a lack of understanding and ignorance, to say it directly.

Ironically, proponents of creationism and intelligent design use basic tenets of science such as tentativeness of scientific explanations, skeptical review, and openness to new explanations as the basis for introducing "alternative theories," thus undermining the school science program. The earlier discussion of the educational core and recommendation that teachers understand the nature of scientific knowledge becomes especially important for this discussion. I believe it is critically important for all science teachers to educate students about the nature of science. The public understanding of science, or more accurately the public's lack of understanding of science, presents a major weakness, one that allows advocates of "intelligent design," make what seems a reasonable case for its inclusion in school science programs. It does sound reasonable to argue that alternative theories should be introduced, because, in science, the presentation of alternative explanations stands as a central reason for progress. In contrast to "intelligent design," however, in science what is offered as an alternative explanation must be based on evidence—not on authoritative assertions, arguments of incompleteness, or, most astonishingly, incredulity. Simply stated, arguments based on "I assert this to be true," "You have not proved the theory beyond a doubt," or "It is beyond my comprehension, so an intelligent designer must be the cause" simply do not meet the criteria of scientific explanations.

The continual assault on biological evolution stands as a major insult to the integrity of science. Every science teacher has a responsibility to uphold the underlying values and tenets of science, and the extension to leadership is clear and direct. Leaders in science education should provide the professional experiences for science teachers to develop a deep and rich understanding of scientific inquiry and the nature of science.

Integrating Professional Development

Everything I have discussed—international perspectives, educational core, inquiry orientation, and integrity of science—requires some level of professional development for those in the science education community. And, that is the personal obligation of science teachers and the professional responsibility of educational leaders. Although listed last, professional development likely is the most significant trend for the first decade of the 21st century. One could view the categories I have presented as topics or themes within which to initiate professional development programs.

I used the term *integrated* in the section title to suggest that the professional development experience should not be instituted as single "events" with topics interesting but nonetheless isolated from the central work of science teaching. So, for example, I recommend that professional development be seen as integral to science curriculum reform in school systems. In this era of NCLB, assessment also could certainly be a central entry point for professional development.

It is probably worth recalling the professional development standards as they serve as an initial orientation for leaders. Following are the essential statements on professional development from the *National Science Education Standards* (NRC 1996):

- Professional development for teachers of science requires learning essential science content through the perspectives and methods of inquiry (p. 59).
- Professional development for teachers of science requires integrating knowledge of science, learning, pedagogy, and students; it also requires applying that knowledge to science teaching (p. 62).
- Professional development for teachers of science requires building understanding and ability for lifelong learning (p. 68).
- Professional development programs for teachers of science must be coherent and integrated (p. 70).

Standards for science education cannot change teachers' beliefs or behavior, but they can provide clear and crucial directions for change, because they define goals and identify directions for improvement. Standards do have the power to change elements at the educational core and provide a vision of what should be maintained and what should be changed within science education.

When developing the national Standards, we recognized professional development as a key component of the science education system, one often neglected when concentrating on core content. The professional development Standards consider *what* teachers should learn and *how* they should learn it. Although the contexts for professional development will vary, leaders can use the standards as a model for designing professional development. Note that the terms *integrating* and *integrated* are used in two of the four Standards, thus reinforcing the idea that professional development be seen as central to leadership activities, especially as it applies to science teachers.

Conclusion

Entering the 21st century presents the occasion to review trends and issues that leaders will encounter. What is common to the work of leaders? I proposed establishing a clear and consistent vision combined with a practical and workable plan. The vision and plan will get the leader started in directions that may involve curriculum reform, instructional improvement, or alignment of assessments. One crucial point that I made for leaders is their ability to realize and resolve paradoxes as they execute their plans. The paradoxes have been referred to as tensions, critical problems, even absurdities. Regardless, effective leadership requires the resolution of the need to, for example, initiate bold, new programs while maintaining established, past traditions, or fulfilling a national mandate such as NCLB while incorporating a local agenda. One of the most disheartening paradoxes is the reality of achieving the established vision and enduring criticism. Given this view of leadership in science education, I described several themes that leaders will confront in the first decades of the 21st century.

I identified five themes that will directly or indirectly influence science education leaders. Teachers will be influenced by international assessments such as PISA and TIMSS, especially as the results for U.S. students influence the public's perception of school programs. The relationship between U.S. achievement and economic progress will provide the rationale for reform initiatives.

I made the case that the educational core—curriculum, instruction, assessment, and professional development—is where our time, money, and effort should be focused. Improvements in the educational core will, in the short- and long-term, bring the greatest advances toward scientific literacy for all students. Among the crucial aspects of the educational core, one has to include the understanding of scientific inquiry by classroom teachers and their subsequent efforts to help students develop the cognitive abilities and conceptual understandings aligned with this aspect of science education.

The science education community has been and will be confronted by groups attempting to control the curriculum and introduce religious ideas in the science. Leaders should recognize this as an attack on the standards and values of science, an assault on the integrity of science. All leaders in the science education community have an obligation to confront these assaults and to support science teachers as they introduce the ideas of scientific inquiry and the nature of science.

Finally, I see the continued needs for professional development. Relative to this theme, I note that it should be integrated with other meaningful activities such as curriculum reform.

Rodger W. Bybee
is the executive director of the Biological Sciences Curriculum Study (BSCS). Before this he was executive director of the Center for Science, Mathematics and Engineering Education at the National Research Council. Author of numerous journal articles, chapters, books, science curricular and textbooks, he also directed the writing of the content standards for the National Science Education Standards. Honors included the National Science Teachers Association Distinguished Service Award.

References and Resources

General

Burns, J. M. 1978. *Leadership*. New York: Harper & Row.

Bybee, R.W. 1997. *Achieving scientific literacy: From purposes to practices.* Portsmouth, NH: Heinemann.

Bybee, R.W., ed. 2002. *Learning science and the science of learning.* Arlington, VA: NSTA Press.

Bybee, R. W. 2005. *Scientific inquiry and science teaching.* In *Scientific inquiry and the nature of science: Implications for teaching, learning, and teacher education*, eds. L. B. Flick and N. G. Lederman. Boston, MA: Kluwer Academic Publishers.

Combs, A. W., A. B. Miser, and K. S. Whitaker. 1999. *On becoming a school leader: A person-centered challenge.* Alexandria, VA: Association for Supervision and Curriculum Development.

Gardner, J. W. 1990. *On leadership.* New York: The Free Press.

National Research Council (NRC). 1996. *National Science Education Standards.* Washington, DC: National Academy Press.

National Research Council (NRC). 2005. *How students learn: Science in the classroom.* Committee on How People Learn, A Targeted Report for Teachers, M. S. Donovan and J. D. Bransford, eds. Washington, DC: The National Academies Press.

No Child Left Behind Act of 2001. 2002. Public Law 107–110–January 8, 2002. 107th Congress. Washington, DC.

Patterson, J. L. 1993. *Leadership for tomorrow's schools.* Alexandria, VA: Association for Supervision and Curriculum Development.

International Perspectives

Bybee, R. W., and D. Kennedy. 2005. Math and science achievement. *Science* 307 (28): 481.

Bybee, R. W., and E. Stage. 2005. No country left behind. *Issues in Science and Technology* (Winter): 69–75.

Gonzales, P., E. Pahlke, J. C. Guzman, L. Partelow, D. Kastberg, L. Jocelyn, and T. Williams. 2004. *Pursuing excellence: Eighth-grade mathematics and science achievement in the United States and other countries from the* Trends in International Mathematics and Science Study (TIMSS) 2003. Washington, DC: National Center for Education Statistics, U.S. Department of Education.

Lemke, M., A. Sen, E. Pahlke, L. Partelow, D. Miller, T. Williams, D. Kasterberg, and L. Jocelyn. 2004. *International outcomes in learning mathematics literacy and problem solving: PISA 2003 results from the American perspective.* (NCES 2005–003). Washington, DC: National Center for Education Statistics, United States Department of Education.

Educational Core

Elmore, R. F. 2004. *School reform from the inside out: Policy, practice, and performance.* Cambridge, MA: Harvard Education Press.

Evans, R. 1996. *The human side of school change: Reform, resistance, and the real-life problems of innovation.* San Francisco, CA: Jossey-Bass.

Inquiry

Bybee, R. W. 2000. Teaching science as inquiry. In *Inquiring into inquiry learning and teaching in science,* eds. J. Minstrell and E. H. van Zee, 20–45. Washington, DC: American Association for the Advancement of Science.

National Research Council (NRC). 2000. *Inquiry and the National Science Education Standards: A guide for teaching and learning.* Washington, DC: National Academy Press.

Integrity of Science

Bybee, R. W. (Ed.). 2004. *Evolution in perspective: The science teacher's compendium.* Arlington, VA: NSTA Press.

Moore, J. A. 2002. *From genesis to genetics: The case of evolution and creationism.* Berkeley and Los Angeles, CA: University of California Press.

National Academy of Sciences (NAS). 1998. *Teaching about evolution and the nature of science.* Washington, DC: National Academy Press.

Professional Development

Loucks-Horsley, S., N. Love, K. Stiles, S. Mundry, and P. Hewson. 2003. *Designing professional development for teachers of science and mathematics.* Thousand Oaks, CA: Corwin Press.

Rhoton, J., and P. Bowers. 2001. *Professional development leadership and the diverse learner.* Arlington, VA: NSTA Press.

Rhoton, J., and P. Bowers. 2001. *Professional development planning and design.* Arlington, VA: NSTA Press.

Wallace, J., and J. Loughran, eds. 2003. *Leadership and professional development in science education: New possibilities for enhancing teacher learning.* New York: RoutledgeFalmer.

CHAPTER 11

The Principal as Leader of Change

Nicole Saginor

As schools approach the era of accountability for student achievement delineated in the No Child Left Behind Act of 2001 (NCLB 2002), the need to elevate the level of science teaching and learning has become more critical. In decades past, efforts at improving science instruction tended to be aimed at the teacher and student, focusing on what should be taught and how. As outlined in the National Science Education Standards (NSES) (NRC 1996), methods of inquiry, standards-based programs, materials, and resources all contributed to a new vision of science instruction.

These were important steps forward. Yet years after the NSES have been established, we still lag behind our goals of high-quality science for all students. To effect systemic change, the first task is to define the basic unit of that change. If the classroom alone were the unit of change, then advances made through the standards movement would have created that change. But to focus only on the classroom while students navigate through a system as complex as a school is inefficient and eventually fails, as individual teachers unsupported by administrators or their peers either wither in their resolve or continue their excellent teaching behind the closed doors of teacher isolation.

Another strategy, most promising in nature, to produce enduring reform in instruction, has been the development of teacher-leaders and the recognition of excellence in teaching. The theory that teachers trained in standards-based content and instructional strategies will seed the changes in their buildings either through direct professional development or informal sharing seemed sensible. This strategy, too, has proven woefully inadequate and even at times counterproductive when unsupported at the building level. While much has been written about the promise of teacher-leadership and the role of the principal in cultivating this resource (Lambert 1998;

Crowther et al. 2004), again the culture of isolation has proven a barrier. Teachers have actively resisted the "interference" of their peers into their teaching practice. The traditionally flat nature of the teaching profession, where the only differentiation between teachers is salary linked to longevity, has discouraged teachers from stepping up to lead change among their peers.

Much research has now revealed that real change occurs only when certain conditions exist. Deep understanding of science content and skill in science content-pedagogy are necessary, but not sufficient. The "reculturing of schools," a concept reiterated in *The New Meaning of Educational Change* (Fullan 2001), means that innovations don't change schools without a concurrent change in the culture. And school culture does not change without the green light from the building principal. The development of professional learning communities (DuFour and Eaker 1998) brings teachers out of their rooms into groups focused on issues directly bearing on curriculum —what is taught; instruction—how it is taught; and assessment—student results. These learning communities rarely form through the efforts of teachers alone. Even poor test results can drive teachers further into their rooms to fret alone about how to get their students to perform better on high-stakes tests. But the most effective use of data that produces results in student performance comes with the collaborative inquiry of teachers who together investigate the conditions producing the data and then collectively own responsibility for altering those conditions (Love 2002). The shift from the focus on teaching to the focus on learning is best expressed by three corollary questions to the statement, "We believe all children can learn" which DuFour and Eaker poses frequently during presentations: "What do we expect them to learn? How will we know when they have learned it? How will we respond when they do not learn?" (p. 59).

This shift in culture must either originate directly from the principal or be heartily and publicly endorsed and actively participated in by the principal. This makes the principal's skill critical in effecting real and measurable improvement in instruction and student achievement. What are the skills the principal needs to pull this off? Now more than ever, as the instructional leader of the school, the principal must:

- manage the culture of change and build professional learning communities
- cultivate teacher-leadership

- advocate for science to be taught in elementary school to support literacy
- provide for proper professional development
- understand standards-based science so when he or she knows what to look for when observing a class
- have tools to supervise teachers in the best instructional practices for producing enduring learning and deep content in science

What Principals Must Know and Do to Achieve Science Excellence

No systemic or enduring change in a school has ever happened successfully without either the driving force or the willing and active support of the principal. That is why the current crisis in the principalship is of much concern. When the average stay of a principal in a particular school is three years, any initiative becomes another thing coming down the pike that teachers can easily resist or simply ignore until the next principal arrives. As long as the job of principal remains as complex and undoable as it is currently, and as long as either teaching faculties or local school boards pressure an innovative principal until that principal chooses to leave, true innovation will be an uphill challenge. But stably building leadership alone is not enough. A principal who stays must be able to not only manage skillfully the day-to-day emergencies and the political pressures but also must be competent enough to be accepted as a true instructional leader. The specific competencies required to guide the successful reform of science with the outcome of improved teaching practice and student achievement are outlined in this chapter.

Managing Change, Building Professional Learning Communities

Throughout our ten-year study, whenever we found an effective school or an effective department within a school, without exception, that school or department has been part of a collaborative professional learning community.... The most promising strategy for sustained, substantive school improvement is building the capacity of school personnel to function as a professional learning community. The path to change in the classroom lies within and through professional learning communities (McLaughlin 1995).

A learning organization (DuFour and Eaker 1998) is a school community in which teachers and administrators engage, as a normal undertaking of their daily work, in substantive conversations about their practice, their students' learning, and relevant trends and research. It is one in which peer mentoring or coaching happens as a matter of course, where teachers observe each other, teach with each other, and learn from each other as well as from outside experts. DuFour and Eaker quote multiple research studies citing the culture of a school that has strong leadership and a clear and common purpose embodied in its policies and procedures as the critical ingredient of success (Lezotte 1997; Newmann and Wehlage 1995; Purkey and Smith 1983). But this does not describe the culture of many of our schools. Fullan, in *Leading in a Culture of Change* (2001a), speaks to the need of not only restructuring for reform, but also "reculturing."

> Effective leaders know that the hard work of reculturing is the sine qua non of progress .... Leading in a culture of change means creating a culture (not just a structure) of change. It does not mean adopting innovations, one after another; it does mean producing the capacity to seek, critically assess, and selectively incorporate new ideas and practices .... (Fullan 2001a, p. 44).

More simply said, "I know of no improving school that doesn't have a principal who is good at leading improvement" (Fullan 2001b). Reculturing does not happen without leadership. Nor does a professional learning community arise spontaneously.

How does a principal alter the culture of a school to create this learning community? DuFour and Eaker (1998) identify the following actions that contribute to the successful generation of a learning community:

- Lead through shared vision and values rather than rules and procedures and model them on a daily basis
- Involve faculty members in the school's decision-making processes and empower individuals to act
- Provide staff with the information, training, and parameters they need to make good decisions
- Create collaborative structures with a focus on teaching and learning
- Foster an approach that focuses on learning rather than teaching
- Encourage teachers to think of themselves as leaders
- Establish personal credibility

- Be fixated on results
- Recognize that continuous improvement requires continuous learning

But more than following these wise guidelines, it is imperative that the principal become a real and contributing member of that learning community. Only in this way can credibility be established and values modeled, demonstrating that learning is everyone's job. Teachers will follow when the principal comes out of his or her office and enters the fray of finding a common strategy for reaching all students.

One of the most efficient ways to engage a faculty as a professional learning community is to give them the tools to understand their student assessment data. Collaborative inquiry (Love 2002) into student results is a complex set of learned skills that includes having access to useful data, understanding how the data is reported, learning tools to analyze that data, establishing the structures and processes (time and support) for collaborative inquiry, and being part of a culture that accepts student learning as a collective endeavor. Ensuring that a faculty possesses these skills and has the opportunity to use them productively is a critical piece of work for every principal.

Cultivating Teacher-Leadership

Teacher-leadership as a formal role has been promulgated as an ideal response to the problem of the increasing complexity of the principalship and the corresponding rate of turnover. Teacher-leadership stands on its own as an appropriate strategy, regardless of whether or not it can relieve the pressure on an overworked administrator. The teaching profession has traditionally been flat. The only differentiation between teachers in most contracts is salary, based solely on number of degrees and longevity. Although some districts have entertained the prospect of merit pay, teacher unions have usually opposed such moves. But teachers are not and never have been created equal. They differ in competence, in ingenuity, risk-taking, intellectual curiosity, and potential for leadership. Injecting teacher-leadership into the profession offers a career ladder for those who would take advantage of it. It introduces an expectation that, in a teacher's career, paths other than classroom teaching or administration can be followed. It enriches the possibilities within each school, allowing and encouraging all professionals to participate in decision making, policy formation, and curriculum and instruction issues. It offers shared responsibility and ownership. Increased responsibility improves instruction as teachers become fully invested in the outcomes.

Teacher-leaders can provide on-site professional development during the school days or provide in-service opportunities at the school. This is what we have called job-embedded professional development. It sounds good; it happens rarely. But when it does, you can count on there being at the helm of that school a principal with a vision and the ability to bring that vision to a living reality.

The published work on teacher-leadership has spoken of "building leadership capacity" (Lambert 1998) and the "role of the principal" (Crowther et al. 2004). But the inherent difficulties in pulling this off gracefully in a school have not received sufficient attention. In Vermont, as a State Systemic Initiative (SSI) of the National Science Foundation (NSF), we (the Vermont Institute of Science, Math, and Technology, now Vermont Institutes) have been experimenting since 1994 with various models of teacher-leadership. Some of these models have taken teachers out of their classrooms for a sabbatical-like experience to offer intensive training and provide opportunities to present school-based workshops, in-class modeling, peer coaching, and other forms of professional development in content-rich inquiry-based instruction. Other models of teacher-leadership have left teachers in their schools but taken them out of the classroom for a period of time to work with their school and district colleagues. Still others have provided masters' degrees with the expectation of recipients' assuming leadership at the culmination of the degree. We have provided summer institutes and ongoing support for science mentors at the high school level, and have supported teachers striving for National Board Certification.

Oddly, the potpourri of models of teacher-leadership has led to similar results. Each year, we offer a teacher-leader conference at which teacher-leaders and their principals gather. At each conference, we highlight three new models of teacher-leadership with their successes and their challenges. It didn't take long to see that the principal was an integral ingredient in both the successes and the challenges.

Training

Teacher-leadership is not automatic. One cannot assume that even the finest teacher can step into a role of leadership successfully. The first issue to attend to is proper training and support. Teachers are trained to teach students. Adult learning is an entirely different ballgame (Vella 1994). There are also differences among the roles of teacher, facilitator, and coach. Teachers need to understand which role they will assume and then learn the most effective ways of approaching their colleagues respectfully.

In addition, if colleagues are to respect the leadership of a peer, the peer must demonstrate expertise in the subject matter. One caution before investing heavily in generic programs of mentoring and leadership: Strong and deep knowledge of content is a critical component of successful teaching. Make sure your leaders can offer sound advice and modeling in their science. If they do not, they will neither win the respect of their peers, nor be of any substantive help to them.

Finally, a frequently overlooked need of teacher-leaders is that of support. The role of teacher-leader can be a lonely one. It is critical that teacher-leaders have access to others who are doing what they do, both for continuous learning and for processing their work. One of our models for doing this was New York City's District II system in which outstanding teachers were tapped to become professional developers. They received intensive training and support from an infrastructure that included the principals, who were in turn supported at the district level. We also joined in a tristate effort with Maine and New Hampshire to create a cadre of high school science teachers (the Northern New England Co-Mentoring Network) trained in depth in content, content-pedagogy, national standards, and tools for mentoring new teachers. Whatever the format, it must be formally organized, ongoing, and in a facilitated venue.

Logistics

The simple need for a place to hang your coat, to put your books, to have a professional conversation has been overlooked all too often by schools whose teachers take time from their classrooms to assist their peers. The classic error of administrators is to assume that teacher-leaders can take on the additional duties of leadership without any reduction or adjustment in teaching load. "We have a teacher-leader who can do that—I don't have to worry about it," is a common administrative misconception that leads quickly to teacher burnout—a common by-product of teacher-leadership. Conversely, neglect and underuse can be as detrimental. Whether it be reduced teaching responsibilities with scheduled times for peer observation and mentoring, faculty meetings partially or fully committed to professional sharing and discussion, or even a modest stipend, teacher-leaders supported by their principals continue to feel good about their work.

Time for the work must be provided for both the teacher-leader and any other faculty members. This work needs to be done during normal work hours unless it is going to be compensated beyond regular salary.

Structures for the work must be created. Whether the structures are workshops, special faculty meetings that have been organized for this purpose, team meetings, pairing of new and experienced teachers for mentoring, or just a buddy system of peer coaching with guidelines and expectations, opportunities for teachers to learn from each other must be created intentionally.

Roles must be made clear by the building administration and must provide the teacher-leader with both the *authority* and the *autonomy* to get the job done. Nothing is more powerful for building leadership capacity in a school than sharing the power and authority by the positional leader.

Goals set by and expectations of the principal must be clear, reasonable, and attainable. Nothing dampens the enthusiasm of teachers more quickly than work that doesn't seem to go anywhere. It helps if those expectations derive directly from the work of teachers and if they have had a hand in developing them. The work, once done, should be seen as adding value to their practice. For example, if at the end of a series of sessions on assessment led by a teacher-leader, the faculty were to emerge with a set of local assessments to track student progress and adjust their instruction, a higher commitment to the task would be more likely achieved.

Perceptions of the community and particularly of the school board should be that a teacher's work consists primarily of direct contact with students. Teachers who take time from their classrooms to assist other teachers face the following possible reactions: Shouldn't they have learned what they needed in college? Are we paying her for that? What's happening to her students in the meantime? Because teacher-leadership doesn't usually come free, a commitment must be made to the benefits of this role and to its funding. Whether paying for substitutes or replacements or offering part-time or job-sharing options, the board and the community need to understand the value added or they will simply not support it. Formal publicity and informational sessions that permit honest discussion and airing of concerns is highly recommended to avoid negative public reactions later that could damage the standing of a particular teacher.

Culture

> The forces reinforcing the status quo are systemic .... Confronting the isolationism and privatism of educational systems is a tall order. It requires intensive action ... to make it possible ... for teachers to work naturally together in joint planning; observation of each other's practice; and seeking, testing, and revising teaching strategies.... (Fullan 2001b, p. 7).

Resistance from within to teacher-leadership can be both subtle and fierce. Only determined leadership from the principal can eradicate it. Although principals cannot do this alone, they must be an insistent force for the change. Teachers traditionally are followers: followers of schedules, curriculum, administrative edicts, and innovations. As is the custom now, it is virtually taboo for a teacher to criticize a fellow teacher or otherwise interfere with another's practice. Principals can inadvertently foster competition among teachers, or what I've come to call "sibling rivalry." Choosing a single teacher to lead or bestowing too much authority on a single teacher can cause resentment. Principals can do many positive things to foster conditions that will allow teacher-leadership to flourish. They can create a culture of collegiality and mutual respect, and a vibrant environment where ideas are freely challenged and readily shared, and multiple opportunities for leadership promoted. They can honor the risk-taker as well as the high achiever and provide support when things don't turn out as planned. They can insist that respect be accorded and that hostility, overt or passive, directed toward a teacher taking the lead in an initiative will not be tolerated. Most of all, principals must understand that this new role can be not just difficult but also the cause of outright ostracism. As long as teachers are allowed to be hurt by their peers, teacher-leadership will not take its proper place in the landscape of our schools. On the bright side, collaboration is contagious. Once teachers get a taste of working together, they are reinvigorated with the enthusiasm that accompanied them to their first jobs.

Advocating for Science to Be Taught in Elementary School to Support Literacy

Reading scores will improve only so much by doing more reading. If we are really serious about improving reading scores, students need a content area such as science to apply their reading and writing skills. (Amaral et al. 2002)

The No Child Left Behind Act of 2001 (2002) has placed very high stakes on the outcomes of state-administered tests in mathematics and literacy. The requirements for science do not come into effect until 2007. This has caused many schools, particularly elementary schools that regularly struggle with implementing quality science programs, to put off their efforts to address science achievement. The work of Michael Klentschy in California has provided us with startling data demonstrating that these choices do not need to be made (Amaral et al. 2002). As part of a Local Systemic Change initiative from the National Science Foundation, his California district, a stone's throw from Mexico with a large Hispanic population and various degrees of limited English proficiency, introduced an inquiry-based science program from kindergarten to grade six in which students engaged in active learning through the use of kits from FOSS, STC, and Insights. A strong emphasis in this program was placed on writing, particularly the writing done in student journals or lab books, and embedded assessments. The instruction was exclusively in English and emphasized learning content and articulating understanding of that learning.

Their findings over a four-year period demonstrated a consistent yearly rise in scores, both in science and in writing (Amaral et al. 2002). Noted as well, although not the original intent of the study, was that scores in reading consistently rose at all grade levels tested, as did those, in general, in mathematics. Particularly significant, in view of the focus of this chapter, was the professional development component of the program. Not only were the teachers targeted for intensive training but the superintendent also. He then organized and led training sessions for principals who, in addition, attended a two-day symposium at the outset and some follow-up sessions.

The data from this study fly in the face of the edict of many a well-meaning principal who has prohibited or severely limited science instruction in the early grades in order to focus on literacy and mathematics. It also demonstrates that the locus of change is the system, not the classroom. The leadership from the superintendent and the understanding and constant support of the principals were key factors in the successful implementation of the training received by teachers. A teaching faculty gets a powerful message when district and building leadership takes an active role in the professional development, in effect saying, "I do not ask you to do anything that I would not devote my own time to."

Providing for Professional Development

Valuable work has been done to inform the development of a comprehensive professional development system for teachers of science (Loucks-Horsley et al. 2003). This work outlines an array of strategies to address the different facets of learning that teachers need to improve their science instruction. Increased science content knowledge, science content pedagogy, collaborative inquiry into student results for a schoolwide commitment, and leadership all must be developed and constantly improved. The strategies described address all these as well as building collaborative structures and practices, and ways in which to ensure a refreshed practice through the application of new learning. Other strategies include mentoring and immersion experiences, case discussions, lesson study, and action research. Deciding which strategies to use and when can be daunting for a principal, particularly one who lacks a science background. These decisions, however, affect budgets and as such are the distinct purview of the principal. A comprehensive program of professional development can be built only by knowing how to assess faculty needs and by understanding the power and limits of each strategy.

The work of Loucks-Horsley et al. speaks not only to the specific strategies for meeting all the professional development needs of teachers of science but also makes the point that principals must also increase their understanding of science and the way it is taught in order to be true leaders of science reform. One of the most effective ways in which to do this and at the same time contribute to the development of a learning community is for the principal to participate in the professional development activities along with the teachers. "Learning together, when it is done in an open and trusting environment, can build respect for different roles and relationships that help school staffs with the difficulties of significant change" (Loucks-Horsley et al. 2003).

Understanding Standards-Based Science and Having Tools for Supervision

Finally, if principals are to increase their science knowledge, they need to have tools that are designed for them. Most principals are not science majors, nor should they be expected to be science content experts. Yet they are responsible for supervising instruction and ultimately for student results. At Vermont Institutes, our approach to increase principals' ability to understand what high-quality standards-based science instruction looks like and how to supervise teachers for improved practice has been the development of the Vermont Classroom Observation Tool (VCOT). Based on extensive research (Horizon Research 1997; SAMPI 1999) as well as standards of practice (Danielson 1986; Marzano 1999; Saphier and Gower 1997), the VCOT is designed to highlight key components of science instruction that have been demonstrated to improve teaching practice.

The VCOT is based on the following assumptions:

1. The best science instruction happens in an investigative environment.
2. Content and process do not eclipse each other; both are critical to successful science instruction.
3. Knowledge is socially constructed and solidified through dialogue and the active engagement of every child in a safe and respectful environment.
4. Instruction is enhanced by the integration of technology.

The VCOT addresses four criteria of quality instruction: *planning and organization, classroom implementation, specific concepts and content,* and *classroom culture and the learning environment.* The tool itself is a helpful document. We have found, however, that without a training program, it is unlikely to be helpful to principals who have little experience with science teaching. We carefully crafted a two-day intensive training with a one-day follow-up designed to immerse principals into the world of science content and pedagogy. A series of taped simulations of instructional events provided practice in and dialogue about the use of the tool. Principals explored the elements of good inquiry with a strong emphasis on assessment of student understanding. The training included an exploration of best practices in using observations during supervision to produce changes in instruction and to minimize resistant or defensive reactions.

Concluding Thoughts

If we are ever to see our students achieve not only improved test scores but also improved understanding of both the content and processes of scientific investigation, we must do more than try to reach their teachers with the lessons learned from the research. Teachers affect one classroom at a time, and their impact on every single child is crucial. But students who progress through a school deserve teachers every year who will build on what they already have and prepare them for what they will need. Therefore, although training teachers is an essential component of programs to improve student results in science, it is at the level of the school at which efforts must be aimed. A knowledgeable and passionate principal who can ensure that *all* teachers are held to a high standard (as high a standard as that to which we now hold our students) is as essential as any professional development strategy. Until we have the active and informed participation of every principal combined with the expectation for a level of quality professional practice from every teacher, our results will continue to disappoint us.

Nicole Saginor

is the associate executive director of the Vermont Institutes, a professional development organization in Montpelier, Vermont. She has developed institutes, workshops, and courses in leadership focusing on the role of principals and teacher-leaders in school reform. She is the principal developer of the Vermont Classroom Observation Tool, a protocol for observing and supervising instruction in math, science, and technology. A member of the faculty of the Vermont Science Initiative at the Vermont State Colleges, she has also served as clinical and adjunct faculty at the University of Vermont.

References

Amaral, O., L. Garrison, and M. Klentschy. 2002. Helping English learners increase achievement through inquiry-based science instruction. *Bi-Lingual Research Journal* 26 (Summer): 2.

Crowther, F., S. Kaagen, M. Fergusen, and L. Hann. 2004. *Developing teacher-leaders.* Thousand Oaks, CA: Corwin Press.

Danielson, C. 1986. *Enhancing professional practice: A framework for teaching.* Alexandria, VA: Association for Supervision and Curriculum Development.

DuFour, R., and R. Eaker. 1998. *Professional learning communities at work: Best practices for enhancing student achievement.* Bloomington, IN: National Educational Service.

Fullan, M. 2001a. *Leading in a culture of change.* San Francisco: Jossey-Bass.

Fullan, M. 2001b. *The new meaning of educational change.* San Francisco: Jossey-Bass.

Horizon Research. 1997. *Local systemic change classroom observation protocol.* Funded by the National Science Foundation, Washington, DC.

Lambert, L. 1998. *Building leadership capacity in schools.* Alexandria, VA: Association for Supervision and Curriculum Development.

Lezotte, L. 1997. *Learning for all.* Okemos, MI: Effective School Products.

Loucks-Horsley, S., N. Love, K. Stiles, S. Mundry, and P. Hewson. 2003. *Designing professional development for teachers of science and mathematics.* Thousand Oaks, CA: Corwin Press.

Love, N. 2002. *Using data/getting results: A practical guide for school improvement in mathematics and science.* Norwood, MA: Christopher-Gordon.

Marzano, R. 1999. *Strategies that impact student achievement.* Presented at Association for Supervision and Curriculum Development Conference, Boston.

McLaughlin, M. December 1995. *Creating Professional Learning Communities.* Keynote address presented at the Annual Conference of the National Staff Development Council, Chicago.

National Research Council (NRC). 1996. *National Science Education Standards.* Washington, DC: National Academy Press.

Newmann, F., and G. Wehlage. 1995. *Successful school restructuring: A report to the public and educators by the Center for Restructuring Schools.* Madison, WI: University of Wisconsin.

No Child Left Behind Act (NCLB) of 2001. 2002. Public Law 107–110–January 8, 2002. 107th Congress. Washington, DC.

Purkey, S., and M. Smith. 1983. Effective schools: A review. *Elementary School Journal* 83(4), 427-452.

Saphier, J., and R. Gower. 1997. *The skillful teacher: Building your teaching skills.* Acton, MA: RBT Publications.

Science and Math Program Improvement (SAMPI). 1999. *Science: Teaching practices observation instrument, Version B.* Kalamazoo, MI: Western Michigan University.

Vella, J. 1994. *Learning to listen, learning to teach: The power of dialogue in educating adults.* San Francisco: Jossey-Bass.

CHAPTER
12

Keeping Good Science Teachers: What Science Leaders Can Do

Linda Darling-Hammond and Mistilina Sato

Substantial evidence suggests that, of all school resources, well-prepared, experienced teachers are the most important determinant of student achievement. Student achievement in science—as in other subjects—has been found to be strongly related to teachers' preparation in both subject matter and teaching methods, as well as to their preparation to work with diverse students (Goldhaber and Brewer 2000; Monk 1994; Wenglinsky 2002). Further, student performance on state tests is significantly higher, both before and after controlling for student poverty, for students whose teachers are fully certified and have higher scores on teacher certification tests (Ferguson 1991; Fetler 1999; Fuller 1998; Goe 2002). Teachers' experience levels also matter, especially the steep gain in effectiveness that typically occurs after the first few years of teaching (Kain and Singleton 1996). (For summaries of this research, see Darling-Hammond 2000b; Wilson et al. 2001.)

Choosing curriculum and supplying textbooks is important, but, to improve student achievement in science, school and district leaders must attract and retain well-prepared and committed science teachers and support their continued learning. Only when teachers have had the kind of training and experience that makes them successful with students can schools become and remain effective. Creating the conditions to retain strong teachers preserves this essential human capital; hiring, training, and losing new teachers is a costly vicious cycle. Evidence suggests that attrition is a much greater problem in the teacher supply picture than is producing enough teachers to fill the nation's needs. School leaders need to understand the reasons for teacher attrition if they are to develop effective strategies for building and maintaining a strong science teaching force. In this chapter, we discuss what influences science teacher recruitment and retention and what science leaders in teaching, teacher education, professional development, and school administration can do to address this problem.

The Supply and Demand of Science Teachers

Because of the growing body of research about how teachers matter to student achievement, the No Child Left Behind Act of 2001 (2002) mandates that all schools be staffed by "highly qualified teachers"—that is, teachers who have a strong base of knowledge of their subject matter and an understanding of how to teach it to students. Recruiting qualified teachers is a major challenge, especially in cities and poor rural areas, even though, as a nation, we produce many more qualified teachers than we hire. There are about four times as many individuals holding teaching credentials as there are jobs in K–12 teaching, and the preparation system produces nearly twice as many teachers annually as there are jobs to be filled by new teachers. But some districts and states have surpluses, while others struggle to fill vacancies and deal with high turnover (Darling-Hammond and Sykes 2003). In addition to distributing teachers more equitably, the teacher quality challenge rests with *keeping* the teachers we prepare.

Since the early 1990s, the annual number of exits from teaching has increasingly surpassed the number of entrants, putting pressure on the nation's hiring systems. For example, while U.S. schools hired 230,000 teachers in 1999, 287,000 left their teaching jobs in that year (Ingersoll 2001). Less than 20% of this attrition is due to retirement. Both teacher dissatisfaction with the conditions of work and teacher lack of preparation are critical components of high turnover, especially in hard-to-staff schools (Ingersoll 2001; Henke et al. 2000).

The technical fields of science and mathematics tend to face greater challenges recruiting and retaining qualified teachers because the opportunity costs for individuals entering teaching—that is, the relative differences in salaries outside of teaching—tend to be very large and have been growing larger since the early 1990s (see Figure 1). Many positions are filled by uncertified teachers or teachers assigned outside their field of expertise, especially in less affluent districts that serve greater numbers of low-income students and students of color (National Commission on Math and Science Teaching for the 21st Century 2000) (see Figure 2). In states without substantial recruitment incentives, the problem of underprepared science teachers has been worsening. For example, a longitudinal examination of teacher preparation in California between 1997–98 and 2002–03 found that the proportion of uncertified secondary teachers (across all subject areas) rose from 6% to 10%, while the proportion of uncertified science teachers increased from 5% to about 13% (Center for the Future of Teaching and Learning 2003). In districts with large concentrations of students of color, the percentage of uncertified teachers were twice as high. Continuing to hire underprepared teachers as a stopgap measure is not an effective, efficient, or moral solution for schools.

Figure 1: Trends in starting salaries of selected majors (as a ratio of teachers' starting salaries)

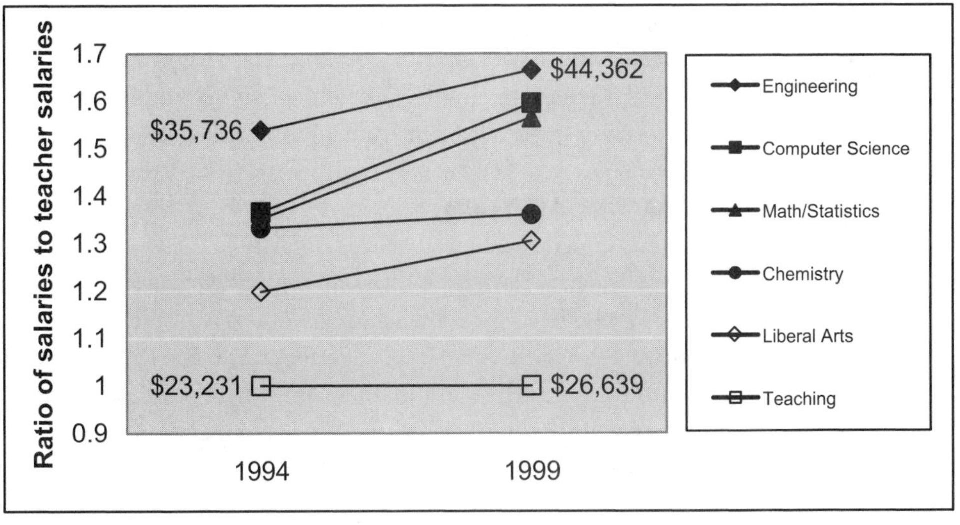

Figure 2: Disparities in access to qualified math and science teachers, 1998

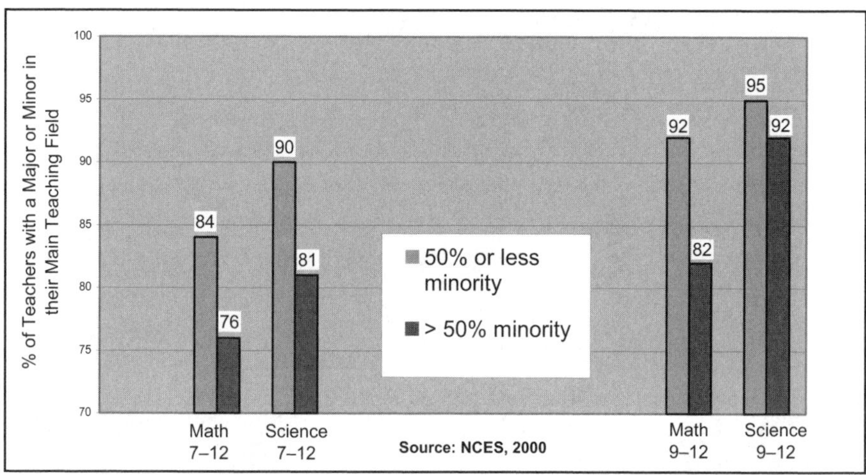

As the nation continues its long-term shift to a knowledge-based service economy, the education profession will find itself in greater contest with other service-providing professions. While employment in public education is projected to increase 17.5% between 2002 and 2012, employment in professional, scientific, and technical services will grow by 27.8% in that same period (Bureau of Labor Statistics 2004). Schools seeking to fill science education positions will compete with an employment market that offers applicants more choices in comparable service-oriented and technically oriented fields and more lucrative jobs. Recruiting and keeping qualified science and math teachers will become even more of a challenge for many school districts if no action is taken to make a teaching career more attractive.

Science Teacher Attrition

Teaching has long experienced steep attrition in the first few years: about one-third of new teachers leave the profession within five years.[1] After this point, individuals who have chosen teaching tend to stay in the profession, and the attrition rate increases again at retirement age. Evidence suggests that annual turnover of science and mathematics teachers, at about 16%, is slightly higher than the average for the teacher population as a whole (Ingersoll 2003). Studies have found that math and science teachers are particularly sensitive to salary levels in their decisions; thus, they tend to leave at higher rates than other teachers, especially when they are in districts with lower salaries (Murnane and Olsen 1990). For example, a longitudinal study of a large urban school district from 1991 to 2001 found that the attrition rate of secondary science teachers was higher than the overall rate for teachers in 10 of 11 years of the study, correcting for retirements (Hansen et al. 2004).

From a district perspective, the costs of early attrition from teaching are enormous. A recent study in Texas conservatively estimated the cost of the state's annual turnover rate of 15%, which includes a 40% turnover rate for public school teachers in their first three years, at $329 million a year, or at least $8,000 per recruit who leaves in the first few years of teaching (Texas Center for Educational Research 2000). This includes the costs of recruiting, selecting, hiring, inducting, and replacing individuals who leave. Taking into account the organizational costs of termination, substitutes, new training, and lost learning produces an estimated national price tag as high as $2.1 billion a year. Instead of going to needed school improvements, funds are spent in a way that produces little long-term payoff for student learning.

Given the strong evidence that teacher effectiveness increases sharply after the first few years of teaching (Kain and Singleton 1996), the churning in the beginning teaching force wastes money and reduces productivity in education, because the system never realizes the eventual payoff from its investment in novices. Schools where most teachers are inexperienced or underqualified or both must continually pour money into recruitment efforts and professional support for new teachers, many of them also untrained, without reaping dividends from the investment. Other teachers, including the few who could serve as mentors, are stretched thin and feel overburdened by the needs of their colleagues as well as their students. Scarce resources are squandered trying to re-teach the basics each year to teachers who come in with few tools and leave before they become skilled (Carroll et al. 2000). As a principal in one such school noted:

> (H)aving that many new teachers on the staff at any given time meant that there was less of a knowledge base. It meant that it was harder for families to be connected to the school because—you know, their child might get a new teacher every year. It meant there was less cohesion on the staff. It meant that every year, we had to recover ground in professional develop-

ment that had already been covered and try to catch people up to sort of where the school was heading (Darling-Hammond 2002, p. 58).

Most important, teacher attrition consigns a large portion of children in high-turnover schools to a continual parade of relatively ineffective teachers. This signals one of the problems with many contemporary approaches to teacher shortages: approaches that bring people into teaching with little training to fill classrooms quickly contribute to the high attrition that creates shortages in the first place. Unless policies and practices are developed to stem such attrition—through better preparation, mentor support, assignment, and working conditions—the goal of ensuring qualified teachers for all students, especially those targeted by No Child Left Behind, cannot be met.

What Science Leaders Can Do

In all schools, regardless of school wealth, student demographics, or staffing patterns, the most important resource for continuing improvement is the knowledge and skill of the schools' best-prepared and most committed teachers. Science leaders can break the cycle of attrition by addressing four major areas that have been found to influence whether and when teachers leave specific schools or the profession entirely:

- Quality preparation
- Supports, including mentoring, for beginning teachers
- Salaries
- Working conditions, including professional teaching conditions

Ensure High-Quality Preparation for New Teachers

School and district leaders have a responsibility to provide students with qualified teachers to teach them. Seeking out and hiring better-prepared science teachers has many benefits, in both lower attrition and higher levels of competence, which reduce later costs of unnecessary teacher failure as well as unnecessary student failure. Although compensation and incentives have been major concerns of those worried about teacher retention, adequate preparation is at least as important. Once people choose to enter teaching, what appears to matter most to their decision to stay is how well-prepared and supported they are and, consequently, how efficacious they feel.

A growing body of evidence indicates that attrition is unusually high for those who lack initial preparation. A recent National Center for Educational

Statistics (NCES) report found that 29% of new teachers who had not had student teaching experience left within five years, compared to only 15% of those who had had student teaching experience as part of a teacher education program (Henke et al. 2000). This same study found that 49% of uncertified entrants left within five years, compared to only 14% of certified entrants. In California, the state standards board found that 40% of teachers holding an emergency permit leave the profession within a year and two-thirds never receive a credential (Darling-Hammond 2002).

Analyses conducted by Richard Ingersoll (NCTAF 2003) using the national Schools and Staffing Surveys found that beginning teachers who lacked student teaching, who had not had the opportunity to be observed or coached in their teaching, and who lacked training in child psychology or learning theory were at least twice as likely to leave in their first year of teaching as those who had had these elements of preparation. In these studies and others, graduates of preservice teacher education programs felt significantly better prepared and more efficacious than those entering through alternative routes or with no training (Darling-Hammond et al. 2002; NCTAF 2003).

Studies have also found that alternate routes into teaching that offer only a few weeks of training before assumption of full teaching responsibilities produce very high attrition rates, ranging from 46% over three years for the Massachusetts Institutes for New Teachers program (Fowler 2003) to an average of 80% attrition after two years in the classroom for Teach for America recruits in Houston, Texas (Raymond et al. 2001). Similar crash courses in teaching have been failing all around the country. A January 2001 report in the *St. Petersburg Times* reported on the loss of nearly 100 area recruits that year, many of them mid-career alternative certification candidates who lacked education training and were supposed to learn on the job. Microbiologist Bill Gaulman, a 56-year-old African-American former Marine and New York City firefighter, left before midyear; his comments reflected the experiences of many: "The word that comes to mind is 'overwhelmed,'" said Gaulman, "People told me 'Just get through that first year.' I was like, 'I don't know if I can get through this week.' I didn't want to shortchange the kids," Gaulman said. "I didn't want to fake it. I wanted to do it right" (Hegarty 2001). Unfortunately, many programs that underprepare candidates ultimately *disrecruit* them from teaching rather than recruit them into a career.

Better-prepared teachers not only continue their teaching careers longer, but also reduce training costs when attrition rates are taken into account. For example, a longitudinal study of 11 teacher education programs found that those who complete redesigned five-year teacher education programs enter and stay in teaching at much higher rates than four-year teacher education graduates from the same institutions (Andrew and Schwab 1995). These five-year programs allow intensive training for teaching and a year or more of student teaching, as well as a major in a disciplinary field. Similarly, both four- and five-year teacher education graduates enter and stay at higher rates than teachers hired through alternative routes that offer only a few weeks of training before recruits are left on their own in the classroom (Darling-Hammond 2000a). These differences are so large that, taking into account the costs to states, universities, and districts for preparation, recruitment, induction, and replacement due to attrition, the cost of preparing career teachers in more intensive five-year programs is much less than that of preparing a greater number of teachers in short-term programs, who then leave earlier (see Figure 3). Graduates of extended five-year programs also report higher levels of satisfaction with their preparation and receive higher ratings from principals and colleagues.

Figure 3: Disparities in access to qualified math and science teachers, 1998

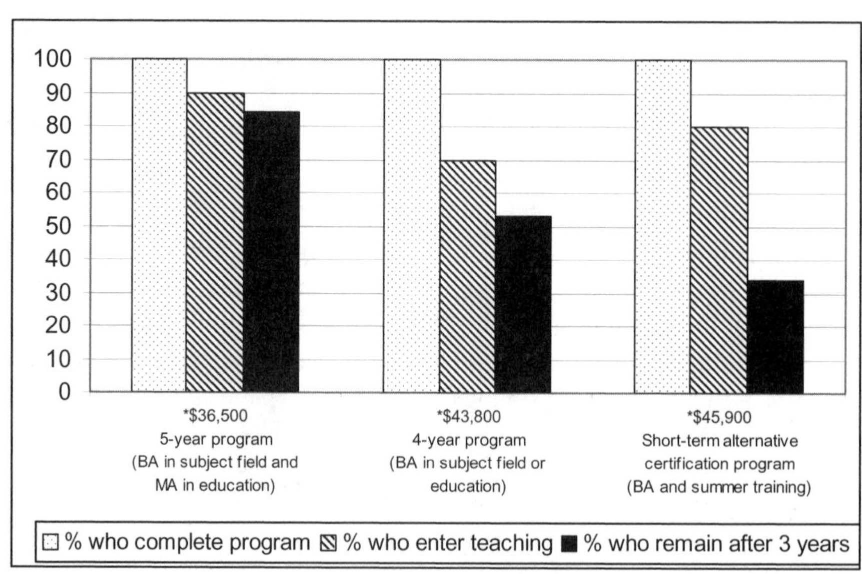

Of course, preparing teachers more comprehensively for teaching, as well as in their content area, also enables them to be more effective. In a study of mathematics and science teachers, Goldhaber and Brewer (2000) concluded that teachers were more effective when they had a content major and when they had full certification in that field, suggesting that what licensed teachers learn in the pedagogical portion of their training adds to what they gain from a strong subject-matter background. When Wenglinsky (2002) studied the mathematics and science achievement of more than 7,000 eighth graders on the 1996 National Assessment of Educational Progress, he found that student achievement was influenced by both teacher content background (such as a major or minor in science or science education) and teacher education in how to work with diverse student populations (including limited-English-proficient students and students with special needs). Measures of teaching practices, which had the strongest effects on achievement, were related to teachers' training: students performed better when teachers provided hands-on learning opportunities and focused on higher-order thinking skills. These practices were, in turn, related to training teachers had received in developing thinking skills, developing laboratory skills, and having students work with real-world problems. The cumulative effect of the combined teacher quality measures, in fact, outweighed the effect of socioeconomic background on student achievement.

Clearly, science teacher educators have a responsibility to prepare teachers adequately for their increasingly complex work in science classrooms. The National Science Teachers Association (NSTA) recommends that elementary and middle school teachers be prepared with course work that represents a balance among life, Earth/space, physical, and environmental sciences, in addition to their pedagogical preparation for teaching science (NSTA 2003). According to a national survey of teachers of science, approximately half of the teachers of grades 1–4 and about two-thirds of the teachers of grades 5–8 teachers meet this requirement (Smith et al. 2002). The preparation of elementary school teachers to teach science continues to challenge teacher education. Of teachers assigned to teach the four major discipline areas in the elementary curriculum, 76% reported feeling very well qualified to teach reading/language arts, approximately 60% reported feeling very well qualified to teach mathematics, and 52% reported feeling very well-qualified to teach social studies, while only 30% reported feeling very well qualified to teach life science (Smith et al. 2002).

Preparing to teach science requires specialized knowledge and skills based in the discipline. With the recent turn toward inquiry-centered teaching in science that is advocated by the National Science Education Standards (NRC 1996), the expectation of many state science frameworks and standards is that students are not only learning factual content in the sciences, but that they also are regularly engaging in the doing of science through empirical investigation. Novice teachers of science must be prepared to organize students for active learning, to manage equipment in laboratory or classroom settings, and to facilitate the activity of the students to support meaningful learning.

Provide Mentoring Support in the Induction Years

When teachers enter the classroom, their professional preparation does not end. In the first years of teaching, they continue to need support from school administrators and colleagues. The commitment effects of strong preparation are enhanced by equally strong induction and mentoring in the first years of teaching. A number of studies have found that well-designed mentoring programs improve retention rates for new teachers and improve their attitudes, feelings of efficacy, and instructional skills (Gold 1996; Huling-Austin 1990).

Districts such as Cincinnati, Columbus, and Toledo, Ohio, and Rochester, New York, have reduced attrition rates of beginning teachers by more than two-thirds, often from levels exceeding 30% to rates of under 5%, by providing expert mentors with release time to coach beginners in their first year on the job (NCTAF 1996). These young teachers not only stay in the profession at higher rates, but become competent more quickly than those who must learn by trial and error. Each program was established through collective bargaining and is governed by a panel of seven to ten teachers and administrators. The governing panel selects consulting teachers through a rigorous evaluation process that examines teaching skills and mentoring abilities.

One reason for the programs' success is the intensive assistance provided by consulting teachers who are freed from responsibilities to focus on this job. A full-time consulting teacher might mentor up to 10 teachers in his or her subject matter area. This ensures that adequate help and documentation will occur over the course of the year. Mentors meet with one another to share what they are learning about mentoring. The value of the advice offered is increased by the high levels of expertise of the consulting teachers, who are selected for teaching excellence and who generally are matched by subject area and grade level with the teacher being helped.

Although the number of state induction programs for beginning teachers has increased from seven in 1996–97 to 33 in 2002, only 22 states fund these programs (NCTAF 2003). At the state level, induction programs that are tied to high-quality preparation can be doubly effective. In Connecticut, for example, common standards guide teacher education and induction for licensing. Cooperating teachers are trained to use the state portfolio assessment system for beginning teachers that their student teachers will encounter when they undertake independent classroom teaching. In this portfolio, science teachers must demonstrate—though lesson plans, videotapes of their teaching, and analyses of student work—how they engage their students in scientific inquiry and how they scaffold students' learning. Districts that hire beginning teachers must provide them with mentors who are trained in the state teaching standards and portfolio assessment system that were introduced as part of reforms during the 1990s. These reforms also raised salaries and standards for teachers, requiring more preparation in content and pedagogy before entry, and created an assessment of teaching for professional licensure modeled after that of the National Board for Professional Teaching Standards (Wilson et al. 2000).

The additional benefit of these programs is a new lease on life for many veteran teachers. Expert veterans need challenges to remain stimulated and excited about staying in the profession. Many say that mentoring and coaching provides an incentive for them to remain in teaching, because they gain by learning from and sharing with other colleagues (Gless and Moir 2001).

Schools and districts should design comprehensive induction and support programs for new teachers to help them build their professional efficacy and learn to navigate the local school and district culture. They should assist new teachers with curriculum development as the teachers become familiar with local resources and expectations for student learning. Britton and Raizen (2003) argue that induction programs for science teachers should attend to early career learning issues of planning for instruction, expanding teaching repertoires, assessing student understanding, working with parents, and promoting a reflective stance toward practice. Based on New Zealand's comprehensive model of induction for science teachers that has been in operation for 25 years, these authors draw the following lessons for induction programs in the United States:

1. Support novices in planning science courses and lessons that are aligned with local, state, or national standards; organize lessons around central ideas or curricular units; tightly link science lessons to central ideas or learning goals; incorporate inquiry into the science classroom; and help them choose the level of detail on which to focus student learning.
2. Support novices in locating or creating instructional resources and in learning methods for inquiry-based teaching.
3. View induction as a multifaceted process that provides a variety of supports to meet the varied needs of the novices and do not place sole responsibility on a single person to provide all of the support and assistance that a new teacher needs.
4. Promote a faculty culture of supporting beginning teachers.
5. Value the role of facilitated peer support through regular gatherings of beginning teachers and skilled facilitators.

In addition to establishing induction programs for new teachers, school and district policies need to support new teachers as they work to establish themselves as teachers of science. Policies on assigning new teachers to less-demanding classes and few course preparations, and policies that limit new teachers' assignment to extracurricular duties, can give new teachers time to focus on developing their teaching practices rather than struggling to stay afloat in their early years in the profession (NCMST 2000).

Improve the Daily Working Conditions of Teachers

Although science teachers overwhelmingly report that they enjoy teaching science (Smith et al. 2002), surveys have long shown that working conditions play a major role in teachers' decisions to move schools or leave the profession. More than 50% of teachers who leave their positions cite job dissatisfaction or pursuing another job as their reasons (Ingersoll 2003). Teachers with greater autonomy, as well as those who feel they have administrative support, appropriate student behavior in class, and control over classroom procedures report high levels of job satisfaction (Perie et al.

1997). These factors generally have stronger relationships to teacher satisfaction than do salaries and benefits.

High school science teachers have the lowest reported job satisfaction among all teachers (Perie et al. 1997). Further, teachers in high-poverty schools are more than twice as likely to leave because of dissatisfaction than those in low-poverty schools (Darling-Hammond 1997). There are large differences in the support teachers receive from high- versus low-wealth schools. Teachers in more-advantaged communities experience easier working conditions, including better access to materials and supplies, smaller class sizes and pupil loads, and greater influence over school decisions (NCES 1997).

In many cases, teachers' satisfaction with their working conditions is tied to having the appropriate resources in order to perform the work competently. Teaching science in a way that is aligned with the National Science Education Standards and many local science frameworks requires access to science equipment, adequate consumable resources, and a teaching space that is conducive to scientific investigation (flat surfaces and a water source at the minimum). In a survey of teachers in Washington, D.C., and Chicago, nearly 60% reported that the science labs in their schools were somewhat or very inadequate, or that they did not have lab space at all. Additionally, close to 50% of Chicago teachers and more than 30% of Washington teachers had insufficient electrical outlets in their classrooms (Schneider 2003). Providing the basic resources, facilities, and teaching materials that a science teacher needs to teach effectively is not only a matter of improving working conditions for teachers but is also a matter of providing access to high-quality science instruction for the students.

In addition to poor physical working conditions, teachers have long suffered from low professional status that results in lower salaries than other professionals, limited input on policy, tight control over the daily work in their classrooms and schools, and lack of support for professional learning and practice. Leaders cannot completely transform the conditions of teaching, but they can provide more opportunities for teachers to take on leadership responsibilities, greater respect for teacher input into policy decisions, and more support for professionally competent teaching.

One critical area, especially for science teachers, is being assigned to teach courses outside of a teachers' area of preparation. A survey conducted by NSTA (2000) reported that more than 20% of science teachers had been assigned to teach out-of-field in the previous three years, with 25% of those teachers reporting they had been assigned to teach a course in which they had no prior college course work or preparation. With qualified science teachers in short supply in some geographic areas, it is understandable how a school administrator may choose to assign a teacher to fill a position for purposes of efficiency. Science teachers, however, have prepared themselves in particular scientific disciplines. Being assigned by a superior to teach outside one's area of preparation is not only professionally challenging, but is also disempowering to the professional. Inviting and enabling teachers to be part of the decision-making processes in schools and districts, on the other hand, can lead to stronger commitment from teachers to the school and to greater ongoing improvement.

Finally, an important aspect of working conditions for teachers is access to their colleagues on a regular basis. Only 27% of high school science teachers report they have time during the regular school week to work with their colleagues on science curriculum and teaching. Even more rare is the opportunity for teachers to observe each other teaching classes (Smith et al. 2002). School structures and teachers' time needs to be reconfigured to allow for regular professional dialogue, sharing of ideas and resources, and collaborative curriculum planning. (For examples, of how this can be done, see Darling-Hammond 1997; NCTAF 1996).

Make Salaries Competitive

Although salaries are not the major factor influencing retention in teaching, compensation does affect who enters and who stays in teaching. Even though teachers may be more altruistically motivated than some other professionals, teaching must compete for talented college and university graduates each year. To attract its share of the nation's college-educated talent and to offer sufficient incentives for professional preparation, the teaching occupation must be competitive in terms of wages and working conditions. From this viewpoint, there is reason for concern because teacher salaries are relatively low and, as we noted earlier, have been declining in relation to other professional salaries throughout the 1990s (see Figure 1). Even after adjusting for the shorter work year in teaching, teachers earn 15% to 40% less than individuals with college degrees who enter other fields. Teachers with a baccalaureate degree in science or mathematics could earn twice as much salary in private industry (Bradley 2000).

Teachers are more likely to quit when they work in districts with lower wages and when their salaries are low relative to alternative wage opportunities, especially for teachers in high demand fields like science and math (Brewer, 1996; Hansen et al. 2004; Mont and Rees 1996; Murnane et al. 1989; Murnane and Olsen 1990; Theobald 1990; Theobald and Gritz 1996). Salary differences seem to matter more at the start of the teaching career (Gritz and Theobald 1996; Hanushek et al. 1999). Nationally, teachers in schools serving the largest concentrations of low-income students earn salaries, at the top of the local pay scale, that are one-third less than those in higher income schools (NCES 1997), while they also face fewer resources, poorer working conditions, and the stresses of working with students and families who have a wide range of needs. The challenge of distributing qualified teachers to all students requires attention to these disparities, a challenge that some states have taken up successfully with subsidies for preparing science teachers, more equalized salaries, and greater investments in high-needs districts (Darling-Hammond 1997).

Closing Remarks

As a number of studies have found, there is a magnetic effect when school systems make it clear they are committed to finding, keeping, and supporting good teachers as a primary focus of school and district management. In urban centers, just as in suburban and rural districts, good teachers gravitate to places where they know they will be appreciated. They are sustained by other good teachers who become their colleagues, and, together, these teachers become a magnet for still others who are attracted to environments where they can learn from their colleagues and create success for their students. When the high costs of attrition are calculated, many of the strategic investments needed to support competent teachers in staying, such as mentoring for beginners and ongoing learning and leadership challenges for veterans, pay for themselves in large degree. These initiatives require the collective effort of science leaders including teachers, teacher-educators, professional developers, and administrators at the school, district, and state levels. The results of such initiatives have demonstrated that great school leaders can create great school environments for accomplished science teaching to flourish and grow.

[1] Ingersoll (2003) extrapolates from cross-sectional data on teacher attrition (from the 1999–2000 Schools and Staffing Surveys) to develop a five-year attrition rate for beginning teachers of 46%; this figure includes private school teachers who have much higher rates of attrition than do public school teachers. He calculates a five-year attrition rate of about 38% for public school teachers. This approach underestimates survival rates because it does not take into account the return to teaching of individuals who left teaching for a year or two for childrearing or further study and re-entered during the first five years—a proportion that, other estimates suggest, could be about 20% of leavers. With this adjustment, the five-year cumulative attrition rate would be just over 30% for public school teachers. Another estimate, using longitudinal data from the 1993-94 Baccalaureate and Beyond surveys, finds a four-year attrition rate of about 20% for teachers who entered teaching directly after college (Henke et al. 2000).

Linda Darling-Hammond

is Charles E. Ducommun Professor of Education at Stanford University, where she is also co-director of the Stanford Educational Leadership Institute and the School Redesign Network. Her research, teaching, and policy work focus on teacher quality, school restructuring, educational policy, and educational equity. She is author of The Right to Learn, *as well as 10 other books and more than 200 journal articles, book chapters, and monographs.*

Mistilina Sato

is an Assistant Professor of Teacher Development and Science Education at the University of Minnesota. As a graduate student and post-doctoral fellow at Stanford University, her research and professional development work with teachers focused on teacher leadership, National Board Certification for teachers, performance assessment for beginning teachers, formative assessment in science classrooms, and elementary science education reform.

References

Andrew, M., and R. L. Schwab. 1995. Has reform in teacher education influenced teacher performance? An outcome assessment of graduates of eleven teacher education programs. *Action in Teacher Education* 17 (3): 43–53.

Bradley, A. 2000. High tech fields luring teachers from education. *Education Week* January 19.

Brewer, D. J. 1996. Career paths and quit decisions: Evidence from teaching. *Journal of Labor Economics* 14 (2): 313–339.

Britton, E., and S. Raizen. 2003. Comprehensive teacher induction in five countries:

Implications for supporting U.S. science teachers. In *Science teacher retention: Mentoring and renewal,* eds J. Rhoton and P. Bowers. Arlington, VA: National Science Education Leadership Association and NSTA Press.

Bureau of Labor Statistics. 2004. *Occupational outlook handbook,* 2004–05 ed. Accessed December 3, 2004, at *http://stats.bls.gov/oco/.*

Carroll, S., R. Reichardt, and C. Guarino. 2000. *The distribution of teachers among California's school districts and schools.* Santa Monica, CA: Rand.

Center for the Future of Teaching and Learning. 2003. Teaching and California's future: The status of the teaching profession 2003 research findings and policy recommendations. Accessed December 3, 2004, at *www.cftl.org/documents/2003fullreportdec10.pdf*.

Darling-Hammond, L. 1997. *Doing what matters most: Investing in quality teaching.* New York: National Commission on Teaching and America's Future.

Darling-Hammond, L. 2000a. *Solving the dilemmas of teacher, supply, demand, and quality.* New York: National Commission on Teaching and America's Future.

Darling-Hammond, L. 2000b. Teacher quality and student achievement: A review of state policy evidence. *Educational Policy Analysis Archives* 8 (1). Accessed December 3, 2004, at *http//:epaa.asu.edu/epaa/v8n1/.*

Darling-Hammond, L. 2002. *Access to quality teaching: An analysis of inequality in California's public schools.* Los Angeles: University of California, Los Angeles, Institute for Democracy, Education, and Access. Accessed December 3, 2004, at *http://repositories.cdlib.org/idea/wws/wws-rr002-1002.*

Darling-Hammond, L., R. Chung, and F. Frelow. 2002. Variation in teacher preparation: How well do different pathways prepare teachers to teach? *Journal of Teacher Education* 53 (4): 286–302.

Darling-Hammond, L., and G. Sykes. 2003. Wanted: A national teacher supply policy for education: The right way to meet the "Highly Qualified Teacher" challenge. *Education Policy Analysis Archives* 11 (33). Accessed December 3, 2004, at *http://epaa.asu.edu/epaa/v11n33/.*

Ferguson, R. F. 1991. Paying for public education: New evidence on how and why money matters. *Harvard Journal of Legislation* 28 (2): 465–98.

Fetler, M. 1999. High school staff characteristics and mathematics test results. *Education Policy Analysis Archives* 7 (9). Accessed December 3, 2004, at *http://epaa.asu.edu/epaa/v7n9.html.*

Fowler, R.C. 2003. The Massachusetts signing bonus program for new teachers: A model of teacher preparation worth copying? *Education Policy Analysis Archives* 11 (13). Accessed December 3, 2004, at *http://epaa.asu.edu/epaa/v11n13/.*

Fuller, E. 1998. *Do properly certified teachers matter? A comparison of elementary school performance on the TAAS in 1997 between schools with high and low percentages of properly certified regular education teachers.* Austin, TX: University of Texas at Austin, The Charles A. Dana Center.

Gless, J., and E. Moir. 2001. Teacher quality squared. *Journal of Staff Development* (22) 1. Accessed December 3, 2004, at *www.newteachercenter.org/article-teacherqualitysq.html.*

Goe, L. 2002. Legislating equity: The distribution of emergency permit teachers in California. *Educational Policy Analysis Archives* 10 (42). Accessed December 3, 2004, at *http://epaa.asu.edu/epaa/v10n42.*

Gold, Y. 1996. Beginning teacher support: Attrition, mentoring, and induction. In *The handbook of research on teacher education.* 2nd ed., eds. J. Sikula, T. J. Buttery, and E. Guyton. New York: MacMillan.

Goldhaber, D. D., and D. J. Brewer. 2000. Does teacher certification matter? High school certification status and student achievement. *Educational Evaluation and Policy Analysis* 22 (2): 129–45.

Gritz, R. M., and N. D. Theobald. 1996. The effects of school district spending priorities on length of stay in teaching. *Journal of Human Resources* 31 (3): 477—512.

Hansen, M. L., D. S. Lien, L. C. Cavalluzzo, and J. W. Wenger. 2004. *Relative pay and teacher retention: An empirical analysis in a large urban district.* Accessed December 3, 2004, at *www.cna.org/documents/IPR11020.1.pdf.*

Hanushek, E. A., J. F. Kain, and S. G. Rivkin. 1999. *Do higher salaries buy better teachers?* (Working Paper 7082). Cambridge, MA: National Bureau of Economic Research.

Hegarty, S. 2001. Newcomers find toll of teaching is too high: Among those quitting are non-education majors thrust into challenging classrooms. *St. Petersburg Times,* January 21.

Henke, R., X. Chen, and S. Geis. 2000. *Progress through the teacher pipeline: 1992—93 college graduates and elementary/secondary school teaching as of 1997.* Washington, DC: National Center for Education Statistics.

Huling-Austin, L. 1990. Teacher induction programs and internships. In *The handbook of research on teacher education,* ed. W. R. Houston. New York: MacMillan.

Ingersoll, R. M. 2001. Teacher turnover and teacher shortages: An organizational analysis. *American Educational Research Journal* 38 (3): 499—534.

Ingersoll, R. M. 2003. Turnover and shortages among math and science teachers in the U.S. In *Science teacher retention: Mentoring and renewal.* J. Rhoton and P. Bowers, eds. Arlington, VA: National Science Education Leadership Association and NSTA Press.

Kain, J. F., and K. Singleton. 1996. Equality of educational opportunity revisited. *New England Economic Review,* (May/June): 87—111.

Monk, D. 1994. Subject area preparation of secondary mathematics and science teachers and student achievement. *Economics of Education Review* 12 (2): 125–42.

Mont, D., and D. I. Rees. 1996. The influence of classroom characteristics on high school teacher turnover. *Economic Inquiry* 34: 152–67.

Murnane, R. J., and R. J. Olsen. 1990. The effects of salaries and opportunity costs on length of stay in teaching: Evidence from North Carolina. *The Journal of Human Resources* 25 (1): 106–24.

Murnane, R. J., J. D. Singer, and J. B. Willett. 1989. The influences of salaries and opportunity costs on teachers' career choices: Evidence from North Carolina. *Harvard Educational Review* 59 (3): 325–46.

National Center for Education Statistics (NCES). 1997. *America's teachers: Profile of a profession, 1993–94.* Washington, DC: U.S. Department of Education.

National Commission on Math and Science Teaching for the 21st Century (NCMST). 2000. *Before it's too late.* Washington, DC: U.S. Department of Education.

National Commission on Teaching and America's Future (NCTAF). 1996. *What matters most: Teaching for America's future.* New York: Author.

National Commission on Teaching and America's Future (NCTAF). 2003. *No dream denied.* New York: Author.

National Research Council (NRC). 1996. *National Science Education Standards.* Washington, DC: National Academy Press.

National Science Teachers Association (NSTA). 2000. NSTA survey: Science teacher credentials, assignments, and job satisfaction. Accessed December 3, 2004, at *www.nsta.org/about/survey2000data.html.*

National Science Teachers Association. 2003. *Standards for science teacher preparation.* Arlington, VA: Author.

No Child Left Behind Act (NCLB) of 2001. 2002. Public Law 107-110-January 8, 2002. 107th Congress. Washington, DC.

Perie, M., D. P. Baker, and S. Whitener. 1997. *Job satisfaction among America's teachers: Effects of workplace conditions, background characteristics, and teacher compensation* (Statistical Analysis Report July 1997). Washington, DC: National Center for Educational Statistics.

Raymond, M., S. Fletcher, and J. Luque. 2001. *Teach for America: An evaluation of teacher differences and student outcomes in Houston, Texas.* Stanford, CA: Center for Research on Educational Outcomes, The Hoover Institution, Stanford University. Accessed December 3, 2004, at *http://credo.stanford.edu/downloads/tfa.pdf.*

Schneider, M. 2003. Linking school facility conditions to teacher satisfaction and success. Washington, DC: National Clearinghouse for Educational Facilities. Accessed December 3, 2004, at *www.edfacilities.org/pubs/teachersurvey.pdf.*

Smith, P. S., E. R. Banilower, K. C. McMahon, and I. Weiss. 2002. *A national survey of trends in science and mathematics education: Trends from 1977 to 2000.* Chapel Hill, NC:

Horizon Research, Inc.

Texas Center for Educational Research. 2000. *The cost of teacher turnover.* Austin, TX: Texas State Board for Teacher Certification.

Theobald, N. D. 1990. An examination of the influences of personal, professional, and school district characteristics on public school teacher retention. *Economics of Education Review* 9 (3): 241–50.

Theobald, N. D., and R. M. Gritz. 1996. The effects of school district spending priorities on the exit paths of beginning teachers leaving the district. *Economics of Education Review* 15 (1): 11– 22.

Wenglinsky, H. 2002. How schools matter: The link between teacher classroom practices and student academic performance. *Education Policy Analysis Archives* 10 (12). Accessed December 3, 2004, at *http://epaa.asu.edu/epaa/v10n12/.*

Wilson, S., L. Darling-Hammond, and B. Berry. 2000. *A case of successful teaching policy: Connecticut's long-term efforts to improve teaching and learning.* Seattle, WA: University of Washington, Center for the Study of Teaching and Policy.

Wilson, S., R. Floden, and J. Ferrini-Mundy. 2001. *Teacher preparation research: Current knowledge, gaps, and recommendations.* Seattle, WA: University of Washington, Center for the Study of Teaching and Policy.

CHAPTER 13

Understanding Supply and Demand Among Mathematics and Science Teachers[1]

Richard M. Ingersoll

Few educational problems have received more attention in recent years than the failure to ensure that elementary and secondary classrooms are staffed with qualified teachers. Severe teacher shortages, education researchers and policy makers have told us, are confronting our elementary and secondary schools. At the root of these problems, we are told, is a dramatic increase in the demand for new teachers resulting primarily from two converging demographic trends—increasing student enrollments and increasing teacher turnover due to a graying teaching force. Shortfalls of teachers, the argument continues, are forcing many school systems to resort to lowering standards to fill teaching openings, inevitably resulting in high levels of underqualified teachers and lower school performance (NCEE 1983; NAS 1987; NCTAF 1997).

These researchers and policy analysts have also stressed that shortages will affect some teaching fields more than others. Special education, mathematics, and science, in particular, have usually been targeted as fields with especially high turnover and those predicted most likely to suffer shortages (Murnane et al. 1991; Boe et al. 1997; Grissmer and Kirby 1992, 1997; Weiss and Boyd 1990). As a result, over the past decade, the inability of schools to adequately staff classrooms with qualified teachers (hereafter, school staffing problems) has increasingly been recognized as a major social problem, has received widespread coverage in the national media, and has been the target of a growing number of reform and policy initiatives.

The prevailing policy response to these school staffing problems has been to attempt to increase the quantity of teacher supply. In recent years a wide range of initiatives have been implemented to recruit new candidates into teaching. Among these are career-change programs, such as troops-to-teachers, designed to entice professionals into midcareer switches to teaching and Peace Corps-like programs, such as Teach for America, designed to lure the best and brightest into understaffed schools. Many states have instituted alternative certification programs, whereby college graduates can postpone formal education training and begin teaching immediately. Financial incentives, such as signing bonuses, student loan forgiveness, housing assistance, and tuition reimbursement have all been instituted to aid recruitment (for a review of these initiatives, see Hirsch et al. 2001). The federal No Child Left Behind Act of 2001 (2002) provides extensive funding for such initiatives.

Concern over school staffing problems has also given impetus to empirical research on teacher shortages and turnover. However, as numerous analysts have noted, it was difficult, initially, to study these issues because of a lack of accurate data, especially at a nationally representative level, on many of the pertinent issues surrounding teacher supply, demand, and quality. In order to obtain such data, the National Center for Education Statistics (NCES), the statistical arm of the U.S. Department of Education, designed the Schools and Staffing Survey (SASS) and its supplement, the Teacher Follow-up Survey (TFS), in the late 1980s.

The Project

Over the past decade and a half I have been undertaking research using SASS and TFS to study a number of issues concerned with teacher supply, demand, and quality (for summaries, see Ingersoll 1999, 2001, 2003a). In this chapter I will briefly summarize what the data tell us about the realities of school staffing problems and teacher shortages, especially for mathematics and science teachers. I will argue that the conventional wisdom on teacher shortages is largely a case of a wrong diagnosis and a wrong prescription and that while the above policy efforts are often worthwhile, the data show they will not solve the teacher staffing problems schools are facing.

SASS and TFS are the largest and most comprehensive data source available on the staffing, occupational, and organizational aspects of schools. SASS administers survey questionnaires to a random sample of about 50,000 teachers from all types of schools and from all 50 states. NCES has administered SASS on a regular basis; to date, four cycles have been completed—1987–88, 1990–91, 1993–94, and 1999–2000. In addition, all those teachers who leave their teaching jobs in the year subsequent to the administration of the initial survey questionnaire are again contacted to obtain information on their departures. This supplemental study—the TFS—is the largest and most comprehensive data source on teacher turnover in the U.S. (For information on the TFS see Chandler et al. 2004.)

The data presented here come primarily from the two most recent cycles of the TFS (1994–95 and 2000–01) and represent all teachers for grades K–12 and from all types of schools, both public and private. Mathematics and science teachers, the primary focus of this chapter, are those identified by their principals as having their main teaching assignment in either mathematics or science. They represent about 11 percent of the total teaching force. About 22 percent of these mathematics and science teachers are employed in elementary or middle schools, another 73 percent are in secondary schools, and about 5 percent are in combined (K–12 grades) schools. Throughout, I will compare the data on mathematics/science teachers with the data for all teachers.

Schools have two types of teacher turnover. The first, often called teacher attrition, refers to those who leave the occupation of teaching altogether. The second type, often called teacher migration, refers to those who transfer or move to different teaching jobs in other schools. Research on teacher supply and demand has often emphasized the first type and neglected the second. Many assume that teacher migration is a less significant form of turnover because it does not increase or decrease the overall supply of teachers, as do retirements and career changes, and, hence, assume it does not contribute to the problem of staffing schools and does not contribute to overall shortages. From a systemic point of view, this is probably correct. However, from the viewpoint of those managing schools, teacher migration and attrition have the same effect—in either case they result in a decrease in staff that usually must be replaced. Hence, from the school's perspective, teacher migration can, indeed, contribute to the problem of keeping schools staffed with qualified teachers. For this reason, this chapter will present data on both teacher migration and teacher attrition. Hereafter, I will refer to teacher migration as *movers*, teacher attrition as *leavers* and total turnover as *departures*.

In the next section I will present data on how many teachers depart from their teaching jobs and establish the importance of teacher turnover for teacher shortages. In the following section I will present statistics on why teachers move from or leave their teaching jobs. These latter data are drawn from items in the TFS questionnaire that asks teachers to indicate from a list provided in the survey questionnaire the most important reasons for their migration or attrition (see appendix). Next, I present the results from a set of questionnaire items that asks those mathematics and science teachers who had departed to suggest things schools could do to encourage teachers to remain in teaching. Then I present data on what difference induction programs make in reducing beginning-teacher turnover. Finally, I conclude by briefly discussing the implications of these findings for understanding and addressing the staffing problems of schools.

Results: The Importance of Teacher Turnover

Consistent with shortage predictions, the data show that the demand for teachers has indeed increased. Since 1984, student enrollments have increased, teacher retirements have also increased, most schools have had job openings for teachers, and the size of the elementary and secondary teaching workforce has increased. More important, the SASS data tell us substantial numbers of those schools with teaching openings have experienced difficulties finding qualified candidates to fill their positions. Overall, the data show that for the 1999–2000 school year, 58 percent of all schools reported at least some difficulty filling one or more teaching job openings, in one or more fields. Forty-two percent of secondary schools indicated they had at least some difficulty filling their mathematics openings (see Figure 1).

But the data also show that the demand for new teachers and subsequent staffing difficulties are not primarily due to student enrollment and teacher retirement increases. Most of the demand and hiring is simply to replace those who recently departed from their teaching jobs and, moreover, most of this teacher turnover has little to do with a graying workforce.

Teaching is a relatively large occupation—it represents 4% of the nationwide civilian workforce. There are, for example, more than twice as

Figure 1: Percent secondary schools with difficulties filling their teaching vacancies, by field

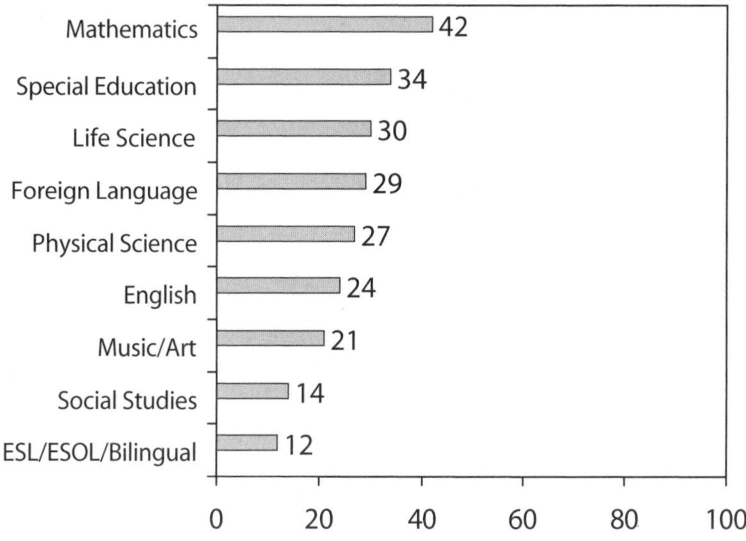

Source: 1999–2000 Schools and Staffing Survey

many K–12 teachers as registered nurses and five times as many teachers as either lawyers or professors (U.S. Bureau of the Census 1998). The TFS data show that teaching has a relatively stable turnover rate: 14.5 percent in 1988–89, 13.2 percent in 1991–92, 14.3 percent in 1994–95, and 15.7 percent in 2000–01. Moreover, total teacher turnover is about evenly split between movers and leavers.

This rate of turnover and the sheer size of the teaching force means that there are large flows in, through, and out of schools each year. For instance, the SASS/TFS data show that about 535,000 teachers (including within-district school-to-school transfers) entered schools just prior to the 1999–2000 school year. But, in the following 12 months even more—about 546,000 teachers—departed their jobs. In other words, in that 12-month period over a million teachers—almost one third of the teaching force—were in job transition. The image that these data suggest is one of a revolving door (see Figure 2).

Figure 2: Numbers of teachers in transition during the 1999-2000 school year

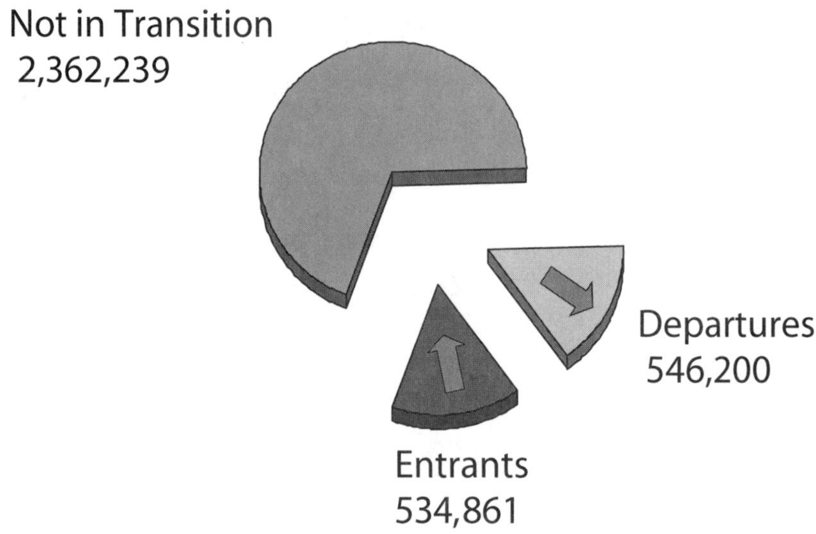

Source: 1999–2000 Schools and Staffing Survey

Of course, not all teacher or employee turnover is detrimental. There is an extensive research literature on employee turnover conducted by those who study organizations and occupations in general (e.g., Price 1977; Mobley 1982). On the one hand, researchers in this tradition have long held that a low level of employee turnover is normal and efficacious in a well-managed organization. Too little turnover of employees is tied to stagnancy in organizations; effective organizations usually both promote and benefit from a limited degree of turnover by eliminating low-caliber performers and bringing in new blood to facilitate innovation. On the other hand, researchers in this tradition have also long held that high levels of employee turnover are both cause and effect of performance problems in organizations (Price 1989).

From this organizational perspective, employee turnover is especially consequential in work sites, like schools, that have production processes requiring extensive interaction among participants (Lortie 1975; Ingersoll 2003b). Such organizations are unusually dependent upon commitment, continuity, and cohesion among employees and, hence, especially vulnerable to employee turnover. From this perspective, high turnover of teachers from schools is of concern not simply because it may be an indicator of sites of potential staffing problems, but because of its relationship to school performance. Moreover, from this perspective, high rates of teacher turnover are of concern not only because they may be an indication of underlying problems in how well a school functions, but also because they can be disruptive, in and of themselves, to the quality of school cohesion and performance.

Although the data show that teaching has relatively high turnover, the data also show that the revolving door varies greatly among different kinds of teachers. Notably, the turnover rate for mathematics/science teachers is higher than for teachers in some other fields (see Figure 3). Moreover, as found in previous research (Murnane et al. 1991), the TFS data show that teaching is an occupation that loses many of its newly trained members very early in their careers—long before the retirement years. I used the TFS data to provide a rough estimate of the cumulative attrition of beginning teachers from the occupation in their first several years of teaching. The data suggest that after just five years, between 40 and 50 percent of all beginning teachers have left teaching altogether.

Figure 3: Percent annual teacher turnover, by field

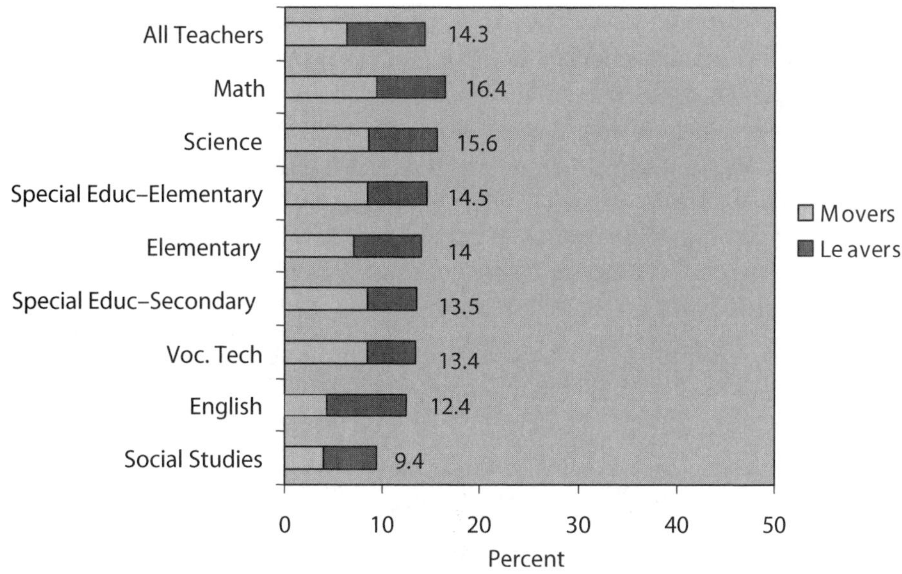

Source: 1994–1995 Schools and Staffing Survey

In short, the demand for new teachers, and the subsequent problems schools face are, to a significant extent, due to teachers moving from or leaving their jobs at higher rates than in many other occupations. These patterns are chronic—similar results are found in all four cycles of the TFS data from the late 1980s to 2001.

These data raise an important question: Why do these teachers depart their jobs?

Results: The Sources of Teacher Turnover

This next section turns to the reasons behind teacher turnover, especially among mathematics and science teachers. Figure 4 presents data on the percentage of teachers who reported particular categories of reasons were important for their departures, separately for all teachers and for mathematics/science teachers. As illustrated in Figure 4, overall, mathematics/science teachers do not greatly differ from other teachers in the reasons why they move from or leave their jobs. Contrary to conventional wisdom, retirement is not an especially prominent factor. It accounts for only a moderate part of total turnover. Notably, retirement also does not account for the relatively high rates of turnover by mathematics/science teachers.

School staffing cutbacks, due to layoffs, school closings and reorganizations, account for an even smaller proportion of turnover than does retirement. Staffing actions more often result in migration to other teaching jobs rather than departure from the teaching occupation altogether.

Personal reasons, such as departures for pregnancy, child rearing, health problems and family moves are far more often given as reasons for turnover than are either retirement or staffing actions (38 percent for all teachers and 44 percent for mathematics/science).

Finally, two related reasons are, together, a very prominent source of turnover. More than half of all teachers who left their jobs give as an important reason either job dissatisfaction or the desire to pursue another job, in or out of education. I have found these findings to be true across different cycles of the data. Moreover, I have found similar factors lie behind both teacher migration and teacher attrition.

What are the sources of this dissatisfaction that lead to turnover and what can schools do to address them? Teachers themselves have offered some ideas. The 1994–95 TFS asked teachers who had moved from or

Figure 4: Percent teachers reporting various reasons were important for their turnover, by field

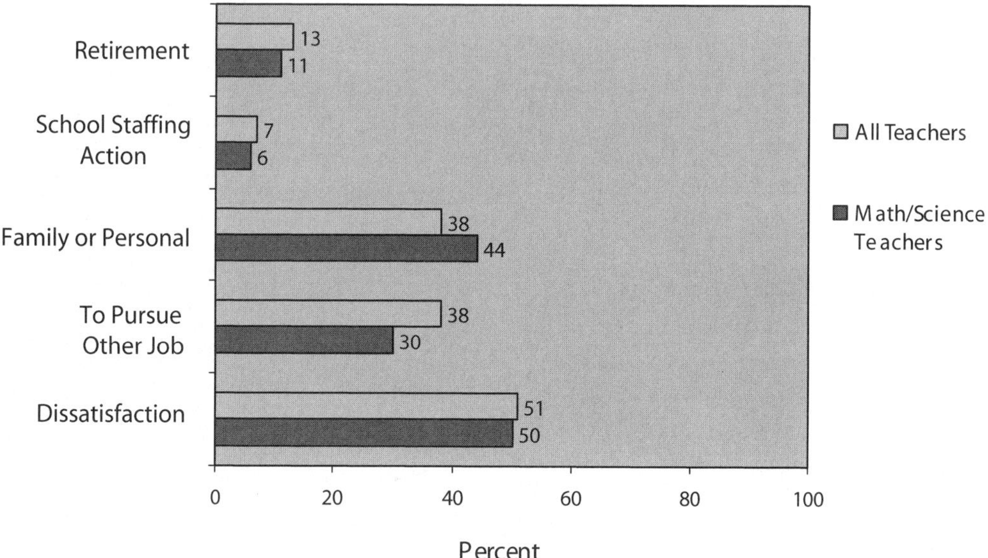

Source: 2000–2001 Teacher Follow-up Survey

left their teaching jobs since the prior year to suggest possible steps schools might take to encourage teachers to remain in teaching. The responses for mathematics/science teachers are summarized in Figure 5.

One strategy suggested by departed teachers to aid retention is increasing salaries, which are, not surprisingly, strongly linked to teacher turnover rates. But salaries are not the only issue, which is important from a policy perspective because increasing overall salaries is expensive, given the sheer size of the occupation.

Reduction of student discipline problems is a second factor frequently suggested by departed teachers. Multivariate analysis of the data also documents that this factor is strongly tied to the rates of teacher turnover. Again, not surprisingly, schools with more student misbehavior problems have more teacher turnover (Ingersoll 2001). But, the data also tell us that, regardless of the background and poverty levels of the student population, schools vary dramatically in their degree of student misbehavior.

Figure 5: Of those math/science teachers who moved from or left their jobs, percent giving various steps schools might take to encourage teachers to remain in teaching

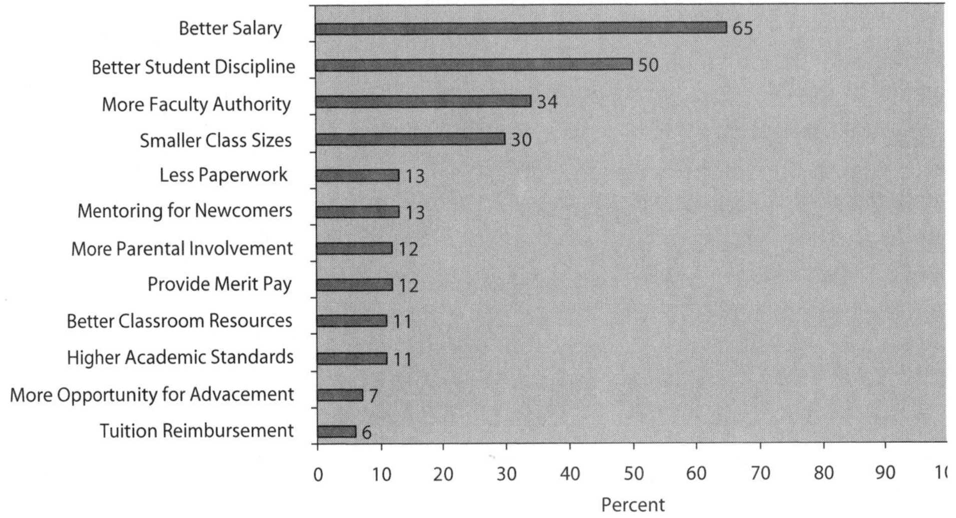

Source: 1994–1995 Teacher Follow-up Survey

One of the factors tied to both student discipline and teacher turnover is how much decision-making influence teachers themselves have over school policies that affect their jobs, especially those concerned with student behavioral rules and sanctions. In a separate multivariate analysis of data from SASS, I have found that, on average, teachers have little say in many of the key decisions that affect their work; but schools where teachers are allowed more input into issues, student discipline in particular, have less conflict between staff and students and less teacher turnover (Ingersoll 2003b). Increasing teacher decision-making power and authority is also, not surprisingly, suggested by teachers as a step to aid retention. Class-size reduction was also frequently suggested by teachers as a step to increase retention. Surprising in Figure 5 is how few teachers suggested increasing support, such as mentoring, for new teachers as one of the main steps necessary for retention.

In a separate multivariate analysis of the 1999–2000 SASS data, we explored the impact of induction supports on the turnover of new teachers. After controlling for the background characteristics of teachers and schools, we found a strong link between participation by beginning teachers in various induction activities and their likelihood of moving or leaving after their first year on the job (Smith and Ingersoll 2004). The data showed that the predicted probability of turnover of first-year, newly hired, inexperienced teachers who did not participate in any induction activities was 41 percent (see Figure 6). In contrast, after controlling for the background characteristics of teachers and schools, the turnover probability was 27 percent for beginning teachers who received what we labeled as some induction (had a mentor from their same field; had regularly scheduled collaboration or common planning time with other teachers in their subject area; had face time with the administration; and participated in beginners' seminars). Twenty-six percent of beginning teachers received just these four components. Finally, a very small number (fewer than 1 percent of beginning teachers in 1999-00) experienced what we labeled as a *full* induction experience that included the above four components, plus three more: participated in an external network, had a reduced number of course preparations, and had a teacher aide. Participation in these activities had a very large and statistically significant impact—the probability of a departure at the end of their first year for those getting this package was less than half of that for those who participated in no induction activities.

Implications

Since the early 1980s, educational policy analysts have predicted that shortfalls of teachers resulting primarily from two converging demographic trends—increasing student enrollments and increasing teacher retirements—will lead to problems staffing schools with qualified teachers and, in turn, lower educational performance.

This analysis suggests, however, that school staffing problems for both mathematics/science and other teachers are not solely or even primarily due to teacher shortfalls resulting from either increases in student enrollment or increases in teacher retirement. In contrast, the data suggest that school staffing problems are also a result of a revolving door—through which large numbers of teachers depart teaching for reasons other than retirement.

Teacher turnover is a significant phenomenon and a dominant factor driving demand for new teachers. The data show that, while it is true that student enrollments are increasing, the demand for new teachers is primarily

Figure 6: Percent turnover after first year of beginning teachers, according to amount of induction support they received

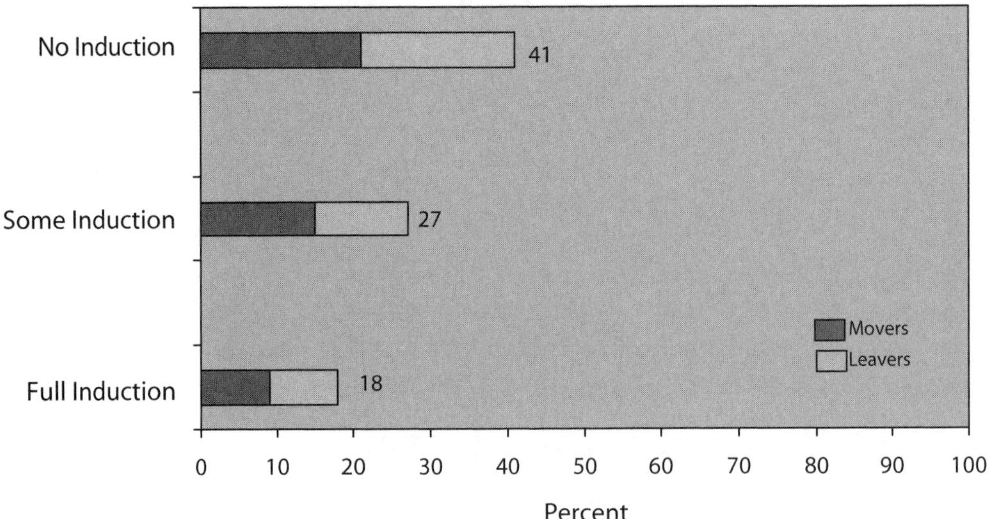

Source: 2000–2001 Teacher Follow-up Survey

due to teachers moving from or leaving their jobs at relatively high rates. Moreover, this analysis shows that, while it is true that teacher retirements are increasing, the overall amount of turnover accounted for by retirement is relatively minor when compared to that resulting from other causes, such as job dissatisfaction and seeking better jobs or other careers.

These findings have important implications for educational policy. Supply and demand theory holds that where the quantity of teachers demanded is greater than the quantity of teachers supplied, there are two basic policy remedies: increase the quantity supplied or decrease the quantity demanded. As noted in the beginning of this chapter, teacher recruitment, an example of the former approach, has been and continues to be a dominant approach to addressing school staffing inadequacies. This analysis suggests, however, that recruitment programs alone will not solve the staffing problems of schools if they do not also address the problem of teacher retention. In short, this analysis suggests that recruiting more teachers will not solve staffing inadequacies if large numbers of such teachers then prematurely leave.

What then can be done? From the perspective of this analysis, schools are not simply victims of inexorable demographic trends, and there is a significant role for the management of schools in both the genesis of and solution to school staffing problems. Rather than increase the quantity of teacher supply, an alternative solution to school staffing problems, documented by this analysis, is to decrease the demand for new teachers by decreasing turnover. The data suggest that the way to improve teacher retention is to improve the conditions of the teaching job. Schools across the country where there is more support from the school administration for new teachers, such as induction and mentoring programs have significantly lower levels of teacher turnover. The same holds for schools with higher salaries, fewer student discipline problems, and enhanced faculty input into school decision-making. The data document that changing these things would all contribute to lower rates of turnover, in turn, diminish school staffing problems and, hence, ultimately, aid the performance of schools.

[1]This chapter draws from an article that appeared in *Science Educator* in Spring 2003.

Appendix

Definitions of Measures of Reasons for Turnover

From a list of 17 reasons, the TFS teachers indicated the level of importance of each in their decision to move from their previous year's school or to leave teaching altogether. I grouped the 17 reasons into 5 categories, as follows:

- **Retirement.**
- **School Staffing Action**: reduction-in-force/lay-off/involuntary transfer.
- **Family or Personal**: change of residence; pregnancy/child rearing; health; other family or personal reason; take sabbatical.
- **To Pursue Other Job**: teach in another state, but certificate not accepted there; to pursue another career; to take courses to improve career opportunities within or outside the field of education; felt job security higher at another school; opportunity for better teaching assignment at another school.
- **Dissatisfaction:** dissatisfied with job; for better salary or benefits; school received little support from community; not agree with, or not feel prepared to implement, new reforms; dissatisfied with workplace conditions; lack of support from administration; lack of autonomy; lack of opportunities for professional development.

Richard M. Ingersoll
a former high school teacher, is a professor of education and sociology at the University of Pennsylvania. His research looks at elementary and secondary schools as workplaces, teachers as employees, and teaching as a job. He is a nationally recognized expert on the problems of underqualifed teachers, teacher turnover, and teacher shortages. His book Who Controls Teachers' Work? Power and Accountability in America's Schools *(Harvard University Press 2003) was the winner of the 2004 Outstanding Writing Award from the American Association of Colleges for Teacher Education.*

References

Boe, E., S. Bobbitt, and L. Cook. 1997. "Whither didst thou go?" *Journal of Special Education* 30: 371–389.

Chandler, K., M. Luekens, D. Lyter, and E. Fox. 2004. *Teacher attrition and mobility: Results from the teacher follow-up survey, 2000–01* Washington, DC: National Center for Education Statistics.

Grissmer, D., and S. Kirby. 1992. *Patterns of attrition among Indiana teachers, 1965–1987.* Santa Monica, CA: Rand Corporation.

Grissmer, D., and S. Kirby. 1997. Teacher turnover and teacher quality. *Teachers College Record 99,* 45–56.

Hirsch, E., J. Koppich, and M. Knapp. 2001. *Revisiting what states are doing to improve the quality of teaching: An update on patterns and trends.* Seattle: University of Washington.

Ingersoll, R. 1999. The problem of underqualified teachers in American secondary schools. *Educational Researcher* 28: 26–37.

Ingersoll, R. 2001. Teacher turnover and teacher shortages: An organizational analysis. *American Educational Research Journal* 38 (3): 499–534.

Ingersoll, R. 2003a. Is there a shortage among mathematics and science teachers? *Science Educator* 12: 1: 1–9

Ingersoll, R. 2003b. *Who controls teachers' work?: Power and accountability in America's schools.* Cambridge, MA: Harvard University Press.

Lortie, D. 1975. *School teacher.* Chicago: University of Chicago Press.

Mobley, W. 1982. *Employee turnover: Causes, consequences and control.* Reading, MA: Addison-Wesley.

Murnane, R., J. Singer, J. Willett, J. Kemple, and R. Olsen. 1991. *Who will teach?: Policies that matter.* Cambridge, MA: Harvard University Press.

National Academy of Sciences. 1987. *Toward understanding teacher supply and demand.* Washington, DC: National Academy Press.

National Commission on Excellence in Education. 1983. *A nation at risk: The imperative for educational reform.* Washington, DC: Government Printing Office.

National Commission on Teaching and America's Future. 1997. *Doing what matters most: Investing in quality teaching.* New York: National Commission on Teaching and America's Future.

Price, J. 1977. *The study of turnover.* Ames, IA: Iowa State University Press.

Price, J. 1989. The impact of turnover on the organization. *Work and Occupations* 16: 461–473.

Smith, T., and R. Ingersoll. 2004. What are the effects of induction and mentoring on beginning teacher turnover? *American Educational Research Journal* 41 (3): 681–714.

U.S. Bureau of the Census. 1998. *Statistical abstract.* 117th ed. Washington, DC: U.S. Department of Commerce.

Weiss, I. R., and S. E. Boyd. 1990. *Where are they now?: A follow-up study of the 1985–86 science and mathematics teaching force.* Chapel Hill, NC: Horizon Research.

Part IV Building Science Partnerships and Collaboration

CHAPTER

14

The Importance of Partnerships in Science Education Reform

George D. Nelson and Carolyn C. Landel

In this chapter, we make the case for the importance of partnerships for science education reform. Building and nurturing appropriate partners for tasks large and small helps to overcome formidable barriers. Good partnerships can shorten the time from planning to implementation and help ensure that reforms are sustained long enough to have the anticipated impact. But partnerships are complex and fragile. To create and sustain them requires expending valuable resources—time, energy, and money—careful planning, and continuous evaluation, feedback, and nurturing (Kingsley and O'Neil 2004). To illustrate our main points we will the use the National Science Foundation- (NSF) funded Mathematics and Science Partnership (MSP) program that we direct as a source of examples.

Realizing the Vision of Science Education Reform

We are optimistic that in spite of the evidence of limited progress after nearly 15 years of standards-based science education reform, the community is poised to build on past experiences and new knowledge to make real strides in improving student learning and closing the achievement gap. The goals of science education reform articulated by the American Association for the Advancement of Science and the National Research Council (AAAS 1989, 1993; NRC 1996) have not changed. If we are successful in achieving them, *every* student will graduate from high school

- knowing a coherent set of important ideas in science, how those ideas were conceived and tested, and how they are used to build technology or to explain natural phenomena;
- confident he or she deeply understands some concepts and possesses some skills, is capable of learning more when necessary and applying scientific habits of mind to new challenges; and
- capable of thinking through issues scientifically, gathering and evaluating evidence, drawing and testing conclusions, and making and communicating sound personal and social decisions.

Everything must come together to meet this ambitious goal: teaching, classroom resources, curriculum materials, assessments, and policies. It should be no surprise that success in achieving universal science literacy will require collaboration among many dedicated partners.

Even though students spend only 14% of their time in school (NRC 1999), the classroom is where learning is motivated, facilitated, and assessed. Effective teaching of all students in those classrooms by effective teachers is the key. But teachers work in complex institutions, steeped in traditions and stubborn habits, under continual pressure to increase student achievement on external assessments, often without sufficient resources or support to make positive changes. Collectively, the larger community expects teachers to help children achieve much more than just science literacy. Science must share the limited instructional time available to children each day with reading, writing, mathematics, and other important subject areas. Though improving science teaching and learning ultimately may rest with students and teachers, they cannot be expected to succeed without help.

A focus on systemic change has resulted in an expanding conception of the important partners and their appropriate roles as they apply to advancing science education reform goals (Ravid and Handler 2001; NNERCC 2004). As progress is made in understanding reform and applying our new understandings, the number of participating partners has expanded and each partner's role in contributing to supporting teachers and students in classrooms has become better defined. Support and action from multiple individuals and institutions are needed for endeavors such as producing high quality curricular materials, developing and delivering professional development, tutoring and supporting all students, and engaging community participation. Given this complex network of needs and partners, planning and implementing science education reform has moved beyond traditional models of acting on good ideas or hunches to making use of relevant research and powerful new tools to affect change. Successful reforms more closely resemble engineering, in which partners carefully direct finite resources to apply new knowledge about teaching, learning, and organizations towards realizing improvements in the function of the education system.

Research supports the idea that real reform cannot be done piecemeal, that sustainable progress towards our vision can be made only through comprehensive partnerships that include the relevant stakeholders. Who are the potential stakeholders who together can drive, support, and sustain reform that will ensure all students succeed in learning important science? Our list starts with students ready to learn and includes teachers, principals, science coordinators, administrators, school boards, parents, business and community members, regional education service agencies, curriculum and assessment developers, local and state politicians, state education leaders, community college science faculty, university science and education faculty and administrators, evaluators and education researchers, outside funders such as NSF or private foundations, and federal entities such as Congress and the U.S. Department of Education.

Each stakeholder has unique needs and vested interests that can motivate or discourage participation in partnerships. Each has specific roles defined by the resources that they can offer and the needs they have. In a successful partnership, all of these stakeholders develop a common vision of what they hope to achieve through working together (Ravid and Handler 2001). Unified by a vision that all can embrace, each partner is motivated to leverage resources to address individual needs, while also serving the larger needs of the partnership as a whole.

In the following sections, we identify the roles relevant stakeholders might assume at important junctions in the preparation of future teachers, beginning with their undergraduate experiences and continuing on into their initial work in schools as new hires. Next, we offer some examples of how these stakeholders contribute to developing, implementing, and sustaining partnerships based on our own experience with the North Cascades and Olympic Science Partnership (NCOSP) (see Table 1). We close with a brief discussion of some common problems that partnerships face as they go about the complex work of science education reform.

Table 1. Excerpts from the NCOSP Year Two Implementation Plan.

Goal 1: All students succeed in challenging science courses aligned with standards.	
Strategy1A	Districts develop five-year strategic plans for effective adoption and implementation of a research-based science curriculum.
Tactic 1	All district partners will attend a Strategic Planning Institute to develop data-driven science education reform plans.
Year 2 Benchmarks	75% of Partner Districts have attended a LASER Strategic Planning Institute 30% of Partner Districts show clear evidence of strategic plans being implemented 30% of Partner Districts support professional development tied to the materials for all teachers
Timeline	**Actions**
Sept 04	Strategic Planning Institute (SPI) promotional materials developed. Strategic Plans from districts who attended the institute in June 04 submitted to partnership to assess the extent to which the professional development plans tie to instructional materials.
Oct 04	Post-SPI meeting for all NCOSP districts who have attended the 2004 institute to support and asses their implementation efforts. Announcements and application materials available to districts.
Nov–Jan 04	Strategic Planning Institute faculty and NCOSP leadership prepare for institute. TOSAs and NCOSP leadership promote institute in the districts.
Feb 05	Post-SPI meeting for all NCOSP districts who have attended the 2004 institute to support and assess their implementation efforts.
March 05	Strategic Planning Institute faculty and NCOSP leadership continue to prepare for institute. TOSAs and NCOSP leadership continue to promote institute in the districts.
April 05	2005 Institute applications due. SPI Faculty assigned to NCOSP districts.
May 05	TOSAs and LASER faculty pre-institute meeting to help prepare districts for the institute. Districts partnered with others who have already attended to provide support and to foster collaboration and coherence across the region. Districts who attended institute in June 04 assess their early implementation efforts.
June 05	Districts attend LASER Strategic Planning Institute and develop five-year strategic plans for science education reform.
July 05	Districts share their plan with the broader stakeholder group and begin to implement select components.
Aug 05	Review evaluations from institute. Address strategies to engage any districts who have not attended an institute nor have an active or effective strategic plan for science education.

(continued on next page)

(continued from preceding page)

Note: This excerpt of the Year Two Implementation Plan features one strategy partner districts will apply to support goal one and one tactic to support that strategy. Year two targets are clearly defined in the plan so that leadership team members have benchmarks to define annual progress toward achieving the goal. A month by month work plan follows, outlining the steps needed for successful implementation. Every NCOSP goal includes multiple strategies and tactics, each detailed in this same fashion. The internal documents also denote the lead person responsible for implementing each component, as well as budget implications. The NCOSP five-year strategic plan (not shown here) describes the baseline data for each goal and annual benchmarks set based on that data.

Partnerships: Diverse Stakeholders, Specific Roles

Research supports the idea that students do better in school if they have a number of good elementary teachers in a row, not just one excellent experience (Amaral et al. 2002; Carey 2004; Sanders et al. 1996). Where do these good elementary teachers come from? Where do they learn about science and how to teach it? How are they prepared, hired, and assigned to classrooms in a building? What stakeholders are involved in the process and what contributions do they make? Starting with their undergraduate experience, future teachers take science and mathematics content courses as part of their certification programs or to meet distribution requirements of the institution. Do these courses address content that is appropriate for future elementary teachers? Does the instruction model the pedagogy that we hope they will use in their own teaching (NRC 1999, 2001)? Providing such learning experiences is the role of the higher education science faculty. They, in turn, must be supported by their peers, chairs, and deans. Are science methods classes able to build on future teachers' content knowledge by familiarizing them with reform curricula, formative assessment techniques, national and state standards, and techniques for effective peer interaction and support? Is there sufficient room in the elementary preservice program for science methods courses and practicum experiences? Are local classrooms where good science instruction is being modeled accessible for field experiences? Do state certification requirements encourage science literacy of the kind we are talking about for elementary teachers? Now we have involved the college of education, local schools and teachers, the state education department, and the legislature.

Once our new teacher earns his or her certification and enters the teaching corps as a new hire in a district, is there sufficient induction support? Does the district have a coherent science curriculum in place that meets the needs of all students? Is there a coherent and comprehensive professional development program, including opportunities to learn additional science content relevant to the materials? Are peer learning opportunities like lesson study or peer coaching encouraged and supported to help teachers focus on student learning and continuous instructional improvement? This is the realm of the principal, the science specialist, the superintendent, the school board, curriculum developers, and professional development providers. Are all students supported and expected to learn mathematics and science by their parents and school personnel? Finally, is the state assessment aligned with the state and national learning goals and constructed to be a valid and reliable criterion-referenced test? Now we have re-engaged politicians, community members, and discipline and education faculty along with psychometricians, state education officials, and commercial testing companies. One can clearly see that for systemic reform, the potential partners are legion. If critical partners are not contributing or not represented, then the reform can stall, or even fail, because the system components are so strongly coupled. Successful partnerships recognize the critical times and places at which the appropriate stakeholders groups must engage to make their unique contributions.

The North Cascades and Olympic Science Partnership

In 2001, the National Science Foundation initiated the Mathematics and Science Partnership (MSP) Program. This program grew out of the research and evaluation findings from previous NSF initiatives, including the state systemic initiatives, rural systemic initiatives, and local systemic change initiatives. The MSP program requires projects to apply the expanding research base on partnerships to their math and science education reform efforts. One major focus of the program is the engagement of university discipline faculty in all appropriate aspects of reform, including contributing to the research base. A complex partnership in northwest Washington responded to this call, resulting in the formation of the North Cascades and Olympic Science Partnership (NCOSP). As of this writing, our partnership is still in its infancy, and it is too soon to say how successfully we will achieve our goals. What we can offer at this stage are a few examples of how we are applying critical components of the partnership research base to our ongoing efforts (Cress et al. 2004; Dierking et al. 1997; Essex 2001; Hord 1986; Kingsley et al. 2004; Ohana 2003; Otterbourg 2004; Ravid and Handler 2001; Trubowitz 1986).

Though all the stakeholders described in the previous section are critical, it is important to consider how each contributes in different ways at different times over the life of the partnership (Otterbourg 2004; Trubowitz 1986). What follows are selected examples of selected strategies that NCOSP is applying during the (1) development and planning; (2) implementation and management; and (3) monitoring and evaluation stages to support and sustain the partnership.

Partnership Development and Planning: Focus on Outcomes

NCOSP is a complex partnership of many diverse stakeholders distributed over a large geographic region, each with its own set of unique contextual factors (see *www.ncosp.wwu.edu*). Early conversations with key stakeholders during the development of the partnership often centered on what we should do. It was clear that most of us associated partnership work with coming together to do something. Few of us came prepared to begin with the end in mind: identifying what we wanted to achieve through the partnership. Partnership activities would be effective only if their purpose was understood and their desired outcomes defined from the outset.

Strategies that would encourage all stakeholders to focus on outcomes *before* planning activities were critical during the development and planning stage. This was true for leadership team members who manage the project as a whole, working group leaders who support the implementation of partnership activities, and district partners who incorporate partnership activities within existing school structures. To chart a long-term course for the partnership, NCOSP Leadership Team members constructed a five-year strategic plan. Annual benchmarks were established in reference to baseline data to provide targets to ensure continued progress toward achieving the long-term outcomes. A detailed annual implementation plan that supports the five-year strategic plan describes and guides all specific actions required for implementation. An excerpt of the Year Two Implementation Plan is shown in Table 1. For NCOSP, these plans help Leadership Team members build and foster coherence across the partnership, provide Working Group

Leaders a scope of work, and assist Evaluation Team members monitor and evaluate partnership achievements.

School district partners also need to develop strategic plans aligned with the vision and goals of the partnership that takes into account the contextual factors and other initiatives present in their setting. A strategic planning process facilitated by Washington State LASER (Leadership and Assistance for Science Education Reform), a supporting partner in NCOSP, is an example of a strategy we are implementing to help districts articulate their own five-year strategic plans for science education reform. Through the six-day Strategic Planning Institute, leadership teams that include administrators, teachers, and community members have the opportunity to begin to

- develop a shared vision about effective science learning and teaching,
- construct models for developing and sustaining a corps of leaders who will champion science education reform in their communities, and
- explore five elements of an effective inquiry-centered science program, including curriculum, professional development, science materials support, assessment, and administrative and community support.

The institute gives districts a mechanism for working collaboratively with local, regional, and national strategic planning experts and time to assess the range of resources available for implementing their own plans. NCOSP district members attending the institute together have a chance to see how the programs and resources of the grant are being applied in other districts. Interacting with non-NCOSP district representatives also attending the institute gives additional insight into other potential models from around the state. Though the strategic plans developed by each partner district vary slightly in design, all are united by their focus on a set of common, long-term outcomes agreed upon by the partners.

Developing a common vision of what we hope to achieve is only a start. NCOSP continues to refine its vision of effective learning and teaching in a reformed science education system, and for the strategies to enact that reform. All partners should be able to articulate clearly the outcomes that the partnership intends to sustain and institutionalize, as well as their specific role in implementing successful short and long-term strategies. This is ongoing work that began during planning and development, continues as we move into implementation and management, and evolves as we learn from monitoring and evaluation efforts.

Partnership Implementation and Management

Just as experiences influenced our thinking about partnerships in the development stage, the same was true as we moved into implementation. For many of us, school-university partnerships historically grew from a desire to resolve a perceived problem in the school system by accessing the necessary solutions that resided in the university (Hord 1986; Ravid and Handler 2001). These models were often very one-sided and suggested that one partner needed to be fixed and the other partner could fix them. In the short term, this model might have limited impact, but for long-term, sustainable, systemic reform, this approach ignored the expertise—and problems—that all stakeholders bring to a partnership. We needed to shift to a model of partnership where *all* stakeholders are learners, *all* have something to gain by participating, and *all* have something essential to contribute. The reciprocal learning inherent in this approach to partnership allows *all* stakeholders to achieve outcomes they would not otherwise achieve (Cress et al. 2004).

Moving into implementation, NCOSP needed to find a way to access and use the resources that all stakeholders brought to the partnership (Ravid and Handler 2001). To begin, it was important to

- acknowledge the expertise of each contributor that was needed and valued,
- identify the bounds of each contributor's influence, and
- highlight the mutual benefits that come from accessing the combined expertise of all stakeholders.

Drawing on the strategic planning that began in the development stage, the partnership began to assemble working groups to implement the actions that targeted the specified outcomes. Because the partnership recognized the needs and expertise in both the school districts and higher education settings during the development and planning phase, the resulting implementation plan called for diverse stakeholders to be represented on each working group.

The Summer Academy Working Group provides an example of how one working group was assembled to reflect the diverse expertise of the group and provide mutual benefit for all participants. The Summer Academy, an intensive two-week professional development experience for NCOSP teacher-leaders, is a central component of the NCOSP. The first academy gave participants an opportunity to engage in an in-depth learning experience consistent with the research on how people learn. The academy asked participants to engage in learning relevant physical science content facilitated by faculty who were striving to model research-based instructional practices shown to foster learning.

To design and deliver this kind of experience in a meaningful way required a wide range of expertise that did not reside with any one individual or one stakeholder group. NCOSP higher-education faculty brought a strong content background, but only a few had experience with constructivist-based instructional practices. Our NCOSP Teachers on Special Assignment, six K–12 teachers hired to work full-time for one year with the project, brought contextual experience that helped ground the academy in content and climate for practicing teachers. This working group devised a three-part facilitation team for each group. These teams included a higher education faculty member as the content lead with a depth of knowledge in both content and pedagogy, a second higher-education faculty member who brought content knowledge but less experience with research-based pedagogy, and a Teacher on Special Assignment who was both an experienced teacher of science and fluent in the norms, values, and culture of K–12 teachers. This combination ensured that participants had access to the expertise they needed for a high-quality and well-rounded learning experience while also allowing each facilitation team member to learn from the knowledge and skills brought to the academy by their fellow team members. This design strategy was consistent with the model of reciprocal learning: all were learners, all were contributors, and all were beneficiaries.

Providing clear short-term and long-term outcomes through strategic planning in the development stages helped define the expertise required for the Summer Academy Working Group as the partnership moved into implementation. Contributions from disciplinary science faculty, science educators, and K–12 teachers were all required to ensure that the program reflected the knowledge and skills of content experts, pedagogy experts, and practitioners who understood the context of schools and children. Drawing on the expertise from diverse groups allowed facilitators and participants alike to have a rich and varied learning experience through the Summer

Academy. This model of partnership advances science learning and teaching for both K–12 teachers and higher education faculty.

Partnership Monitoring and Evaluation: A Culture of Improvement

Strategic planning tied to outcomes and carefully designed implementation plans that apply the knowledge and skills of diverse working group members may get a partnership up and running, but it is only with a commitment to regular monitoring and assessment that partners can be sure their actions are achieving their intended outcomes (Kingsley et al. 2004). There is no guidebook for complex systemic reform. These kinds of partnerships are breaking new ground and, in doing so, have an obligation to themselves and the field to monitor carefully the extent to which their plans succeed. Action plans for working groups must contain benchmarks to allow for monitoring progress toward meeting objectives aligned with the vision and goals. At every stage and every level, partners must be prepared to respond to evaluation data and make necessary midcourse corrections to continue forward progress.

NCOSP has attempted to make evaluation a regular and routine process. The NCOSP evaluation team meets bimonthly with the principal investigator and project director and reports quarterly to the Partnership Leadership Team, in addition to constructing annual evaluation reports. In addition to formal evaluation efforts, NCOSP working groups establish norms, self-evaluate the extent to which their meetings or activities reflect those norms, and subsequently self-adjust based on their observations and insights. Listening without interrupting is a frequently stated norm in working groups. Self-reflection often reveals that this norm is not honored during discussions. Recognizing this, groups brainstormed strategies to foster more respectful dialogue and then determine whether that strategy led to changes in behavior.

A process we are preparing to implement provides another example of an approach we are taking to foster a culture of evidence and commitment to continuous improvement. As our partnership entered its second year, activities in the districts and higher-education institutions increased substantially. Each partner had signed an agreement when the partnership was formed during the planning and development stage. As implementation began, it was clear we would need a way to help each district and higher education institution assess the fulfillment of their agreement to monitor how effectively their implementation plan was supporting success.

To do this, the partnership is carefully designing rubrics aligned with the original agreements that describe the long-term progression toward achieving the partnership outcomes. Data will be collected to chart each institution's progress toward satisfying the terms of the agreement. This analysis will be used in an annual reflection with each institution and to inform any needed midcourse corrections unique to each site. This kind of process is useful at many levels. Defining the long-term progression identifies small steps toward success and makes the process less mysterious or vague. Assessing progress helps individual institutions recognize their strengths and challenges so that they can focus their efforts. It allows the partnership to identify areas where partners are struggling to succeed so that activities and resources can be redirected. It also identifies partners that are succeeding in specific areas, highlighting potential pockets of expertise that can then be replicated throughout the partnership. Perhaps most important it keeps all of us focused on our outcomes—not just on completing a series of activities—and working together, as a partnership, to make steady, forward progress. All of these efforts connect back to overarching vision and goals for the partnership and are used to inform the selected strategies and actions outlined in the implementation plans in support of the larger strategic plan.

Partnership Challenges

Even when every effort is made to carefully apply the emerging partnership research base, partnership work is just not easy (Kingsley 2004; Trubowitz 1986; Cress et al. 2004). Here, we share some of the challenges we are encountering so that others can consider how they will respond when they face similar obstacles. In the years ahead we hope to be able to share the strategies we applied to overcome these challenges as part of our own contribution to the research base on partnerships.

Geographic Separation

Distance between partners makes partnership work more challenging. In the early stages of partnership development, cultivating relationships is critical. Geographic separation makes relationship building harder as it precludes informal interactions that happen around the water cooler. Travel time is downtime, and, with the busy schedules all of us maintain, spending time on the road can be a burden and a source of frustration, regardless of the quality or importance of a meeting. Cultural contexts change from school to school, district to district, and region to region. Emerging solutions that make perfect sense in urban or suburban settings with large communities of teachers located within relative proximity may be completely unworkable in a rural setting with only a few teachers, all separated by large driving distances. The needs and contexts are different and may require different solutions to get the same outcome. Understanding the cultural and contextual factors in rural and remote regions is essential. Despite these challenges, rural and remote areas must have access to partnerships if they are to succeed, and the science education community needs to learn more about the unique context of learning and teaching in these settings.

One-Size-Fits-All Expectations

An outcomes-driven partnership must remember that it is the outcomes that are important. All partners are committed to common outcomes. However, the process to get there—the implementation strategies—can, and will, vary among sites. The context is critical—existing resources, the current capacity of the institution, administrative commitment, teacher commitment—and must be considered in establishing an effective implementation plan. Having flexibility in the process of achieving the partnership outcomes can be misinterpreted as anything goes. For others, the lack of a single, common implementation plan creates confusion because they are looking for clear guidance on what to do. Particularly in the early stages of a partnership, having different implementation plans at different sites can cause additional confusion. Stakeholders across sites often talk with one another and when they learn that they are not all doing the same thing, it raises questions and concerns. Our partnership is struggling to offer sufficient flexibility, while also providing necessary clarity.

Implementing a Systems Approach

The American curriculum has often been criticized for being "a mile wide and an inch deep" (Schmidt et al. 1997). Partnerships run the risk of falling into that same trap by engaging too many stakeholders and taking on too many facets of the system. At the same time, systemic reform is complex and all components of the system have to change if partnership outcomes are to be realized, institutionalized, and lasting. Patience, tempered by a long term outlook, is important. The partnership leadership team will continually face challenging questions as they plan, implement, and monitor changes to the system. Does the partnership leadership team have sufficient depth to support a new change element? Will delaying implementation of a new element have negative consequences on other partnership components? To successfully implement a systems approach, partnerships must build sufficient capacity to support the many stakeholders and program components to avoid overextending leadership team members.

Conclusion

The complex work of science education reform will require equally complex partnerships in order to realize the vision and goals described by AAAS and the NRC. Bringing to bear the knowledge and skills of a diverse set of stakeholders is essential for success. We advocate for a new notion of partnership where these stakeholders are

- focused on what the partnership wants to achieve;
- engaged as learners, contributors, and beneficiaries; and
- committed to continuous improvement through careful monitoring and evaluation.

Hopefully, these few examples taken from the work of the North Cascades and Olympic Science Partnership provide some clues into partnerships for science education reform. We are optimistic that over the next few years much will be learned from the experiments like NCOSP that are currently under way.

George D. Nelson

is the director of science, mathematics, and technology education at Western Washington University, and the principal investigator for the North Cascades and Olympic Science Partnership. He previously served as director of Project 2061 at the American Association for the Advancement of Science, and associate vice provost for research/associate professor of astronomy and education at the University of Washington in Seattle and as a NASA astronaut. His research interests are science education reform and the effective preparation of future science teachers.

Carolyn C. Landel

is a research associate at Western Washington University and the project director for the North Cascades and Olympic Science Partnership. She has performed biomedical research at Fred Hutchinson Cancer Research Center and the University of Massachusetts Medical Center, served as the educational programs manager for the Washington Association for Biomedical Research, and is a former fellow in the National Academy for Science and Mathematics Education Leadership. Her current interests include engaging higher education scientists and K–12 teachers in efforts to improve science learning and teaching at all levels.

References

Amaral, O. M., L. Garrison, and M. P. Klentschy. 2002. Helping English learners increase achievement through inquiry-based science instruction. *Bilingual Research Journal* 26 (2): 213–239.

American Association for the Advancement of Science (AAAS). 1989. *Science for all Americans.* Washington, DC: Oxford University Press.

American Association for the Advancement of Science (AAAS). 1993. *Benchmarks for science literacy.* Washington, DC: Oxford University Press.

Carey, K. 2004. The real value of teachers. *Thinking K–16* 8 (1).

Cress, K., D. J. Heck, B. A. Miller, and I. R. Weiss. Handbook for enhancing strategic leadership in the math and science partnerships. Retrieved December 2004 from Horizon Research at *www.horizon–research.com/reports/2004/mspta_handbook.php.*

Dierking, L. D., J. H. Falk, S. Fisher, D. G. Holland, D. Schatz, and L. Wilke. 1997. *Collaboration: Critical criteria for success.* Washington, DC: Association of Science-Technology Centers.

Essex, N. L. 2001. Effective school-college partnerships: A key to educational renewal and instructional improvement. *Education* 121: 732–736.

Hord, S. 1986. A synthesis of research on organizational collaboration. *Educational Leadership* 43: 22–26.

Kingsley, G., and D. V. O'Neil. 2004. Performance measurement in public-private partnerships: Learning from Praxis, Construction a conceptual model. A paper presented at the American Society for Public Administration 65th National Conference. Portland, OR.

National Network of Eisenhower Regional Consortia and Clearinghouse (NNERCC). 2004. *What experience has taught us about collaboration.* Retrieved December 2004 from Eisenhower Network at *www.mathsciencenetwork.org/collaboration.pdf.*

National Research Council (NRC). 1996. *National Science Education Standards.* Washington, DC: National Academy Press.

National Research Council (NRC). 1999. *How people learn: brain, mind, experience, and school.* Washington, DC: National Academy Press.

National Research Council (NRC). 2001. *Knowing what students know: the science and design of educational assessment.* Washington, DC: National Academy Press.

Ohana, C. 2003. *Partnerships in math education: The power of university-school collaboration.* Portsmouth, NH: Heinemann.

Otterbourg, S. D. 2004. Investing in partnerships for student success: A basic tool for community stakeholders to guide educational partnership development and management. Retrieved December 2004 from Partnership for Family Involvement in Education at *www.ed.gov/pubs/investpartner/index.html.*

Ravid, R., and M. Handler. 2001. *The many faces of school-university collaboration: Characteristics of successful partnerships.* Englewood, CO: Teacher Ideas Press.

Sanders, William L., and J. C. Rivers. 1996. *Cumulative and residual effects of teachers on future student academic achievement.* Knoxville, TN: University of Tennessee Value–Added Research and Assessment Center.

Schmidt, W., C. McKnight, and S. Raizen. 1997. *A splintered vision: An investigation of U.S. science and mathematics education.* Lansing, MI: U.S. National Research Center, Michigan State University.

Trubowitz, S. 1986. Stages in the development of school-college collaboration. *Educational Leadership* 43: 18–21.

CHAPTER

15

Developing Professional Learning Communities

Beth Giglio

The creation of professional learning communities does not call for the completion of a series of tasks, but rather for a process of continuous improvement and perpetual renewal. It is a constant challenge that is never quite completely solved (DuFour et al. 2004, 140).

Adlai E. Stevenson High School (AESHS) is a suburban school in Illinois that has been consistently cited in educational literature as an exemplary professional learning community (DuFour et al. 2004; Richardson 2004; Schmoker 2001). How did this happen, and what has been the impact on the science program as a result of this district's commitment to professional learning? What distinguishes any school or district as a professional learning community (PLC)? The purpose of this chapter is to examine experiences of the science division of AESHS and the vision of the teachers who are members of this science PLC. Four "how" questions guide the discourse:

1. How do science educators develop and sustain PLCs?
2. How do PLCs promote science learning for our students?
3. How do school and professional environments promote and affect science learning communities?
4. How do we measure the effectiveness of science learning communities?

How Do Science Educators Develop and Sustain PLCs?

National Science Education Standards (NSES) (NRC 1996) calls on science educators to create professional learning communities. The chapters on "Science Teaching Standards" and "Standards for Professional Development for Teachers of Science" both reference changing emphases within science education, emphasizing the importance of teacher collaboration and collegiality (NRC). *Professional learning community* is a term widely used throughout professional development literature. Richard DuFour, former principal and former superintendent at AESHS and a nationally recognized author and speaker on PLCs, wrote in an article in *Educational Leadership*:

> The idea of improving schools by developing professional learning communities is currently in vogue. People use this term to describe every imaginable combination of individuals with an interest in education . . . the term has been used so ubiquitously that it is in danger of losing meaning (2004, p. 6).

DuFour's article identifies three big ideas of PLCs. He encourages educators to define the benchmarks of student learning, develop a collaborative teaching culture, and analyze student achievement results (DuFour 2004). DuFour and Eaker's *Professional Learning Communities at Work* documents more specific information on building and maintaining a PLC (1998). This book also chronicles the template used to build learning communities at Stevenson High School.

To develop science PLCs, educators need to stay focused. The NSES have provided us with a common vision. However, its Standards and benchmarks can seem overwhelming. How can leaders use the national standards to develop local documents that have personal and professional meaning for their own teachers? The AESHS science teachers used the NSES as a template for developing their own science vision, beginning when the NSES were first circulated in draft form. Science teachers used staff development time to discuss and craft their vision. The resulting vision is a working document used as a template for science goal-setting and professional development. The current version is titled "Science Vision: 2000–2005" and has a format aligned to the district vision of the high school.

CHAPTER 15

Table 1. Science vision 2000–2005

Mission Statement
The science division of Adlai E. Stevenson High School has a vision for the future. Our intent is to provide standards which will produce responsible learners who use science as a process to make informed decisions, solve problems, and enrich their lives.
Vision Statement
1. Curriculum and Assessment
Science has many disciplines, all interrelated. It is our goal to provide intellectually challenging science curriculum that emphasizes the connections between the physical, biological, and Earth sciences. Continuous and varied assessments of student achievement and instructional programs are crucial. Therefore, the science division will: Create science courses that articulate the connections between physical, biological,and Earth sciences. Utilize a wide range of diverse and authentic assessments. All assessment plans will include formative and authentic pieces. Collect longitudinal student achievement data as part of our commitment to continuous improvement of the science curriculum and instruction.
2. Equity and Access: Attention to Individual Students
The practical application of science requires both individual and group efforts. With this in mind, the science division will provide multiple opportunities for students to accept responsibility for their own learning and to work collaboratively within teams. Decision-making skills will be promoted and practiced. The science division will: Provide opportunities for individual students to accept responsibility for their own learning. Create a learning environment in which students work with others responsibly and respectfully. Utilize strategies which involve students in decision-making processes throughout their science course work.
3. Personnel: Working Within a Professional Learning Community
Science teachers are life-long learners. These professionals continue to participate in a variety of professional activities which increase their knowledge of science content, pedagogy, and assessment of student learning and program success. The division will: Engage in ongoing professional development as curricular teams and as a division. Collaborate within curricular teams, as well as vertically and horizontally between courses to ensure exemplary science curriculum (content and process skills), instructional practices, and student assessment. Continue to promote educational connections between the science division and other SHS divisions (e.g. science and applied arts, science and mathematics), as well as with educational institutions and business/industry.

(continued on next page)

(continued from preceding page)

4. The Climate of Teaching and Learning
An exemplary science program provides opportunities for students to become engaged in their own learning. Science knowledge is best studied within real-life contexts. The science division will: Promote inquiry-based learning which allows students to effectively use science as a process. This will include student use of technology, mathematical analysis of data, critical thinking skills, communication of data/conclusions, and discrimination of relevant concepts/facts. Provide authentic learning opportunities.These allow students to apply scientific principles to real-life situations. Connections to historical perspectives, home and community, and careers will be emphasized. Provide opportunities for students to understand the impact of scientific ethical issues within local and global communities.

Note that "Working Within a Professional Learning Community" is a major component of the AESHS vision. The science division sets annual goals; teacher teams identify student achievement or SMART (specific and strategic, measurable, attainable, results-oriented, time-bound) goals for each science course; and individual teachers identify professional development goals. All are tied to the science vision. For example, one science division goal for the 2004–05 school year promoted vertical articulation across the curriculum to identify the status of the science reading initiative and analyze available student achievement data in science content reading. The science core leadership team, consisting of the science directors and four teacher-leaders, collaboratively sets annual goals and references these back to the district goals and the science vision. The SMART goal for the sophomore Biology Team since fall 2000 has been to improve students' performance on science reading assessments. Student achievement data from chapter and final exam assessments are available for the Biology Team to review and discuss. This longitudinal data drives instructional and assessment decisions by the team. This SMART goal was developed and continues to be sustained by the teachers on the Biology Team, which consists of all teachers who teach biology during any given year.

All AESHS teachers use 15 critical questions to guide discussions within the curricular teams. The development of team SMART goals and other learning initiatives for courses often result from the teacher discourse that has surrounded the consideration of these questions. Team members use a 1-to-10 scale to rank each critical question. Examples of these questions include

- Is each member of our team clear on the intended outcomes of our course in general as well as the specific outcomes of each unit?
- Have we aligned the outcomes of our course to state goals and to high-stakes tests such as the ACT and Prairie State exams?
- Have we developed formative assessments that help us identify the strengths and weaknesses of individual students?
- Have we analyzed student achievement data and established measurable team goals that we are working together to achieve?

The science teachers at AESHS set for themselves professional development goals that encompass a two-year span. Working with the division director, each teacher identifies his or her own professional goals and how they correlate to the division vision. The teacher then lists the professional development activities he or she will complete to accomplish the goals. Needed resources are also discussed. Throughout the two years, each teacher meets periodically with the science director to discuss progress. Examples of recent individual professional goals in the science division include

- Enhance my knowledge and use of the available software options . . . [and] increase students' utilization of inquiry-based technology tools and provide opportunities for students to accept responsibility for their own learning. This ties to our vision 2A and 4A.
- Complete my master's in biology. This is tied to point 3 of the vision.
- Investigate implementation of a science department peer-tutoring program. This is tied to points 2 and 3 in our science vision. (See Table 1).

How Do PLCs Promote Science Learning?

As science educators, our primary focus is to provide opportunities for all students to learn science. The quality of the instruction we can provide hinges on our own knowledge as science teachers. What promotes science-educator learning? Where do we need to focus within our schools? Will our professional development focus on content? standards? assessment? *How People Learn* (Bransford et al. 2000) tells us that:

> Teacher learning is relatively new as a research topic, so there is not a great deal of data on it. But the research that does exist . . . provides important information about teachers as they attempt to change their practices . . . (and) . . . is based on the assumption that what is known about learning applies to teachers as well as to their students (p. 190).

In the science classrooms at AESHS, students do not learn in isolation. The science teachers consciously use instructional techniques and tools to encourage student collaboration. Many of the AESHS science teachers were not taught in collaborative classrooms and may be unfamiliar and uncomfortable with these types of learning situations. Establishing our own "teacher PLC" will help us learn and, in turn, create and model collaborative learning for our science students. During spring 1997, the AESHS science division decided to adopt *BSCS Biology: A Human Approach* for the sophomore biology curriculum. The biology teachers were excited about adopting this inquiry-based curriculum aligned with the NSES, yet were also apprehensive about their abilities to teach this curriculum. They were able to schedule a week-long summer workshop organized and facilitated by Janet Carlson Powell from BSCS (Biological Science Curriculum Study). This served as a starting point for building a community of teacher-learners. Teachers learned about the organization of the new textbook while using the BSCS 5E Model for their own learning! These science teachers were "learning how to learn," using the new curriculum.

Bransford et al. (2000) identifies five major pathways for practicing teachers to continue their own learning. Included are formal graduate programs, professional development with teacher-educators and educational consultants, experiences separate from classroom teaching such as parenting and coaching, the teacher's own teaching practice, and interactions with other teachers. Four of the five pathways involve collaboration with other teachers or practitioners. The NRC discusses continuing professional development in *Inquiry and the National Science Education Standards* (2000):

> A commitment to inquiry . . . is an important theme for professional development, in addition to its other goals. The most effective professional development not only stimulates the need to continue to learn, it also provides knowledge about where to look for information, it provides opportunities to improve teaching and learning; and it introduces teachers to tools for continuous improvement (p. 109).

The AESHS science division commits to inquiry in professional development in a number of ways. The high school science teachers collaborate with each other and with other teacher colleagues. An example follows:

Ted and Amerigo are second-year teachers at AESHS. They share a classroom for sophomore biology and often collaborate on lab preparations.

This year they are determined to provide their students with additional experiences in collecting, organizing, and analyzing data. A "new" lab will be integrated into the unit on natural selection. Amerigo teaches three sections of biology in the morning; Ted does the same, but in the afternoon. During his morning prep period, Ted visits Amerigo's class. Ted observes student progress and success, and constructs a data-collection device for use in subsequent class periods. This device allows student pairs to share their data more efficiently with the rest of the class. Between classes, Ted and Amerigo continue to discuss their satisfaction with the organization of the activity.

As a result of this minicollaboration, the students in the classrooms of these two teachers benefited from a more organized and engaging learning experience. But wait! Amerigo and Ted are members of the Biology Team and have reaped the benefits of the work and collaboration of the more veteran members of the team. It is second nature for the duo to share the new lab and the discoveries about data collection with the rest of their team. In this way, additional students benefit.

The science PLC at AESHS extends beyond the curricular course teams. Formalized staff development occurs within the science division. During the 2004–2005 school year, science teachers at AESHS used the book *Learning Science and the Science of Learning* (Bybee 2002) to guide discussions in staff development. The environmental science teachers have teamed with teachers from one of the sender schools to provide an "ecobuddy" program. In this program, junior and senior students from the high school act as mentors to the second graders. Coordinated visits throughout the school year, some at the high school and others at the primary district, allow students to collaboratively investigate concepts of environmental science. Additional learning community efforts between the high school and its K–8 sender schools include scheduled science articulation meetings. In 2003 the K–8 teacher representatives asked if the high school teachers would be willing to act as content area specialists. The K–8 teachers identified specific science content—such as magnetism, biodiversity, and weather—and the AESHS science teachers provided minilessons during the science articulation meetings.

In their study of four schools committed to the PLC model, DuFour et al. noted, "In each of the four schools, building shared knowledge was a critical step in finding common ground. Teachers were more likely to acknowledge the need for improvement when they jointly studied evidence of the strengths and weaknesses of their school" (2004, p. 137).

How Does School Environment Promote Professional Learning Communities?

Establishing professional learning communities in science takes leadership, a common vision, time, and commitment to the process. In *The Results Fieldbook,* Schmoker writes about the teacher-leadership at AESHS (2001). He notes that:

> Opportunities for leadership experience provide another source of pride for teachers. A crying need exists for excellent, practicing teachers to advance—to lead—by taking a more formal and explicit role in the supervision and improvement of instruction. At AESHS, a host of new, redefined positions have emerged (p. 25).

Within the AESHS science division, the leadership consists of a director (science administrator), four core leaders (in the areas of Earth science, physics, chemistry, and biology), and team leaders for each curricular team. The science teachers are the leaders within their own divisions. The core leadership team determines staff development for science. Science teachers write individual professional development goals biannually. The SMART goals for each course are determined within the curricular teams, under the leadership of science team leaders. Major continuing initiatives such as reading in the science content areas and further enhancement of critical-thinking skills are collaborative efforts within and between the teams of teachers.

As discussed, the science division uses a common vision to guide curricular, instructional, and assessment decisions. How is this vision communicated to new hires? How is the vision being interpreted within and across curricular teams? Many schools now provide mentorship programs for teachers new to the district. AESHS is no exception. At AESHS each new teacher is assigned a mentor teacher from the same teaching area. In science, biology teachers mentor new biology colleagues, chemistry veterans mentor new chemistry teachers, and so on. There is a two-day orientation prior to the beginning of school. Teachers new to the building also attend monthly after-school meetings with the principal and his assistant.

The most direct mentoring occurs within the collaborative curricular teams. An example is the Natural Science team. Natural Science is a freshman level course, incorporating concepts from physical, Earth, and space sciences, that is often taught by new teachers. The Natural Science teachers meet on a regular basis during time built into the school schedule. For each unit, a different veteran Natural Science teacher shares instructional tips, packets of materials, and content expertise with the team. At a recent Natural Science team meeting, the teacher-presenter showed demonstrations that could be used during the unit on physics concepts. Demonstration equipment was in the room, questions were posed and answered, and other teachers shared additional instructional ideas. The students of all of the Natural Science teachers will benefit from this shared information.

Teacher interactions and requests for additional professional development demonstrate commitment to the PLC model. During the 2004–05 school year, four science teachers—one chemistry and three physics—designed a project in which they collaboratively researched the newest developments in particle physics that relate to atomic structure. The team discussed the information, organized it into a PowerPoint presentation, and presented the PowerPoint at a chemistry and physics meeting. Another example was a proposal by one of the natural science teachers. She wanted to collaborate with colleagues who also taught natural science and biology or chemistry. The three science teachers met with two special education teachers, a reading specialist and a reading specialist in training. The team of five discussed reading strategies for use in science classrooms. A brief overview and a handout were shared at a science division meeting, and additional resources were placed in science offices.

How Do We Measure Effectiveness?

The effectiveness of any science learning community can be measured in one of two ways. First and most important, student progress and achievement can be observed and analyzed. Second, the professional growth and collaborative efforts of the science teachers can be documented—often by the teachers themselves.

What indicators will be used to ascertain student achievement in science? AESHS science teachers track achievement history as measured by external assessments such as PLAN and ACT Science Reasoning Tests, the science portion of the Illinois Prairie State Achievement Exam (PSAE), and participation in and scores for the College Board's advanced placement science programs. Primary attention, however, goes to the school's local assessments. Historical student achievement data is used to gauge progress. Here's how it works. Science teacher teams use common assessments. For chapter or unit tests, these assessments may be exactly the same or may have core questions included in each teacher's assessment. Finals (semester exams) are criterion-referenced tests (CRT). Each science course has a course description that lists the major concepts taught within a semester, and the finals are referenced to these concepts. Data from the multiple-choice portions of the exams are graded using Mastery Manager. Teachers use the data generated by this software to measure not only the success of individual students but also the efficacy of the course in terms of instructional methodologies and assessments. As Joan Richardson notes about AESHS in *From the Inside Out* (2004):

> The "common assessment piece" is perhaps the ultimate puzzle piece in a school that wants to ensure consistently high quality for all students. Common assessments—both formative and summative—cannot be done successfully unless teachers are willing to work together closely in aligning curriculum and writing assessments and sharing results (p. 114).

At AESHS, common assessments have been expanded to include formative evaluations. Curricular teams in science select appropriate methods based on the needs of their courses and students. Formative science assessments include, but are not limited to, such tools as midterms, research projects, reading assignment questions, and graphical analysis problems. Student assessment data from the formative assessments are collected and analyzed by the science teacher teams. Are students learning? Which concepts need to be retaught or revisited? This focus on formative assessment relates to the previous section on creating the environment for collaboration. Results of common assessments are used to inform instructional practices, not to evaluate teachers. There is an atmosphere of professional trust. A good example of this was a 2003 Accelerated Biology Teacher's presentation about their Accelerated Biology SMART goal to the AESHS Board of Education. Included in their information was consolidated student data, listed by teacher name. The teacher team was comfortable providing this information and trusted that all adults at the meeting were focused on a common objective: improving student achievement.

AESHS asks both students and teachers to reflect on the curricular programs. Each year the school's Student Services division compiles student survey responses and reports to the faculty as well as to the Board of Education. The survey contains information from current students and from one-year and five-year graduates. The one-year graduates are asked to answer the question, "How well did AESHS prepare you for college in the area of science?" Teacher teams complete End of Year Team Assessment forms collaboratively and share this information with the division director. Prompts for the team assessment include such questions as

- Provide evidence of your team's attention to and development of higher-order thinking skills for students.
- Describe the types of formative assessments used by your team ... (and) the learning experiences that occurred during discussion of these results.
- Examine your SMART student achievement goals for this year ... (and) list evidence of measurable student achievement gains as it relates to those goals.

Conclusion

Professional learning communities need vision, time, and commitment. The Science PLC at AESHS is the result of goal setting, teamwork, and attention to student achievement. Teachers realize their teamwork never truly ends. To repeat a quote from the beginning of this chapter: "[This is] a process of continuous improvement and perpetual renewal" (DuFour et al. 2004, p. 40).

Beth Giglio

is the director of science at Adlai E. Stevenson High School (AESHS) in Lincolnshire, Illinois, where she supervises 40 science teachers and 6 support staff. Coordination of the science curriculum, instruction, and assessment is her responsibility. She also organizes and implements staff development, evaluates classroom teaching performance, and plans articulation between the high school and its K–8 science colleagues. She has presented at state and national conferences and has worked collaboratively to pilot new courses at AESHS such as Careers in Medicine and Healthcare and Sheltered Biology.

References

Bransford, J. D., A. L. Brown, and R. R. Cocking, eds. 2000. *How people learn: Brain, mind, experience, and school.* Washington, DC: National Academy Press.

Bybee, R. 2002. Scientific inquiry, student learning, and the science curriculum. *Learning science and the science of learning,* ed. R. Bybee. Arlington, VA: NSTA Press.

DuFour, R. 2004. What is a "professional learning community?" *Educational Leadership* 61 (8): 6–11.

DuFour, R., and R. Eaker. 1998. *Professional learning communities at work: Best practices for enhancing student achievement.* Bloomington, IN: National Educational Service.

DuFour, R., R. DuFour, R. Eaker, and G. Karhanek. 2004. *Whatever it takes: How professional learning communities respond when kids don't learn.* Bloomington, IN: National Educational Service.

National Research Council (NRC). 1996. *National science education standards.* Washington, DC: National Academy Press.

National Research Council (NRC). 2000. *Inquiry and the national science education standards: A guide for teaching and learning.* Washington, DC: National Academy Press.

Richardson, J. 2004. *From the inside out: Learning from the positive deviance in your organization.* Oxford, OH: National Staff Development Council.

Schmoker, M. 2001. *The results fieldbook: Practical strategies from dramatically improved schools.* Alexandria, VA: Association for Supervision and Curriculum Development.

CHAPTER

16

No Child Left Behind: Implications for Science Education

Susan Mundry

Few institutions have as great an influence on society as the education system. It touches everyone—learners, parents, employers, and citizens. As a result, many people have a stake in seeing that the nation's schools provide the best education to all students. State and national politicians shape their election campaigns on improving education. Parent groups have brought suit against states for equal funding for their children's school's. Business leaders call for schools to better prepare students to contribute to an increasingly technological workplace. Teacher unions and professional associations stress the need for increased professional development and opportunities to attract and retain qualified teachers, especially in urban and rural areas.

The recently enacted No Child Left Behind Act of 2001 (NCLB 2002) acknowledges and supports the need for partnership and collaboration among these many stakeholder groups to increase learning for all students—especially students in poverty who have traditionally fared poorly in school. NCLB asks each of education's stakeholders to share in this vision and to play a key role in carrying out the vision. In her confirmation hearing, Secretary of Education Margaret Spellings said that all stakeholders have a rightful place in education and that different groups will play unique roles in supporting quality education (Spellings 2005). NCLB, for example, asks teachers and other educators to rethink their expectations of who can learn and benefit from proven practices and policies; it stresses the importance of engaging parents and providing them with information about their children's schools and teachers; and it calls for researchers to conduct more rigorous studies to inform best practice and faculty in higher education institutions to collaborate with K–12 educators on the improvement of mathematics and science education.

Although NCLB has its detractors who worry that sanctions for low-performing schools threaten the future of public education and that funding is inadequate to accomplish the goals, it is hard to argue with the law's vision for learning for all. For too long, poor and nonwhite students have achieved well below their wealthier, white counterparts. Everyone wants to see all students succeed, teachers want access to the best methods and tools for teaching, and parents want the best educational opportunities for their children. Yet there are major hurdles to reaching the vision of NCLB.

Learning is complex and is influenced by many factors—ensuring learning for all will take time and require additional resources. The research base needed to confirm best practice is not yet in place and is unlikely to ever be comprehensive enough to provide guidance on every decision a science teacher needs to make. Education's best resource will continue to be teachers who have the background, experience, and resulting professional judgment to make key instructional decisions.

Perhaps the biggest barrier to achieving the vision of NCLB is that the structures and beliefs operating in many schools run counter to the law's basic premise—that all students can meet academic standards. To reach the vision of learning for all manifested in NCLB, all stakeholder groups need to think differently about who can learn and what it takes for all students to learn. Rick Dufour, for example, a former school leader in Illinois, demonstrated that all students could reach high standards when the school is organized to support learning. He now works with other school faculties to challenge and change their beliefs about learning. He identified four types of schools: 1) The "Charles Darwin School" believes all kids can learn, based on their ability. The teachers in these schools see aptitude as relatively fixed and do not believe they can have a great influence on the extent of student learning. 2) The "Pontius Pilate School" operates on the belief all kids can learn if they take advantage of the opportunity the school provides and put forth the necessary effort. 3) The "Chicago Cubs Fan School" is based on the belief that all kids can learn something and helps students experience academic growth in a warm and nurturing environment. 4) The

"Henry Higgins School" operates on the belief that all kids can achieve high standards of learning as long as they receive enough support and help. These schools establish standards that all students are expected to achieve and continue to work with students until they meet the standards (Dufour et al. 2004, pp. 30–31).

Although NCLB faces many hurdles, particularly at the local level, the idea that we can design a system of education where more children are educated in the "Henry Higgins School" is a reasonable and worthwhile goal. In its first years of implementation NCLB emphasized systems for ensuring learning in reading and mathematics in elementary and middle schools, but in the coming years other subjects, especially science, will gain more attention and prominence. Science educators at all levels should understand the major provisions of the law, work to build effective partnerships with stakeholders, push for adequate funding to reach the vision, and take advantage of the opportunity presented by increased accountability for student learning in science. The remainder of this chapter discusses major provisions of NCLB with implications for science education.

No Child Left Behind and Science Education

The U. S. Department of Education cites four overall strategies for enhancing science achievement in the No Child Left Behind Act (NCLB) of 2001 (2002). These are

1. Ensure that schools use research-based methods to teach science.
2. Establish partnerships with institutions of higher education and others to ensure that teachers are well prepared to provide the best instruction.
3. Measure student progress in science learning at least once in each of three grade spans (grades 3–5, grades 6–9, and grades 10–12) each year.
4. Provide all public school teachers of core academic subjects with high-quality professional development.

Each of these is discussed further in the next sections.

Use Research-Based Methods to Teach Science

NCLB calls for educators to use instructional programs and practices that have been shown by research to be effective. NCLB does not endorse any particular approach to teaching and learning science, but calls on educators to use research evidence as criteria for making instructional decisions. One implication of this provision is that science teachers need to have access to a professional knowledge base of teaching and learning science. There has been increasing attention to building teachers' understanding of research—particularly the new research on cognition that helps teachers understand more about the conditions and environments that support student learning. As Stigler and Hiebert (2004) write, the teaching profession needs its own knowledge base to provide teachers with the "theories, empirical research, and alternative images of what implementation looks like" (p. 16). For example, a recent report from the Board on Behavioral, Cognitive, and Sensory Sciences and Education (2005) provides a thorough synthesis of research on how students learn. The report points out that the research has not yet found all the answers, but that that it "can point to the strengths and weaknesses of instructional strategies and the classroom environments that support those strategies" (p. 586). This and similar research-based resources should be used routinely by teachers and become the subject of teacher book discussion and study groups.

Another implication of this NCLB provision is that teachers become good consumers of research. According to the *U.S. Department of Education Policy Guidance* (2002), educators should rely on research studies that are scientifically based, meaning that they use rigorous data analysis; provide reliable and valid data; use experimental or quasiexperimental designs that assign subjects to different conditions with appropriate controls, with a preference for random-assignment experiments; and have been accepted by a peer-reviewed journal or approved by a panel of independent experts through a comparably rigorous, objective, and scientific review. This provision presents a tremendous challenge in the education field because there is no history of investing in scientifically based research and the context of education makes it difficult to carry out such research. Recently the U.S. Department of Education has funded more studies using rigorous experimental designs. In addition, the federally supported What Works Clearinghouse is screening existing studies of programs, practices, and educational interventions to provide educators and the public with the evidence of what works from studies that are scientifically based. The clearinghouse has a current slate of topics for review, including middle and elementary mathematics, beginning reading, education for English language learners, and several other areas and will review science programs in the future.

In the near term, how can science educators increase their use of research-based methods to teach science? One way is through Curriculum Topic Study (Keeley 2005). Through this process, teachers do a guided systematic study of research and standards documents specifically related to a topic they teach. They examine the research on teaching the topic and identify what is important for their students to understand—what are the essential core ideas? They reflect on and review their own curriculum and practices to assess the extent to which they focus on developing students' understanding of the essential core ideas. They also conduct a systematic study of the research to learn the typical naïve ideas students can have about science topics, the places at which students often face learning difficulties, and the teaching strategies that are effective in addressing these difficulties. Teachers who incorporate Curriculum Topic Study into their practice report that they can make curricula choices that are better aligned with standards and research and ensure that students are learning important core ideas in science (Keeley 2005).

In addition to using ongoing processes like Curriculum Topic Study to learn and apply research findings, teachers should have opportunities to attend regional and national meetings of their professional associations such as the National Science Teachers Association, National Science Education Leadership Association, and the National Association for Research in Science Teaching. These meetings include important current information on how students learn science and the effects of using specific instructional strategies such as inquiry and technology, as well as findings on students' conceptions of science concepts. Like professionals in other career areas, educators should have a solid understanding of the research base in their field and keep abreast of new developments from research.

Partnerships With Other Professional Development Organizations

NCLB calls for institutions of higher education and others to work in partnership with K–12 schools to support the development of qualified teachers and enhance teaching practice. NCLB sees colleges and universities as uniquely positioned to improve science teacher education by providing teacher candidates with content-rich learning experiences, including use of technology and advanced laboratory equipment as part of their undergraduate and graduate programs. The law authorizes the establishment of mathematics and science partnerships (MSPs) that are designed to tap the rich content knowledge of institutions of higher education and strengthen subject matter teaching and learning in K–12 schools. To enhance teacher education and professional development, NCLB provides funding on a competitive basis for partnerships between high-need school districts and institutions of higher education.

Research supports the idea that effective teaching requires the development of content knowledge (Monk 1994; Goldhaber and Brewer 2000.) As a recent National Research Council report states: "Efforts to teach for understanding without a solid grasp of disciplinary concepts fall short" (Board on Behavioral, Cognitive, and Sensory Sciences and Education 2005, p. 577). "Knowing the core concepts of the discipline itself—the standards of evidence, what constitutes proof and disproof and modes of reasoning and engaging in inquiry—is clearly required" (Board, p. 576).

But teachers need more than content knowledge to prepare for success in the classroom. They must also develop specialized teacher knowledge called pedagogical content knowledge. *Pedagogical content knowledge* is an understanding of what makes learning concepts easy or difficult for students and knowledge of effective methods for representing and presenting concepts to make them comprehensible to different learners of different ages and developmental levels (Shulman 1986.) Teacher development programs that focus on content knowledge and on how students learn subject matter produce greater positive effects on student learning (Kennedy 1999; Weiss et al. 2003).

Public schools and districts and institutions of higher education are beginning to create new relationships to enhance teacher education. It has not been easy for these two very different institutions to establish productive patterns of collaboration. Each institution brings its own perspective and talents to the table, and they need to be integrated into a common vision and approach. Based on interviews and site visits we conducted with MSPs funded by the National Science Foundation, new MSPs needed time to get to know one another's contexts and work together to develop programs that were not only content rich but also grounded in effective pedagogy *and* reflective of the realities of the schools. Initially, some higher education faculty brought the strong sense that teachers just needed more content learning, whereas science educators argued that teachers needed more pedagogy and strategies for using inquiry in the classroom. School personnel cited the need for help with content and curriculum and ideas for teaching students with varied needs. The vision of MSPs is for these various stakeholders to bring their varied perspectives together and draw on each of the institutions' unique capacity to design programs and approaches that address specific teacher and student learning goals.

The MSPs are learning to work together, often through trial and error. At one MSP site, the higher education partners began planning an entire program for their participating schools without talking with the school personnel to assess their needs and learn how the program might work. A savvy school superintendent intervened and suggested that any program the university offered needed to be "co-planned" with the school personnel who would be involved. This advice helped the MSP develop a plan to gain support and design the program to better address the specific needs of the schools.

NCLB also encourages higher education and other partners such as science centers, professional development organizations, and research labs to partner with schools, specifically to offer content-rich summer institutes of two weeks duration or more with appropriate follow-up to support teachers as they apply their learning in the classroom (U. S. Department of Education 2004). Likewise, to achieve the vision of NCLB, these partners must work closely with schools and districts to assess teachers' needs, backgrounds and interests, identify the highest needs in terms of student learning, and use this data to design appropriate programs.

Measure Student Progress in Science Learning

By the 2005–2006 school year all states must have challenging academic content standards in place for science education. The standards will "include the same knowledge, skills, and levels of achievement expected of all children" (NCLB 2002, Title I, Part A, Subpart 1, Sec. 1111 [C]). States will also "develop more rigorous mathematics and science curricula that are aligned with challenging State and local academic content standards and with the standards expected for postsecondary study in engineering, mathematics, and science" (NCLB, Title II, Part B, Sec. 2201 [a-4]). Beginning in 2007, NCLB will require districts to assess student learning in science at least once in each of three grade spans (grades 3–5, grades 6–9, and grades 10–12). The assessments must be aligned to state standards and measure higher-order thinking skills and understanding.

The inclusion of science testing in the state accountability system will raise the profile of science achievement throughout the country. In recent years, attention to science learning has suffered as schools, especially elementary schools, have focused more on reading and mathematics. We know from the many states that already test students in science and from participation in international assessments and the National Assessment of Education Progress (NAEP), that we have not yet come close to reaching the goal of high achievement for all students in science. Science educators can proactively use the occasion of the upcoming science testing to convince decision makers of the need to increase instructional time in science in the elementary schools and to ensure that the local curriculum at all grade levels reflects challenging content for students.

Since the real value of student assessments is that they serve as a feedback mechanism, schools should prepare now to help teachers use summative assessment information collected under NCLB to improve teaching, curriculum, and student learning. The Using Data–Getting Results Process (Love 2002) is one way teachers are learning to examine results from tests and other student data to make changes in practice that increase student learning. In addition, through WestEd's Center for Assessment and Evaluation of Student Learning, school teams learn to use continuous classroom assessment to document what students understand in science and inform instructional decisions. The use of ongoing mechanisms for student assessment provides teachers with more current information than most state-required testing and helps to pinpoint areas in which students are struggling before they fail a higher-stakes test. Teachers can deepen learning and re-teach in areas in which student understanding is weak to bring about improvements in student learning (Black and Wiliam 1998).

Provide Public School Teachers With High-Quality Professional Development

Clearly the vision of NCLB cannot be attained without implementing ongoing and effective professional development focused on teaching and learning. That all teachers are highly qualified and effective is a critical component of the No Child Left Behind Act, and the law requires that all public school teachers of core academic subjects receive high-quality professional development. School districts receiving Title I funds must spend at least 5% of their Title I allocation on professional development activities. Any school not meeting its adequate yearly progress target for two consecutive years must use at least 10% of its Title I funds for professional development.

In planning for the provision of high-quality professional development, schools and districts need to abandon the entrenched practices that treat all teacher needs as the same and realize that one-size-fits-all professional development does not work (Loucks-Horsley et al. 2003). NCLB calls for professional development that enhances teachers' knowledge of their academic subject matter and advances teacher understanding of effective pedagogy and instructional strategies that are based on scientifically based research, including how to teach students with special needs and English language learners. As outlined in the National Science Education Standards

> "Effective teaching requires that teachers know what students of certain ages are likely to know, understand, and be able to do; what they will learn quickly; and what will be a struggle. Teachers of science need to anticipate typical misunderstandings and to judge the appropriateness of concepts for the developmental level of their students. In addition, teachers of science must develop understanding of how students with different learning styles, abilities, and interests learn science. Teachers use all of that knowledge to make effective decisions about learning objectives, teaching strategies, assessment tasks, and curriculum materials" (NRC 1996, p. 62).

Other important characteristics of effective professional development highlighted in NCLB include that they are

- integrated with school and district educational improvement plans and state and local standards and curriculum;
- sustained, intensive, and classroom-focused, not one-day or short-term workshops or conferences;
- developed with extensive participation of teachers, principals, parents, and administrators; and
- regularly evaluated for their impact on increased teacher effectiveness and improved student academic achievement and the findings are used to enhance professional development.

NCLB also stresses the importance of increasing the effective use of technology to enhance teaching and learning and calls for professional development for teachers and principals in this area. NCLB's Enhancing Education Through Technology Program, requires recipients of funds to use "at least 25 percent of those funds for ongoing, sustained, and high-quality professional development on the integration of advanced technologies into curriculum and instruction and on the use of those technologies to create new learning environments" (NCLB 2002, Sec. 2416[a]).

Increasingly, schools and districts also see the need to develop teacher-leaders and provide advancement opportunities that retain good teachers and build the infrastructure for ongoing professional development. NCLB allows districts to use federal funding for "teacher advancement initiatives that promote professional growth and emphasize multiple career paths, such as paths to becoming a career teacher, mentor teacher, or exemplary teacher …" Career teachers grow in their knowledge and skills while their duties remain focused in the classroom and on instruction of their students. Mentor teachers maintain instructional responsibilities in the classroom and also take on additional duties such as mentoring new or reassigned teachers. NCLB refers to "exemplary" teachers as those who have a distinguished record of increasing student academic achievement and provide professional development for other teachers to increase student learning. Creating the capacity for teachers to continue to grow in the profession and support the growth of other teachers is a good investment.

In WestEd's work in the Northern New England Co-Mentoring Network, we support teacher-leaders in developing the capacity to play the roles of both "mentor" teachers and "exemplary" teachers. This has paid off for the mentors, their mentees and colleagues, and the districts. The teacher-leaders provide content-based mentoring that includes supporting new and reassigned teachers to increase their knowledge of science content and pedagogy. Many also take on the broader role of building a professional learning community in their schools and districts to support other teachers to adopt standards-based science instruction and roles of aligning curriculum across grade spans and supporting a common vision for science education throughout the district. (More information about this program is at *www.nnecn.org*.)

Summary

The NCLB Act reflects and supports high standards of learning for all students in all public schools. By calling for states to establish and implement challenging standards for science education and measuring student progress toward the standards, it underscores the national priority for all students to develop scientific understanding. Its major strategies include ensuring that teachers know and use research-based knowledge and approaches; that schools, institutions of higher education and other service providers work in partnership to make science learning the best it can be; that states implement assessment systems to measure student progress in science learning at least once in each of three grade spans (grades 3–5, grades 6–9, and grades 10–12) each year; and that all teachers have high-quality professional development opportunities throughout their careers to ensure that they continue to develop the knowledge, skills, and strategies to support students in meeting the standards.

To achieve the vision of NCLB requires rethinking many of our beliefs about who can learn and what the role of the teacher is in the classroom. It requires building bridges within and across institutions and developing a much deeper knowledge base in science education on which teachers can draw. Since education's very best resource is teachers who have the background, experience, and strong professional judgment to make effective instructional decisions, programs supported by NCLB should focus on supporting the research, partnerships, and programs that contribute to enhancing teaching practice.

Susan Mundry

is associate director of Mathematics, Science, and Technology at WestEd. She co-directs the National Academy for Science and Mathematics Education Leadership. Susan was senior research associate for the National Institute for Science Education's professional development study team. She is coauthor of Designing Effective Professional Development for Teachers of Science and Mathematics; Global Perspectives for Local Action: Using TIMSS to Improve U.S. Mathematics and Science Education; Teachers as Learners: A Multimedia Kit for Professional Development in Science; *and* Mathematics and Leading Every Day: 124 Actions for Effective Leadership.

References

Black, P., and D. Wiliam. 1998. Inside the black box: Raising standards through classroom assessment. *Phi Delta Kappan* 80 (2): 139–148.

Board on Behavioral, Cognitive, and Sensory Sciences and Education. 2005. *How students learn: History, mathematics and science in the classroom.* Washington, DC: National Academy Press.

DuFour, R., R. DuFour, R. Eaker, and G. Karhanek. 2004. *Whatever it takes: How professional learning communities respond when kids don't learn.* Bloomington, IN: National Educational Service.

Goldhaber, D. D., and D. J. Brewer. 2000. Does teacher certification matter? High school teacher certification status and student achievement. *Educational Evaluation and Policy Analysis* 22 (2): 129–146.

Improving Teacher Quality—State Grants Title II Part A, Non Regulatory Guidance, January 16, 2004 Revised, Academic Improvement and Teacher Quality Programs, Office of Elementary and Secondary Education, U.S. Department of Education. Retrieved December 27, 2004, from *www.ed.gov/programs/teacherqual/guidance.doc.*

Keeley, P. 2005. *Science curriculum topic study: Bridging the gap between standards and practice.* Thousand Oaks, CA: Corwin Press.

Kennedy, M. 1999. Form and substance in mathematics and science professional development. *National Institute for Science Education Brief* (November): 1–7.

Loucks-Horsley, S., N. Love, K. E. Stiles, S. Mundry, and P. W. Hewson. 2003. *Designing professional development for teachers of science and mathematics.* Thousand Oaks, CA: Corwin Press.

Love, N. 2002. *Using data–getting results: Collaborative inquiry for school-based mathematics and science reform.* Norwood, MA: Christopher-Gordon.

Monk, D. H. 1994. Subject area preparation of secondary mathematics and science teachers and student achievement. *Economics of Education Review* 13: 125–145.

National Research Council (NRC). 1996. *National Science Education Standards.* Washington, DC: National Academy Press.

No Child Left Behind Act (NCLB) of 2001. 2002. Public Law 107–110–January 8, 2002. 107th Congress. Washington, DC.

Shulman, L. S. 1986. Those who understand: Knowledge growth in teaching. *Educational Researcher* 15 (2): 4–14.

Spellings, M. 2005. Confirmation testimony before congressional committee. *Congressional Record,* (January 6, 2005).

Stigler, J. W., and J. Hiebert. 2004. Improving mathematics teaching. *Educational Leadership* 61 (5): 12–17.

U. S. Department of Education. 2002. *No child left behind: A desktop reference.* Washington, DC: Author.

U.S. Department of Education Policy Guidance "Guidance for the Reading First Program"

April 1, 2002. Retrieved December 27, 2004, from *www.ed.gov/ programs/readingfirst/ guidance.doc.*

U.S. Department of Education Policy Guidance "Non-Regulatory Guidance for NCLB's Improving Teacher Quality State Grants" January 16, 2004. Retrieved December 27, 2004, from *www.ed.gov/programs/teacherqual/guidance.doc.*

U. S. Department of Education. n.d. The facts about science achievement. Washington, DC: Author. Retrieved December 29, 2004, from *www.ed.gov/nclb/methods/science/ science.pdf.*

Weiss, I. R., J. D. Pasley, P. S. Smith, E. R. Banilower, and D. J. Heck. 2003. *Looking inside the classroom: A study of K–12 mathematics and science education in the United States.* Chapel Hill, NC: Horizon Research.

What Works Clearinghouse. *www.whatworks.ed.gov.*

CHAPTER 17

Alternative Certification: Aspirations and Realities

Norman G. Lederman, Judith S. Lederman, and Fouad Abd-El-Khalick

We live in an increasingly scientific and technology-laden world. Science and technology permeate almost every facet of our lives at the personal, social, economic, and cultural levels (AAAS 1990; NRC 1996). Educating students—our future voting citizens—in science, mathematics, and technology is crucial for the well being of our nation and its people in, at least, three major ways: ensuring our economic competitiveness in an increasingly interdependent global economy that emphasizes science, mathematics, and technology-related understandings and skills; empowering our citizens to make informed decisions about science and technology-related personal and societal issues; and enabling our populace to experience the profound intrinsic value of understanding and participating in the production of scientific and mathematical knowledge that has shaped and continues to shape our life, history, and culture (AAAS 1990, 1993; NRC 1996).

Yet, as the National Commission on Mathematics and Science Teaching for the 21st Century (NCMST 2000) firmly indicated, "the current preparation that students in the United States receive in mathematics and science is, in a word, unacceptable" (p. 7). Dissatisfaction with the current state of K–12 science and mathematics education largely hinges on the consistently dismal performance of our students on national and international measures and comparisons such as the National Assessment of Educational Progress (NAEP) and the Third International Mathematics and Science Study (TIMSS). In educational circles, however, such dissatisfaction preceded the publication and publicity of the aforementioned reports on performance indicators. As early as the mid-1980s, professional organizations, such as the AAAS (1989), National Science Teachers Association (NSTA; 1982), and National Council of Teachers of Mathematics (NCTM; 1989), voiced concerns about the ways in which science and mathematics were being taught in precollege classrooms. For example, more than a decade ago AAAS (1990) noted that the methods of teaching K–12 science "emphasize the learning of answers more than the exploration of questions, memory at the expense of critical thought, bits and pieces of information instead of understandings in context, recitation over argument, [and] reading in lieu of doing" (p. xvi). These organizations have since put forward a number of documents articulating the priorities and agendas for reforming precollege science and mathematics education at the curricular, pedagogical, instructional, professional, and institutional levels (AAAS 1993, 1997, 2001; NCTM 1991, 2000; NRC 1996, 2000, 2001).

Among these priorities is the preparation of qualified science and mathematics teachers who are capable of addressing the needs of an increasingly diverse student population; developing curricular materials that focus on depth of exploration and conceptual understanding rather than breadth of coverage and rote memorization; building and maintaining active, student-centered learning environments that are conducive to inquiry, meaningful construction of knowledge, and development of critical and higher-order thinking skills and habits of mind; and engaging in self-critique, reflection, and lifelong learning at the personal and professional levels. Obviously, the preparation of teachers capable of enacting the reforms vision for pre-college science and mathematics teaching necessitates a new breed of teacher preparation programs.

The Problem: Shortages of Qualified Science Teachers

Educational problems are often too complex to be attributed to a single factor or a small number of factors (Ingersoll 1999). Yet few would argue the assertion that "the most direct route to improving science and mathematics achievement for all students is better mathematics and science teaching" (NCMST 2000, p. 7). Better teachers are central to better teaching: Evidence strongly indicates that student learning is affected by the qualifications of teachers (AAAS 1990; Darling-Hammond and Hudson 1990; Ferguson 1991; Hanushek 1986; Hedges et al. 1994; NRC 1996, 2000; Shavelson et al. 1989). Indeed, "the most consistent and powerful predictors of student achievement in mathematics and science are full teaching certification and a college major in the field being taught" (NCMST 2000, p. 7). Research has shown that teachers holding teaching certificates in specific subject areas—in-field teachers—are more effective in affecting student learning and achievement than out-of-field teachers (Druva and Anderson 1983; Ferguson and Ladd 1996; Fetler 1999; Ingersoll 1999; Sanders and Rivers 1996).

There is a severe shortage of qualified science and mathematics teachers. In a recent survey, Allen (2003) reported that 48% and 61% of all responding middle and high schools respectively reported difficulty in finding qualified science teachers. Nationwide, about one-fifth of all secondary school science teachers are out-of-field teachers. In particular, 33.1% of life science and 56.5% of physical science high school teachers are not certified to teach science (Ingersoll 1999). It is important to note, however, that the No Child Left Behind (NCLB) of 2001 (2002) legislation provides a much narrower definition of qualified (or highly qualified) and that all teachers in all core subject areas must be highly qualified by the start of the 2005–2006 school year.

Teacher shortages are more pronounced in the case of urban and rural communities. The magnitude of the problem in urban settings is reflected in data reported by the Urban Teacher Collaborative (UTC; 2000), which represents about 40 major city school districts including Chicago Public Schools. The Great City School Districts, which serve about 50% of the students who are not proficient in English, about 50% of minority students, and 40% of the nation's low-income students, are experiencing "real teacher shortages in specific subject fields, across grade levels, and in the ranks of minority teachers. Shortages are most severe in special education, science, and mathematics" (UTC 2000, p. 19). In a survey conducted by the UTC, 97.5% and 95% of the responding districts respectively indicated an immediate need for qualified science and mathematics teachers.

Moreover, 75% of the responding districts indicated an immediate need for teachers of color. Similar patterns and trends are evident in rural areas where demand for science and mathematics teachers is almost always catalogued under the "considerable shortage" category and comes second only to special education (Allen 2003). Additionally, teacher shortages are not likely to diminish any time soon (UTC 2000). The NCMST (2000) anticipates an increase in these shortages due to massive reshuffling in the current teaching force through fast-approaching retirements, attrition, and job changes, and estimates that 240,000 middle and high school science and mathematics teachers will be needed over the next 10 years.

Addressing Teacher Shortages: The Issue of Quality

In their attempts to meet the demand for science and mathematics teachers, school districts have resorted to a range of recruitment and retention strategies. In its survey of the Great City School Districts recruitment strategies, the UTC (2000) reported that 65% of the responding districts offered alternative routes to certification, sponsored job fairs, and/or offered on-the-spot contracts. What is noteworthy is that 82.5% of the surveyed districts allowed noncredentialed teachers to teach under some form of emergency permit, long-term teacher substitutes, or certification waivers. Retention strategies in these districts ranged from offering induction programs (67.5%), to tuition assistance for graduate coursework (25%), to bonuses for enhanced student achievement (7.5%) (UTC 2000).

The alternative certification program is one approach to alleviating the problem of shortages of qualified teachers. It is important to note that some people prefer to distinguish between *alternative certification*, which refers specifically to credentialing, and *alternate route*, which refers specifically to teacher preparation programs. We will use these terms interchangeably in this report with our primary focus being on teacher preparation as opposed to the policy issues surrounding credentialing. These programs come in many varieties but generally have in common an accelerated or shortened path for individuals to become certified teachers. The idea is not new. Alternative teacher certification programs have existed since as early as 1982. Immediately before this time, high-ability individuals began to find teaching less than desirable, and the conditions of the workplace caused many teachers to exit the field. The result, of course, was a decrease in the number of highly qualified individuals in the teaching profession. Institutions of higher learning saw alternative certification programs as means to alleviate the teacher shortage as well as provide a more financially feasible alternative to traditional teacher education programs. A study of the finances of alternative certification programs (Denton and Smith 1983) showed, however, that the typical alternative program cost 1.67 times more than the teacher education program it replaced. Nevertheless, alternative certification programs have remained and continue to be advocated as a viable way to relieve the strain of teacher shortages in a more cost-efficient manner.

Alternative certification programs come in many varieties, in both name and structure. Alternative pathway, emergency certificate, temporary certificate, residence program, and apprenticeship programs are just a few of labels. One very popular format is the boot-camp-type program, characterized by an intense, but short, training period—two to three weeks during the summer—followed by an extended supervised internship in a classroom. This approach may place more teachers in K–12 science classrooms, but does it begin to address the problem? Many would argue that we have more than a problem of quantity; a problem of quality exists as well. We should not limit ourselves to asking how many more teachers we are able to put in classrooms. We should be equally concerned with asking questions about the qualifications of these new teachers. Major reform documents in precollege science and mathematics education (e.g., AAAS 1990, 1993, 2001; NCTM 1991, 2000; NRC 1996, 2000) articulate images of teaching that place great demands on teachers' content knowledge and pedagogical expertise. Teachers are expected to develop curricula, plan student-centered units and lessons, and orchestrate instruction that will: (a) foster equity and excellence for all students irrespective of their age, sex, cultural or ethnic background, aspirations, disabilities, or interest and motivation in science and mathematics; (b) actively engage students in extended inquiries to help them build deep conceptual understandings of key concepts and theories in physical, life, and mathematical sciences; (c) help students understand the nature of science, mathematics, and technology, and their interactions with the social, economic, and cultural spheres; and (d) provide students with opportunities to develop attitudes, values, skills, and habits of mind, such as decisionmaking and higher-order and critical-thinking skills that would enable them to engage in lifelong learning.

These alternative pathways or certification programs are often contrasted with traditional teacher preparation programs that typically entail having or earning a major in the target content area, completing substantial coursework in education, and going through some form of supervised student teaching experience. However, the forms that alternative certification programs have come to assume are far different, to say the least. By and large, with some exceptions, such programs have come to mean that "college graduates can postpone formal education training, obtain an emergency teaching certificate, and begin teaching immediately" (Ingersoll 1999, p. 26). A growing number of states—including Kentucky, Massachusetts, and Pennsylvania—and cities—including Baton Rouge, Kansas City, Los Angeles, and New York City—are short-circuiting well-thought-out, evidence-based practices undertaken in traditional teacher preparation programs and offering crash courses that put new teachers in classrooms after as little as three weeks of training (Zernike 2000). In some cases teaching assignments go to individuals who have had hardly any preparation at all (Goodnough 2000). Although we would prefer to use the word *education* when discussing the preparation of teachers, *training* appears to be a more accurate descriptor when it comes to alternative certification programs.

The Various Forms of Alternative Certification Programs

Two main varieties of alternative certification programs exist: state-mandated programs that permit school districts to initiate the process and programs that allow postsecondary institutions to initiate the process. A third category is joint university-school district programs that provide campus-based training and on-the-job supervision.

School-Initiated Programs

The New Jersey Provisional Teacher Program, begun in 1985, is the first program of this type. The program was developed by the Department of Education, and it invited well-prepared liberal arts graduates without traditional training to teach in one of the 600 school districts in New Jersey. By the beginning of the 1985 school year, 121 individuals had been hired as provisional teachers by school districts. A year later the number had increased to 391. They were required to work full-time at full salary for one year. These provisional teachers received feedback and help from an on-site support team, and they were required to attend 200 hours of state-sponsored seminar classes on topics such as curriculum, students, and school setting. After one year, they were offered full certification. Since the inception of the New Jersey program, there have been similar initiatives in various states—among them California, Oregon, and Georgia. One of the primary drawbacks has been financing. In particular, schools and school districts have lacked the funds to provide release time for those professionals responsible for supervising individuals pursuing the alternative pathway to certification (Dill 1996). When the Council for Basic Education did one of the first follow-up studies of the New Jersey program, it found that most administrators preferred to hire certified teachers rather than provisionally certified teachers because of the expense of the mandated supervisory time. Administrators felt the same way even if they had hired a successful provisionally certified individual (Gray and Linn 1988).

Institution-Initiated Programs

Institution-initiated programs are administered by institutions of higher learning and are typically some shortened variation of the regular teacher education program in place. In general, individuals in these programs must have a degree in a subject matter field as a prerequisite to enrollment. The idea is that the individual's path to learning pedagogy can be shortened significantly. These programs, because they are based in universities, maintain some coursework and have less on-the-job training than what is seen in the school-initiated programs. It is important to note that these programs are different from programs leading to a master's of arts in teaching. Both typically require a subject matter degree for entrance, but the alternative programs require far less coursework prior to certification. Several large-scale descriptive studies have been completed for such programs by the Policy Study Associates (Adelman 1986) and the Southern Regional Education Board (Cornett 1988). These studies indicated that institution-initiated programs were responsible and innovative ways to address the problems of teacher shortages. In particular, the data indicated that applicants for such programs had stronger subject matter backgrounds than individuals in traditional programs and were more strongly committed to a career in teaching. It was also noted that the alternative certification programs tended to have more selective admissions requirements. On the surface, it would appear that the alternative certification programs have not sacrificed quality in its candidates. However, very little data was available on the effectiveness of alternatively certified individuals. Specific research related to effectiveness will be discussed later in this chapter.

Recently, the number of institution-initiated programs has proliferated, and little is known about how many such programs actually exist. Variations in program structure abound, with the major differences relating to the induction or internship level. In short, experiences in schools vary from the complete length of the program to capstone experiences. In addition, field experiences often vary with intensity during the program to take advantage of the interplay between campus coursework and field experiences. The supervision of field experiences is as varied, with either precollege personnel totally responsible or with university and school personnel sharing responsibility. When it comes to professional development and support, variations in programs can be dramatic. At times professional support is provided onsite, while at other times such support is provided on a university campus. In addition, independent of site, school personnel or university personnel may provide professional development coursework. Just about any configuration possible probably exists, making systematic evaluation difficult.

NCLB provides specific guidelines for alternative-route teachers, specifying that a teacher in an alternative certification program must receive high-quality professional development that is sustained, intensive, and classroom-focused before and while teaching. They must also receive intensive supervision that consists of regular and ongoing support.

What Does the Research Say About Alternative Certification?

The earliest research on alternative teacher education programs indicated that administrators felt that alternatively prepared teachers were as competent as those prepared traditionally and that student achievement data and teacher appraisal scores did not vary between first-year alternative teachers and those with regular certifications (Goebel 1986; Hutton 1987; Million 1987). The Rand Study (Darling-Hammond et al. 1989) looked at 64 mathematics and science certification programs and found that students in alternative certification programs possessed a stronger commitment to subject matter, while those prepared in traditional programs were most interested in working with students. In terms of student achievement, the students of alternatively certified teachers tended to do as well or slightly better than students of teachers certified in a traditional manner (Brown et al. 1989). Darling-Hammond (1990) did an extensive review of alternative and traditional certification programs and found that

1. when adequate preservice education is added to intensive on-the-job supervision, job satisfaction is higher and attrition is lower;
2. subject matter knowledge is important for effectiveness up to a point;
3. stronger relationships were noted between education coursework and teacher performance than were demonstrated between subject matter coursework and teacher effectiveness; and
4. thoroughly supervised, high-quality, intensive clinical learning experiences were significantly related to teacher effectiveness.

As a consequence, she concluded that alternative certification routes as well as traditional routes should be evaluated in terms of how well they provide high-quality clinical experiences to support subject matter knowledge and pedagogical knowledge.

In an effort to assess whether alternatively certified teachers were as competent as traditionally certified teachers, Knight et al. (1991) compared students' perceptions of their learning environments. The results indicated that students in classes of traditionally certified teachers thought their classroom environment promoted more higher-thought processes, better pacing, and more group cohesiveness. Alternatively, Ball and Wilson (1990), in a study of mathematics teachers, found each group possessed less-than-adequate instructional skills. The overwhelming number of studies performed during the 1990s tended to focus on the characteristics of teachers produced through alternative routes rather than direct comparisons of effectiveness. Few differences were generally found. Among the more consistent differences noted were that alternatively certified teachers tended to be more receptive to teaching disadvantaged youth in urban areas, but they were also more negative about the teaching profession after several years on the job.

As noted, alternative certification programs are quite varied. The same, however, can be said concerning traditional certification programs. The consequence of such variety is difficulty in making any direct and fair comparisons concerning the effectiveness of teachers derived from alternative and traditional programs. More important, separating the impact of various program types from the selection criteria of its students is almost impossible. Rather than not try, however, some notable attempts have been made to compare alternate route and traditional programs.

Goebel et al. (1989) compared 177 alternative certification program teachers with 192 experienced teachers and 158 fully certified first-year teachers. The study found virtually no differences in student achievement across the three groups. They did find that the students of the more experienced teachers, regardless of program, performed slightly better than the less experienced teachers. In Georgia, Guyton et al. (1991) compared 23 beginning teachers in an alternative certification program with 26 beginning teachers who were prepared in a traditional program. Although data were not collected on student achievement, no differences were found on periodic evaluations of performance completed by mentors, peers, and principals. Hawk and Schmidt (1989) compared 16 beginning math and science teachers enrolled in an alternative certification program with 53 first-year teachers from a traditional program. The traditionally prepared group had more teachers ranked at the "above standard" level on an end-of-year teacher performance appraisal, but both groups had 85% achieving at least at the "standard" level. Hutton et al. (1990) also compared first-year teachers from traditional and alternative programs. Sixty-two teachers from a traditional program were compared with 110 teachers from an alternative program. In additional to various findings related to demographics and job satisfaction, it was noted that both groups equally met statewide (Texas) teacher performance evaluations and virtually no difference existed related to supervisor and principal ratings of performance.

Jelmberg (1996) compared 30 alternatively certified teachers with 200 traditionally prepared teachers. Unlike in other studies, the teachers in this investigation had been teaching for two to three years. Also unlike other investigations, the traditionally prepared teachers were considered superior based on principals' evaluations of performance. Karge et al. (1992) found similar results comparing first-year teachers in California. Sandlin et al. (1992–1993) followed these same teachers for an additional year and found that eventually there was no difference between the groups.

Using a quasi-experimental design, Miller et al. (1998) compared the performance of two matched—by subjects taught, grade level, and school characteristics—sets of 41 traditionally prepared and alternatively prepared teachers. Data were collected from 350 students with respect to mathematics and reading achievement. No differences were found for student achievement across the two groups. It is significant to note that the teachers in this investigation had been teaching for three years. One of the better-known alternative route programs is Teach for America. The 117 participants in this program were compared to 8,500 beginning and veteran teachers in Houston Public Schools (Raymond et al. 2001). The study found no differences in their pupils' achievement scores.

In summary, there are wide variations in both alternative route programs and traditional preparation programs. The biggest differences between the two groups tend to be that alternative certification teachers are more committed to teaching, more willing to work in disadvantaged areas, more willing to work with lower-ability students, and more diverse in terms of ethnicity. Alternative path teachers also tend to become more disenchanted with teaching as a profession after several years, and they more frequently experience classroom management and general adjustment problems during their first few years. The research on teaching ability and student learning is equivocal at best. And, disregarding the difficulties in comparing samples from widely differing programs and work situations, the research on achievement and teacher competency is equivocal at best. If there is any difference, it seems to be in the area of administrator perceptions, favoring traditionally certified teachers during the first two to three years of teaching.

Quo Vadis?

It appears that alternative certification or alternative route programs are here to stay. They are quite varied in structure, but so are traditional programs. Limited research suggests that successful alternative-route programs can be characterized by strong partnerships between schools and the preparation program, rigorous selection criteria for admittance, a strong and intensive supervision component during field placements, and a program curriculum that includes attention to teaching methods and classroom management. It also appears that the more extensive the coursework prior to full-time teaching the better. These program characteristics are consistent with NCLB guidelines for alternative-route teachers. However, the empirical research does not support that programs possessing these characteristics contribute to better teaching. Clearly, considering a program a success is independent of student achievement.

Although the number of alternative programs is ever increasing, shortages in the number of qualified science teachers continue. These programs have not solved the teacher shortage problem alone, but they should not bear full responsibility. Numerous societal and financial reasons make teaching a less than desirable profession. The more contentious issue is whether alternative programs prepare qualified teachers or, in terms of No Child Left Behind, "highly qualified" teachers. We believed that alternative programs did not produce competent teachers when we started our review. The limited research appears to indicate otherwise. More accurately stated, the research indicates that teachers completing alternative pathways do as well as those completing traditional programs. However, it is important to realize that most of the relatively limited research was done with beginning teachers. We hold to a conviction that the first few years of any teacher's career are primarily occupied with classroom management and simply learning the ropes. We are also a bit biased, having all come from traditional programs. There is a significant need, nevertheless, for more research comparing the teaching skills, abilities, and attitudes of experienced alternative and traditionally certified teachers.

Norman G. Lederman
is chair and professor of mathematics and science education at the Illinois Institute of Technology. A former high school teacher of biology and chemistry, he is internationally known for his research on the development of students' and teachers' conceptions of nature of science and scientific inquiry. He is a former president of the National Association for Research in Science Teaching and the Association for the Education of Teachers in Science, and has also served as director of Teacher Education for the National Science Teachers Association.

Judith Sweeney Lederman
is the director of teacher education in the Department of Mathematics and Science Education at Illinois Institute of Technology. She regularly presents nationally and internationally on the teaching and learning of science in both formal and informal settings. In addition to numerous book chapters, she recently published an elementary science teaching methods text and is writing a

secondary methods text and two books on the nature of science. She is presently CESI president and a member of the NSTA Council.

Fouad Abd-El-Khalick

is associate professor of science education at the University of Illinois, Urbana-Champaign. He is known for his research on students' and teachers' conceptions of nature of science and currently serves on the Board of Directors of the National Association for Research in Science Teaching. He has also developed and received external funds for an alternative teacher certification program centered in Champaign and Chicago, Illinois.

References

Adelman, N. E. 1986. *An exploratory study of teacher alternative certification and retraining programs* (U.S. Department of Education, Data Analysis Support Center, Contract No. 300–85–0103). Washington, DC: Policy Studies Associates.

Allen, M. B. 2003. Eight questions on teacher preparation: What does the research say? *The Education Commission of the States.* Denver, CO.

American Association for the Advancement of Science (AAAS). 1989. *Science for all Americans.* Washington, DC: Author.

American Association for the Advancement of Science (AAAS). 1990. *Science for all Americans.* New York: Oxford University Press.

American Association for the Advancement of Science (AAAS). 1993. *Benchmarks for science literacy.* New York: Oxford University Press.

American Association for the Advancement of Science (AAAS). 1997. *Blueprints for reform: Science, mathematics, and technology education.* New York: Oxford University Press.

American Association for the Advancement of Science (AAAS). 2001. *Designs for science literacy.* New York: Oxford University Press.

Ball, D. L., and S. M. Wilson. 1990. *Knowing the subject and learning to teach it: Examining assumptions about becoming a mathematics teacher.* Paper presented at the annual meeting of the American Educational Research Association, Boston, MA.

Brown, D., E. Edington, D. A. Spencer, and J. Tinafero. 1989. A comparison of alternative certification, traditionally trained, and emergency permit teachers. *Teacher Education & Practice* 5 (2): 21–23.

Cornett, L. M. 1988. *Alternative teacher certification programs: Are they working?* Atlanta: Southern Regional Education Board.

Darling-Hamnond, L. 1990. Teaching and knowledge: Policy issues posed by alternate certification for teachers. *Peabody Journal of Education* 67 (3): 123–154.

Darling-Hammond, L., and L. Hudson. 1990. Pre-college science and mathematics teachers: Supply, demand and quality. *Review of Research in Education* 16: 223–264.

Darling-Hammond, L., L. Hudson, and S. Kirby. 1989. *Redesigning teacher education: Opening the door for new recruits to science and mathematics teaching.* (RAND–R–3661–FF/CSTP, ERIC No. ED 309 144). Santa Monica, CA: Rand.

Denton, J., and N. Smith. 1983. *Alternative teacher preparation programs: A cost-effectiveness comparison.* No. 86. Portland, OR: Northwest Regional Educational Laboratory.

Dill, V. S. 1996. Alternative teacher certification. In *Handbook of research on teacher education*, ed. J.Sikula, 932–960. New York: Macmillan

Druva, C. A., and R. D. Anderson. 1983. Science teacher characteristics by teacher behavior and student outcome: A meta-analysis of research. *Journal of Research in Science Training* 20 (5): 467–479.

Ferguson, R. F. 1991. Paying for public education: New evidence on how and why money matters. *Harvard Journal on Legislation* 28: 465–498.

Ferguson, R. F., and H. F. Ladd. 1996. How and why money matters: An analysis of Alabama schools. In *Holding schools accountable*, ed. H. Ladd, 265–298. Washington, DC: The Brookings Institution.

Fetler, M. 1999. High school staff characteristics and mathematics test results. *Education Policy Analysis Archives* 7 (9): 1–19.

Goebel, S. D. 1986. *Alternative certification program final report.* Austin: Texas Education Agency State Board of Education Minutes.

Goebel, S. D., K. Ronacher, and K. A. Sanchez. 1989. *Alternative certification program, 1988–1989: Houston Independent School District.* Unpublished manuscript. (ERIC Document 332 103). Houston, TX: Department of Research and Evaluation, Houston Independent School District.

Goodnough, A. 2000. State to sue over uncertified teachers. *The New York Times,* August 1.

Gray, D., and D. H. Lynn. 1988. *EW teachers, EHER teachers: A report on two initiatives in New Jersey.* Washington, DC: Council for Basic Education.

Guyton, E., M. C. Fox, and K. A. Sisk. 1991. Comparison of teaching attitudes, teacher efficacy and teacher performance of first-year teachers prepared by alternative and traditional teacher education programs. *Action in Teacher Education* 13 (2): 1–9.

Hanushek, E. 1986. The economics of schooling: Production and efficiency in public schools. *Journal of Economic Literature* 24: 1141–1178.

Hawk, P., and M. W. Schmidt. September-October, 1989. Teacher preparation: A comparison of traditional and alternative programs. *Journal of Teacher Education* 40: 53–58.

Hedges, L., R. Laine, and R. Greenwald. 1994. A meta-analysis of the effects of differential school inputs on student outcomes. *Educational Researcher* 23 (3): 5–14.

Hutton, J. B. 1987. *Alternative teacher certification: Its policy implications for classroom and personnel practice.* Monograph Number 5. Commerce, TX: Center for Policy Studies and Research in Elementary and Secondary Education. (ERIC Reproduction Service No. ED 286 264)

Hutton, J. B., F. W. Lutz, and J. L. Williamson. 1990. Characteristics, attitudes, and performance of alternative certification interns. *Educational Research Quarterly* 14: 38–48.

Ingersoll, R. M. 1999. The problem of underqualified teachers in American secondary schools. *Educational Researcher 28* (2): 26–37.

Jelmberg, J. 1996. College-based teacher education versus state-sponsored alternative programs. *Journal of Teacher Education* 47, 60–66.

Karge, B. D., B. L. Young, and R. A. Sandlin. Summer 1992. Teaching internships: Are they a viable route to California alternative certification. *Teacher Education Quarterly* 9–18.

Knight, S., E. Owens, and H. Waxman. 1991. Comparing the classroom learning environments of traditionally and alternatively certified teachers. *Action in Teacher Education 12* (4), 29–34.

Miller, J.W., M. C. McKenna, and B. A. McKenna. 1998. A comparison of alternatively and traditionally prepared teachers. *Journal of Teacher Education* 49, 165–176.

Million, S. 1987. *Maintaining academic integrity in the midst of educational reform: An alternative certification program.* Paper presented at the meeting of the annual national conference of the National Conference on Inservice Education, San Diego, CA.

National Commission on Mathematics and Science Teaching for the 21st Century (NCMST). 2000. *Before it's too late.* Jessup, MD: Education Publications Center.

National Council of Teachers of Mathematics (NCTM). 1989. *Professional standards for teaching mathematics.* Reston, VA: Author.

National Council of Teachers of Mathematics (NCTM). 2000. *Principles and standards for school mathematics.* Reston, VA: Author.

National Research Council (NRC). 1996. *National Science Education Standards.* Washington, DC: National Academy Press.

National Research Council (NRC). 2000. *Educating teachers of science, mathematics, and technology: New practices for the new millennium.* Washington, DC: National Academy Press.

National Research Council (NRC). 2001. Adding it up: Helping children learn mathematics. Washington, DC: National Academy Press.

National Science Teachers Association (NSTA). 1982. *Science-technology-society: Science education for the 1980s.* Washington, DC: Author.

No Child Left Behind Act (NCLB) of 2001. 2002. Public Law 107–110–January 8, 2002. 107th Congress. Washington, DC.

Raymond, M., S. H. Fletcher, and J. Luque. 2001. *Teach for America: An evaluation of teacher differences and student outcomes in Houston, Texas.* Unpublished manuscript. Stanford, CA: CREDO, Hoover Institution.

Sanders, W. L., and J. C. Rivers. 1996. *Cumulative and residual effects of teachers on future students academic achievement.* Knoxville, TN: University of Tennessee Value-Added Research and Assessment Center.

Sandlin, R. A., B. L. Young, and B. D. Karge. 1992–93. Regularly and alternatively credentialed beginning teachers: Comparison and contrast of their development. *Action in Teacher Education* 14: 16–23.

Shavelson, R., L. McDonnell, and J. Oakes. 1989. *Indicators for monitoring mathematics and science education.* Santa Monica, CA: Rand.

Urban Teacher Collaborative. 2000. *The urban teacher challenge: Teacher demand in the great city schools.* Washington, DC: Council of the Great City Schools.

Zernike, K. 2000. Less training, more teachers: New math for staffing classes. *The New York Times,* August 24.

Part V Science of Learning Science

CHAPTER

18

Brain Research: Implications for Teaching and Learning

James E. Hamos[1]

"To be done with caution and a realization of the limitations"—this is the summary comment of this chapter on applying understandings derived from brain research, as of the year 2005, to the context of education. Certainly, learning—be it the learning of subject matter in science or the learning of another discipline—is a byproduct of brain function. As knowledge of many aspects of the brain has exploded over the past few decades, there has been a strong desire to link the study of the brain, i.e., neuroscience, with education, the applied learning endeavor of students. This interest accelerated in the 1990s, a period dubbed as the Decade of the Brain by the 101st Congress (1989), and continues in the earliest part of the 21st century. Although our knowledge of brain function on many levels continues to grow impressively, we are still limited in our ability to fully comprehend this complex organ and should be wary of over-selling applications of brain research in classrooms.

The chapter that follows is an effort to bring together some basic facts about the brain with a variety of thinking on how ongoing brain research may contribute to teaching and learning in general and, perhaps, to science teaching and learning more specifically. A caveat—the author is a neurobiologist by training; a teacher of neuroscience to students of many age groups (but especially medical students) for many years; and, over the past decade, a participant in the broader discussion and policy-setting environment of mathematics and science standards and assessment. Although able to cover much ground in the topic of this chapter, the author does not, and cannot, represent every voice interested in the application of brain research to education. The base of brain research, however, can be framed from a number of perspectives, and the reader is highly encouraged to pursue the literature that exists and will continue to expand as a science of learning evolves over the coming years.

The Cellular and Chemical Brain

Any organ, in any animal, is made up of cells. Further, any animal that contains cells responsible for even basic actions responding to the environment (e.g., movement, reflexes, sensing light) has a group of specialized cells responsible for this response that are called neurons. These are the nerve cells or, if the animal has a complicated structure that can be called a brain, brain cells. Although not the only type of cell that exists in the brain, neurons underlie the messaging system that makes the nervous system different from other systems of the body.

An appreciation of learning as it is related to brain research, then, must begin with a review of the basic biology of the neuron. Understanding the reality of neurons is not necessarily a new phenomenon, although new findings of how they work continue to become evident. Indeed, the intense study of neurons is a relatively new phenomenon in the biological sciences, and the belief that the brain is made up of individual elements is roughly only 100 years old (see, for example, *Neuron Theory or Reticular Theory?* written in 1954 by Ramón y Cajal, one of the founders of brain research, as a summation of his impressive, Nobel Prize–winning work).

Neurons come in many shapes and forms, but they do have distinctive common components that serve as the cellular foundation for their function. While this chapter will simplify the cellular anatomy and physiology of neurons, the reader is encouraged to examine very readable and more detailed reviews of these complex cells in *Neuroscience: Exploring the Brain* (Bear et al. 2001), a text for early undergraduates, or *A Celebration of Neurons* (Sylwester 1995), a book aptly written for educators. Ultimately, neurons are designed for communication; and the nervous system and brain is a means to maintain, hold, and organize the many billions of neurons that communicate for a myriad of motor, sensory and cognitive functions.

To communicate, each neuron has regions—called the *cell body* and *dendrites*—that receive the preponderance of input information as well as a single output structure that sends information—its *axon*. The cell body is the portion of a neuron that makes it most similar to other cells of the body as the cell body contains the genetic material, DNA and RNA, as well as the majority of the protein-producing structures. The dendrites are highly specialized for neurons as the dendrites enable each neuron to tremendously increase its surface area to receive information, much as in the way that branches on a tree significantly increase its surface area to display leaves for their function. Although a neuron can have one, two, or many primary dendrites with countless smaller branches, each neuron has only one axon to send information. This results in an all-or-none phenomenon in terms of output function for a neuron at any given moment in time since its axon is either sending information or not.

How, then, is communication accomplished in the nervous system? Ultimately, this is a result of electricity and chemistry. The electricity is propagated along the membranes of the neurons. For the dendrites, the propagated electricity stays relatively close to the cell body. Because of specializations along the axon's membrane, the electricity is propagated extremely rapidly and can travel quite a distance from the cell body. For example, some neurons that reside in the brain have axons that extend two or three feet into the spinal cord (proportionally, this is equivalent to a human being having a living process that extends roughly 50 miles away and then being able to communicate extremely rapidly with something at the end of the process).

So, electricity is used as the mechanism of moving information about the nervous system along a single neuron's membrane. The mechanism of transferring information from one neuron to another neuron involves chemistry and a specialized region between the two cells called the *synapse* or the *synaptic junction.* This means of communication, known as *synaptic transmission,* is a large topic in neuroscience, and the reader is encouraged, once again, to delve into other reviews. It involves subjects such as neurotransmitters (small chemical substances such as dopamine, acetylcholine, serotonin, and glycine), storage mechanisms for the neurotransmitters inside specialized parts of the ends of axons, and receptors on the receiving portions of neurons, especially along the dendrites, which respond when the neurotransmitter is released. A key point for the current chapter is that this elegant design is true for the simplest animal, with but a few neurons to maintain all of its reflex functions, to the most complicated parts of the human brain that serve as the biological foundation of cognition, utilizing ensembles of scores of neurons to achieve higher order functions.

A final consideration about these means of communication is that not all of the activity from a neuron to the next is one of stimulation, what the neurophysiologist would call excitation. Rather, depending on the neurotransmitter involved and the type of receptor on the receiving neuron, synaptic activity can be excitatory or inhibitory, a dampening of the ability of the second neuron in the circuit to send electricity along its axon. Since a single neuron receives synaptic input from hundreds, thousands, or even more other cells, a neuron must sum all of the excitatory and inhibitory inputs that are active at any given moment in time to activate or not activate its axon, i.e., the all-or-none phenomenon described previously. The sheer numbers of neurons that exist in a human brain, the degree and precision of wiring among these neurons, and the ability to stimulate (excite) or dampen (inhibit) the next neuron in a chain of neurons are all factors in increasing the incredible complexity that underlies every neural function.

Brain Functions Are Distributed in Multiple Brain Regions

The brain is responsible for a wide variety of responses to the internal and external environment. There are extremely basic neural functions that keep a body working, such as controlling the heart, the other vital organs, and the muscles of our musculoskeletal system. The basic senses—sight, hearing, smell, taste, and touch—are means by which the brain gathers information from the outside world. Reflexes typically are survival mechanisms by which the nervous system automatically responds to external stimuli to protect the organism. Some forms of memory are relatively simple functions by which the nervous system maintains an awareness of prior events. Elementary behavior can be considered as a means by which the brain expresses itself, enabling the organism to further respond to the outside world. Higher cognitive functions—such as abstract thinking or language—have evolved as special aspects of the brains of human beings. Spectacularly, underlying every one of these functions—be it the most basic or the most complex—are neurons communicating with each other via synaptic activity that is excitatory or inhibitory.

The nervous system is not a hodgepodge of these special cells that randomly find each other whenever there is a need for communication. Over the years, it has been learned that different neural functions are localized to specific areas of the spinal cord and brain. This can be observed across species (phylogeny) and as it occurs through development (ontogeny). Interestingly, elements of each function are distributed across multiple regions of the brain (and, depending on the function, the spinal cord). For example, for movement, the majority of neurons activating the muscles of our skeleton reside in the spinal cord. Neurons responsible for an individual's decision to move reside quite a bit away, in the brain. Still other neurons, responsible neither for the actual activation of muscles nor for deciding to move them, but rather for ensuring that the movements are smoothly coordinated, reside in a number of other regions of the brain.

The intricacy by which neural functions are distributed in multiple brain regions has been especially well studied in the visual system, the sensory system responsible for sight. Over a number of decades, the visual system has been a model system in neuroscience because scientists have learned that they can easily manipulate the input to the system—photons of light—and then study areas of the brain that respond. As the visual systems of many animals, including humans, have been studied, a compelling truth stands out: although light of varying wavelengths enters the eye and is the stimulus for a cascade of brain stimuli, the eye, initially, and then the brain parcels this information for use in a number of ways. (This topic in neuroscience has been extensively studied and discussed, including a recent article by Tong in 2003.)

What seems simple—light comes in and an individual sees—becomes a complex activity in the brain as the sensory information is distributed to a number of different brain regions for finer aspects of "seeing" itself (i.e., visualizing the outside world), for behaviors (e.g., interacting with the motor system to move the head to bring some new objects into the field of view, or recognizing an object by recalling a visual memory), for defensive reflexes (e.g., to duck one's head when some object comes into view of the peripheral visual system), or to adapt the organism to daily light and dark cycles called circadian rhythms.

As other neural systems have been studied, it has become clear that all of them utilize multiple brain regions to conduct the function for which they are responsible, indicating that this property of distributing information in multiple regions is likely to be a ubiquitous property of the nervous system, which has been co-opted for every brain function, including higher-order cognitive functions such as learning. Communication among the neurons in these multiple regions, then, becomes a key issue during the initial laying down of synaptic wiring in development and for efficiency in adulthood. Also, because each brain function has multiple neural regions underlying its wiring, it is not at all unreasonable to expect that some regions would work especially well in certain individuals and not as well in other individuals, or that a single person could have highly functioning brain regions at work for certain abilities but less well for others. The levels of functioning are likely determined by a combination of genetic disposition and experience, and some may be amenable to improvement. Described later in this chapter, this distribution of information to multiple regions likely has consequences for teaching and learning.

The Brain During Prenatal Development

How, then, does a brain develop—one that must have all of the billions of neurons necessary, must have them in the correct places of the brain, must wire them up for appropriate communication, and that then can use and adapt to information that appears over a lifetime? One of the major beliefs for much of the first 100 years of the field of studying the brain is that the production of all neurons needed for a mammalian organism's lifetime occurs prenatally. Studies suggested that the entire process was done *in utero* due to the complexity of just getting the brain cells and crude wiring into place. Compelling evidence supported the notion that cell division, the process of producing new cells, stopped for neurons after birth while it continued robustly for almost all of other cell types throughout the body.

Over the past decade, newer studies indicate that some neurons in a few brain locations have a limited ability to undergo cell division, to connect with other neurons, and to begin to share communication. While this is a new and interesting phenomenon to consider, it still is valid to consider that the vast majority of brain cells utilized over a lifetime are in place at the time of birth with only a small percentage of neurons continuing to divide after birth.

Indeed, a host of studies indicate that the prenatal brain contains many more developing neurons than will be active and functioning in childhood and adulthood. The process of creating a brain *in utero* involves an exuberant production of huge quantities of neurons followed by a period of neuronal cell death as the brain selectively develops in response to genetic signals and to the beginning communication between developing neurons. Similarly, during the early formation of synaptic connections, there is a period of an exuberant overproduction of synapses (studies by Huttenlocher and colleagues—for example, Huttenlocher and Dabholkar [1997]—formed the early literature on this phenomenon). The initial process of overproduction of neurons seems to be one that helps get the cell bodies of neurons into their correct locations throughout the brain. As the neuronal appendages—dendrites and axons—begin to extend from the cell bodies, chemical gradients guide the axons to the correct sites of their termination (remember, sometimes many inches or feet away from the cell body) while the dendrites begin to display their branching patterns, receive tentative synaptic information, and then become active. As initial neuronal communication begins, the end processes of dendrites and axons become selectively pruned, and neurons that do not become part of a functioning circuitry die off. All of this results in a well-sculpted brain, with neurons and circuitry in place for a lifetime.

The Brain After Birth

As the nervous system becomes operational, first at a cellular level, then at a circuit or communication level, and then at a systems level, the specific brain systems follow a genetically driven period of order, followed by adaptability to change, then followed by long-term functioning that is much less responsive to change. Once again, as described below, the visual system has been a wonderful model system to elucidate how this happens (Wiesel 1982, one of a series of key insights deriving from the pioneering work of Hubel and Wiesel); and the lessons learned in studying this system seem to be generalizable to many, if not all, brain functions.

One of the key aspects of vision is the ability to take photons of light—the visual signal—into the eyes and transfer this into a message that the brain understands. All of this begins in the retina, an outcropping of the brain that exists in the back of the eye. Single eyes work independently of each other and thus are considered to function monocularly. However, many animals function binocularly, meaning that they perceive the outside world as if information from both eyes is brought together. This is an ability that is particularly useful in a visual ability such as depth perception, the capacity to understand the outside world in three-dimensional space. Since the retinas act independently, where then does binocular vision occur? It turns out that binocular vision is largely a by-product of neural circuitry when retinal information is shared at progressively different levels of the brain.

Developmental neurobiologists have studied the development of binocular vision and observed the requirement for brain activity to concretize the function on a genetically ready template (Katz and Shatz 1996). That is, much of the regions that will become part of the functioning visual circuits are laid down prenatally. As cellular activity in the developing retinas begins spontaneously, there is some initial sorting out of the messages that proceed into the brain. However, since there is no light *in utero*, the developing fetus does not develop the ability to see. Very rapidly after birth, though, light begins to enter the eyes, serving as a powerful sensory stimulus that drives brain activity, and binocular vision then flourishes as an important aspect of visual function.

This aspect of the visual system is modified if the system is perturbed. For example, in children with amblyopia, wherein something (such as a congenital cataract or misalignment of the eyes) interrupts there being a normal image on the two retinas during postnatal development, the child develops diminished visual capacity unless corrective measures are taken. When amblyopia is mimicked in experimental animals, one finds that the brain mechanisms responsible for developing binocular vision do not do so normally. Of tremendous interest, though, is that the loss of visual ability can be reversed if corrective measures are done during a narrow postnatal time window during which the brain maintains a postnatal plasticity to adapt to aberrational events. This has become known as the "critical period," a time of brain plasticity during which an aspect of brain development is sensitive to change.

The critical period—or, more broadly, a "sensitive" period (Knudsen 2004)—seems to be a consistent phenomenon for various brain functions with the length of the period varying for different brain functions and in different species. For example, the critical period for most visual functions in humans lasts for roughly the first six years of life. Critical periods have been identified for other sensory systems as well as for aspects of the motor system.

For higher cognitive functions, there is debate about critical periods among those who study child development. In behavior, the Austrian biologist Konrad Lorenz found that there is an extremely short critical period during which imprinting, the identification of a mother and a father by a newborn, occurs. For functions such as language, some contend that there are critical periods, or at least "sensitive periods" (Locke 1997). For each brain function, once a critical period of time ends, the long-term functioning is set in place and any alteration that might have occurred is almost completely locked in place for a lifetime.

The Brain and Learning

This chapter has reviewed some key insights into the brain, scaffolding these on some model brain functions. To generalize these to the fields of teaching and learning, it is important to ask if studies of the basic neurobiology of learning indicate that this aspect of brain function generally follows the same rules—and the answer is that a body of research evidence suggests that learning does. A series of elegant experiments have derived the basic cellular and molecular biology for memory which, when built upon, becomes learning (Squire and Kandel 1999). These building blocks are distributed in multiple brain regions, especially in the human brain. Although there is a specific developmental scheme that seems to extend significantly longer for memory and learning than for a basic sensory system such as vision, there is not clear evidence that all of the substrates of learning have critical periods.

For much of the 20th century, psychology—the study of the mind—was a field independent from neuroscience. However, key understandings regarding the biological constructs for higher cognitive functions such as learning have occurred, especially during the past decade as noninvasive techniques such as PET (Positron Emission Tomography) and fMRI (Functional Magnetic Resonance Imaging) have been developed and enhanced. These tools enable researchers from previously separate fields to study the functional activity of the brain as it is involved in specific tasks; they have reinforced prior conceptions of where and how the brain learns; and they are opening up new insights into the brain during normal behavior as well as when it is dysfunctional in a range of learning disorders.

Reasonable Applications to Teaching and Learning

Noting that the field of neuroscience has exploded and provided new insights into many brain functions, including learning, some educators maintain that this information is useful as currently understood and can be adapted into teaching and learning in actual classrooms (Caine and Caine 1997; Jensen 1998; Gram and Germinario 2000). A host of books, materials, and websites are available in which aspects of understandings gleaned from brain research are used to support particular approaches to teaching and learning. Although these are based in the same neurobiology that has been explored above, the author, as stated at the start of this chapter, recommends a more cautious approach but does agree there are some current understandings of the brain that already seem relevant to learning in general and to science teaching in a few ways.

Certainly the distinctive development of the brain during the early years of life argues that early childhood (Gopnik et al. 1999; Skonkoff and Phillips 2000) must be a protected period during which traumas are minimized, if not completely avoided, and normal development is allowed to proceed unencumbered. This enables the completion of the period of neuron development, lays the framework for appropriate synaptic connections, and allows the normal process of selective neuron death and pruning of the overabundance of synapses. Scourges such as drug and alcohol abuse during pregnancy or malnutrition and lack of stimulation in the earliest years of life have devastating effects on brain development.

Understandings about the critical period suggest that many, if not all, brain functions have periods of time when the related system can adapt to—but not always totally overcome—shocks. However, these time windows in life are perilously short, lasting just a few years or, perhaps, the first decade(s) of life in some aspects of brain function. This knowledge spawned a series of discussions in 1990s about the first three years of life as years that demanded extraordinary sanctity, protected by policy and encouraging special behaviors from parents and caregivers. Countervailing viewpoints argue that, although brain research highlights the importance of the early postnatal years, it does not suggest that this is the exclusive period of brain development and related cognitive development—so all of society's emphasis must not support sole attention to the first three years while neglecting later periods important to teaching and learning (Bruer 1999).

Many researchers have pondered the phenomenon of exuberant production of synaptic connections in early life and wondered if maintaining the extra synapses or stimulating the brain to produce additional synapses would help or hinder behaviors. Studies by Diamond and colleagues (Diamond et al. 1964) suggest that certain stimuli can indeed produce structural changes in some brain cells. Whether or not such changes are of benefit still is highly conjectural. Remember, the nervous system functions as an elegant mixture of inhibition and excitation that for each neuron must sum to produce an all-or-none electrical potential along an axon. Additional sites of synaptic connections have as much potential to "short-circuit" the system as they do to have a positive benefit. The evidence that extra stimulation can lead to direct, measurable increases in cognitive function, let alone structural changes in the brain, is inconclusive. The clamor that occurred when phenomena such as the Mozart effect were revealed (Rauscher et al. 1993)—which grew into a concept that listening to Mozart, an external stimulus for the brain, will increase a child's intelligence—has been significantly reduced despite the public interest.

As an organ of the body, the evolution of the human brain over the past tens of thousands of years has resulted in a body system that seems to thrive and grow within a "normal" childhood that has balanced nutrition and external stimulation. Early learning—much of which is informal but also including the earliest aspects of formal education—seems to start off naturally for many children, although all aspects of this learning are not understood. Much work has been done to understand aspects of higher-order cognitive function such as language acquisition and early reading abilities. Much less has been done to understand when and how children acquire abilities and interests in mathematics and science. A very recent workshop at the National Academies of Science highlights the issues and points to future directions (National Research Council 2005).

The concept that many brain regions must be activated during any given brain function is supportive of the theory of multiple intelligences (Gardner 1985), which argues that intelligence should not be considered as a singular aspect of behavior but rather that in each individual there exists a number of intelligences that work independently of each other. Further, in a given individual, some intelligences may be significantly stronger than others. As described earlier, any given brain function requires that a number of brain regions be involved in order for proper functioning. The outside observer often discerns behaviors—for example, seeing, speaking, thinking, learning—as unimodal, while the brain actually parcels the work among many brain areas; and these regions operate in different ways for different individuals, based on genetics and experience.

Although a biological substrate for intelligence or intelligences has not been identified, it makes sense that multiple brain regions would underlie such functions and that they would display themselves as strengths and weaknesses in cognitive abilities. For the teaching and learning enterprise, it then becomes significant to attend to the various ways of learning to garner the greatest capacity of the learner. A similar argument can be made for learning styles and attempts to integrate learning styles and multiple intelligences (Silver et al. 2000).

A classroom based on an appreciation that students are individuals with a variety of intelligences operating at different levels would offer an opportunity for more students to utilize their full range of cognitive, and brain-based, skills. Building on cognitive strengths and bolstering of cognitive weaknesses would be attempts to fully utilize the biological substrates for learning. It is in this regard that the multimodal science classroom (although there are applications within the teaching of all disciplines), which involves a mixture of direct instruction, investigations, and inquiry learning, is likely to provide good stimuli for students with multiple intelligences (Armstrong 1994). Most importantly, such classrooms must be available to all students because there is no evidence from a neurobiological perspective that the overall construct of the brain is different for one group of students compared to another group. Failure to offer such opportunities limits students' capacities.

Lastly, if teaching and learning are conducted with an appreciation of multiple intelligences, then accurate and appropriate assessment should also tap into multiple intelligences. Failure to do so only results in the capturing of knowledge in a single aspect of brain function, and only for those students who excel—for whatever reasons of genetics and experience—in that function.

CHAPTER 18

Horizons for Brain Research and Learning

The confluence and advancement of the fields of neuroscience and developmental psychology have resulted in new thinking and an evolving science of learning, which has strong possibilities for influencing the future of teaching and learning (Brandt 2000). The belief that now, more than ever, there may be relevance of the basic science of the brain to education has furthered excitement. A good portion of the literature that exists has been brought together in a seminal series, initiated as *How People Learn* (Bransford et al. 1999) but followed by other texts on teaching, learning, and assessment (Chudowsky and Glaser 2001), under the auspices of the National Research Council. These compiled learnings even have suggestions for advanced study—Advanced Placement and the International Baccalaureate—in high schools with recommendations such as "curricula for advanced study should emphasize depth of understanding over exhaustive coverage of content" (Gollub et al. 2002, p. 199).

Funding is just now becoming available for significant efforts to provide a 21st century context for understanding what learning is and how it is affected in all domains. Tools and approaches that span an interdisciplinary array of closely allied fields—such as neuroscience, psychology in all of its many aspects, cognitive science, and computational science—are expected to yield new insights. Modern theories of cognition have already begun to articulate original thinking on assessment (Pellegrino et al. 1999), so one might expect that stronger linkages of brain research with cognitive neuroscience and cognitive psychology might offer new insights as well.

In summary, the full application of brain research to education is still on the horizon, as our understanding of the brain and its relationship to classroom learning remains in the early stages. The interdisciplinary approach of a science of learning holds much promise for the future, and, while fledging, needs to be watched actively by educators as they consider further changes in their teaching during the 21st century. As this approach matures, transferring learning research to teaching and learning practice is especially critical.

[1]Opinions and conclusions expressed in this chapter are those of the author and do not necessarily reflect the views of the National Science Foundation.

James E. Hamos
is a program director at the National Science Foundation (NSF) where he helps manage a broad national portfolio of projects in the Math and Science Partnership program. Originally trained as a neuroscientist, his work on Alzheimer's disease brought him into discussions of science literacy and illiteracy and, finally, to local, state, and national issues in mathematics and science education. Honors include a Public Service Award from the University of Massachusetts system and a Director's Award of Excellence at NSF.

References

101st Congress. 1989. The Decade of the Brain. *Congressional Record, Vol. 135.*, Public Law 101–58.

Armstrong, T. 1994. *Multiple intelligences in the classroom.* Alexandria, VA: Association for Supervision and Curriculum Development.

Bear, M. F., B. W. Connors, and M. A. Paradiso. 2001. *Neuroscience: Exploring the brain.* 2nd ed. Baltimore, MD: Lippincott Williams & Wilkins.

Brandt, R. S., ed. 2000. *Education in a new era.* Alexandria, VA: Association for Supervision and Curriculum Development.

Bransford, J. D., A. L. Brown, and R. R. Cocking (eds.). 1999. *How people learn: Brain, mind, experience, and school.* Committee on Developments in the Science of Learning, Center for Education, Division of Behavioral and Social Sciences and Education, National Research Council. Washington, DC: National Academy Press.

Bruer, J. T. 1999. *The myth of the first three years.* New York: The Free Press.

Caine, R. N., and G. Caine. 1997. *Unleashing the power of perceptual change: The potential of brain-based teaching.* Alexandria, VA: Association for Supervision and Curriculum Development.

Chudowsky, N., and R. Glaser, eds. 2001. *Knowing what students know: The science and design of educational assessment.* Board on Teaching and Assessment, Center for Education, Division of Behavioral and Social Sciences and Education, National Research Council. Washington, DC: National Academy Press.

Diamond, M. C., D. Krech, and M. R. Rosenzweig. 1964. The effects of an enriched environment on the histology of the rat cerebral cortex. *Journal of Comparative Neurology* 123: 111–119.

Gardner, H. 1985. *Frames of mind: The theory of multiple intelligences.* New York, NY: Basic Books.

Gollub, J. P., M. W. Bertenthal, J. B. Labov, and P. C. Curtis. 2002. *Learning and understanding: Improving advanced study of mathematics and science in U.S. high schools.* Committee on Programs for Advanced Study of Mathematics and Science in American High Schools, Center for Education, Division of Behavioral and Social Sciences and Education, National Research Council. Washington, DC: National Academy Press.

Gopnik, A., A. N. Meltzoff, and P. K. Kuhl. 1999. *The scientist in the crib.* New York: William Morrow.

Gram, H. G., and V. Germinario. 2000. *Leading and learning in schools: Brain-based practices.* Lanham, MD: Scarecrow Press.

Huttenlocher, P. R., and A. S. Dabholkar. 1997. Regional differences in synaptogenesis in human cerebral cortex. *Journal of Comparative Neurology* 387: 167–178.

Jensen, E. 1998. *Teaching with the brain in mind.* Alexandria, VA: Association for Supervision and Curriculum Development.

Katz, L. C., and C. J. Shatz 1996. Synaptic activity and the construction of cortical circuits. *Science* 274: 1133–1138.

Knudsen, E. I. 2004. Sensitive periods in the development of the brain and behavior. *Journal of Cognitive Neuroscience* 16: 1412–1425.

Locke, J. L. 1997. A theory of neurolinguistic development. *Brain and Language* 58(2): 265–326.

National Research Council (NRC). 2005. *Mathematical and scientific development in early childhood: A workshop summary.* Beatty, A., rapporteur. Mathematical Science Education Board, Board on Science Education, Center for Education, Division of Behavioral and Social Sciences and Education. Washington, DC: National Academy Press.

Pellegrino, J. W., G. P. Baxter, and R. Glaser. 1999. Addressing the "two disciplines" problem: Linking theories of cognition and learning with assessment and instructional practice. *Review of Research in Education* 24: 307–353.

Ramón y Cajal, S. 1954. *Neuron theory or reticular theory? Objective evidence of the anatomical unity of nerve cells.* Madrid: Consejo Superior de Investigaciones Cientificas.

Rauscher, F. H., G. L. Shaw, and K. N. Ky. 1993. Music and spatial task performance. *Nature* 365: 611.

Silver, H. F., R. W. Strong, and M. J. Perini. 2000. *So each may learn: Integrating leaning styles and multiple intelligences.* Alexandria, VA: Association for Supervision and Curriculum Development.

Skonkoff, J. P., and D. A. Phillips (eds.). 2000. *From neurons to neighborhoods: The science of early child development.* Committee on Integrating the Science of Early Childhood Development, Center for Education, Division of Behavioral and Social Sciences and Education, National Research Council. Washington, DC: National Academy Press.

Squire, L. R., and E. R. Kandel. 1999. Memory: From mind to molecules. *Scientific American Library.* New York: WH Freeman.

Sylwester, R. 1995. A *celebration of neurons: An educator's guide to the human brain.* Alexandria, VA: Association for Supervision and Curriculum Development.

Tong, F. 2003. Primary visual cortex and visual awareness. *Nature Reviews Neuroscience* 4: 219–229.

Wiesel, T. 1982. Postnatal development of the visual cortex and the influence of the environment. *Nature* 299: 583–592.

CHAPTER

19

How Do Students Learn Science?

Nancy P. Moreno and Barbara Z. Tharp

Science is neither a philosophy nor a belief system. It is a combination of mental operations that has become increasingly the habit of educated peoples, a culture of illuminations hit upon by a fortunate turn of history that yielded the most effective way of learning about the real world ever conceived.

—E. O. Wilson (1998, p. 45)

Type "science learning" into the web search engine Google, and you will get 19,600,000 results within 0.17 seconds. Pick up the *National Science Education Standards* (NSES) (NRC 1996), and find a systemwide blueprint for developing students' science understanding and skills developed by more than 3,000 scientists and educators. Take a look at the federal budget for 2004, and see millions of dollars allocated to educational research.

Despite the commitment of such immense attention, energy, and funding, our system for science education continues to fall short. U.S. students are performing at or below the levels attained by students in other countries in the developed world; U.S. student performance becomes increasingly weaker at higher grade levels; and achievement gaps between various racial/ethnic subgroups persist and have shown no signs of narrowing since 1990 (NSF 2004; Martin et al. 2004).

As we search for ways to improve classroom science experiences for students, we repeat the same question over and over: "How do students learn science?" In one sense, how students learn science falls within the realm of cognitive neuroscience. Perhaps a more pragmatic question is, "Which factors or practices most contribute to students' learning of science?"

To address this question, it is important to clarify the meaning of "science learning." Noted biology educator John Moore (1993, 502) says that "Science is both knowledge of the natural world expressed in naturalistic terms and the procedures for obtaining that knowledge." Thus, the learning of science involves the acquisition of a body of knowledge and an understanding of the process by which that knowledge was built. The NSES go one step further, recommending that students develop "abilities necessary to do scientific inquiry," in addition to understanding the nature of scientific inquiry (p. 121).

Ask a scientist how she or he learned science, and inevitably the scientist will describe training and study culminating in graduate education experience not unlike a medieval apprenticeship, which engaged the apprentice in hands-on and inquiry processes. Most important, for professional scientists, the learning of science involves doing science at some point along the educational continuum, in addition to mastering a body of knowledge about an aspect of the natural world.

Unfortunately, very few practicing scientists are teaching K–12 science, and very few science teachers have the opportunity to participate in real scientific investigations. In K–12 schools, all too often, science is viewed as a collection of facts to be memorized—and then forgotten. Even undergraduate-level science instructors fall into the trap of emphasizing rote learning of science information (NRC 2003). All too rarely do educators focus on helping their students to achieve understanding, which implies grasping a rich cluster of facts, concepts, and examples associated with a major idea (NRC 1996). All too seldom do students have an opportunity to develop and conduct simple scientific investigations.

In the broadest sense, we already know what promotes meaningful learning of real science by students. As described by the NSES (NRC 1996) and supporting documents (NRC 1999, 2000), students should experience a coherent, accurate, and developmentally appropriate science curriculum and conduct scientific inquiries throughout their K–12 experience. Analysis of the recently published findings from the Trends in Mathematics and Science Study (TIMSS) (Martin et al. 2004) identified two important factors related to instruction that contributed to measurable gains in science learning: effective delivery of the content to be assessed and schools with positive climates for learning.

It is no surprise that higher levels of teacher science content knowledge have been found to correlate positively with effective teaching practices (Supovitz and Turner 2000) and student science achievement (Rowan et al. 2000). However, it is important to acknowledge that not all teachers of science have strong science backgrounds. In fact, only 24% of U.S. public school elementary teachers majored in a subject-specific content area (including science) for their graduate or undergraduate degrees (NCES 2002). At the secondary level, even though most teachers majored in a subject-specific content area or in a subject area specialization in education (NCES 2002), approximately 24% of secondary school classes in core subjects are taught by teachers lacking even a minor in those subjects (Jerald 2002).

Although this clearly is not ideal, even teachers with incomplete science backgrounds can facilitate students' learning of science knowledge and skills through a number of practical approaches. The following sections discuss factors that we and others have found to contribute to students' science learning.

Engaging Subject Matter

The notion of science as an exciting, knowledge-building endeavor is implicit even in informal conversations among scientists. When two scientists meet, the first question they pose to each other usually is, "What are you working on?" Embedded in this simple query are the notions that science is active and ongoing—and intrinsically interesting. Like scientists, young students often perceive the world as interesting and are eager to learn more about how it works. In his introduction to *Inquiry and the National Science Education Standards* (NRC 2000, p. xii), Bruce Alberts, former president of the National Academy of Sciences, refers to the importance of curiosity to science and building science knowledge: "Visit any second-grade classroom, and you will generally find a class bursting with energy and excitement, where children are eager to make new observations and figure things out."

Somewhere along the educational continuum, however, school science manages to squelch most students' enthusiasm toward learning about the natural world. Many programs of science instruction, unfortunately, reduce science knowledge to rote learning of disconnected facts. These approaches ignore the potential of real-world issues that can engage students in meaningful learning (Mintzes and Wandersee 1998). For learning to be meaningful (as opposed to rote), the material itself must have meaning (as opposed to being random), the learner must be able to incorporate the new ideas into an existing conceptual framework, and he or she must choose to incorporate the new knowledge in a non-verbatim way (Mintzes and Wandersee 1998).

In many situations, students choose to expend effort to learn something when they perceive it to be interesting and relevant. Their interest can be piqued during the introduction to a lesson—sometimes referred to as the "engage" phase (Bybee 1997)—or when the teacher asks questions, shows a discrepant event, or poses a problem related to the community or natural world. Students also can be motivated to learn something for themselves when they have a need to apply information to resolve an intriguing problem. This happens, for example, when students test predictions and hypotheses during the exploration of a science question. Students who are interested in a task are more likely to use higher-level thinking strategies, as opposed to memorization or other superficial learning strategies, and be more persistent in their efforts to follow through with an idea (Chin and Brown 2000).

Opportunities for Guided Inquiry

An engaging topic that motivates students to learn is the first step. Students also need opportunities to investigate scientific questions, collect and apply evidence, and communicate the outcomes of their investigations. These processes, all part of the science inquiry model described in NSES, can contribute to students' understanding of science concepts and how science knowledge has been developed over time. Guided inquiry, in which students explore a question or a variation of a question posed by the teacher, is a particularly valuable approach (Moreno et al. 2001). Over time, such experiences can help develop students' abilities to ask and investigate their own questions—a process sometimes referred to as open inquiry (NRC 2000).

In guided inquiry, the teacher assumes responsibility for establishing the parameters of the investigation. This role may involve directly posing the question to be explored and defining the variables and/or data to be used or simply guiding students in the selection and investigation of an appropriate question and variables. Teachers facilitate the acquisition of needed materials and the learning of new procedures or techniques in addition to establishing guidelines for the communication of results and explanations. Guided inquiry is goal-oriented, in the sense that it is directed at helping learners develop knowledge related to a specific domain.

Inquiry learning often is equated with constructivist learning, and there is no denying the influence of constructivist theories on science education research and practice in the U.S. At the same time, we acknowledge the considerable discussion about what actually constitutes constructivist teaching and learning. At the very least, as noted by Matthews (2002, p. 132), the attention to constructivism has served science education by "alerting teachers to the function of prior learning and extant concepts in the process of learning new material, by stressing the importance of understanding as a goal of science instruction, [and] by fostering pupil engagement in lessons," in addition to building awareness of the human dimension of science.

Evidence is emerging that standards-aligned, guided inquiry does facilitate student science learning. Published evaluations of systemic change projects funded by the National Science Foundation are beginning to relate standards-aligned science teaching, which includes inquiry experiences, with measurable increases in higher-order thinking and problem-solving skills, science process skills, and understanding of concepts (Kahle et al. 2000; Marx et al. 2004; Rivet and Krajcik 2004; Von Secker and Lissitz 1999).

In addition, the inquiry-based programs are effective with urban or other disadvantaged students, who cope with challenges not faced by other learners. Urban students, for example, face larger class sizes, fewer opportunities for instruction by teachers certified in the subject area (NCES 2002; Haycock 2001), fewer opportunities to conduct laboratory investigations (Von Secker and Lissitz 1999), and greater exposure to instruction that emphasizes rote learning (Haberman 1991).

We are finding, as part of the Environment as a Context for Opportunities in Schools (ECOS) project, that inquiry-based science teaching can close the gap between students in English-speaking and Spanish-speaking elementary school classes, as measured by subject-specific content knowledge tests. The ECOS project is promoting the implementation of an integrated curriculum in seven urban elementary schools and is examining the effects of the approach on student science learning and language skills development. Each participating school uses environmental health science inquiry units, developed at Baylor College of Medicine (BCM) with funding from the National Institute of Environmental Health Sciences, as the basis for science, reading and language arts, mathematics, and health instruction for at least one semester per school year. During 2003–2004, the first full year of full program implementation, Spanish-speaking elementary students performed at much lower levels on content pretests, but their scores were indistinguishable statistically from other groups on posttest (Moreno et al. 2005). Kahle et al. (2000) reported that standards-aligned teaching practices, which include opportunities to learn through inquiry, positively influenced urban African-American students' science achievement and attitudes. These effects were particularly pronounced among boys. Similarly, Freedman (1997) found that hands-on laboratory experiences raised achievement levels and promoted positive attitudes toward science among all members of a multiracial and multiethnic student population enrolled in a ninth-grade physical science course.

Experience With Concepts and Models of Science

Complementary to inquiry learning are opportunities to develop deep understandings of complex ideas. As part of the inquiry process, students learn to use evidence to construct explanations of natural phenomena and to apply new knowledge to new situations. Thus, inquiry contributes to the development of students' critical thinking abilities while building subject-specific knowledge.

Of course, students cannot possibly experience all science concepts firsthand, but other learner-centered strategies can help them develop additional content knowledge and science skills. Analogies, open-ended problems, models, and explanations all allow students to connect new information with past experiences (Chin and Brown 2000). Explanation by the learner (self-explanation), in particular, has been found to facilitate the integration of new knowledge with existing knowledge (Chi et al. 1994). As students acquire more sophisticated ways of processing and assimilating science knowledge, the foci of their explanations shift from descriptive accounts to delineating relationships and even causality (Woodruff and Meyer 1997).

Accommodation of New Knowledge Relative to Prior Knowledge

Piaget's models for knowledge acquisition have been applied extensively in science education (1975). As most commonly interpreted, these models assert that real-world experiences cause learners either to assimilate new knowledge into an existing cognitive structure or to experience disequilibrium, in which new knowledge is not consistent with the existing structure (Bybee 1997; Weaver 1998). Disequilibrium, considered by some to be essential for the construction of new knowledge, can lead to conceptual change by the learner.

The role of prior knowledge in shaping science beliefs and understandings has been highlighted very effectively by the Private Universe in Science Project (Harvard-Smithsonian Center for Astrophysics 1995). As illustrated in several of the video resources created by the project, students create their own explanations for phenomena in the natural world and hold tightly to those explanations. Even though many of these explanations or conceptual frameworks are inaccurate, students will alter them to accommodate new knowledge only when they experience situations that cannot be reconciled with their existing conceptual frameworks (Weaver 1998). According to Posner (1992), in order for conceptual change to occur, the new conception must be plausible and have better predictive value than the original one. Some investigators have found that students with high logical thinking abilities undergo more cognitive dissonance after experiencing a discrepant event than those with less developed logical thinking abilities (Kang et al. 2004). The challenge for teachers is to assess students' preconceptions prior to introducing new topics, so that appropriate learning experiences can be provided (Meyer 2004).

Opportunities to Communicate

The social dimension of science learning also must be considered, for science is a social endeavor that involves consensus building, peer review, and communication in a variety of formats. Scientists do not always agree. Consequently, written and verbal discourse are part of the process of developing scientific knowledge. Students of science, ideally, should have opportunities to work as small groups to conduct investigations, evaluate evidence, and formulate explanations. Meyer and Woodruff (1997) found, for example, that seventh-grade students who engaged in inquiry, followed by small and large group discussion and evaluation, were able to achieve consensus and develop a coherent explanation of light and shadows. In addition, the students were able to connect their own ideas with expert text and move from situation-specific explanations to more unified explanations of all of the observed effects.

Peer-peer discussion can help clarify concepts for students and aid meaningful learning. A learner at the same developmental level is sometimes more effective than a teacher at reinterpreting or explaining a difficult concept to another learner (Jones and Carter 1998).

The quality of questions posed by students is an important indicator of whether a science lesson is promoting in-depth, meaningful learning. Students who are engaged in their own science learning tend to ask questions focused on explanations, causes, or predictions, or on resolving discrepancies in knowledge (Chin and Brown 2000).

Exposure to Teachers With Positive Attitudes Toward Science

We have found that students' enthusiasm for science can be shaped by teacher attitude, regardless of a teacher's personal level of content knowledge. Successful teachers provide a learning environment in which curiosity is encouraged openly and students have opportunities to explore ideas and physical objects. Much has been written about addressing teachers' reluctance to teach science, particularly in elementary schools (NRC 1997; NSF 1997). It is possible, however, through sustained, standards-aligned professional development, to change teachers' attitudes toward science and beliefs about their own abilities to teach science (Roberts and Moreno 2003; Roberts et al. 2001).

Teacher enthusiasm and attitude has been related to improved learning by students, particularly when the enthusiasm is reflected in a willingness to use a variety of approaches to meet students' needs (Darling-Hammond 1999). Radford (1998) found that an NSES-aligned approach to science teaching, coincidentally perceived by students as fun, was linked to greater student understanding of science processes.

Over the past 10 years, at Baylor College of Medicine, we have conducted in-depth summer and school-year science professional development for more than 1,200 Houston-area elementary and middle school teachers through programs funded by the National Science Foundation and the National Institutes of Health. Most participants were certified in areas other than science. Many of them, nevertheless, have become successful teachers of science and schoolwide science leaders. Examples include program graduates who have become schoolwide science specialists, districtwide master science lead teachers, and even a district-level supervisor of elementary science.

The catalyst for much of this success has been the empowerment of teachers to overcome their stated reluctance to teach science and encourage an attitude open to learning and experimenting with approaches to science teaching. In fact, a follow-up conducted three years after graduation with elementary teachers who participated in the NSF-funded Baylor Science Leadership Program found statistically significant changes in science teaching efficacy beliefs ($N=28$, $p \leq 0.001$, Cohen's $d = 1.83$) as measured using the Self Efficacy Teaching and Knowledge Instrument for Science Teachers (SETAKIST) (Roberts 2000). Over a three-year period, these teachers participated in more than 100 hours per year of professional development provided by BCM and other partners in the Houston Urban Systemic Initiative.

An important step in building a positive attitude toward science teaching is realizing that it is not necessary—and indeed not possible—to know everything about a given science field. In fact, most effective science teachers openly acknowledge this fact and encourage students to use a variety of resources to resolve questions and issues that come up during class discussions.

Guidance Through Appropriate Questions

Related to overall attitude is a teacher's willingness to move beyond asking questions that emphasize rote recall of information. Many teachers consider questions that echo facts covered in class or in a textbook to be safe, because the answers are laid forth clearly in the text or answer key. In our experience, once teachers start to ask questions that are open-ended, for which there may not be a single "right" answer, they discover that students become more engaged and science class becomes more interesting.

Even teachers with minimal science backgrounds can develop their questioning skills to promote in-depth science learning. Indeed, effective science questions can emphasize prediction ("What if…?"), focus students' attention

("Have you seen ...?"), provide opportunities for comparison ("How are they alike?"), help students uncover relationships ("What happens if ...?") or pose new problems ("Can you find a way to ...?") (Eltgeest 1985).

In 2000, we conducted classroom observations of 13 randomly selected graduates (10% of the total enrollment) of the two-week summer Baylor Science Leadership Program (BSLP) for Houston-area elementary science teachers. Trained personnel observed the selected teachers' classes on two different occasions using the electronic version of the Stallings Observation System (Stallings et al. 1979), which monitors the types of questions that teachers and students ask during a lesson. We found that program graduates spent less time asking direct questions and providing direct instruction and more time asking higher-order questions and receiving questions from students than the criterion values established for these activities (equated with "good teaching") by the developers of the instrument (Moreno et al. 2004). Although BSLP teachers did not have strong science backgrounds, they were able to improve learning opportunities by engaging students through appropriate questions and encouraging students to ask their own questions.

Opportunities to Work With Scientists

Although it is not possible for all science learners to engage with research scientists, such experiences can profoundly increase students' motivation to learn science and their comprehension of complex scientific ideas. Naturally, the impact of the experience is dependent on the dynamics between students and mentor scientists. And even when students gain knowledge about the process of scientific inquiry, they do not necessarily change their conceptions about the nature of science (Bell et al. 2003). When students are allowed to conduct "real" research alongside practicing scientists, however, they can acquire insight into data collection and use of evidence (Etkina et al. 2003), develop and use sophisticated laboratory skills (Knox et al. 2003), and build abilities to plan and conduct their own investigations (Korman and Dixon 1997).

Even co-teaching by scientists or graduate students in regular school classrooms can motivate student science learning. At Baylor College of Medicine, we conduct two separate programs that place graduate students or postdoctoral fellows in elementary (Science Education Leadership Fellows) or high school (Graduate Teaching Fellows in K–12 Education) classrooms. Evaluations of these partnership initiatives are showing that regular classroom visits by scientists can contribute to students' becoming more enthusiastic about science, and, in some cases, increased student science learning. Student achievement on statewide standardized tests, for example, has improved in 75% of the elementary schools participating in the Science Education Leadership Fellows program since 1999.

Summary

Science assumes that "nature is, in principle, knowable" (Moore 1993, 502). Accomplished teachers use a variety of instructional approaches to guide learners toward knowledge about the natural world and about how science, as a discipline, gathers knowledge and condenses knowledge about the world. Since the needs and interests of each learner are unique, it is important to provide different kinds of opportunities for students to experience the natural world and test and refine their conceptual frameworks. Chances to participate in guided inquiry, develop explanations with peers, communicate ideas, and interact with enthusiastic teachers and scientists can enhance students' efforts to learn science. Most important, in order for students to learn science, they must be motivated and engaged in the exploration of topics and questions that are interesting and relevant.

Nancy P. Moreno

is associate professor in the Department of Family and Community Medicine and associate director of the Center for Educational Outreach at Baylor College of Medicine, Houston. Trained as a botanist, she now focuses on developing collaborations among scientists and educators and leads science education partnerships funded by the National Institutes of Health, the Howard Hughes Medical Institute, and the National Science Foundation.

Barbara Z. Tharp

is assistant director of the Center for Educational Outreach and assistant professor of Family and Community Medicine at Baylor College of Medicine in Houston, Texas. She is a former elementary teacher who has co-authored a number of articles on teaching elementary science as well as several integrated curriculum series including BrainLink, My Health My World, From Outerspace to Innerspace, *and* My World and Me.

Acknowledgments

We express our appreciation to James Denk, senior editor in Baylor College of Medicine's Center for Educational Outreach, and an anonymous reviewer for their valuable suggestions. We gratefully acknowledge the following agencies for their support of educational programs described in this chapter: Howard Hughes Medical Institute (grant number 51004102); Science Education Partnership Award program, National Center for Research Resources, National Institutes of Health (NIH) (grant number R25 RR14354); National Institute of Environmental Health Sciences, NIH (grant number R25 ES10698); the National Space Biomedical Research Institute (NASA cooperative agreement NCC9-58); and the National Science Foundation (grant numbers DGE0086397 and ESI9816227). The opinions, findings, and conclusions expressed are solely those of the authors and do not necessarily reflect the views of BCM or the funding agencies. The partnerships described would not be possible without the numerous contributions of faculty and staff of the Center for Educational Outreach at BCM and the participating K–12 teachers and administrators.

References

Bell, R. L., L. M. Blair, B. A. Crawford, and N. G. Lederman. 2003. Just do it? Impact of a science apprenticeship program on high school students' understanding of the nature of science and scientific inquiry. *Journal of Research in Science Teaching* 40 (5): 487–509.

Bybee, R. 1997. *Achieving scientific literacy: From purposes to practice.* Portsmouth, NH: Heinemann.

Chi, M. T. H., N. deLeeuw, M. H. Chiu, and C. LaVancher. 1994. Eliciting self-explanations improves understanding. *Cognitive Science* 18: 439–477.

Chin, C., and D. E. Brown. 2000. Learning in science: A comparison of deep and surface approaches. *Journal of Research in Science Teaching* 37 (2): 109–138.

Darling-Hammond, L. 1999. Teacher quality and student achievement: A review of state policy evidence. *Center for the Study of Teaching and Policy, University of Washington, Document R–99–1*, Seattle, WA.

Eltgeest, J. 1985. The right question at the right time. In *Primary Science: Taking the Plunge,* ed. W. Harlen, 36–46. Oxford: Heinemann.

Etkina, E., T. Matilsky, and M. Lawrence. 2003. Pushing to the edge: Rutgers Astrophysics Institute motivates talented high school students. *Journal of Research in Science Teaching* 40 (10): 958–985.

Freedman, M. P. 1997. Relationship among laboratory instruction, attitude toward science, and achievement in science knowledge. *Journal of Research in Science Teaching* 34 (4): 343–357.

Haberman, M. 1991. The pedagogy of poverty versus good teaching. *Phi Delta Kappan* 73: 290–294.

Harvard-Smithsonian Center for Astrophysics. 1995 Private Universe Project. Retrieved January 14, 2005, from *www.learner.org/resources/series29.html.*

Haycock, K. 2001. Closing the achievement gap. *Educational Leadership* 6 (58): 6–11.

Jerald, C. D. 2002. All talk, no action: Putting an end to out-of-field teaching. Based on data analysis by Richard M. Ingersoll, University of Pennsylvania. Original analysis for the Education Trust of the 1999–2000 Schools and Staffing Survey. Education Trust, August. Retrieved November 18, 2004, from *www.edtrust.org/main.*

Jones, M. G., and G. Carter. 1998. Small groups and shared constructions. In *Teaching science for understanding: A human constructivist view,* eds. J. Mintzes, J. Wandersee, and J. Novak. New York: Academic Press.

Kahle, J. B., J. Meece, and K. Scantlebury. 2000. Urban African-American middle school science students: Does standards-based teaching make a difference? *Journal of Research in Science Teaching* 37 (9): 1019–1041.

Kang, S., L. C. Scharmann, and T. Noh. 2004. Reexamining the role of cognitive conflict in science concept learning. *Research in Science Education* 34: 71–96.

Korman, M. S., and B. S. Dixon. 1997. Research projects in acoustics for high school mentorship students. *The Journal of the Acoustical Society of America* 102 (5): 3126.

Knox, K. L., J. A. Moynihan, and D. G. Markowitz. 2003. Evaluation of short-term impact of a high school summer science program on students' perceived knowledge and skills. *Journal of Science Education and Technology* 12 (4): 471–478.

Martin, M. O., I. V. S. Mullis, E. J. Gonzalez, and S. J. Chrostowski. 2004. Findings from IEA's trends in international mathematics and science study at the fourth and eighth grades. Chestnut Hill, MA: TIMSS and PIRLS International Study Center, Boston College.

Marx, R. W., P. C. Blumenfield, J. S. Krajcik, B. Fishman, E. Soloway, R. Geier, and R. T. Tal. 2004. Inquiry-based science in the middle grades: Assessment of learning in urban systemic reform. *Journal of Research in Science Teaching* 41(10): 1063–1080.

Matthews, M. R. 2002. Constructivism and science education: A further appraisal. *Journal of Science Education and Technology* 11 (2): 121–132.

Meyer, K., and E. Woodruff. 1997. Consensually driven explanation in science teaching. *Science Education* 81 (2): 173–192.

Meyer, H. 2004. Novice and expert teachers' conceptions of learners' prior knowledge. *Science Education* 88: 970–983.

Mintzes, J. J., and J. H. Wandersee. 1998. Reform and innovation in science teaching: A human constructivist view. In J. Mintzes, J. Wandersee and J. Novak, *Teaching science for understanding: A human constructivist view.* New York: Academic Press.

Moore, J. A. 1993. *Science as a way of knowing: The foundations of modern biology.* Cambridge, MA: Harvard University Press.

Moreno, N., B. Tharp, and J. K. Roberts. 2005. Does inquiry science teaching impact teacher behaviors and student learning? American Association for the Advancement of Science Annual Meeting Abstracts, A85. Washington, D.C. 1721

Moreno N., J. Denk, J. K. Roberts, B. Tharp, M. Bost, and W. Thomson. 2004. An approach to improving science knowledge about energy balance and nutrition among elementary and middle school students. *Cell Biology Education* 3:122–130.

Moreno N., K. Chang, B. Tharp, J. Denk, J. K. Roberts, P. Cutler, and S. Rahmati. 2001. Teaming up with scientists. *Science and Children* 39 (1): 42–45.

National Research Council (NRC). 1996. *National Science Education Standards.* Washington, DC: The National Academy Press.

National Research Council (NRC). 1997. *Science for all children.* Washington, DC: The National Academy Press.

National Research Council (NRC). 1999. *Designing mathematics or science curriculum programs: A guide for using mathematics and science education standards.* Washington, DC: The National Academy Press.

National Research Council (NRC). 2000. *Inquiry and the National Science Education Standards: A guide for teaching and learning.* Washington, DC: The National Academy Press.

National Research Council (NRC). 2003. Improving undergraduate instruction in science, technology, engineering, and mathematics: report of a workshop. Steering Committee on Criteria and Benchmarks for Increased Learning from Undergraduate STEM Instruction. In Committee on undergraduate science education, eds. R. A. McCray, R. DeHaan, and J. A. Schuck . Washington, DC: The National Academy Press.

National Science Board. 2004. *Science and engineering indicators* 2004. Two volumes. Arlington, VA: National Science Foundation (volume 1, NSB 04–1; volume 2, NSB 04–1A).

National Science Foundation (NSF). 1997. *The challenge and promise of K–8 science education reform.* NSF 97–76. Arlington, VA: National Science Foundation.

National Center for Educational Statistics (NCES). 2002. Contexts of elementary and secondary education. In: The Condition of Education. Indicator 32 (2002). Retrieved January 14 from *www.nces.ed.gov//programs/coe/2002/section4/indicator32.asp.*

Piaget. J. 1975. *The development of thought.* New York: Viking Press.

Posner, G. J. 1992. *Analyzing the curriculum.* New York: McGraw Hill.

Radford, D. L. 1998. Transferring theory into practice: A model for professional development for science education reform. *Journal of Research in Science Teaching* 35 (1): 73–88.

Rivet, A. E., and J. S. Krajcik. 2004. Achieving standards in urban systemic reform: An example of a sixth grade project-based science curriculum. *Journal of Research in Science Teaching* 41 (7): 669–692.

Roberts, J. K. 2000. Self efficacy knowledge and teaching instrument for science teachers (SETAKIST): A proposal for a new efficacy instrument. Paper presented at the annual meeting of the Mid-South Educational Research Association, Bowling Green, KY. ERIC Document Reproduction Service No. TM032238.

Roberts, J. K, and N. Moreno. 2003. Teacher self-efficacy is NOT enough! The problem of interpreting measures of teacher self-efficacy apart from other measures of teacher performance. Paper presented at the 2003 annual meeting of the American Educational Research Association, April 22 (session #29.025), Chicago, IL.

Roberts, J., R. Henson, B. Tharp, and N. Moreno. 2001. An examination of change in teacher self-efficacy beliefs in science education based on duration of inservice activities. *Journal of Science Teacher Education* 12 (3): 199–213.

Rowan, R., R. Correnti, and R. J. Miller. 2002. What large-scale survey research tells us about teacher effects on student achievement: Insights from the prospects study of elementary schools. Consortium for Policy Research in Education, University of Pennsylvania, CPRE Research Report Series RR–051.

Stallings, J., M. Needels, and N. Staybrook. 1979. How to change the process of teaching basic skills in secondary schools, Phase II and III. Final report for National Institute of Education. Menlo Park, CA: SRI International.

Supovitz, J. A., and H. M. Turner. 2000. The effects of professional development on science teaching practices and classroom culture. *Journal of Research in Science Teaching* 37 (9): 963–980.

Von Secker, C. E., and R. W. Lissitz. 1999. Estimating the impact of instructional practices on student achievement in science. *Journal of Research in Science Teaching* 36 (10): 1110–1126.

Weaver, G. C. 1998. Strategies in K–12 science instruction to promote conceptual change. *Science Education* 82: 455–472.

Wilson, E. O. 1998. *Consilience: The unity of knowledge.* New York: Alfred A. Knopf. p 45.

CHAPTER

20

The Psychology of Scientific Thinking: Implications for Science Teaching and Learning

Junlei Li and David Klahr

Science education has two primary aims: to teach children about our accumulated knowledge of the natural world and to help them employ the methods, procedures, and reasoning processes used to acquire that knowledge—in other words, to "think scientifically." The content of science education comprises examples sampled from the vast and ever-expanding collection of knowledge in different domains and disciplines. The process of scientific thinking is generalized from the practices shared across domains and disciplines. Researchers in psychological science have paid increasing attention to this generalized form of scientific thinking. In this chapter, we suggest ways in which the emerging psychological understanding of scientific thinking can inform practical questions in science education.

Our examination of science education through the lens of the psychology of scientific thinking is prompted, in part, by the No Child Left Behind Act (NCLB) of 2001, in which the phrase "scientifically based research" appears more than 100 times (Traub 2002). In addition to NCLB, publication of the National Academy of Science's *Scientific Research in Education* (SRE)

(Shavelson and Towne 2002) and its sequel, *Advancing Scientific Research in Education* (Towne et al. 2004), has generated extensive discourse about the definition of scientific research as well as its validity and relevance in educational settings (Berliner 2002; Darling-Hammond and Youngs 2002; Erickson and Gutierrez 2002; Feuer et al. 2002; Pelligrino and Goldman 2002; St. Pierre 2002).

The key message of NCLB and SRE is that educational practice should incorporate "what works" solutions validated by scientifically based research (see *www.whatwork.ed.gov*). The problem is that few of the scientifically rigorous psychological studies of scientific thinking were ever intended to provide practical recommendations for what works in the classroom. Instead, these psychological inquiries have asked "what is" scientific thinking in children, lay adults, and present and past scientists (Klahr and Simon 1999). Can the psychological investigations of scientific thinking inform practical questions in science education? We think this question is worth exploring for both psychological researchers and science educators.

Given the limited space and scope of this chapter, we chose to delve deeply into just one theoretical description of scientific thinking. For more comprehensive reviews of relevant psychological research, see Kuhn (1997), Lehrer and Schauble (forthcoming), Metz (1995, 1997), and Zimmerman (2000). Our particular theoretical framework can be viewed as an elaboration of an insight voiced by Einstein in his characterization of the relationship between scientific thinking and everyday thinking.

> The scientific way of forming concepts differs from that which we use in our daily life, not basically, but merely in the more precise definitions of concepts and conclusions; more painstaking and systematic choice of experimental material, and great logical economy (Einstein 1936/1950, p. 98).

In proposing "precise definitions of concepts" for the scientific thinking process itself, we characterize scientific thinking as a set of cognitive processes underlying general problem solving but constrained by the unique features of the scientific problem (Klahr 2000; Klahr and Dunbar 1988; Newell and Simon 1972; Simon et al. 1981). We use this framework to connect the basic research on scientific thinking with the practice of science teaching, particularly with reference to inquiry, the goal and means of science education advocated by the National Science Education Standards (NSES) (NRC 1996).

CHAPTER
20

Psychological Research and Science Teaching

Psychologists who study scientific thinking seek answers to questions such as "What is thinking?" and "How does knowledge develop?" Teachers and educational developers seek answers to questions such as, "How should we teach (a particular aspect of) science?" and "Do some teaching methods work better than others?" The psychologists' questions—in pursuit of fundamental understanding of human cognition—are characteristic of basic research in the science laboratory aimed at structured problems. The questions asked by teachers and educational developers—aiming toward usability and efficacy—are characteristic of an engineering design, aimed at solving practical problems. Ideally, these two types of questions and their approaches are complementary in advancing our understanding of the natural world and engendering practical applications. Scientific research provides causal and correlational information (e.g., factors that stimulate the development of thinking and initial knowledge of children at various ages) helpful to engineer effective applications. In return, practical uses reveal obstacles and challenges that energize and enlighten scientific research (Stokes 1997). The integration of educational research and practice, however, has fallen short of its potential for reciprocal, productive, and sustainable interaction (Brown 1992; Hiebert et al. 2002; Lagemann 1996, 2000; Strauss 1998).

At least in the area of psychology, one primary reason for this lack of mutual influence derives from inherent incompatibilities between the goals and methods of basic psychological research and those of science teaching in classrooms (Klahr and Li 2005). For example, research in the psychological laboratory has tried to distinguish between domain-specific knowledge and domain-general strategy. Researchers often studied one type of knowledge or the other, but both simultaneously (Kuhn and Angelev 1976; McCloskey 1983; Tschirgi 1980). The complexity of scientific thinking was divided into a more manageable set of distinguishable processes (e.g., hypothesis generation, experimentation, and evidence evaluation) and then each process was studied in relative isolation (Zimmerman 2000). Furthermore, researchers were typically interested in examining what, how, and why children think, rather than in how to teach children to think more scientifically (Metz 1995, 1997).

In stark contrast, science teachers generally do not seek to isolate every minute aspect of science in everyday teaching: one does not teach process without any content or vice versa. Integration across the traditional boundaries of content knowledge and process skills is explicitly emphasized in the standards of science teaching (AAAS 1993; NRC 1996). In addition, the standards and accountability reforms, by their very definitions, ask teachers to help students master a predefined set of educational objectives within a predefined period of time—in grade blocks, fifth to eighth grade, for instance—regardless of an individual child's natural competency or developmental pace. These highly contrasting goals and approaches of researchers and teachers make it difficult to translate researchers' understanding of children's competence—and lack of competence—in scientific thinking into educational practice. Much of the misinterpretation and misapplication of psychological research in science education is evidence of such difficulty (Metz 1995, 1997).

In summary, psychological research on scientific thinking cannot readily provide the kind of what-works information demanded by the NCLB model of research-to-practice pipeline. We want to explore the possibility that basic psychological research can inform practice without necessarily having to produce what-works prescriptions. To design effective teaching practices, teachers need to understand the goal they are teaching toward. Psychological research, as we have described, adopts goals and employs methodologies for the explicit purpose of seeking such an understanding. Informed by the piecemeal understanding of scientific thinking produced by earlier studies, psychologists over the last two decades have sought to unravel the interdependencies among domain-specific knowledge, experimental strategy, hypothesis generation, and experimentation (Klahr and Dunbar 1988; Kuhn et al. 1995; Schauble 1990, 1996; Schauble et al. 1991).

A more integrated psychological account of scientific thinking to describe the interplay between content knowledge and process skills in children, adults, and practicing scientists has emerged (Klahr and Simon 1999; Zimmerman 2000). We see an opportunity to synthesize the emerging integrative account of scientific thinking with what NSES has broadly defined as the inquiry goal and approach of science education.

Translating psychological theories into educational implications is a daunting and undervalued task. The topic domains studied by researchers, even when relevant, constitute a small subset of the content standards to which teachers are held accountable. Of the few studies that do involve training children to think more scientifically, even fewer training procedures have been validated beyond the one-on-one laboratory studies (e.g., Chen and Klahr 1999; Toth et al. 2000). In articles about scientific thinking in psychological journals, it has been and is still common to find brief and generic "educational implications" sections relegated to the very end of a paper, occupying only the space of a footnote. In this chapter, we expand the "footnote" with more substantive and pragmatic analyses.

Scientific Thinking as Problem Solving

We first describe a theoretical model of scientific thinking: Scientific Discovery as Dual Search (SDDS). The SDDS model describes scientific thinking by integrating domain-specific knowledge (content) and domain-general strategy (process). This theoretical perspective has guided two decades of empirical research in our own research program (Klahr 2000; Klahr and Dunbar 1988; Klahr et al. 1993). Although it is by no means the only theory of scientific thinking, SDDS is emerging as a promising framework to synthesize the accumulated research on scientific thinking (Zimmerman 2000).

The defining feature of SDDS is its conceptualization of scientific thinking as a complex problem-solving process, involving the coordination of hypothesis-search and experiment-search. The claim that scientific discovery is a type of problem solving is neither controversial nor informative unless we go beyond a generic interpretation of "problem solving" as a synonym for "thinking."

SDDS is based on the theoretical perspective of Newell and Simon (1972) that defines a problem as consisting of an *initial state* and a *goal state*, between which may exist a hierarchy of intermediate *subgoal* states. For example, to find out which factors influence the period of a pendulum, a middle-school child's initial state may consist of some hunches about pendulums. The goal state is to find out which hunch is right. The subgoal states may include specifying a hypothesis ("I think the weight of the bob matters"), testing the hypothesis (measuring the period with bobs of different weights), and then evaluating the outcomes ("The period did not change when I changed the bob's weight"). To accomplish each subgoal, the child needs to know a few *operators*: the set of permissible transformations from one state to another. To test whether the weight of the bob matters, knowing how to design a controlled and informative experimental comparison and make a precise prediction from the hypothesis being tested would be helpful. To determine whether the experimental outcome matters one way or the other, differentiating experimental error (e.g., random counting errors) from experimental effect (e.g., the difference actually created by changing a variable) and guarding against one's own confirmation bias in data interpretation would help. Executed proficiently, a sequence of operators can result in a solution path from the initial state to the goal state.

Operators have constraints that must be satisfied before they can be applied. Not just any controlled experiment would correctly test the effect of the bob weight. The experiment must compare the weight difference rather than some other variables like the string length. The total set of states, operators, goals, and constraints is called a *problem space*. The problem-solving process can be conceptualized as a search for a path in the entire problem space that progresses from the initial state to the goal state.

Each of the elements of SDDS—initial states, goal states, operators, and constraints—can vary along a well- to ill-defined continuum in a classroom or professional scientific task. For example, in a "mix these chemicals and see what happens" scenario, one has a well-defined initial state—the set of chemicals—but an ill-defined goal state—what one is expected to find. Or, in a "use strings and weights to find out what determines the period of a pendulum" scenario, one has well-defined initial and goal states—the lab materials and the purpose—but ill-defined operators —how one should design experiments to isolate the causal variable.

Table 1 and Figure 1 summarize how the three phases of SDDS—search hypothesis space, test hypothesis, and evaluate evidence—iteratively advance the scientific thinking process. The output from search hypothesis space is a fully specified hypothesis, which is passed forward as the input to test hypothesis. The output of test hypothesis is a description of evidence for or against the hypothesis, based on the match between the prediction derived from the current hypothesis and the actual experimental result. Next, evaluate evidence decides whether the cumulative evidence—as well as other considerations—warrants the acceptance, rejection, or continued consideration of the hypothesis. The rejection or continuing consideration of a hypothesis starts the process all over again.

Table 1: Scientific discovery as dual-search problem solving (SDDS)

<table>
<tr><td rowspan="5">Search Hypothesis Space</td><td>Evoke partial hypothesis based on prior knowledge</td><td colspan="2">Recall from memory, combined with analogical mapping, heuristic search, priming, and other cognitive mechanisms.</td></tr>
<tr><td rowspan="4">Complete partially specified hypothesis</td><td rowspan="3">Generate Outcome</td><td>Search Experiment Space
Generate some useful data (low constraint) that present intriguing and informative phenomenon. Low constraint: engineering approach acceptable.</td></tr>
<tr><td>Run
Execute experiments or collect data via observation.</td></tr>
<tr><td>Decide data
Accept, reject, or continue collecting data. Rejection reasons include measurement, methodology, or description. Continue collecting if data is not clearly interpretable.</td></tr>
<tr><td>Generalize Outcomes</td><td>If fail to generalize pattern, do more generate outcomes.</td></tr>
<tr><td rowspan="4">Test Hypothesis</td><td>Search Experiment Space</td><td colspan="2">High constraint: controlled experimentation, focused data collection, scientific approach preferred, need to inform and discriminate.</td></tr>
<tr><td>Make Prediction</td><td colspan="2">Constrained by theory, not hunch.</td></tr>
<tr><td>Run</td><td colspan="2">Execute experiments or collect data via observation.</td></tr>
<tr><td>Match</td><td colspan="2">Does the prediction match the experimental outcome?</td></tr>
<tr><td rowspan="2">Evaluate Evidence</td><td>Review Outcomes</td><td colspan="2">Evaluate theory vs. accumulated evidence: how to respond to anomalous data, can theories explain data, are there alternative hypotheses?</td></tr>
<tr><td>Decide</td><td colspan="2">Accept, reject, modify, or continue?</td></tr>
</table>

Figure 1 Scientific discovery as dual search (modified from Klahr 2000)

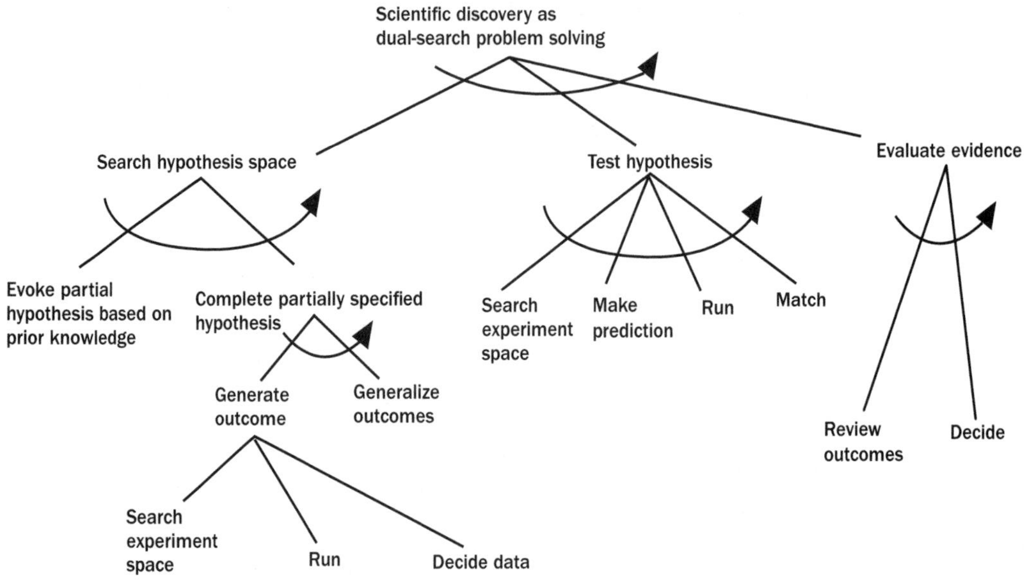

Note: See detailed explanations of the terminologies in Table 1.

The progression within phase and across phases is driven by a coordinated search in two problem spaces: the hypothesis space and the experiment space. Each space has its own initial states, goal states, operators, and constraints. The hypothesis space starts with an initial state consisting of prior content knowledge. Its goal state is to produce a fully specified and testable hypothesis that can account for some or all of that knowledge in a concise or universal form. When prior knowledge is not sufficient to evoke a testable hypothesis, one may supplement prior knowledge by generating additional experimental outcomes.

This is the first of the two places where the search in the experiment space is coordinated with search in the hypothesis space. For brevity, we use the term *experiment* to refer to both active experimental manipulations of variables, such as a physics experiment, and procedures of passive observations, such as a geological field expedition or astronomical data collection. Within the search hypothesis phase, the goal of searching experiment space is to produce outcomes that will allow some generalization toward a testable hypothesis. The method of experimentation is not tightly constrained. For example, if your goal is to develop some hunches about what makes a pendulum swing faster, then putting everything you think would speed up the swing into the same pendulum design is an efficient and acceptable strategy. The critical testing of each hunch comes later.

Once a testable hypothesis is formed, the problem-solving process proceeds to test the hypothesis. This is the second instance in which searching in the experiment space is required, but the constraint is more stringent. The goal state in the experiment space is to produce informative and logically unambiguous outcomes to which the hypothesis' prediction is compared. Generally, the aforementioned engineering approach, in a case such as building a fast car, with confounding variables would not be acceptable and would most certainly be uninformative.

Based on cumulative experimental outcomes, the evidence evaluation process produces a decision regarding the acceptance, rejection, or continued consideration of the hypothesis. Both the evidence and prior knowledge constrain decisions in this process. When children, adults, and practicing scientists are reasoning about real-world contexts, their prior knowledge imposes strong theoretical biases on their reasoning (Brewer and Chinn 1994; Tschirgi 1980). These biases influence not only the initial strength with which people hold these hypotheses—and hence the amount of disconfirming evidence necessary to refute the hypotheses—but also the features in the evidence that will be attended to and encoded. In scientific reasoning, such confirmation bias is seen paradoxically: necessary, so that one does not readily change a reasonable theory based only on small amounts of contradictory data; and problematic, when one refuses to change a theory despite the preponderance of evidence.

Following this theoretical introduction, we anticipate a pragmatic question: "So what?" Haven't science educators always regarded science as "problem solving," albeit in a generic and less operational sense? Technical jargon aside, what practically does this model add to the six-step "scientific method" found on posters in nearly every grade-school science classroom or the more elaborate definition of inquiry or scientific process found in science standards or textbooks?

We readily admit that the integration of this theoretical perspective with educational practice is at an early and exploratory stage. In our own research, we have begun to conduct laboratory and classroom studies towards this effort only since the late 1990s (Chen and Klahr 1999; Klahr and Li 2005; Klahr and Nigam 2004; Masnick and Klahr 2003; Toth et al. 2000; Triona and Klahr 2003). Based on our experience observing and teaching in the elementary school classrooms, however, we believe that educational practice can be much informed by the understanding of what scientific thinking is. We suggest why SDDS differs from traditional educational conceptualizations of the scientific method and how it may serve as an organizing framework to connect psychological research to inquiry-based science teaching.

Theory, Standards, and Science Teaching

To connect research to practice, we relate the rest of our discussion to the KWHL chart (Table 2), a tool originally intended to help teachers plan instruction (Kujawa and Huske 1995; Ogle 1986). We suggest how SDDS and relevant research can inform the first three questions of the KWHL chart with respect to science education. The fourth question, "what students learned," is explored in a separate report (Klahr and Li 2005).

The "K"—What Do Students Know?

Of the four KWHL questions, psychological research has provided the most extensive answers for this one. Many psychological investigations explicitly address this question within one or more aspects of scientific thinking. The consensus emerging from researchers is that even very young children can demonstrate partial competency in various aspects of scientific thinking. A short list of examples includes: preschoolers infer causal relations from data patterns (Gopnik et al. 2001); children in first and second grade

Table 2: KWHL chart

What students *know* ***(K)***
What we *want* ***(W)*** students to know
How ***(H)*** students will find out (about scientific thinking)
What students have *learned* ***(L)***

Note: The "W" question is paraphrased to suit the present discussion. A more common version is "What students want to know."

understand the difference between a conclusive and an inconclusive test of a simple hypotheses (Sodian et al. 1991); and children from the sixth to the ninth grades provide and incorporate causal explanations into their evaluation of evidence (Koslowski 1996).

More impressively, elementary-school-age children are ready to develop and refine their thinking when provided with carefully designed instruction and/or task environment (Klahr and Chen 2003; see also Kuhn 1997; Metz 1995, 1997). The cumulative research data convincingly argue against the once commonly held notion that elementary or middle school children lack developmental readiness to engage in abstract reasoning about evidence and hypotheses and must be taught science using only developmentally-appropriate tasks such as concrete manipulation of objects, procedural execution, categorization, classification, and description (Metz 1995; Lehrer and Schauble, forthcoming).

Children's developmental readiness for scientific thinking is impressive, but it should not be mistaken for robust competence. Many studies have found significant gaps between children's and adults' scientific thinking, even though adults are far from being proficient across many aspects of reasoning (Fay and Klahr 1996; Klahr et al. 1993; Kuhn et al. 1988; Kuhn et al. 1995). Children struggle much more than adults in evaluating evidence that contradicts their prior beliefs about causal relationships (Amsel and Brock 1996; Kuhn et. al. 1988); children lack conscious awareness that contradictory evidence should result in a reexamination of prior hypotheses (Kuhn et. al. 1988); children's use of experimentation to test a hypothesis is often driven by an engineering approach to create desirable effects. For example, when children were asked to test which features cause a car to go fast or slow, they designed experiments to create the fastest car instead (Schauble 1990).

What are the practical implications of these research findings? We suggest that SDDS can be used as an instructional analysis framework to map research findings onto classroom practices. To illustrate, we found two instances of "search experiment space" in an NSES fifth- through eighth-grade sample lesson. In the sample lesson, a teacher facilitates lesson activities in which students are to discover which factors determine the period of a pendulum (NRC 1996, 146–147). To start the lesson, the teacher engages the students to search the hypothesis space to suggest potential causal variables.

Instead of asking the students to evoke such hypotheses directly from prior knowledge, she guides the students to set up pendulums, count swings, and discuss why pendulums swing at different rates. Viewed through a SDDS lens, this teaching strategy is productive in two ways:

- It enables the students to generate testable hypotheses from data when their prior knowledge may only offer partially specified hypotheses.
- It helps the teacher to anticipate how the students' causal beliefs may subsequently affect their choice of experimentation and evidence evaluation strategies.

Because generating explanatory hypotheses is a natural inclination found in middle-school children (Koslowski 1996), the teacher could afford to focus less on instruction and more on facilitating the exploration and discussion.

The sample lesson began sounding too good to be true when the students, having thus searched the hypotheses space, spontaneously proceeded to test each hypothesis by designing unconfounded experiments—experiments in which only the focal variable is varied and all others are held constant. The psychological research suggests that students' strategy would falter precisely at the point of searching experiment space under the constraining goal of hypothesis testing (Chen and Klahr 1999; Schauble 1990; Schauble et al. 1991). Connecting such research findings to this particular point of inquiry may help the teacher anticipate the less optimal but more likely scenario in which students, instead of carefully isolating variables, confound experimental variables either in favor of their prior beliefs or to create what they consider a favorable effect. For example, students might set up a fast-swinging pendulum with short string, high release, and light weight bob to compare against a slow swinging pendulum with all the opposite features only to conclude that the high drop-point is what makes the difference.

The stated goal of this NSES sample lesson was for "students to develop an understanding of variables in inquiry and how and why to change one variable at a time" (NRC 1996, p. 146). This second instance of search experiment space is the critical point at which psychological research would suggest more teacher guidance or instruction. Yet the narrative for this lesson segment was so idealistically understated that it mentions neither teacher instruction nor guidance.

Understanding what students know in generic terms of developmental readiness or appropriateness is insufficient to implement effective inquiry in science education. Using the sample lesson above, we suggest that SDDS could serve as a framework to organize the teacher's knowledge of children's particular strengths and weaknesses. Such knowledge needs to come from both research and classroom practice, as science teachers accumulate a wealth of understanding from experience. SDDS can help facilitate a task analysis process by which a teacher structurally examines each component of scientific thinking involved in the lesson plan (e.g., search experiment space, search hypothesis, evaluate evidence) and asks, "Is this well-defined or ill-defined in the students' minds?" If hypotheses are ill-defined, the teacher may choose to add experimentation to allow students to explore and explain. If the experimental strategy to test a hypothesis is ill-defined, the teacher may choose to offer more explicit instruction or guidance. If the strategy to evaluate evidence is influenced by students' strong prior beliefs, the teacher may anticipate students' biased interpretation of contradictory data and help students become aware of their biases. The task analysis helps the teacher anticipate trouble spots, understand dependencies of one thinking process on another, and adjust the degree of constraint and guidance in instruction.

The "W"—What Do We Want Students to Know?

NSES uses the term *inquiry* to define broadly the ends and means of science education and emphasize the integration of individual process skills with content knowledge. This matches the theoretical motivation of SDDS, which is to integrate various scientific thinking skills studied in isolation into a coherent whole along with content knowledge. In fact, the list of "science as inquiry" objectives for fifth- through eighth- grade content Standards (NRC 1996, pp. 143–148) contains many of the same aspects of scientific thinking described by SDDS. So what can SDDS add to the inquiry standards beyond what is already stated in *NSES*?

The most important contrast between SDDS and inquiry in *NSES* is how differently each organizes the elements of scientific thinking. *NSES*, as well as the many state science standards developed during the standards reform, uses lists (bulleted, numbered, or simply organized as such) to define inquiry objectives. SDDS adopts a hierarchical and cyclical representation. Such representational differences are not superficial, because they lead to substantively different conceptualizations of the inquiry goal. Using lists to present complex information has been criticized as being too generic, leaving critical relationships unspecified and critical assumptions unstated (Shaw et al. 1998; cited by Tufte 2003). Although the vagueness and unstated assumptions of NSES as a whole have been critiqued (Donmoyer 1995; Rodriguez 1997; Shiland 1998), we as psychological researchers are most concerned by the lack of operational specificity in NSES regarding the relationships among the inquiry components. Without relationships, entities such as *prediction, experimentation, hypothesis generation,* and *evidence evaluation* are liable to be treated as a laundry list, with no sense of relative sequences or mutual contingencies. In fact, a common practice adopted by educational developers, publishers, and teachers in response to the standards reform was to make and complete checklists to show how curriculum and teaching align with the list items in the standards.

We believe the list representation of inquiry and the subsequent checklist implementation of inquiry standards overlook the fundamental structure of the nature of scientific thinking and ultimately mislead instruction. Without understanding the contingent relationships among the problem states and operators within scientific thinking, a teacher could easily engage a process skill out of context, a practice that *NSES* explicitly deemphasizes. We find examples of such practice even among the *NSES* sample lessons that are intended to convey exemplary inquiry-based teaching. In a density lesson unit (NRC 1996, pp. 150–153) used to illustrate inquiry teaching standards for fifth through eighth grades, the teacher asks students to make predictions for novel demonstrations on four separate occasions in three lessons. Does that indicate the lessons have helped students to "develop … predictions … using evidence" and "recognize and analyze … predictions"? (NRC 1996, pp. 147–148) Recall that in SDDS, prediction is an operator under the "test hypothesis" phase (see Figure 1), which requires a fully specified and testable hypothesis as input (from the phase "search for hypothesis") and produces as output (toward the phase "evaluate evidence") a matching between the prediction and the experimental outcome.

In each of the four cases in which the teacher asks students to make predictions, the teacher presents them with new and interesting experimental setups (i.e., the teacher conducted "search experiment space" for the students) without suggesting or asking students to formulate any specifiable hypotheses (i.e., the students are given experiments, but are not required to first "search hypothesis space"). Naturally, the students' responses focus on the outcomes—which of several objects will sink in a column of layered liquids—and not on the hypotheses that might explain their predictions—relative density and buoyancy.

Although we acknowledge that such practices can be very interesting and engaging to the students, we question whether they improve students' scientific thinking processes or content knowledge. In this particular instance, the lesson simply did not press the students to link their predictions with some testable hypotheses. Thus, even when the evidence contradicts or confirms prediction, it would unlikely result in students' revising or affirming their explanatory hypotheses, but more likely push them further along a course of guessing by trial and error. Such use of "prediction" reminds us of the "Will it float?" segment from David Letterman's Late Show, in which regulars on the show make guesses about various objects before dropping them into the water, rarely justifying or explaining the underlying reasons. The segment is entertaining, though the people making the guesses do not seem to improve their accuracy over time.

We use this example to illustrate the instructional consequences of viewing scientific thinking as an unordered list of relevant skills, rather than as a set of problem-solving goals and operators that are mutually contingent and constrained within explicitly structured relationships. Although we offer a critique of the NSES with regard to its presentation of inquiry objectives, we appreciate that the intent of NSES was to counter the practice of rigidly defining scientific thinking as a sequence of unalterable steps—state the problem, collect data, communicate results—as still seen on posters titled "The Scientific Method" in many science classrooms. Despite our concerns with inquiry standards and some sample lessons, we generally agree with the emphasis NSES places upon integrating various process skills. We suggest that, for the practitioner who aims to understand and implement inquiry, a theoretical model such as SDDS is a well-specified middle ground between the inflexible six-step "scientific method" and the vague bullet lists used by science standards.

The "H"—How Do Students Learn and Develop "Scientific Thinking"?

Of the four KWHL questions, the "H" is least answerable by the psychological studies of scientific thinking. As we said earlier, most psychological research does not directly ask "What works"? Recognizing this limitation, we refrain from discussing prescriptions for science teaching, but suggest how SDDS and psychological research can help in examining the what-works question.

How does one decide the fit between an instructional method and a particular learning goal? In such an analysis, SDDS can serve as a framework for connecting psychological research to educational practice. For example, if the goal is to develop students' understanding of the control-of-variable strategy (as in the NSES sample lesson described earlier, NRC 1996, pp. 146–147), should a teacher let students discover on their own, guide the students by asking them to justify their experimental design and conclusions, or offer explicit instruction on the concept of good experimental design?

Viewing this problem through an SDDS lens, we suggest that the discovery process does not provide nearly as much corrective feedback to the search for experiments as it does the search for hypotheses. If a hypothesis is wrong, then evidence collected via proper experimentation would at least contradict its prediction. This offers the learner feedback about the quality of the hypothesis. But if the learner chooses an incorrect experimental strategy that intentionally favors the confirmation of a prior belief, the subsequent confirmation would satisfy the goal of confirming one's prior belief and mask the deficiency of the experimental strategy. Therefore, in order to develop sound experimental strategy, the teacher must compensate for misleading feedback inherent within the discovery process.

In our own research, we have found that a brief period of explicit instruction, combined with probing questions and hands-on experiments, is more effective in helping students learn to control variables than either probing or hands-on experiments without explicit instruction (Chen and Klahr 1999; see review of replication studies by Klahr and Li 2005). Other researchers have found that, across a period of sustained engagement, children improve their use of controlled comparisons to make inferences without explicit instruction, provided the discovery task was designed to make desirable outcomes difficult to attain without first understanding underlying causal relationships (Schauble 1990, 1996; Schauble et al. 1991). Sustained engagement and task complexity can thus offer performance feedback that helps students improve experimental strategies.

These examples make a broader point about searching for what works in science education. Recently, proponents of direct instruction have challenged the long-advocated hands-on science approach. The sides of the debate over instructional approaches were particularly polarized in deciding whether California's science curriculum should require either a maximum or a minimum of 25% hands-on science (Adelson 2004; Begley 2004; California Department of Education 2004; Cavanagh 2004; "Stand and deliver … or let them discover?" 2004).

We disagree with the perception that instructional approaches such as hands-on science, discovery learning, and direct instruction are mutually exclusive rather than intersecting and complementary. As our examples illustrate, (1) explicit instruction can be particularly useful when the hands-on experience itself offers little corrective feedback; (2) sustained exploration can be effective if the discovery task is explicitly designed to afford performance feedback; and (3) a thoughtful combination of explicit instruction and self-guided exploration, both within the context of hands-on experience, can effectively help children develop both process skills and content knowledge.

Examining the policy debate through an SDDS lens, one finds that, despite the passionate advocacy on both sides, it is hardly a well-defined debate. The direct-instruction label is sometimes intended to mean a highly specified instructional procedure, mainly for reading and math, developed by Engelmann and colleagues (Engelmann and Carnine 1991). At other times it is used much more diffusely to mean a wide range of teacher-controlled talking, showing, questioning, and demonstrating.

Hands-on science and *discovery learning* are even less well-defined terms that usually allude to various mixtures of physical manipulation, guided inquiry, and student exploration. Such lack of precise operational definitions has allowed earnest and passionate, but empirically ungrounded, debates to flourish in the area of science instruction policy. Only a handful of empirical studies have directly compared an operationally defined exemplar of one approach versus another in science education (Klahr and Nigam 2004). Thus, it seems scientifically premature to even begin a debate (i.e., entering the evaluate evidence phase of SDDS) when the terms of the debate have not yet passed muster of the "search hypothesis space" phase. Perhaps, in addition to applying SDDS towards science teaching, we may be informed by applying SDDS to the debates about science teaching!

The Teacher and the Researcher

If we envision the end goal of improving science education as painting a masterpiece, then the painter (whether teacher or researcher) needs to possess not only great techniques but perceptive vision. A painter spends just as much time seeing the picture as painting it. The champion of inquiry in education, John Dewey, remarked, "Abstract thought is imagination seeing familiar objects in a new light" (cited by Prawat 2002). In that spirit, we have described a relatively abstract theoretical framework that has guided and synthesized the psychological studies of scientific thinking. We suggest how such a model may be applied to the examination of the means and ends of science education. By viewing scientific thinking as a model of problem solving, one can use the model's descriptive power (the contingencies, relationships, inputs, and outputs) to analyze a topic area, evaluate instruction, and integrate available research findings into instructional design.

Although we recognize that our suggestions are theoretical in nature, we arrived at this tentative stage by placing ourselves and our research under the environmental constraints of the classrooms and the policy constraints of standards and accountability (Klahr and Li 2005). By attempting to translate our abstract and theoretical formulation of scientific thinking into instructional analysis, we hope to encourage teachers to become researchers, not in the sense that teachers should do our kind of research in classrooms, but in the sense that teachers would supplement their professional knowledge by viewing scientific thinking from the researchers' perspective.

We hope we have continued along the paths trodden by other basic researchers to put theoretical findings to the test of educational relevancy and usefulness. Before drawing conclusions about what works in science education, teachers and researchers may be well served by seeing scientific thinking in a different light—and we could all begin by seeing it through the other's eyes.

Junlei Li

is a postdoctoral research fellow at the Department of Psychology at Carnegie Mellon University. He investigates the practical implications of educational policy and cognitive research by co-teaching with teachers in urban school science classrooms.

David Klahr

is Professor of Psychology at Carnegie Mellon University. He has written many articles and books on the analysis of complex cognitive processes in such diverse areas as voting behavior, college admissions, consumer choice, peer review, problem solving, and scientific reasoning, and has more recently worked on how to better teach children to design and interpret simple experiments. He has served on several recent NRC committees on cognitive development, assessment, and early science learning.

Acknowledgments

The work reported here was supported in part by grants from NICHD (HD 25211), NIH (MH19102), the James S. McDonnell Foundation (96–37), the National Science Foundation (BCS-0132315), and the Cognition and Student Learning program at the Institute of Education Science (R305H030229).

References

Adelson, R. 2004. Instruction versus exploration in science learning. *Monitor on Psychology* 35 (6): 34–36.

American Association for the Advancement of Science (AAAS). 1993. *Benchmarks for science literacy.* New York: Oxford University Press.

Amsel, E., and S. Brock. 1996. The development of evidence evaluation skills. *Cognitive Development* 11: 523–550

Begley, S. 2004. The best ways to make school children learn? We just don't know. *The Wall Street Journal Online,* p. B1. Retrieved December 10, 2004, from *http://online.wsj.com/article/0,,SB110263537231796249,00.html.*

Berliner, D. C. 2002. Educational research: The hardest science of all. *Educational Researcher* 31 (8): 18–20.

Brewer, W. R., and C. A. Chinn. 1994. The theory-ladenness of data: An experimental demonstration. In *Proceedings of the Sixteenth Annual Conference of the Cognitive Science Society,* eds. A. Ram and K. Eiselt, 61–65. Hillsdale, NJ: Lawrence Erlbaum.

Brown, A. L. 1992. Design experiments: Theoretical and methodological challenges in creating complex interventions in classroom settings. *Journal of Learning Sciences* 2 (2): 141–178.

California Department of Education. January 29, 2004. Curriculum commission: Approval of criteria for evaluating k–8 science instructional materials for 2006 primary action. Retrieved on April 7, 2004, from *www.cde.ca.gov/be/pn/im/documents/infocibcfirfeb04item01.pdf.*

Cavanagh, S. November 10, 2004. NCLB could alter science teaching. *Education Week* 24 (11): 1, 12–13.

Chen, Z., and D. Klahr. 1999. All other things being equal: Children's acquisition of the control of variables strategy. *Child Development* 70 (5): 1098–1120.

Darling-Hammond, L., and P. Youngs. 2002. Defining "highly qualified teachers": What does "scientifically-based research" actually tell us? *Educational Researcher* 31 (9):13–25.

Donmoyer, R. 1995. The rhetoric and reality of systemic reform: A critique of the proposed national science education standards. *Theory into Practice* 34 (1): 30–34.

Einstein, A. 1950. Physics and reality. In A. Einstein, *Out of my later years* (59–111). New York: Philosophical Library. (Original work published 1936.)

Engelmann, S., and D. Carnine. 1991. *Theory of instruction: Principles and applications.* Eugene, OR: ADI Press.

Erickson, R., and K. Gutierrez. 2002. Culture, rigor and science in educational research. *Educational Researcher* 31 (8): 21–24.

Fay, A., and D. Klahr. 1996. Knowing about guessing and guessing about knowing: Preschoolers' understanding of indeterminacy. *Child Development* 67: 689–716.

Feuer, M.J., L. Towne, and R. J. Shavelson. 2002. Scientific culture and educational research. *Educational Researcher* 31 (8): 4–14.

Gopnik, A., D. Sobel, L. Schultz, and C. Glymour. 2001. Causal learning mechanisms in very young children: Two, three, and four-year-olds infer causal relations from patterns of variation and covariation. *Developmental Psychology* 37 (5): 620–629

Hiebert, J., R. Gallimore, and W. Stigler. 2002. A knowledge base for the teaching profession: What would it look like and how can we get one? *Educational Researcher* 31 (5), 3–15.

Klahr, D., and Z. Chen. 2003. Overcoming the "positive capture" strategy in young children: Learning about indeterminacy. *Child Development* 74, 1256–1277.

Klahr, D., and K. Dunbar. 1988. Dual space search during scientific reasoning. *Cognitive Science* 12, 1–48.

Klahr, D., and J. Li. 2005. Cognitive research and elementary science instruction: From the laboratory, to the classroom, and back. *Journal of Science Education and Technology,* Special Issue, Science Education in Review.

Klahr, D., and M. Nigam. 2004. The equivalence of learning paths in early science instruction: Effects of direct instruction and discovery learning. *Psychological Science* 15(10), 661–667.

Klahr, D., and H. A. Simon. 1999. Studies of scientific discovery: Complementary approaches and convergent findings. *Psychological Bulletin 125 (5): 524–543.*

Klahr, D. 2000. *Exploring science.* Cambridge, MA: MIT Press.

Klahr, D., A. L. Fay, and K. Dunbar. 1993. Heuristics for scientific experimentation: A developmental study. *Cognitive Psychology* 24(1): 111–146.

Koslowski, B. 1996. *Theory and evidence: The development of scientific reasoning.* Cambridge, MA: MIT Press.

Kuhn, D. 1997. Constraints or guideposts? Developmental psychology and science education. *Review of Educational Research* 67 (1): 141–150.

Kuhn, D., and J. Angelev. 1976. An experimental study of the development of formal operational thought. *Child Development* 47: 697–706.

Kuhn, D., E. Amsel, and M. O'Loughlin. 1988. *The development of scientific thinking.* New York: Harcourt, Brace and Jovanovich.

Kuhn, D., M. Garcia-Mila, A. Zohar, and C. Anderson. 1995. Strategies of knowledge acquisition. Monographs of the Society for Research in *Child Development,* Serial No. 245 60 (40): 1–128.

Kujawa, S., and L. Huske. 1995. *The strategic teaching and reading project guidebook,* rev. ed. Oak Brook, IL: North Central Regional Educational Laboratory.

Lagemann, E. C. 1996. Contested terrain: A history of education research in the United States, 1890–1990. *Educational Researcher* 26 (9): 5.

Lagemann, E. C. 2000. *An elusive science: The troubling history of educational research.* Chicago: University of Chicago Press.

Lehrer, R., and L. Schauble. (forthcoming). *Scientific thinking and science literacy: Supporting development in learning contexts.* Handbook of Child Psychology.

Masnick, A. M., and D. Klahr. 2003. Error matters: An initial exploration of elementary school children's understanding of experimental error. *Journal of Cognition and Development* 4: 67–98.

McCloskey, M. 1983 Naive theories of motion, In *Mental Models,* eds. D. Gentner and A. Stevens, 229–324. Hillsdale, NJ: Lawrence Erlbaum.

Metz, K. E. 1995. Reassessment of developmental constraints on children's science instruction. *Review of Educational Research* 65 (2:) 93–127.

Metz, K. E. 1997. On the complex relation between cognitive developmental research and children's science curricula. *Review of Educational Research* 67 (1): 151–163.

National Research Council (NRC). 1996. *National Science Education Standards.* Washington, DC: National Academy Press.

Newell, A., and H. A. Simon. 1972. *Human problem solving.* Englewood Cliffs, NJ: Prentice Hall.

No Child Left Behind Act (NCLB) of 2001. 2002. Public Law 107-110-January 8, 2002. 107th Congress. Washington, DC.

Ogle, D. S. 1986. K–W–L group instructional strategy. In *Teaching reading as thinking,* eds. A. S. Palincsar, D. S. Ogle, B. F. Jones, and E. G. Carr (Teleconference Resource Guide, 11–17). Alexandria, VA: Association for Supervision and Curriculum Development.

Pelligrino, J. W., and S. R. Goldman. 2002. Be careful what you wish for—you may get it: Educational research in the spotlight. *Educational Researcher* 31 (8): 15–17.

Prawat, R.S. 2002. Dewey and Vygotsky viewed through the rearview mirror—and dimly at that. *Educational Researcher* 31 (5): 16–20.

Rodriguez, A.J. 1997. The dangerous discourse of invisibility: A critique of the national research council's national science education standards. *Journal of Research in Science*

Teaching 34: 19–37.

Schauble, L. 1990. Belief revision in children: The role of prior knowledge and strategies for generating evidence. *Journal of Experimental Child Psychology* 49: 31–57.

Schauble, L. 1996. The development of scientific reasoning in knowledge-rich contexts. *Developmental Psychology* 32: 102–119.

Schauble, L., L. Klopfer, and K. Raghavan. 1991. Students' transition from an engineering model to a science model of experimentation. *Journal of Research in Science Teaching* 18 (9): 859–882.

Shavelson, R. J., and L. Towne, eds. 2002. *Scientific research in education.* Washington, DC: National Academy Press.

Shaw, G., R. Brown, and P. Bromiley. May–June 1998. Strategic stories: How 3M is rewriting business planning. *Harvard Business Review* 76: 3–8.

Shiland, T. W. 1998. The atheoretical nature of the national science education standards. *Science Education* 82 (5): 615–617.

Simon, H. A., P. Langley, and G. L. Bradshaw. 1981. Scientific discovery as problem solving. *Synthese* 47: 1–27.

Sodian, B., E. Zaitchik, and S. Carey. 1991. Young children's differentiation of hypothetical beliefs from evidence. *Child Development* 62: 753–766.

St. Pierre, E. A. 2002. "Science" rejects postmodernism. *Educational Researcher* 31 (8): 25–27.

Stand and deliver…or let them discover? 2004. *District Administration* (November): 79.

Stokes, D. E. 1997. *Pasteur's quadrant: Basic science and technological innovation.* Washington, DC: Brookings Institution Press.

Strauss, S. 1998. Cognitive development and science education: Toward a middle level model. In *Handbook of child psychology: Vol. 4. Child psychology in practice*, eds. I. Sigel and K. A. Renninger , series ed. W. Damon, 357–400. New York: John Wiley & Sons.

Toth, E., D. Klahr, and Z. Chen. 2000. Bridging research and practice: A cognitively-based classroom intervention for teaching experimentation skills to elementary school children. *Cognition & Instruction* 18 (4): 423–459.

Towne, L., L. L. Wise, and T. M. Winters. 2004. *Advancing scientific research in education.* Washington, DC: The National Academy Press.

Traub, J. November 10, 2002. No child left behind: Does it work? *New York Times.* Retrieved December 9, 2002, from *www.nytimes.com.*

Triona, L. M., and D. Klahr. 2003. Point and click or grab and heft: Comparing the influence of physical and virtual instructional materials on elementary school students' ability to design experiments. *Cognition & Instruction* 21: 149–173.

Tschirgi, J. E. 1980. Sensible reasoning: A hypothesis about hypotheses. *Child Development* 51: 1–10.

Tufte, E. R. 2003. *The cognitive style of powerpoint.* Cheshire, CT: Graphics Press LLC.

Zimmerman, C. 2000. The development of scientific reasoning skills. *Developmental Review* 20: 99–149.

CHAPTER

21

Research in Science Education: An Interdisciplinary Perspective[1]

Michael R. Vitale and Nancy R. Romance

The continuing goal of science education research is the generation of pedagogical knowledge that can be used to improve meaningful understanding of science concepts by students. Using present initiatives in science education as a foundation, we provide an overview of developments in cognitive science and instructional psychology and associated exemplary research findings and implications that provide researchers and practitioners with an interdisciplinary framework for improving the quality of school science instruction.

As a subject of formal study, the discipline of science consists of two complementary components (AAAS 1993). The first is the conceptual and factual knowledge that pertains to understanding the different domains of science—understanding the operations of the physical world, the living environment, and the human organism. The second addresses the nature of scientific inquiry, which represents the process through which the cumulative knowledge of science is established—understanding the process of scientific research. Even though the teaching and learning of science within elementary, secondary, and postsecondary educational settings differ substantially in sophistication, all three are linked pedagogically by these two common components of science content and process. In turn, at any level of sophistication, these two components are fundamental to the concept of scientific literacy.

The purpose of the field of science education is applying the methods of scientific inquiry to advance pedagogical knowledge of how students are gain a meaningful understanding of science content and the nature of science. In other words, the goal of the field of science education is to use the processes of science to establish knowledge that, when applied, results in science being taught more effectively. The resulting pedagogical knowledge represents the content of the field of science education—how to teach, for example, physics, Earth science, or biological principles more effectively.

Within science education, a primary methodological issue is identifying what students must do to demonstrate an in-depth understanding of science. This issue is important because all science education research requires that student performance be observed, measured, and evaluated in some form. Although different approaches to classroom assessment—such as multiple choice, performance, portfolios—are topics current in science education (Pellegrino et al. 2001), the methods of science themselves prescribe an overall framework for assessing student understanding (Metzenberg et al. 2004; Mintzes et al. 1999; Ruiz-Primo et al. 2002). Specifically, students demonstrate understanding of scientific concepts and principles in the same manner as scientists (Vitale and Romance, forthcoming)

- by linking knowledge to observable phenomena,
- by applying their knowledge to make specific predictions of future events—such as predicting that when a substance is heated, the substances will expand—and/or to manipulate conditions to make future events occur—such as making a substance expand by heating the substance, and
- by organizing their knowledge in terms of core concepts and concept relationships as a form of expertise (Bransford et al. 1999).

In a complementary fashion, students who have such forms of understanding also can

- apply science knowledge abductively by suggesting plausible reasons why phenomena may have occurred—such as if something expanded, a possible reason is that it was heated).

Although not always addressed explicitly in science education, the preceding suggests how meaningful understanding of discipline-specific science concepts (and principles) provides students at all levels with a substantive framework for applying both scientific knowledge—why expansion joints are used in bridges—and the processes of science —scientifically testing the plausibility of whether a substance expanded because it was heated.

Although science and science education are complex and overlap, certain characteristics clearly distinguish them.

- First, *science* can be considered broadly as a process for establishing and organizing cumulative knowledge that leads to prediction or control of events.
- Second, the *processes of science* can be considered as the means for generating such knowledge in the different domains of science (e.g., physics, Earth science, biology).
- Third, student learning of both the resulting knowledge of science and the process of scientific inquiry in school settings is the domain of *science education*, and,
- Fourth, the domain of *science education research*, using the processes of science, focuses upon the development of pedagogical knowledge that improves teaching of science content and process.

Research Overview: An Interdisciplinary Perspective

This section consists of three parts whose combined understanding serves as an interdisciplinary-oriented guide for science educators and science education researchers.

The first part of this section informally summarizes and interprets the status of research activity in science education.

The second part overviews recently emerging principles in cognitive science and related disciplines that offer a strong research-based foundation for the future advancement of science education.

The third part presents examples of research in science education that embody these principles and provide concrete models for researchers and practitioners.

Building upon the three parts in this section, the following sections provide an overview of the implications of interdisciplinary research perspectives along with recommendations for science education research and practice.

Status of Research in Science Education: An Informal Appraisal

An informal review of recent research by science educators in scholarly journals—such as *International Journal of Science Education, Journal of Research in Science Teaching,* and *Science Education*; handbooks (Fraser and Tobin 1998a, 1998b; Gabel 1994); and textbooks revealed a surprising finding. Relatively few studies in science education involve experimental, or field experimental, research that demonstrates the effect of approaches to or characteristics of science instruction on meaningful conceptual understanding by students in school settings. Rather, the majority of science education studies (a) describe teacher experiences in science instructional settings, (b) evaluate student misconceptions—including reporting teachers' frustration on the resistance of student misconceptions to conceptual change, or (c) use science content as an incidental research context for investigating other issues such as equity/gender issues, professional development strategies, and focusing on the processes of teaching, versus achievement outcomes, using constructivist, cooperative learning, or inquiry/questioning strategies.

In comparison to research on science education, recent research from related disciplines such as cognitive science (Bransford et al. 1999), educational psychology (Mayer 2004), and instructional psychology (Grossen et al. 2001) offers a rich source of interdisciplinary perspectives and findings (see Romance and Vitale 2002). The field of science education is largely unaware of this research, despite its potential for systemically improving the understanding of how students gain in-depth science knowledge from school instruction. The remainder of this section presents principles and exemplary interdisciplinary research findings whose foundations are grounded in these related fields and that offer implications for systemically improving student science learning.

Research-Based Principles for Science Education

A recent publication by the National Research Panel, *How People Learn* (Bransford et al. 1999) serves as an important guide for research in science education. Focusing on meaningful student learning, the publication stresses that to teach effectively in any discipline, the information being taught must be linked to the key organizing principles, or core concepts, of that discipline. Well-organized and readily accessible prior student conceptual knowledge is the major determinant of the forms of cumulative meaningful student learning characteristic of scientists, a principle also expressed by Hirsch (1996). From this research perspective, all forms of science pedagogy should focus instructional, and assessment, activities on the core concepts that reflect the underlying logic of the discipline.

Prior knowledge and meaningful learning: Expert versus novice research. A major area of research relating to the role of prior knowledge in meaningful learning that Bransford et al. reviewed focused on the cognitive differences between experts and novices. This research has shown repeatedly that expert knowledge is organized in a conceptual fashion very different from that of novices' knowledge and that the use of knowledge by experts in application tasks such as analyzing and solving problems is primarily a matter of accessing and applying prior knowledge (Kolodner 1993, 1997) under conditions of automaticity. Related to this view is earlier work by Anderson and others (Anderson 1992, 1993, 1996), who distinguished the "strong" problem-solving process of experts that is highly knowledge-based and automatic from the "weak" strategies that novices with minimal knowledge must adopt in a trial-and-error fashion. Directly related are key elements in Anderson's cognitive theory that (a) consider all cognitive skills as forms of proficiency that are knowledge-based, (b) distinguish between declarative and procedural knowledge (i.e., knowing about versus applying knowledge), and (c) identify the conditions in learning environments—extensive practice—that determine the transformation of declarative to procedural knowledge, learning to apply knowledge in various ways.

This research emphasizes that extensive amounts of varied experiences—practice—involving the core concept relationships to be learned are critical to the development of expert mastery in any discipline. In related research, Sidman (1994) and others (Dougher and Markham 1994; Artzen and Holth 1997) have explored the conditions under which extensive practice to the stage of automaticity focusing on one subset of relationships can result in the learning of additional subsets of relationships. In their work, these additional relationships were not taught but rather were implied by the original subset of relationships that were taught (i.e., equivalence relationships). In other relevant work, Niedelman (1992), Anderson (1996), and Goldstone and Son (2005) have offered interpretations of the research issues relating to how the amount and kinds of initial learning—such as degree of original mastery and interaction of concrete experiences in varied contexts and abstract perspectives—are related to transfer of initial learning to applied settings.

Explicit knowledge representation: Research on intelligent tutoring systems. A parallel area of research addresses the knowledge-based architecture of computer-based intelligent tutoring systems (ITS) developed in the early 1980s (Kearsley 1987; Luger and Stubblefield 1998). In these systems, an explicit representation of the knowledge to be learned provides an organizational framework for all elements of instruction, including the determination of learning sequences, the selection of teaching methods, the specific activities required of learners, and the evaluative assessment of student learning success. Specifically, from the standpoint of assessment, knowledge-based instructional models provide a sequence of interrelated activities that provided teachers with an authentic context for evaluating cumulative student meaningful understanding.

Knowledge-based instruction versus metacognitive strategies. Although there is a well-established research literature (Bransford et al. 1999) that focuses on the importance of "content-free" metacognitive strategies—such as use of general strategies by students to facilitate their learning, a knowledge-based approach primarily emphasizes the development and organization of prior knowledge in a manner that is reflected in three research areas: (a) the development of expertise summarized by Bransford et al. (1999) and Anderson (1992, 1993, 1996); (b) the work on case-based knowledge representation and reasoning—remembering and applying past problem-solving scenarios provides a powerful context for approaching the next problem—developed by Kolodner and her colleagues (1997); and (c) the general development of knowledge categories offered by Sowa (2000).

From a knowledge-based approach, research on the use of general metacognitive strategies has greater potential relevance for novices than for experts who have an in-depth understanding of science conceptual content (see Anderson 1987). Because such general metacognitive research is contextualized within a framework of science learning by novices, it has minimal relevance to enhancing the forms of meaningful in-depth science understanding that are characteristic of experts. Rather, a more promising view of meaningful science learning as knowledge-based has a greater potential value for researchers and practitioners. Specifically, a knowledge-based perspective holds that the cumulative experiences of students in developing in-depth conceptual understanding (i.e., expertise) results in the development of a framework of general knowledge categories (Dansereau 1995; Vitale and Medland 2004) in the form of core concepts and concept relationships. Within such a framework, additional knowledge is first assimilated and then used by students as prior knowledge for new learning as a form of expertise (see Mayer 2004). In turn, this expertise facilitates students' cumulatively acquiring, organizing, accessing, and thinking about new information that is embedded in reading comprehension and meaningful learning tasks to which the new knowledge is relevant (Vitale et al. 2002).

Implications for science education research from cognitive science. From a knowledge-based perspective, the overall principles of relevance to both researchers and practitioners for sound science instruction are as follows:

- All aspects of science instruction should focus on the development and organization of core science concepts;
- Both the curricular structure of instruction and curricular mastery by students should be considered to be and approached as a form of expertise (i.e., representing the form of science understanding characteristic of experts); and
- The development of conceptual prior knowledge is the most critical determinant of future success in meaningful learning.

In this regard, the study of how cumulatively focusing on the core concepts and relationships that reflect the logical structure of the discipline and enhancing the development of prior knowledge are of paramount importance for meaningful learning to occur is an expanding research trend. Additionally, the preceding, as potential standards for sound science instruction that focuses on both science content and science processes are consistent with the results of the Third International Math and Science Study (TIMSS) presented as a framework for the following section (Schmidt et al. 1999, 2001).

Exemplars of Science Education Research

This section presents five research exemplars that serve two major functions. The first is that they illustrate one or more major points presented above within a research context that is directly relevant to applied science learning settings. The second is that, considered together, they provide systemic implications for improving the quality of science instruction in schools, and therefore for broadening the foundation of science education research. The exemplars are presented using the major curricular findings of the TIMSS study (Schmidt et al. 1999, 2001) as an overall conceptual framework in a fashion that complements the parallel ideas presented in the Bransford et al. (1999) report.

The TIMSS study as a framework for research exemplars. The curricular findings of the highly-respected TIMSS study (Schmidt et al. 1999, 2001) provide a strong intellectual framework for the research exemplars presented. In comparing the science and mathematics curricula of high-achieving and low-achieving countries, the TIMSS study reported a major conclusion that is consistent with the research above. Specifically, the TIMSS study found that the curricula of high-achieving countries was characterized as focused around big ideas, conceptually coherent, and carefully articulated across grade levels. In contrast, the curricula in low-achieving countries (including the U.S.) emphasized superficial, highly-fragmented coverage of a wide range of topics with little conceptual emphasis or depth (i.e., U.S. curriculum was "a mile wide and an inch deep"). In general, the findings of the TIMSS study and the supporting perspectives from Bransford et al. (1999) offer a useful framework for the exemplars that follow. The small number of research studies reported here are intended to provide researchers and practitioners with examples that facilitate understanding of the implications of the research.

Using concept mapping as a knowledge-elaboration tool. The first exemplar consists of work by Novak and Gowin (1984) who studied the developmental understanding of science concepts by elementary students over a 12-year period. Their work, which was based on Ausubel's theory of cognitive learning (1968), is highly consistent with contemporary cognitive science research principles. In a longitudinal study, they used concept maps to represent the cumulative development of student understanding of science topics based on interviews. As their original work evolved, these two researchers initiated the use of concept maps by students to enhance meaningful understanding of science. Related work has been reported by Fisher et al. (2000), Mintzes et al. (1998), and Romance et al. (2000). These studies have demonstrated the importance of students' having the means to perceive and reflect on the development of their own views of core concept relationships.

Focusing instruction directly on core concepts. The second exemplar is a videodisc-based instructional program by Hofmeister et al. (1989) that focuses on the development of core science concepts in physical science (e.g., heating, cooling, force, density, and pressure) to understand phenomena in Earth science (e.g., understanding how the concept of convection causes crustal, oceanic, and atmospheric movement). Two representative studies are relevant here. Muthukrishna et al. (1993) demonstrated experimentally that instructional use of the videodisc-based materials to directly teach core-concepts was an effective way to eliminate common misconceptions (e.g., seasons and day and night) of elementary students in science. Vitale and Romance (1992) showed in a controlled study that the use of the same core-concept-focused instructional program resulted in mastery of the same core concepts by elementary teachers (versus control teachers who demonstrated virtually no conceptual understanding of the same content). In much the same way as did TIMSS (Schmidt et al., 1999, 2001) and Novak and Gowin (1984), these studies suggest that focusing instruction on core concepts, including principles, is an important element in developing meaningful student learning.

Using direct instruction to enhance student learning. The third exemplar is an experimental study by Klahr and Nigam (2004) that found teacher-guided direct instruction far more effective than a discovery approach not only on student initial acquisition of a procedure for designing and interpreting simple unconfounded experiments, but also on subsequent application/transfer. In interpreting their findings, the perspectives offered by Klahr and Nigam were consistent with a more general analysis of the potential role of direct/guided instruction in meaningful science learning presented by Mayer (2004). In turn, both perspectives are consistent with more general approaches in instructional science (e.g., Engelmann and Carnine 1982; Grossen et al. 2001) that address technical issues in the design of optimally effective learning environments.

Using the conceptual structure of the discipline as a basis for problem solving. The fourth exemplar is a series of studies at the elementary and postsecondary levels. In an analysis of learning by elementary students and of associated instructional materials, Vosniadou (1996) emphasized the importance of focusing instruction on the relational nature of science concepts in order for students to gain meaningful understanding. Dufresne et al. (1992) found that postsecondary students who engaged in analyses of physics problems based upon a conceptual hierarchy of relevant principles and procedures were more effective in solving problems. Complementing these two studies, carefully designed experiments by Leonard et al. (1994), Chi et al. (1981), and Heller and Reif (1984) showed that success in application of science concepts was facilitated by amplifying student understanding of the hierarchical organization of science concepts. The findings of these experimental studies parallel the descriptive findings of the TIMSS study and ideas presented by Bransford et al. (1999).

Using meaningful learning in science as a basis for improving reading comprehension. The fifth exemplar is a series of experimental studies with upper elementary students by Romance and Vitale (2001) that encompass many of the preceding research principles. Their integrated instructional model, Science IDEAS, combined science, reading comprehension, and writing within a daily two-hour block that replaced regular reading and language arts instruction. During that time students engaged in science learning activities that involved hands-on science experiments and projects; reading science texts, trade books, and internet-accessed science materials; writing about science; journaling; and using concept mapping as a knowledge representation tool. As an intervention implemented within a broad inquiry-oriented framework, teachers used core science concepts as curricular guidelines for identifying, organizing, and sequencing the different instructional activities in which students engaged. Both within and across lessons, all aspects of teaching emphasized students' learning more about what had been learned previously in order to engender cumulative student in-depth science understanding.

A series of studies exploring the effectiveness of the model (Romance and Vitale 2001) showed that students participating in Science IDEAS instruction obtained significantly higher levels of achievement in both science and reading comprehension as measured by nationally normed standardized tests such as the Metropolitan Achievement Test—Science and the Iowa Tests of Basic Skills—Reading Comprehension. In addition, compared to controls, Science IDEAS students displayed significantly more positive attitudes toward science learning both in and out of school, greater self-confidence in learning science, and more positive attitudes toward reading in school. In addition, in follow-up studies, the researchers extended elements of the Science IDEAS intervention to postsecondary science instruction in chemistry and biology (Haky et al. 2001; Romance, Haky, et al. 2002). These extensions emphasized (a) the use of core concepts and concept relationships as a curricular framework for teaching and (b) student use of propositional concept mapping to enhance reading comprehension of science texts and to guide review and study. Considered together, this combined series of studies supports the effectiveness of a knowledge-based approach to science instruction.

Integration of major points of the science education research exemplars. The following summarizes the major points of the research exemplars from two perspectives:

- As instructional guidelines for practitioners, and
- As a set of contextual characteristics that are required for the ecological validity of research investigating science instruction as a cumulative learning process.

Specifically, these points are:

- A comprehensive science curriculum should include the study of both science knowledge and the nature of science (not just one of the two) as a requirement for science literacy,
- The curriculum focus of science instruction at all levels should be on the core concepts and concept relationships (i.e., principles) within the areas of science to be taught and learned (consistent with the conceptual organization of experts and representing the logic of the discipline),
- The overall framework of core concepts and core concept relationships should be articulated across grade levels in a clear and coherent fashion,
- All student learning activities, assessment practices, and teaching strategies should be directly related to the overall core concept framework,
- Students should experience a variety of learning activities for developing meaningful science understanding of core concepts, including the use of concept mapping as a knowledge representation tool,
- Students should engage in a variety of application and problem-solving experiences after the initial development of meaningful science understanding of the relevant science content, and

- Cumulative development of science understanding as students progress through school should be accomplished through the elaboration and detailing of core ideas previously introduced as much as is possible.

Implications of an Interdisciplinary Research Perspective for Improving Science Instruction

In this section, the implications of interdisciplinary research are considered from three perspectives: (a) directions for research in science education, (b) transformation of research into practice, and (c) building standards for research utilization by practitioners.

Implications for Science Education Research

Perhaps the most important implication of the preceding is that science education researchers should strive toward forming interdisciplinary perspectives that result in integrating their research with that of related disciplines. In doing so, researchers should recognize that such an initiative is consistent with both a constructivist view of knowledge development and the cumulative inquiry processes on which all science is based. Further, the integration of diverse disciplines should be recognized as a means for pursuing systemic disciplinary advancements (e.g., see Kuhn 1996; Hirsch 1996; Mayer 2004).

To advance understanding of science learning, science education researchers should consider the benefits of incorporating three emerging interdisciplinary areas of investigation into science education research. The first of these research areas is Engelmann and Carnine's (1982) Direct Instruction (DI) Model from instructional psychology. The DI Model attempts to provide an algorithmic framework that includes strategies for effectively teaching concepts, concept relationships, intellectual skills (as procedures), and cognitive routines that apply complex knowledge and skills. Additionally, the model includes strategies for the developmental articulation of curriculum-emphasizing core concepts that optimize retention, application, and use of knowledge and skills learned as facilitative knowledge for new learning. All of the algorithmic components of the DI Model could be applied and investigated in science learning frameworks. Of particular promise is using elements of the model to preteach core science concepts. These concepts would then serve as prior knowledge for students participating in the more informal, open-ended, and problem-based settings that are using the small-group inquiry formats that are favored by constructivist-oriented science educators (see Mayer 2004). Because the fields of DI and science education have different emphases, the present ontological framework of science education cannot represent the operational dynamics of the DI Model at the level of detail required for research without substantial interdisciplinary integration.

The second research area is Anderson's cognitive-science-based Adaptive Control of Thought (ACT) Model. Anderson's research (1992, 1993, 1996) provides a theoretical framework that focuses on the transition from novice to expert in terms of the interplay between the dynamics of the learning environment on one hand and the forms of declarative and procedural knowledge on the other. In one fashion or another, these are among the critical issues associated with the use of formal science instruction to build conceptual understanding from a knowledge-based and meaningful learning perspective.

Although complex, Anderson's and related work have yielded many important research findings (Blessing and Anderson 1996; Anderson and Fincham 1994, 1996; Anderson et al. 1997; Anderson and Sheu 1995; Wisniewski 1995). Included are techniques for the differential representation of declarative and procedural knowledge, processes for the development and refinement of cognitive skills, models addressing the transformation of declarative to procedural knowledge, models distinguishing between expert and novice problem solving, and models explaining the reorganization of skill patterns and knowledge structure in the development of expertise.

Anderson, with others, also has used his work as a foundation for critiquing research and policy issues in education (Anderson, Corbett et al. 1995; Anderson, Reder et al. 1995, 1996). Again, the point is that adapting Anderson's ACT model to research in science teaching—both of which depend on the observed structure of the environment in combination with prior knowledge as the basis for learning—could well advance the goals of science education. As with the DI model, the present ontological framework of science education cannot represent Anderson's ACT model at the level of detail required for research without substantial interdisciplinary integration.

As with DI, Anderson's ACT Model could be readily investigated, or applied, within science instruction scenarios. Of particular interest to science educators would be studies conducted with meaningful science content that addresses such issues as knowledge acquisition, automaticity, and the development of expertise, all in a fashion that would investigate characteristics of the instructional environment which, in terms of variables in the ACT model, engender such outcomes.

The third area is the area of equivalence relations in learning, or stimulus equivalence, conducted in behavior analysis research. Although highly experimental at present, this research (Sidman 1994) addresses how to engender learning outcomes that arise indirectly from instruction because they are based upon the structural properties (i.e., element relationships) of the knowledge to be learned. Because science is a structured content domain that is meaningful, it is an area that could benefit greatly from increased understanding of the equivalence relations phenomenon.

This research area addresses a general question of the development of generative inferential processes in learning (Baer 1997; Dougher and Markham 1994; Sidman 1994). More specifically, stimulus equivalence research focuses on understanding how the structure of knowledge and the conditions under which the parts of a structure that are taught can be made to result in learning outcomes that—in relation to the original knowledge structure—are far broader than what was taught explicitly (Artzen and Holth 1997; Eilseth and Baer 1997; Lane and Critchfield 1996; Lynch and Cuvo 1995).

These and other examples from the area of equivalence relations have significant implications for the development of curriculum design strategies that maximize student learning outcomes resulting from formal instruction in terms of learned-but-not-taught relationship-based content. In addition, the implications from this research area complement instructional design models, such as DI and Anderson's ACT model, that emphasize the direct teaching of conceptual relationships and strategies to pursue the development of prescriptive guidelines for accomplishing learned-but-not-taught outcomes through K–12 science instruction. Again, as with the DI and ACT models, the present ontological framework of science education cannot represent behavior analysis equivalence relations at the level of detail required for research without substantial interdisciplinary integration.

Perspectives for Transforming Research Into Practice

A second important interdisciplinary perspective for science education research is the transformation of research into practice. As represented in the specifications for federally funded proposals, such as those from the U.S. Department of Education Institute of the Education Sciences, the development of research knowledge can be approached as a multiphase process that (1) involves initial proof-of-concept demonstrations that (2) then evolve into controlled replicable research studies that, in turn, (3) evolve into scale-up initiatives within applied settings (see Coburn 2003; Vitale and Romance 2004) and, that, in the present context, (4) emphasize development of the capacity of school systems to sustain an application.

Although such a broad perspective may be of limited interest to many science education researchers, it is of primary importance to the discipline because of its implications for curricular policy. For example, Jones et al. (1999) found that school reform initiatives resulted in instructional time for science being reallocated to reading and language arts, raising a significant policy issue for science education. On the other hand, Romance et al. (forthcoming) reported research findings that replacing reading/language arts with science increased achievement in reading comprehension and language arts, while Guthrie et al. (2004) have consistently found that enhancing traditional elementary-level literature-oriented reading programs with science reading content enhanced reading achievement. The point is that while such research findings (see also, Duke et al. 2003; Walsh 2003) have implications for curriculum policy (see Romance et al. 2002), systemic changes in curricular practices require researchers themselves to address the question of the scale-up of their work to applied settings, an issue that is an active area of research and development (Coburn 2003; Vitale and Romance 2004).

Building Standards for Research

The effective use of and advocacy for research in science education must come from practitioners as societal representatives (Johnson and Pennypacker 1992). Although the U.S.-mandated No Child Left Behind initiative will include science, schools tend to meet accountability requirements by emphasizing short-term, within-grade test preparation rather than systemic change. As a result, the practice of "evidence-based" decision making by schools is far from optimal. In this regard, Hirsch (1996), Carnine (1995), and Mayer (2004) have offered a number of perspectives to which researchers should be sensitive. Primarily, science education researchers should first be advocates for the use of empirical research findings as a basis for school decision-making and, second, relate any form of advocacy of their or others' research findings to that general principle. By doing so, researchers are able to contribute toward the acceptance of a general evidence-based criterion of effectiveness that potential instructional initiatives must display prior to large-scale adoption in reform (see Carnine 1995).

Interdisciplinary-Based Recommendations for Research

We offer the following recommendations as a foundation for advancing the scope of future science education research by broadening its interdisciplinary foundations. Specifically, in planning their studies, science education researchers should consider recognizing and addressing issues relating to

- the ontological implications of interdisciplinary research perspectives,
- the ecological validity of findings by conducting research within environments that provide a valid curricular and assessment context for the cumulative in-depth learning of science,
- distinguishing among categories of science concepts (directly observable, real but not observable, constructed but not real) to be learned within different developmentally appropriate instructional contexts (see Romance and Vitale 1998),
- adapting a knowledge-based perspective for conceptual understanding as expertise and the role of such knowledge in understanding the nature of science and the use of metacognitive strategies,
- the importance of focusing research on identification and refinement of conditions that result in improved student understanding of science (as the goal of science education research), and
- the broadening of programmatic research design to encompass an evolution from proof-of-concept to controlled experimentation to demonstrated replicability in applied settings (i.e., scale up).

A Methodological Addendum [2]

Although this chapter's focus and research recommendations are substantive rather than methodological, it would not be complete without briefly recognizing three perspectives that together provide an important methodological foundation for modern science education research.

The first perspective has to do with the present advocacy for the importance of using completely randomized designs (CRDs) as a standard for experimentation whenever possible. Although included as a topic in most introductory textbooks, perhaps the most precise and clearest explanation of the rationale for using CRDs can be found in Raudenbush (2001). On a more general level, it should be recognized that the present emphasis on CRDs in the literature has a decidedly "per-separate-experiment" focus, despite the fact that the replicability of experimental findings across the widest possible range of settings is the key requirement for the acceptance of scientific knowledge. In this regard, researchers should consider a classic work by Sidman (1960) that presents methodological strategies that address the role of randomization within the broader research context of establishing the generalizability of research findings.

The second perspective, related to the first, has to do with estimating and reporting "effect size" as necessary methodological enhancements to the reported results of statistical tests of significance. A methodological overview of such approaches can be found in the recent *Publication Manual of the American Psychological Association* (2001) and is an active topic in the literature (also see Wilkinson 1999).

The third perspective is related to both of the preceding and addresses strategies for cumulative research design in applied settings as outlined by Slavin (1990, 2002). In these papers, Slavin distinguished between model-oriented and variable-oriented research by pointing to the fact that despite all systemic instructional interventions in applied settings being highly complex, such multifaceted models are the form of applications that practitioners must implement to enhance instructional quality through research. Within this context, he suggested a sequential design process in which applications of such models with fidelity (as a complex variable) are first validated as effective within experimental (CRD) studies. Then, after validation, the dynamics of the model are explored systematically.

Although beyond the scope of this chapter, the three perspectives represent methodological standards essential to incorporate in the pursuit of any of the recommendations for interdisciplinary research in science education developed in this chapter.

[1] This research was supported by Grant No. 0228353 from the National Science Foundation Interagency Research Initiative and by Grant No. R305G04089 from the USDOE-Institute of the Education Sciences.

[2] The authors are indebted to an anonymous reviewer's suggestion that chapter would be of greater value if a brief note on methodological standards of practice was added.

Michael R. Vitale

is a professor of curriculum, instruction, and research at East Carolina University. He has professional experience in both higher education (educational psychology—University of Hawaii; instructional technology—Florida Atlantic University) and public school settings (Director of Applied Research, Director of Instructional Technology—Dallas Public Schools). His research interests involve applying principles from cognitive science and instructional design to the study of systemic problems in meaningful learning across grades K–12.

Nancy R. Romance

is a professor of science education in the Charles E. Schmidt College of Science and Biomedical Science at Florida Atlantic University and principal investigator of two major research initiatives addressing science learning and literacy development funded by the National Science Foundation and the United States Department of Education Institute of the Education Sciences. Author of numerous journal articles, chapters, and two K–6 science textbook series, she has also served as the director of Florida's Region V Area Center for Educational Enhancement and the Higher Education Consortium for Mathematics and Science. Her honors include Florida Atlantic University's 2003 Researcher of the Year and the Florida Science Teachers Association Science Educator of the Year award.

References

American Association for the Advancement of Science (AAAS). 1993. *Benchmarks for science literacy.* New York: Oxford University Press.

American Psychological Association. 2001. *Publication manual of the American Psychological Association.* 5th ed. Washington, DC: American Psychological Association.

Anderson, J. R. 1987. Skill acquisition: Compilation of weak-method problem solutions. *Psychological Review* 94 (2): 192–210.

Anderson, J. R. 1992. Automaticity and the ACT theory. *American Journal of Psychology* 105: 15–180.

Anderson, J. R. 1993. Problem solving and learning. *American Psychologist* 47: 35–44.

Anderson, J. R. 1996. ACT: A simple theory of complex cognition. *American Psychologist* 51: 335–365.

Anderson, J. R., A. T. Corbett, K. Koedinger, and R. Pellitier. 1995. Cognitive tutors: Lessons learned. *The Journal of the Learning Sciences* 4: 167–207.

Anderson, J. R., and J. M. Fincham. 1994. Acquisition of procedural skills from examples. *Journal of Experimental Psychology* 47: 1322–1340.

Anderson, J. R., and J. M. Fincham. 1996. Categorization and sensitivity to correlation. *Journal of Experimental Psychology* 22 (2): 259–277.

Anderson, J. R., J. M. Fincham, and S. Douglass. 1997. The role of examples and rules in the acquisition of a cognitive skill. *Journal of Experimental Psychology* 23 (4): 932–945.

Anderson, J. R., L. M. Reder, and H. A. Simon. 1995. *Applications and misapplications of cognitive science to mathematics education.* ACT Research Group, Pittsburgh, PA: Carnegie Mellon University, ACT Research Group.

Anderson, J. R., L. M. Reder, and H. A. Simon. 1996. Situated learning and education. *Educational Researcher* 25 (4): 5–11.

Anderson, J. R., and C. Sheu. 1995. Causal inferences as perceptual judgments. *Memory and Cognition* 23 (4): 510–524.

Artzen, E., and P. Holth. 1997. Probability of stimulus equivalence as a function of training design. *Psychological Record* 47: 309–320.

Ausubel, D. 1968. *Educational psychology: A cognitive view.* New York: Holt, Rinehart, and Winston.

Baer, D. M. 1997. Some meanings of antecedent and environmental control. In *Environment and Behavior*, eds. D. M. Baer and E. M. Pinkston, 15–29. Boulder, CO: Westview Press.

Blessing, S. B., and J. R. Anderson. 1996. How people learn to skip steps. *Journal of Experimental Psychology* 22 (3): 576–598.

Bransford, J. D., A. L. Brown, and R. R. Cocking. 1999. *How people learn.* Washington, DC: National Academy Press.

Carnine, D. 1995. Standards for educational leaders. *Education Week,* October 11, 1995.

Chi, M. T. H., P. J. Feltovich, and R. Glaser. 1981. Categorization and representation of physics problems by experts and novices. *Cognitive Science* 5: 121–152.

Coburn, C. E. 2003. Rethinking scale: Moving beyond numbers to deep and lasting change. *Educational Researcher* 32: 3–12.

Dansereau, D. F. 1995. Derived structural schemas and the transfer of knowledge. In *Teaching for transfer,* eds. A. McKeough, Lupart, and A. Marini, 93–121. Mahwah, NJ: Lawrence Erlbaum.

Dougher, M. J., and M. R. Markham. 1994. Stimulus equivalence, functional equivalence and the transfer of function. In *Behavior analysis of language and cognition,* eds. S.C. Hays, L J. Hays, M. Santo, and O. Koichi, 71–90. Reno, NV: Context Press.

Dufresne, R. J., W. J. Gerance, P. Hardiman, and J. P. Mestre. 1992. Constraining novices to perform expert-like problem analyses: Effects of schema acquisition. *The Journal of the Learning Science,* 2 (3): 307–331.

Duke, N. K., V. S. Bennett-Armistead, and E. M. Roberts. 2003. Filling the nonfiction void. *American Educator* (Spring): 30–35.

Eilseth, S., and D. M. Baer. 1997. Use of a preexisting verbal relation to prevent the properties of stimulus equivalence from emerging in new relations. In *Environment and behavior,* eds. D. M. Baer and E. M. Pinkston, 138–144. Boulder, CO: Westview Press.

Engelmann, S., and D. Carnine. 1982. *Theory of instruction: Principles and applications.* New York: Irvington.

Fisher, K. M., J. H. Wandersee, and D. E. Moody. 2000. *Mapping biology knowledge.* The Netherlands: Kluwer Academic Publishers.

Fraser, B. J., and K. G. Tobin. 1998a. *International handbook of science education.* Part One. Boston: Kluwer Academic Publishers.

Fraser, B. J., and K. G. Tobin. 1998b. *International handbook of science education.* Part Two. Boston: Kluwer Academic Publishers.

Gabel, D. L., ed. 1994. *Handbook of research on science teaching and learning.* New York: Macmillan.

Goldstone, R. L., and J. Y. Son. 2005. The transfer of scientific principles using concrete and idealized simulations. *The Journal of the Learning Sciences* 14 (1): 69–110.

Grossen, B. J., D. W. Carnine, N. R. Romance, and M. R. Vitale. 2001. Effective strategies for teaching science. In *Effective teaching strategies that accommodate diverse learners,* eds. E. J. Kameenui and D. Carnine, 113–137. Upper Saddle River, NJ: Prentice Hall.

Guthrie, J. T., A. Wigfield, and K. C. Perencevich, eds. 2004. *Motivating reading comprehension: Concept-oriented reading instruction.* Mahwah, NJ: Lawrence Erlbaum.

Haky, J., N. R. Romance, D. Baird, and D. Louda. 2001. Using multiple pathways to improve student retention and achievement in first semester chemistry. Paper presented at the Annual Meeting of the National Association for Research in Science Teaching, St. Louis, Missouri.

Heller, J. I., and F. Reif. 1984. Prescribing effective human problem solving processes: Problem description in physics. *Cognition and Instruction* 1, 177–216.

Hirsch, E. D. 1996. *The schools we need. And why we don't have them.* New York: Doubleday.

Hofmeister, A. M., S. Engelmann, and D. Carnine. 1989. Developing and validating science education videodisks. *Journal of Research in Science Teaching* 26 (8): 665–667.

Johnson, J., and H. Pennypacker. 1992. *Strategies and tactics of human behavioral research,* 2nd ed. Hillsdale, NJ: Lawrence Erlbaum.

Jones, M. G., B. D. Jones, L. Chapman, T. Yarbrough, and M. Davis. 1999. The impact of high-stakes testing on teachers and students in North Carolina. *Phi Delta Kappan* 81: 199–203.

Kearsley, G. P., ed. 1987. *Artificial intelligence and instruction: Applications and methods.* New

York: Addison-Wesley.

Klahr, D., and M. Nigam. 2004. The equivalence of learning paths in early science instruction: Effects of direct instruction and discovery learning. *Psychological Science* 15: 661–667.

Kolodner, J. L. 1993. *Case-based reasoning.* San Mateo, CA.: Morgan Kaufmann.

Kolodner, J. L. 1997. Educational implications of analogy: A view from case-based reasoning. *American Psychologist* 82: 57–66.

Kuhn, T. 1996. *The structure of scientific revolution.* Chicago: University of Chicago Press.

Lane, S. D., and T. S. Critchfield. 1996. Verbal self-reports of emergent relations in a stimulus equivalence procedure. *Journal of the Experimental Analysis of Behavior* 65 (2): 355–374.

Leonard, W. J., R. J. Dufresne, and J. P. Mestre. 1994. Using qualitative problem solving strategies to highlight the role of conceptual knowledge in solving problems. *American Journal of Physics* 64: 1495–1503.

Luger, G. F., and W. A. Stubblefield. 1998. *Artificial intelligence: Structures and strategies for complex problem-solving.* Reading, MA: Addison Wesley.

Lynch, D. C., and A. J. Cuvo. 1995. Stimulus equivalence instruction of fraction-decimal relations. *Journal of Applied Behavior Analysis* 28 (2): 115–126.

Mayer, R. E. 2004. Should there be a three-strikes rule against pure discovery learning? The case for guided methods of instruction. *American Psychologist* 59 (1): 14–19.

Metzenberg, S., S. Miller, and D. Carnine. 2004. Avoiding science "lite." *Education Week* 23 (18): 30–44.

Mintzes, J. J., J. H. Wandersee, and J. D. Novak. 1999. *Assessing science understanding: A human constructivist view.* San Diego, CA.: Academic Press.

Mintzes, J. J., J. H. Wandersee, and J. D. Novak. 1998. *Teaching science for understanding: A human constructivist view.* Englewood Cliffs, NJ: Academic Press.

Muthukrishna, A., D. Carnine, B. Grossen, and S. Miller. 1993. Children's alternative frameworks: Should they be directly addressed in science instruction? *Journal of Research in Science Teaching* 28 (10): 233–248.

Niedelman, M. 1992. Problem solving and transfer. In *Higher order thinking,* eds. D. Carnine and E. J. Kameenui. Austin, TX: Pro-Ed.

Novak, J. D., and D. B. Gowin. 1984. *Learning how to learn.* Cambridge, United Kingdom: Cambridge University Press.

Pellegrino, J. W., N. Chudowsky, and R. Glaser, eds. 2001. *Knowing what students know: The science and design of educational assessment.* Washington, DC: National Academy Press.

Raudenbush, S. W. 2001. Comparing personal trajectories and drawing causal inferences from longitudinal data. *Annual Review of Psychology* 52: 501–525

Romance, N. R., J. Haky, G. Mayer, and M. R. Vitale. 2002. Improving student-based performance in introductory college biology and chemistry using conceptually-based models. Paper presented at the Annual Meeting of the National Association for Research in Science Teaching, New Orleans, Louisiana.

Romance, N. R., and M. R. Vitale. 1994. Developing science conceptual understanding through knowledge-based teaching: Implications for research. Paper presented at the annual meeting of the National Association for Research in Science Teaching, Anaheim, California.

Romance, N. R., and M. R. Vitale. 1998. How should children's alternative conceptions be considered in teaching and learning science concepts: Research-based perspectives. Paper presented at the Annual Meeting of the National Association for Research in Science Teaching, San Diego, CA.

Romance, N. R., and M. R. Vitale. 2001. Implementing an in-depth expanded science model in elementary schools: Multi-year findings, research issues, and policy implications. *International Journal of Science Education* 23: 373–404.

Romance, N. R., and M. R. Vitale. 2002. Knowledge-based instructional models as a framework for developing ontological perspectives in science learning: Implications for research and practice in science teaching. Paper presented at the First International Conference on Philosophical, Psychological, and Linguistic Foundations for Language and Science Literacy Research, University of Victoria, Victoria, BC, Canada.

Romance, N. R., M. R. Vitale, and M. F. Dolan. 2002. *What is scientifically based research in science education.* Boca Raton, FL: Florida Atlantic University, Region V Area Center for Educational Enhancement.

Romance, N. R., M. R. Vitale, and J. Haky. 2000. Concept mapping as a knowledge-based strategy for enhancing student understanding. *The NSF Workshop Project Newsletter* 2, 5–8.

Romance, N. R., M. R. Vitale, and M. Klentschy. (forthcoming). Improving K–12 science literacy outcomes by expanding instructional time for science in grades K–5: Implications and opportunities for changing curricular policies and practices in elementary schools. *Journal of Science Education and Technology.*

Ruiz-Primo, M. A., R. J. Shavelson, L. Hamilton, and S. Klein. 2002. On the evaluation of systemic science education reform: Searching for instructional sensitivity. *Journal of Research in Science Teaching* 39 (5): 369–393.

Schmidt, W. H., C. C. McKnight, L. S. Cogan, P. M. Jakwerth, and R. T. Houang. 1999. *Facing the consequences: Using TIMSS for a closer look at U.S. mathematics and science education.* Boston: Kluwer Academic Publishers.

Schmidt, W. H., C. C. McKnight, R. T. Houang, H. C. Wang, D. Wiley, L. Cogan, and R. Wolfe. 2001. *Why schools matter: A cross-national comparison of curriculum and learning.* San Francisco, CA: Jossey-Bass.

Sidman, M. 1960. *Tactics of scientific research.* New York: Basic Books.

Sidman, M. 1994. *Stimulus equivalence.* Boston: Author's Cooperative.

Slavin, R. E. 1990. On making a difference. *Educational Researcher* 19 (3): 30–34, 44.

Slavin, R. E. 2002. Evidence-based educational policies: Transforming educational practice and research. *Educational Researcher* 31 (7): 15–21.

Sowa, J. F. 2000. *Knowledge representation: Logical, philosophical, and computational foundations.* New York: Brooks Cole.

Vitale, M. R., and M. B. Medland. 2004. *Knowledge structure development.* Boca Raton, FL.: Successful Learning Systems.

Vitale, M. R., and N. R. Romance. 1992. Using video disk technology in an elementary science methods course to remediate science knowledge deficiencies and facilitate science teaching attitudes. *Journal of Research in Science Teaching* 29 (9): 915–928.

Vitale, M. R., and N. R. Romance. 2004. *Using an instructional systems development model as a framework for research on scale up.* Technical Report Number 2.002. NSF/IERI Project Number 0228353, College of Science, Florida Atlantic University, Boca Raton, FL.

Vitale, M. R., and N. R. Romance. (forthcoming). A knowledge–based framework for the classroom assessment of student science understanding. *Peers matter.* National Science Teachers Association/National Association for Research in Science Teaching.

Vitale, M. R., N. R. Romance, and M. Dolan. 2002. A rationale for improving school reform by expanding time for science teaching: Implications and opportunities for changing curricular policy and practice in elementary schools. Paper presented at the Annual Meeting of the National Association for Research in Science Teaching, New Orleans, Louisiana.

Vosniadou, S. 1996. Learning environments for representational growth and cognitive science. In *International perspectives on the design of technology-supported learning environments,* eds. S. Vosniadou, E. DeCorte, R. Glaser, and H. Mandl, 13–24. Mahwah, NJ: Lawrence Erlbaum.

Walsh, K. 2003. Lost opportunity. *American Educator* (Spring): 24–29.

Wilkinson, L. W. 1999. Statistical methods in psychology journals: Guidelines and explanations. *American Psychologist* 54 (8): 594–604.

Wisniewski, E. J. 1995. Prior knowledge and functionally relevant features in concept learning. *Journal of Experimental Psychology* 21 (2): 449–468.